# Introducing Buddhism



*Introducing Buddhism* is the ideal resource for all students beginning the study of this fascinating religion. **Charles S. Prebish** and **Damien Keown**, two of today's leading Buddhist scholars, explain the key teachings of Buddhism and trace the historical development and spread of the religion from its beginnings down to the present day. A chapter is devoted to each of the major regions where Buddhism has flourished: India, South-east Asia, East Asia and Tibet. In addition to this regional focus, the introduction takes contemporary concerns into account, covering important and relevant topics such as Engaged Buddhism, Buddhist Ethics, and Buddhism and the Western World, as well as a chapter devoted to Meditation.

*Introducing Buddhism* also includes illustrations, lively quotations from original sources, learning goals, summary boxes, questions for discussion, and suggestions for further reading, to aid study and revision.

**Charles S. Prebish** is Professor of Religious Studies at Pennsylvania State University. **Damien Keown** is Professor of Buddhist Ethics at Goldsmiths College, University of London. They are the editors of the Routledge Curzon series *Critical Studies in Buddhism* and of the *Routledge Encyclopedia of Buddhism*.

## World Religions series

Edited by Damien Keown and Charles S. Prebish

This exciting series introduces students to the major world religious traditions. Each religion is explored in a lively and clear fashion by experienced teachers and leading scholars in the field of world religion. Up-to-date scholarship is presented in a student-friendly fashion, covering history, core beliefs, sacred texts, key figures, religious practice and culture, and key contemporary issues. To aid learning and revision, each text includes illustrations, summaries, explanations of key terms, and further reading.

**Introducing Buddhism**
*Charles S. Prebish and Damien Keown*

**Introducing Hinduism**
*Hillary Rodrigues*

### Forthcoming:

**Introducing Christianity**
**Introducing Islam**

# Introducing Buddhism

Charles S. Prebish and Damien Keown

Routledge
Taylor & Francis Group
NEW YORK AND LONDON

First published 2006
by Routledge
270 Madison Ave, New York, NY 10016

Simultaneously published in the UK
by Routledge
2 Park Square, Milton Park, Abingdon, Oxon OX14 4RN

Reprinted 2007

*Routledge is an imprint of the Taylor & Francis Group, an informa business*



First published in e-book form 2005 by Journal of Buddhist Ethics Online Books

Typeset in Jenson and Tahoma by
HWA Text and Data Management, Tunbridge Wells
Printed and bound in Great Britain by
TJ International Ltd, Padstow, Cornwall



*British Library Cataloguing in Publication Data*
A catalogue record for this book is available from the British Library

*Library of Congress Cataloging-in-Publication Data*
A catalog record for this book has been applied for

ISBN10: 0–415–39234–9 (hbk)
ISBN10: 0–415–39235–7 (pbk)

ISBN13: 978–0–415–39324–1 (hbk)
ISBN13: 978–0–415–39235–8 (pbk)

# Contents

# *Illustrations*

# Acknowledgments

'The Background to Buddhism', 'The Doctrine of Meditation in the Hīnayāna', and 'The Doctrine of Meditation in the Mahāyāna' by Stephan V. Beyer, from Charles S. Prebish (editor), *Buddhism: A Modern Perspective* (University Park, Pennsylvania: The Pennsylvania University Press, 1975), pp. 3–9, 137–147, and 148–158, are reproduced by permission of the publisher.

Material in Chapters 1, 12 and 13 from *Buddhist Ethics: A Very Short Introduction* by Damien Keown (Oxford University Press, 2005) reproduced by permission of Oxford University Press.

Our thanks to Pragati Sahni for permission to use material from her 2003 D.Phil. thesis 'Environmental Ethics in Early Buddhism' in Chapter 12.

All photographic images are copyright John Powers, and are reproduced by permission, except for Figure 8.1, which is copyright Robert Hood.

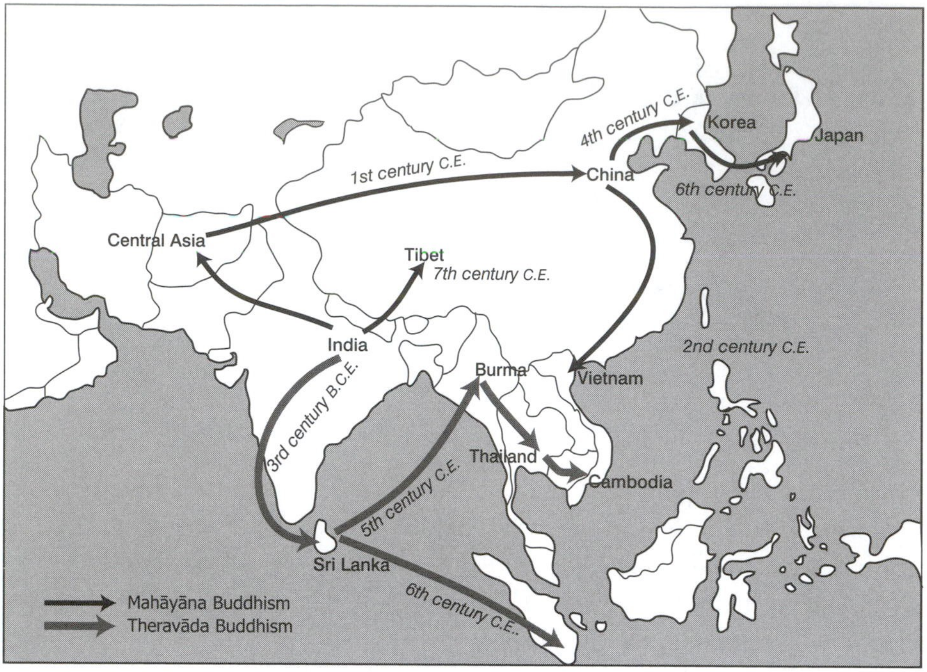


*Map of the spread of Buddhism*

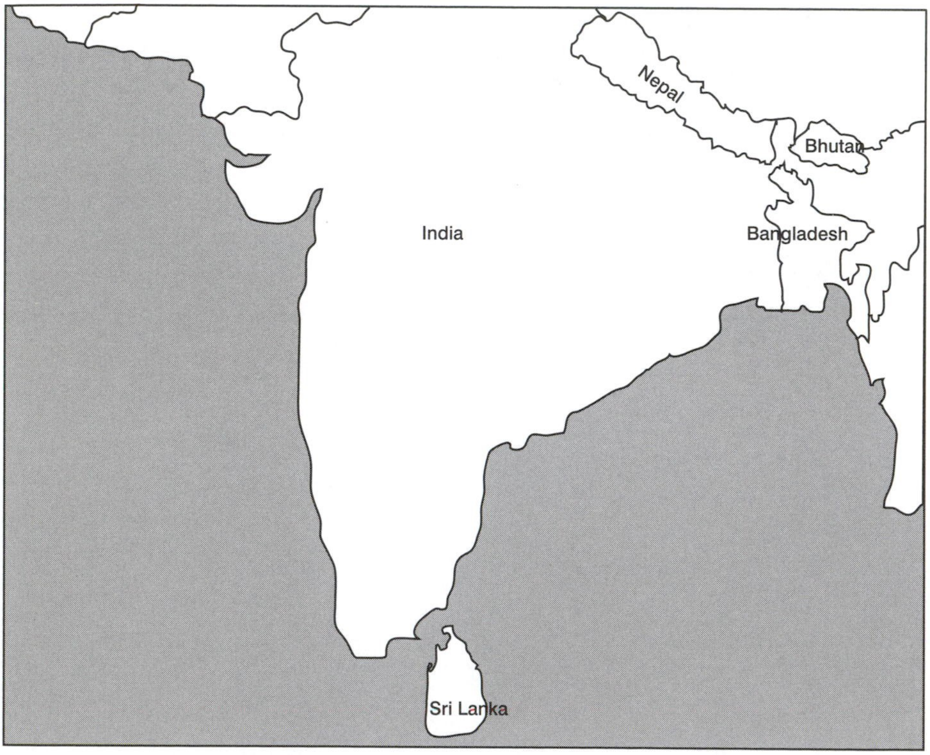


*Map of India*

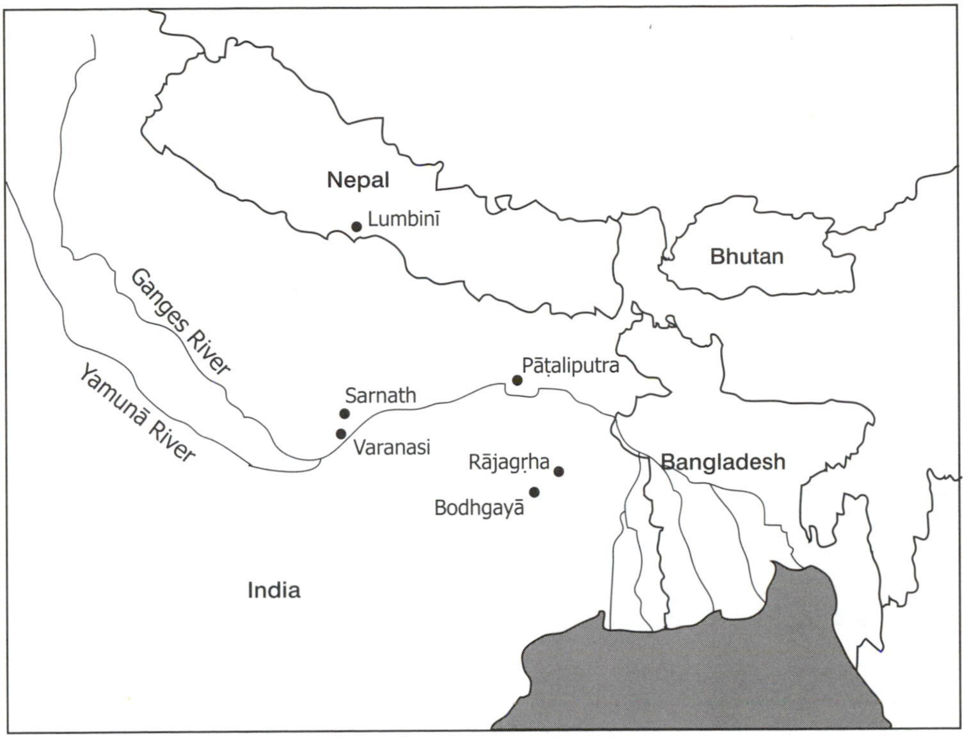


*Map of the region where Buddhism began*

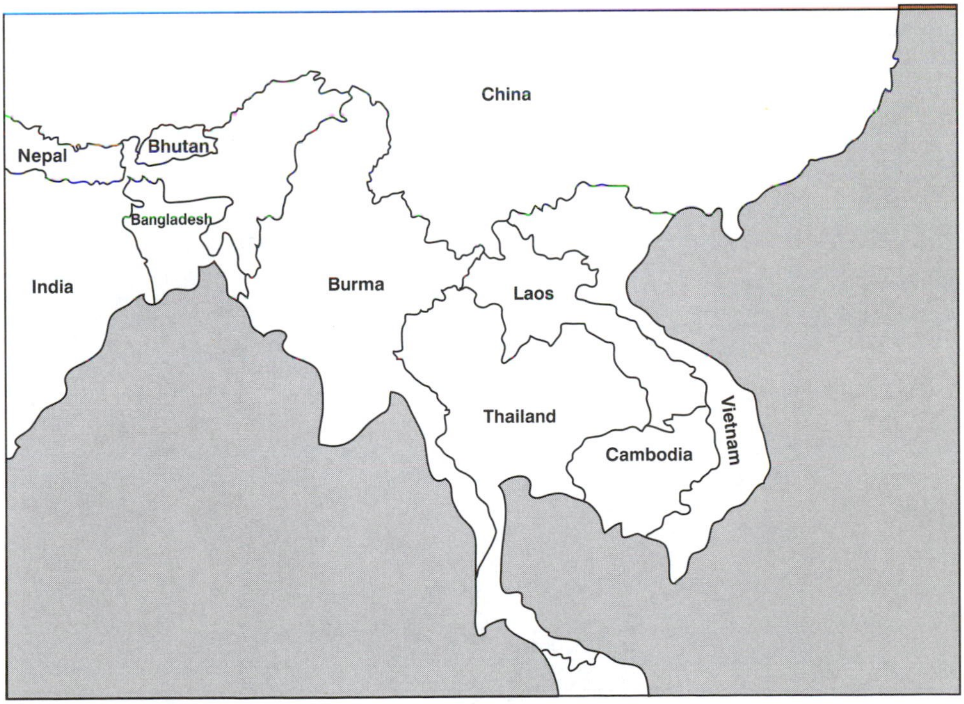


*Map of South-east Asia*

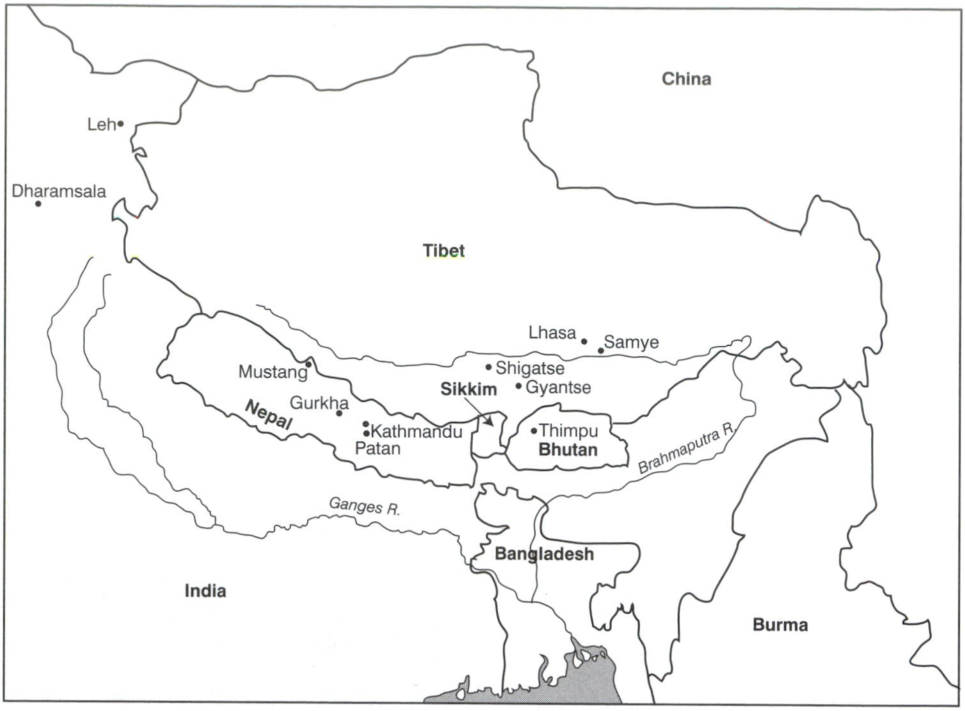


*Map of Tibet*

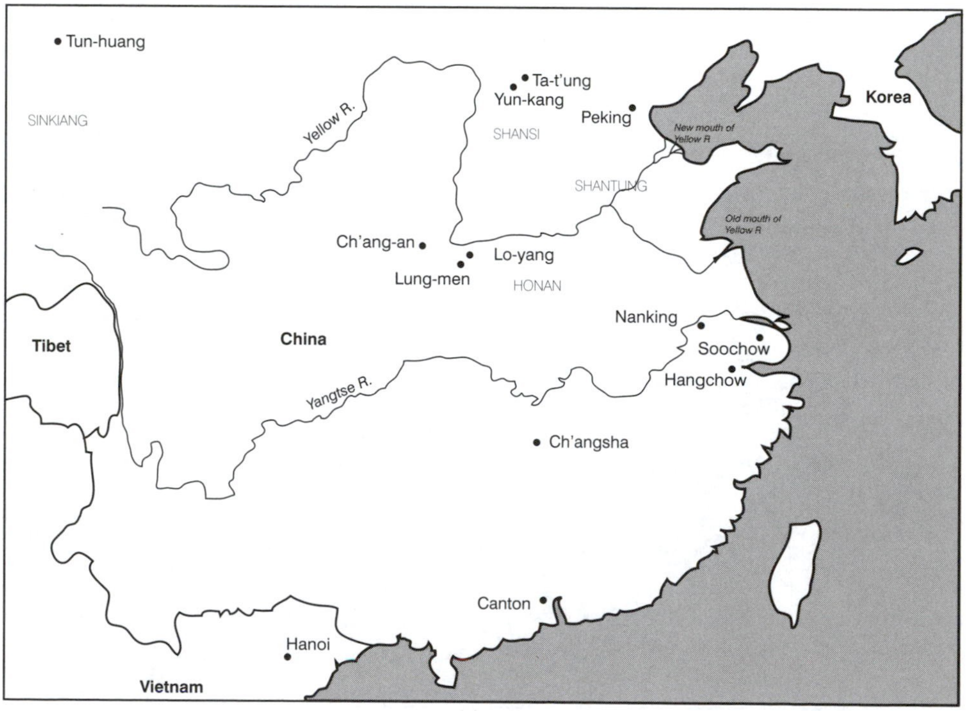


*Map of China*

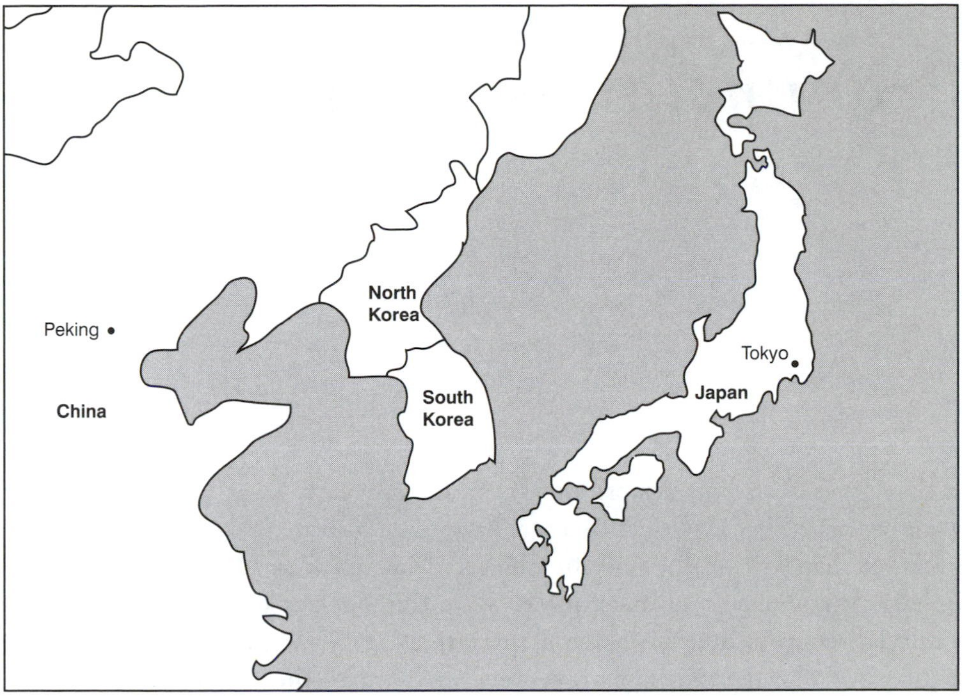


*Map of East Asia*

# *Pronunciation guide*

In the course of its long history Buddhism has spread to every part of Asia. One result of this is that Buddhist concepts have come to be expressed in languages as diverse as Sanskrit, Pāli, Tibetan, Chinese, Mongolian, Japanese, Korean, Thai, Sinhala, Vietnamese and many more. Since this book is intended to reflect the cultural diversity of Buddhism, it contains terms drawn from all the major Buddhist languages. Following the scholarly convention, however, the primary language used is Sanskrit. Sanskrit served as the lingua franca of ancient India, just as Latin did in medieval Europe, and most of the translations made into other Asian languages were based on Sanskrit originals. The most important scriptures of Mahāyāna Buddhism were composed in a variant of Sanskrit known as Buddhist Hybrid Sanskrit, while the earliest Buddhist scriptures are preserved in Pāli, a literary language derived from Sanskrit.

## Sanskrit and Pāli

One feature of Asian languages like Sanskrit is that their alphabets are larger than those of Western languages. In order to represent the additional characters diacritical marks have to be added to the Roman letters. These typically take the form of symbols such as dots and dashes placed above or below certain characters. These symbols affect pronunciation in various ways. As far as Sanskrit is concerned, the most important of these is that a macron above a vowel serves to lengthen it, roughly doubling the length of the sound. Thus the character 'ā' is pronounced as in 'far' rather than 'fat'. With respect to consonants, an underdot (ṭ, ḍ, etc.) indicates that the tongue touches the roof of the mouth when pronouncing these letters, giving the characteristic sound of English when spoken with an Indian accent. For the most part the other marks do not affect pronunciation enough to be of any special concern. A summary of the most important points in connection with the pronunciation of Sanskrit and Pāli terms is shown below:

| | |
|---|---|
| ā | pronounced as in far |
| ī | pronounced as in seek |
| ū | pronounced as in brute |
| ṛ | pronounced as in risk |
| ñ | pronounced as in Spanish mañana |
| ś or ṣ | pronounced as in shoe |
| ṅ/ṃ | pronounced with a nasal sound as in ring |
| c | pronounced ch, as in church |

More detailed guidance on the pronunciation of Sanskrit can be found in Chapter 1 of Michael Coulson, *Sanskrit: An Introduction to the Classical Language* (London: Hodder and Stoughton, 1976).

## Chinese

The transcription and pronunciation of Chinese poses special problems due to the fact that there are two systems in use for transcribing it, namely Wade-Giles and Pinyin. The latter was introduced in 1979 by the People's Republic of China as its official system, but the earlier Wade-Giles method of transcription is still in widespread use. Pinyin has gained acceptance among specialists, and we use it here, but students are more likely to encounter Wade-Giles in introductory and popular literature. A helpful guide on converting from Wade-Giles to Pinyin can be found in A. C. Graham, *Disputers of the Tao* (La Salle, Illinois: Open Court, 1989, 441–4). Neither Pinyin or Wade-Giles, however, provides a way of representing the sounds of spoken Chinese with any accuracy since the same characters in Chinese may be pronounced in one of four different tones.

## Japanese

The transcription of Japanese is relatively unproblematic, and this book uses the widely-adopted Hepburn system. The characters used correspond closely to their Roman equivalents, with the exception of the long vowels ō and ū. As in the transliteration of Sanskrit, the macron over the letter indicates that the sound of the vowel is emphasized and lengthened, thus *kōan* is pronounced 'koh-an', with the emphasis on the first syllable.

## Tibetan

In contrast to Japanese, Tibetan orthography and pronunciation pose many complex problems. This is despite the fact that a standard system of transliteration exists that does not rely on diacritics, namely the system devised by Turrell Wylie and explained in his article, 'A Standard System of Tibetan Transcription' (*Harvard Journal of Asiatic Studies*, vol. 22, 1959: 261–7). The present work adopts this method of transliteration, but difficulties still remain. Not least among these is the fact that Tibetan words frequently contain letters that are not pronounced (this is also a feature of English, as in words such as 'through', 'ought', and so forth). Even more problematic from the point of view of alphabetization is that in Tibetan these redundant letters are often found at the start of a word: thus the term for a senior monk – lama – is in fact spelled 'blama'. Since this book is intended primarily for a general readership, the policy of using a simplified phonetic form for the spelling of Tibetan words has been adopted while putting the correct transliteration from the Tibetan in brackets, thus: lama (blama).

## Korean

The Korean system of writing is known as Hangŭl, and the present work uses the standard conventions for transcription into English. This method uses the standard Roman alphabet pronounced for the most part as in English, with the exception of the two vowels ŏ (pronounced as in cot) and ŭ (pronounced as in burn).

# *Background to Buddhism*

Main topics covered[1]

- The Indus Valley Civilization
- The Indus religion
- The Indus inheritance
- The Vedic culture
- Vedic literature
- The Vedic inheritance
- The Age of the Wanderers
- The two traditions
- The philosophical problematic

## *The Indus Valley Civilization*

In the third millennium B.C.E., peoples from the neolithic cultures of Baluchistan moved into the fertile flood plains of the Indus River and established cities at Harappā, Mohenjodaro, and other sites. They engaged in considerable trading as far as Mesopotamia; the southern city at Lothal had a sophisticated dry dock system. The well laid-out streets, consistent city plans, almost modern sanitation facilities, centralized food storage areas, and the presence of citadels in the hearts of the cities all suggest a strong and conservative system of government.

This Indus Valley Civilization developed its own writing system, which is as yet undecipherable, although there has been some fruitful speculation that it was used to write a proto-Dravidian language. This writing is found in short inscriptions on beautifully carved seals, probably giving the name of the owner, with well-conceived and naturalistic pictures of animals and what may well be gods. Another clue to the religious life of these people is found in the presence of large ritual baths associated

1 Stephan V. Beyer is the author of this chapter, which is reproduced by kind permission of The Pennsylvania University Press. 'The Background to Buddhism' has been published previously in *Buddhism: A Modern Perspective,* edited by Charles S. Prebish.

with the central city and indicating a profound concern for bodily purity – a concern reflected also in the sophisticated sewage system.

By the time this civilization had reached its full growth, it covered a territory over a thousand miles long, greater than that of any other ancient civilization. By around 1200 B.C.E. the cities were dying: craftsmanship and organization were disappearing, and huddled skeletons with crushed skulls in the most recent levels suggest either invasions or internecine warfare. The Indus River seems to have no longer been under control, perhaps because of a shift in its flow, and there may have been excessive floods. It is debated whether the Indo-European invaders from the north-west were the actual destroyers of the cities; but in any case they probably found a civilization in the final process of decay.

## *The Indus religion*

From the seals and the baths we can make some uncertain inferences about the religion of the cities. They seem to have shared in the cult of the Mother Goddess common in the Near East, producing terracotta figurines of female figures, nude except for a short skirt. This goddess, as represented on the seals, seems often to have been associated with horned animals, even being represented herself as a theriomorph. We find scenes of religious processions approaching what seem to be sacred trees, occasionally with a goddess – or a tree spirit – depicted in the branches; one seal depicts a female figure, upside down, with a tree growing from between her parted legs.

Several figures are shown sitting in what came to be called a yogic posture, with legs tightly crossed and the hands placed on the knees, often being paid homage by others. Here too we may mention the ritual baths, and the extreme importance that seems to have been laid upon bodily purity and the proper disposal of human wastes: water itself seems to have carried considerable religious significance. We find, finally, large numbers of seemingly phallic objects, perhaps presented as offerings to the goddess as part of rituals of growth and fertility.

## *The Indus inheritance*

We may speculate on the elements of this religious culture that were passed on to its scattered descendants and absorbed into the mainstream of Indian religion. The Mother Goddess especially reappears in later Hinduism, but played almost no role at all in the Buddhist cult. But we find local spirits of trees and streams as central figures in early Buddhism: these are the *yakṣas* and serpent-like *nāgas* who appear constantly in the canonical texts. The sacred tree, too, appears in Buddhism as the tree of enlightenment. There are, for example, any number of Buddhist representations of the Buddha seated cross-legged beneath the tree, protected by the giant hood of the serpent Mucalinda. The three basic elements in the portrayal may all be derived from the Indus Civilization.

The Indus emphasis on purity of the body and the presence of what may have been yogic practices give some evidence of a basically transcendent perspective in Indus religion. We may postulate the presence of a sacerdotal class who ran the sacred baths and interceded with the goddess for the fertility of the crops. But even more, there may well have been a special class of religious practitioners whose aim lay in the induction of trance-like states of bodily immobility, and the impenetrability of the body to pollution. The entire yogic ideal of absolute withdrawal from sensory input cannot easily be traced to Indo-European antecedents; but in the Indus concern for the integrity of the bodily integument and in their representation of figures in cross-legged immobility, we may find a clue to what would become a major element of Indian religion.

## *The Vedic culture*

The Indo-European invaders who trod upon the warm corpse of the Indus Civilization were, by their own account, a hard-drinking, hard-riding band of stalwart warriors, who used with considerable efficacy their own invention of war, the horse-drawn chariot. They brought with them a pantheon of sky gods, families of professional reciters of hymns and performers of ritual, and a substance called *soma* that produced states of divine ecstasy and magical power.

This *soma* may well have been the psychotropic mushroom *Amanita muscaria*. The religious professionals – the technicians of the sacred – opened up the shining world of the gods, and in their rituals of offerings and praise asked boons of the *devas*, the shining ones. Yet in their ecstatic power they were able to control even the gods themselves, and the rituals grew with time into complex magical simulacra for the processes of the entire cosmos, owned and controlled by human agency.

This growing homologization of the ritual to the universe took place as the secret of *soma* was being lost among the priests. But the ideal of ecstatic trance and magic power continued to be expressed, and paradox and metaphor became the vehicles for a literary alteration of consciousness. The magical correspondences of the ritual were expanded, and even in the latest hymns we find the sacrificer still flying in space, his spirit among the gods, while mortals see only his body here below.

## *Vedic literature*

### The basic texts

This visionary tradition was early formulated into orally transmitted texts. The priestly families kept collections of their own inherited hymns, and shortly before the first millenium B.C.E. these were in turn collected into an anthology known as the Ṛg-veda. As the rituals grew more complex, specialized functions were introduced. A priest was appointed specifically to handle the physical actions of the sacrifice and to manipulate the sacred implements, each of which had to be empowered by the recitation of stereotyped magical formulas. The utterances of this performance were then collected into another anthology, the *Yajur-Veda*. Again, another specialized priest took on the role of cantor, and chanted the sacred verses to special melodies, and these verses were collected, along with their musical notation, in the *Sāma-Veda*.

In addition to these texts, the threefold sacred knowledge, a fourth collection of hymns called the *Atharva-Veda* was made specifically for the magical averting of evil. These rituals against death, disease, and hostile witchcraft seem to have been the property of less orthodox religious specialists who lived somewhat closer to the everyday life of the people.

## The expositions

Around 800 B.C.E. there began the composition of compendious prose expositions of the Vedic ritual. These *Brāhmaṇas* deal in sacerdotal detail with the homologies of the sacrifice and the cosmos, and there are the first hints of later doctrines of liberation. If the ritual granted magical power and control of the universe through the magic namings of the priest, then might there not be the single thing whose name is the name of all? There had already been some speculation that all the gods and the universe itself came from the One: if this one thing could be known, then the ultimate power, and the ultimate freedom, might be gained.

These doctrines were expanded upon in the *Āraṇyakas*, books whose secret and sacred lore could be learned only in the solitude of the forests. The archaic modes of ecstasy were turned to realization, and in meditations called *vidyās*, the practitioner internalized the cosmic dimensions of the ritual and could gain the knowledge and power of the ritual without its actual performance.

Very shortly before the time of the Buddha himself, there began to be composed the earliest prose *Upaniṣads*, teachings imparted only from a master to a disciple. Here the quest for the One was carried on in true earnest. Ritual elements increasingly disappear, and the secret and shockingly new truth of transmigration and its terror of repeated death becomes the central motivation for knowledge. The single thing whose name is the essence of the world process is identified as that which is changeless in the midst of change, the ultimate cause of all effects, that which cannot nonexist : to know it – and thus to possess it – is the key to liberation from death.

The One was approached from several directions. It was considered to be the substance of which all things were made, and thus the unchanging ground of phenomenal appearances. As such it was identified with the magic oral powers that created and sustained the cosmos, and was called the *Brahman*. Again, the One was sought within the individual, as that without which life and consciousness could not be, and was thus the unchanging ground of the transmigrating self. As such it was identified with earlier speculations upon the sustaining power of the breath and was called the *ātman*. A final step was taken in the most secret teaching of all, that in reality this Brahman and this *ātman* were the same.

This teaching is enshrined in the most sacred utterances of the *Upaniṣads*, the great sayings such as '*Tat tvam asi*' ('You are That') or '*Brahmo 'ham*' ('I am Brahman'). It was by meditation upon such sayings that the practitioner gained knowledge in a flash of realization; he perceived directly the unchanging reality that underlay the shifting panorama of experience, and his knowledge freed him forever from the terrible round of death.

## The Vedic inheritance

Such teachings were of paramount importance for developing Buddhism. The Buddha's own enlightenment was a visionary and ecstatic experience in the mythic mode of the earliest Vedic tradition. The doctrine of transmigration is central to the Buddhist quest, and the idea of nirvana would be unintelligible without it. The Buddhist process of insight meditation is a direct continuation of the meditations on the great sayings of the *Upaniṣads*, wherein the practitioner internalizes a concise doctrinal formula as a direct and personal realization of the truth. However much the metaphysical superstructure may have differed – and it differed considerably – the quest for freedom as a state of being within the phenomenal world, and the contemplative techniques used in the search, were inherited from the Vedic tradition.

## The Age of the Wanderers

For several centuries before the birth of the Buddha, a revolution had been under way in India. Iron technology had developed, creating a new type of military specialist and a new impersonal mode of warfare. Iron implements cleared great forests for cultivation and constructed the vast timber palisades of fortified cities. The iron-tipped plough produced a surplus economy that could support great governmental and religious institutions. And from the West came the new concept of the centralized imperium, the world-conquering monarch, and the uses of war for power rather than for gain.

There was vast social upheaval as rival kings sought to establish their empires, as religious ritual was increasingly turned to the support of centralized government, and as the family and tribal structures of earlier times dissolved under the pressures of impersonal imperialism. Independent tribal groups were swept up into larger political units, until by the time of the Buddha only sixteen city-states ruled over what had once been a vast series of independent peoples. Some tribal groups in the foothills of the Himalayas held to their independence, but the writing was clearly on the wall. Soon the state of Magadha would inaugurate a final solution to the tribal question.

## *The two traditions*

Opposition to these new forces took many forms, including military resistance. The philosophical quest for freedom was inextricably bound up with a new social movement, the wanderers (*parivrājakas*) who left home and family to seek a way of liberation in the world. Social *anomie* was expressed creatively in religious seeking, and it was from this movement that Buddhism directly derived. We may note that the movement was inherently conservative politically, a reaction against the release of new social forces; the Buddha himself modeled his monastic institution upon the old customs of the independent tribes.

We may distinguish two main religious postures in the wanderer movement itself. Some sought freedom in transcendence, in an enstatic withdrawal from all sensory input, and in total immobility of the body, the breath, and the mind. Progressive states of trance gradually drew the meditator further and further from the realm of phenomena, until he achieved a state of isolation and monadic impenetrability. This practice was closely bound up with concepts of purity and pollution, for action was seen as a sort of defiling substance that weighted the soul and bound it to the world. The process of trance was often viewed as a means of burning away impurities. If our speculations concerning the Indus Valley religion are valid, we have a clear source for these ideas and practices. The basic functional term would seem to be inviolability: the purity of body is a way of preserving its unitary integrity, establishing the skin as the ultimate ego-boundary, just as the immobility of the mind becomes a means of transcending the defilements of sensory input. Other wanderers sought freedom in immanence, in the visionary and ecstatic experience that rendered all things new, and in the magic knowledge that granted power over the world. The quest was for insight rather than for isolation, for the infinite manoeuvrability available to the one who knew how the universe worked. Here was the direct continuation of the Vedic tradition, which was to culminate in the vision of the *Upaniṣads*.

## *The philosophical problematic*

The above is a much simplified view of a complex phenomenon. Although transcendence and immanence remained the basic polarities of the entire Indian contemplative tradition, there was considerable borrowing of techniques from one tradition to the other. We shall see later how Buddhism dealt with the implicit contradictions of its dual contemplative inheritance. These contradictions further generated an entire series of philosophical problems that both Buddhism and Hinduism had to deal with. If ultimate reality is immanent, then there arises the epistemological question of why the practitioner has not realized it already. The choice of transcendence raised ontological problems, and the choice of immanence raised epistemological ones.

What is the relationship between the body and the soul? If the soul is a permanent and unchanging entity somehow trapped within the phenomenal world in spite of its transcendence, then what is the historical process by which this ontological fall took place? Or if the soul participates in change, then what is the psychological process by which it enters into an epistemological relation with an unchanging reality? We must account for personal change and the possibility of spiritual progress on the one hand and for personal continuity and the persistence of memory on the other. If the soul is permanent and unchanging, then how can it be said to transmigrate?

Problems such as these were early put in specifically Buddhist terms. The problem of karma remained a central issue for over a thousand years, for the Buddhist maintained that there was no permanent entity within the personality: how then can we say that it is the same person who suffers for his past deeds, or who attains enlightenment? The problem of perception remained equally central: how can one impermanent entity perceive another that is already past?

But even more important were the most fundamental soteriological issues raised by the implicit contradictions of the tradition. What is the moral value of action in the world? What happens to an enlightened person when he dies? The Buddha is taken for the model for all religious action, but what was the central act of his life – the enlightenment or the nirvana?

The entire history of Buddhist thought can be seen as a search for answers to these questions.

## Discussion questions

1. What role did the Mother Goddess and yoga play in the religion of the Indus Valley?
2. How important was sacrifice in Vedic religion?
3. What was innovative about the teachings of the *Upaniṣads*?
4. What goal did the 'wanderers' (*parivrājakas*) seek, and what methods did they use to attain it?
5. Describe the pattern of social change that was taking place in the Buddha's day.

# Part I

# Foundations

# 1 *Karma and cosmology*

## In this chapter

Cosmologies provide existential orientation and give meaning and direction to human life. Buddhism has a variety of cosmological notions, and sometimes later models are mapped onto earlier ones, resulting in a somewhat untidy picture. The beliefs described in this chapter are not set out neatly in Buddhist literature but are implicit in the myths and legends which are transmitted as part of the common cultural lore of Buddhist societies. These cosmological beliefs provide the background to Buddhism's understanding of the meaning of human life and its destiny and are the presuppositions upon which its formal doctrines are founded. The chapter begins by introducing perspectives on time, history and destiny which are quite different from the familiar Western ones. It then explains ideas about karma and rebirth which are key to understanding the meaning and purpose of human existence from a Buddhist perspective.

## Main topics covered

- The cosmos in Indian thought
- The inhabitants of the cosmos
- The Six Realms of Rebirth
- Karma
- The concept of merit
- Merit transference
- Western perspectives

## *The cosmos in Indian thought*

Buddhism and Hinduism share a perspective on human life that is in important respects very different to that found in the West. Western conceptions of individual

*Figure 1.1* 1,000 Buddha images, Taeansa Monastery, South Kyongsang, Korea

existence have been profoundly shaped by the teachings of its three main religions – Christianity, Judaism and Islam – which have their roots in the common cultural soil of the Middle East. All three of these religions teach that human life is a unique event: we are born, we live, and we die.

This view of individual life derives from an underlying perspective on time. Broadly speaking, time is understood in the West as linear and punctuated by a series of unique events. In the East, however, time is commonly conceptualized as repetitive and cyclic. Thus while the West tends to see history as a generally forward-moving drama (interpreted in secular terms as 'progress' or religiously as the working-out of divine providence), in parts of Asia – and particularly in India – history is seen as a series of potentially infinite cycles in which similar patterns of events recur with no fixed goal or purpose. Whereas Western religions teach that the universe came into being as the result of a unique act of creation, Indian religions believe that the cosmos has always existed, undergoing vast cycles of evolution and decline lasting for billions of years.

Indian cosmology is in some respects closer to the natural patterns observed in nature, which are predominantly cyclic. The seasons follow their regular course, and the agricultural cycles of birth, growth, death, and renewal are repeated year after year. Periodically nature seems to die and be reborn, as when flowers bloom in the spring after a bleak winter (in India the seasons are different, and the renewal of nature comes each year with the monsoon rains which fall between May and June).

Since human beings are a part of nature, it did not seem strange to Indian thinkers to conceive of human life following a similar pattern and passing through an extended series of births and deaths. Individual existences were thought of like pearls on a necklace – each one separate but strung together in an endless series. The origin of such ideas is pre-Buddhist and they are first mentioned in mystical writings known as the Upaniṣads composed over several centuries beginning around the eighth century B.C.E. Since then belief in reincarnation has been deeply engrained in the Indian worldview and forms a fundamental part of the Buddhist outlook on life.

Buddhist cosmology came to envisage the world as divided into two categories: animate and inanimate. It pictures the inanimate part as a kind of receptacle or container (*bhājana*) in which various kinds of living beings (*sattva*) make their homes. The physical universe is formed out of the interaction of the five primary elements, namely earth, water, fire, air, and space (*ākāśa*). In Indian thought space is considered as an element in its own right rather than just a void or the absence of other elements. From the interaction of these elements worlds are formed, such as the one we now inhabit. This world is not unique, however, and there are thought to be other worlds 'as numerous as the sands of the Ganges' inhabited by beings like ourselves. Groups of these worlds cluster together to form 'world-systems' (roughly equivalent to the modern concept of a galaxy) which are found throughout the six directions of space (to the north, south, east, west, above, and below).

These world-systems were believed to evolve and be destroyed over vast periods of time known as *kalpas*, which last for millions of years. Worlds come into being through the interaction of material forces, flourish for a while, and then embark on a downward spiral at the end of which they are destroyed in a great cataclysm caused by natural elements such as fire, water or wind. In due course the process starts up again and the worlds once again evolve to complete a full cycle of time known as a 'great eon' (*mahākalpa*). Up to this point, Buddhist cosmological notions are not greatly different from those of modern astronomy, and it is when we turn to consider Buddhist notions about the inhabitants of these universes that distinctive conceptions arise.

## *The inhabitants of the cosmos*

The natural forces which shape the universe naturally have an impact on the living creatures who inhabit the worlds which are created and destroyed. Interestingly, some sources see the effect as two-way, and suggest that it is the actions of the inhabitants of the various worlds that to a large extent determine their fate. For instance, when people are greedy and selfish the rate of decline is accelerated, and when they are virtuous it slows down. This view at first seems at variance with the contemporary scientific viewpoint, but on reflection is in harmony with modern ecology, which holds that the selfish exploitation of natural resources involved, for example, in burning large quantities of fossil fuels, plays a part in the decline of the natural environment by causing global warming. According to Buddhist belief, a world in which people are wise and virtuous would last considerably longer and be a more pleasant place to live than one inhabited by an ignorant and selfish population. Buddhist cosmology, therefore, seems to have important implications for contemporary ecology, a subject we will return to in Chapter Twelve.

In Buddhism there is no creation myth as such, but a well-known early text called the *Aggañña Sutta* tells an interesting story about how the world began. It takes us back to the time when a previous world-system had been destroyed, and a new one was once just beginning to evolve. When a world is destroyed, the living beings which inhabit it are reborn into a spiritual realm where they await the eventual evolution of a new world. When the new world begins to appear, they are reborn into it as ethereal beings with translucent bodies showing no distinction between the male and female genders. Slowly, as the fabric of the new world becomes denser, the spirit-like beings reborn there begin to consume its material substance like food. As they do this, their bodies become grosser and more solid, like the bodies we have now. As the food is consumed, the myth recounts, it becomes scarcer, and competition for it leads to violent conflict. In order to keep the peace the people elect a king, who then imposes laws and punishes those who break them. This event marks the beginning of social and political life.

Some scholars interpret this text not so much as a creation myth as a satire on the beliefs of the Buddha's Brahmin rivals who believed that the structure of society envisaged in the caste system was divinely ordained. Whichever way we read it, however, the myth presents a view of the origins of the world which is quite unlike the one taught in Christianity. In the Buddhist account the world is not the work of a divine creator, and creation is not a once-and-for-all event. Both faiths do seem to agree on one thing, however: that mankind is in its present predicament because of a primordial fall caused by a moral failing. The difference is that the Judeo-Christian tradition attributes the fall to pride and disobedience, while Buddhism attributes it to craving and desire.

## *The Six Realms of Rebirth*

Within any given world-system there exist qualitatively different modes of existence, some more pleasant than others. The sources commonly speak of six domains or 'realms' into which an individual can be reborn. Some of these realms are visible to us here and now, while others are not. The ones we can see are the human and animal realms, and the ones we cannot see are those of the gods, the *asuras* (explained below), and hell. On the borderline is the realm of the ghosts, beings who hover on the fringes of the human world and who are occasionally glimpsed as they flit among the shadows. As the wheel of *saṃsāra* moves around, beings migrate through the

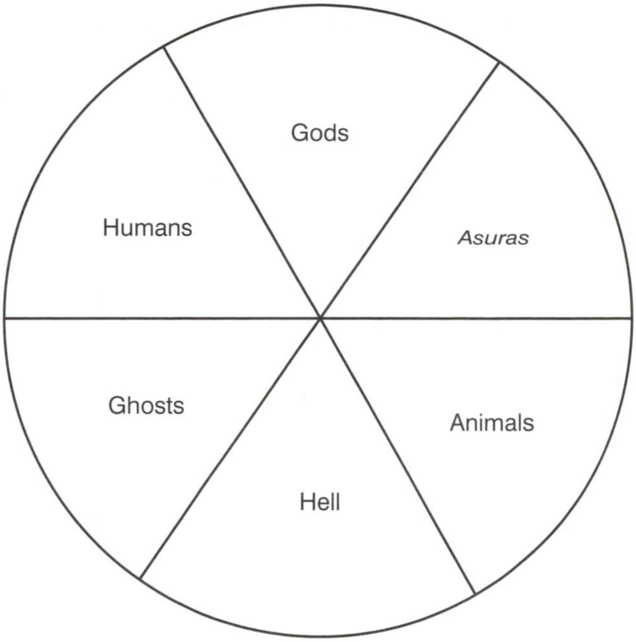


*Figure 1.2* The Six Realms of Rebirth depicted in the wheel of life

various realms of rebirth in accordance with their karma, or the good and evil deeds committed in each life. The scheme of the six realms is commonly depicted in the form of a wheel known as the 'wheel of life' (*bhavacakra*), which sets out the relative position of each of the six domains.

If we look at the circular diagram of the wheel of life, we see three realms below the line and three above. This simple division reflects a qualitative difference in that the three realms below the middle line (hell, the ghosts, and animals) are unfortunate places to be reborn, while those above the line (heaven, the *asuras*, and the human world) are more pleasant. The wheel of life is often depicted in Tibetan *thangkas* or wall hangings. The wheel is a symbolic representation of the process of cyclic rebirth or *saṃsāra*, and is sometimes depicted as showing the six realms of rebirth in the grasp of the demon Yama, the Lord of Death (also known as Māra and by other names). Skulls in Yama's head-dress show that he represents death, time and impermanence. On some accounts the wheel represents a mirror held up by Yama to a dying person revealing the various possibilities for the next rebirth open to them.

The very center of the wheel often shows three animals: a cock, a pig and a snake, which represent the 'three poisons' of greed, hatred and delusion. It is these forces that create bad karma and fuel the endless cycle of rebirth. Placing these mental forces at the center of the diagram reveals the important place that Buddhism accords to psychology and the profound influence it has on our experience of the world by causing us to be reborn in one realm or another. The close connection between psychology and cosmology is also seen in meditational theory, where the various levels of trance (*dhyāna*) are classified in the manner of physical planes in the scheme of thirty-one levels explained below.

Most schools of Buddhism believe that the transition from one realm to another at death is instantaneous (one authority compares it to someone swinging across a river on a rope tied to the branch of a tree). Some Buddhist schools, however, notably those in Tibet, believe there is an intermediate state known as the *bardo* which acts as a buffer between lives and in which the spirit of the deceased person remains for up to forty-nine days before being reborn. During this time the spirit glimpses all six realms of rebirth before being attracted – as if by magnetism – to the one most in keeping with its karmic state.

Perhaps the view of the world just described seems alien and strange, but the notion of the cosmos having various realms or divisions is not unfamiliar in the West. Traditional Christian teachings depict God dwelling at the summit of his creation surrounded by angels and saints, while Satan inhabits an infernal region beneath our feet. Human beings are somewhere in between, poised, so to speak, between two eternal destinies. Traditional teachings also speak of a fourth domain – purgatory – existing as a temporary abode for departed souls undergoing purification in order to be worthy to enter heaven. This gives us a total of four possible states or modes of existence, all of which are found in the Buddhist scheme. To these four Buddhism adds another by subdividing the world we now inhabit into separate domains for animals and humans. It then adds a final one, namely the domain of the *asuras* mentioned above. These are figures from Indian mythology who did battle with the gods as part of an eternal struggle between good and evil. In Buddhist teachings they are depicted as warlike demons consumed by hatred and a lust for power who cannot refrain from expressing their violent impulses in a futile struggle for a victory they never achieve. Instead, their conduct reveals that hatred breeds only hatred, and one battle leads simply to the next. However, as noted, the *asuras* are not of great importance in this scheme of things and are omitted in the earliest descriptions, which speak only of five realms (it is not impossible that they were added to the scheme simply to balance the circle).

There are also some important differences to the Christian conception of the cosmos. The most notable is that in the Buddhist scheme no one is condemned to abide permanently in any given realm. Hell is not a place of permanent damnation, and heaven is not a place of eternal happiness. The wheel revolves continuously, and individuals may move repeatedly in and out of any of the six destinations or '*gatis*', as they are known. In this respect the Buddhist hell is more like the Christian concept of purgatory. The second difference is that the Buddhist hell is more varied, and is thought to have cold as well as hot areas in which the departed spirits suffer until their evil karma is purged.

The world of the ghosts is a realm of suffering of a special kind. The denizens of this realm are pictured as beings who were selfish and greedy in their previous life and who are now suffering the consequences by being denied the ability to enjoy the pleasures they crave. In popular art they are depicted with swollen stomachs and tiny mouths through which they can never pass enough food to satisfy their constant hunger. Generosity (*dāna*) is highly valued in Buddhism, and the greedy seem to merit a special punishment all of their own. These sad wraiths live in the shadows of the human realm, coming out at night to consume the food left out for them as offerings by pious layfolk.

The last of the three unfortunate realms is that of the animals. Rebirth in animal form involves physical suffering due to being hunted both by humans and other predators, as well as the inability to reason and to understand the cause of their predicament. Driven mainly by instincts they cannot control, and without a language capable of communicating the subtleties of Buddhist teachings, animals can only hope for an existence relatively free from pain and to be born in a better condition in the next life. Buddhist folk-tales depict animals as being capable of virtuous behavior to some degree, and modern studies also suggest that the higher mammals are capable of altruistic behavior, but for the most part animals are limited in their capacity for autonomous moral choices. Although there is no dogma on this point Buddhism seems to envisage the realm of animal rebirth as limited to mammals, which means that, contrary to popular belief, you are unlikely to come back as an ant. The *Jātakas* – a collection of stories about the Buddha's previous lives – depict the Buddha at various times as having been a deer (no. 12), a monkey (no. 20), a dog (no. 22), a bull (no. 28), a bird (no. 36), an elephant (no. 72), and many other creatures. However, there are also some early sources which speak of human beings being reborn as scorpions and centipedes (A.v.289) or even worms and maggots (M.iii.168), so it is not possible to be categorical on this point.

The most pleasant of the six realms of rebirth is undoubtedly heaven, which appears at the top of the diagram. Heaven is the residence of the gods (*deva*), namely beings who have accumulated sufficient good karma to justify a rebirth in paradise. These are somewhat like angels in the Christian tradition who reside in the various mansions of heaven. In Buddhism there are no special theological implications associated with a heavenly rebirth: the gods do not create the cosmos, control human destiny, forgive sins, or pass judgement on human beings. Humans may make offerings to the gods and seek their help, but while the gods are revered they are not worshipped in the fashion of the theistic traditions. Nor is heaven a place of permanent salvation: the gods are subject to the law of karma just like anyone else, and in due course they will be reborn in a lower realm when their good karma expires.

Mythology locates the heavens above a great mountain known as Meru which was believed to lie at the center of the world. Later sources (from the fifth century C.E. onwards) subdivide the heavenly realm into twenty-six different levels or 'mansions' which are increasingly sublime. If we add to these the five other realms of rebirth shown in the wheel of life (*bhavacakra*) we reach a total of thirty-one possible rebirth destinations. The lower heavens were thought of as being on the slopes of Mount Meru, the higher terrestrial ones on its summit, and the more sublime heavens floating above it in space. The gods at different levels live for different periods of time. At the lower levels their lifespans are hundreds of times those of humans, and at the top their lives are measured in millions of years. Time is believed to be relative, however, and the gods perceive it differently according to their station: thus a million years of human time might seem like a week to the gods on the lower levels, and a day to the gods at the summit. The top five heavens are known as the 'Pure Abodes', and are reserved for those known as 'non-returners' (*anāgāmin*): these are individuals in the human world who are on the point of gaining enlightenment and will not be reborn again as human beings.

It might seem strange to Western ears to hear that rebirth in heaven is not the ultimate goal, and this statement needs some explanation. In practice, many (if not most) Buddhists would be only too happy to find themselves in heaven in their next rebirth, and almost all (both monks and laymen) make efforts to bring this about. However, Buddhists believe that heaven is only a proximate goal, and the final aim is to attain nirvana and put an end to rebirth altogether. There can even be a danger in being reborn in heaven – that one may become complacent and lose sight of the omnipresence of suffering and impermanence. It is thought that being insulated from suffering causes the gods to lose sight of the painful realities of life the Buddha drew attention to in the First Noble Truth (see Chapter Three), and to slacken their efforts to reach nirvana. For this reason the human world is thought preferable as a place of rebirth since it contains a better balance of pleasure and suffering.

The human world is found in the fifth segment of the *bhavacakra* and is thought to be very difficult to attain. The great advantage of human existence is that it reminds us constantly of the realities of suffering and impermanence, and so keeps our minds focused on those factors which spurred the Buddha to attain enlightenment. Had he remained cosseted within the palace walls as a young prince (a situation analogous to that of the gods) he would never have found a permanent solution to life's problems. Human beings, unlike animals, are also endowed with reason and free will, and are in position to use these faculties to understand Buddhist teachings and choose to follow the Noble Eightfold Path. While suffering certainly exists in human life, so does pleasure, such that the human realm offers a 'middle way' between the higher and lower realms which are either too pleasant (heaven) or too painful (hell). It is thus believed that suffering works like the grit in the oyster to produce the pearl of nirvana.

## *Karma*

In the cosmology set out above, karma is the mechanism that moves people around from one realm of rebirth to another. We could picture it as a kind of elevator

## The Three Spheres of Rebirth

Buddhist cosmology often seems untidy and contradictory, and this is because it is made up of competing schemes which do not always integrate perfectly with one another. Different conceptions of the world developed in a random fashion in myths and legends, and Buddhism absorbed many popular ideas from folklore and local tradition. Alongside the scheme of the six realms of rebirth, for example, is found an ancient Indo-European conception of the world as divided into three layers – known variously as *avacaras*, *dhātus* or *lokas* – and probably based originally on the idea of earth, atmosphere, and sky.

In this tripartite model the surface of the earth is the world of human beings, and above that are various atmospheric phenomena such as clouds, lightning and thunder, which became personified and regarded as divinities. Just as the earth's atmosphere becomes more rarified in higher levels like the stratosphere, in the scheme of the three spheres matter becomes increasingly refined at the upper levels, eventually tapering off into realms which appear to consist of pure thought. The lowest and most earthly of the three spheres is known as the 'sphere of sense-desires' (*kāmāvacara*), and includes all of the realms up to the sixth heaven above the human world. Next is the 'sphere of pure form' (*rūpāvacara*), a rarefied spiritual space in which the gods perceive and communicate by a kind of telepathy. This extends up to level twenty-seven. Highest of all is the 'sphere of formlessness' (*arūpāvacara*), a state without material shape or form (*rūpa*) in which beings exist as pure mental energy.

The gods in the four highest levels, those of the sphere of formlessness (*arūpāvacara*), are thought to apprehend phenomena in four increasingly subtle ways: in the lowest (level twenty-eight) as if all that existed was infinite space; in the second (level twenty-nine) as if there were nothing but infinite consciousness; in the third (level thirty) as 'nothingness', or the idea that even consciousness has been transcended. After leaving behind even the thought of 'nothingness', there arises an ineffable state of mind known as 'neither perception nor non-perception' (level thirty-one). This is the summit of existence and the highest state in which anyone can be reborn. As already noted, Buddhist ideas about cosmology dovetail with its meditational theory, and the names of the two highest levels of rebirth (levels thirty and thirty-one) bear the same names as the two highest stages of meditation. Access to these places or states can thus be gained either by being reborn in them or by tuning into their 'frequency' through meditation. Here we see the close association between psychology and cosmology in Buddhist teachings.

that takes people up and down inside a building. Good deeds result in an upward movement and bad deeds in a downward one. In popular usage in the West karma is thought of simply as the good and bad things that happen to a person, like good and bad luck. However, this oversimplifies what for Buddhists is a complex of interrelated ideas which embraces both ethics and belief in rebirth, and which is summed up in the word *saṃsāra* ('flowing on').

The doctrine of karma is concerned with the ethical implications of *Dharma*, or the Buddha's teachings. Karma is concerned primarily with the moral dimension of those teachings and denotes primarily the consequences of moral behavior. For Buddhism, karma is thus neither random – like luck – nor a system of rewards and punishments meted out by God. Nor is it destiny or fate: instead it is best understood as a natural – if complex – sequence of causes and effects. In the Buddhist scholastic tradition known as *Abhidharma* it is classified (for example, *Atthasālinī* 2.360) as *karma-niyama*: this means that it is seen as just one aspect of the natural order, specifically as one function of the universal law of causation known as dependent origination (*pratītya-samutpāda*) which will be explained in Chapter Three.

The literal meaning of the Sanskrit word karma is 'action', but karma as a religious concept is concerned not with just any actions but with actions of a particular kind. The Buddha defined karma by reference to moral choices and the acts consequent upon them. He stated 'It is intention (*cetanā*), O monks, that I call karma; having willed one acts through body, speech, or mind' (A.3.415). In this emphasis on intention the Buddha modified the traditional understanding of karma, which tended to see it as a product of ritual rather than moral acts. In a discussion with a follower of Jainism concerning which of the three modes of actions – body, speech or mind – is most reprehensible, the Jain states that bodily action has the greatest power to produce bad karma. The Buddha disagrees, stating that mental actions are the most potent of the three, thereby illustrating the innovative ethical perspective adopted by Buddhism.

So how can we tell if an action is good or bad in terms of karma? From the way the Buddha defined it the main criterion seems to be one of intention or free choice. In Buddhist psychology there are said to be three basic kinds of motivation known as 'roots'. These have two forms, good and bad, giving a total of six in all. Actions motivated by greed (*rāga*), hatred (*dveṣa*), and delusion (*moha*) are bad (*akuśala*) while actions motivated by their opposites – non-attachment, benevolence, and understanding – are good (*kuśala*). It will be recalled that these are the same as the 'three poisons' depicted at the center of the wheel of life (*bhavacakra*). Sometimes these terms go by different names, for instance 'craving' (*rāga*) is often called 'attachment' (*lobha*), but the different terminology is of little importance. What matters to a Buddhist is to ensure that his or her motivation is always of a wholesome kind, since this is the way that good karma is accumulated and progress to nirvana is made.

Agriculture provides a familiar metaphor for karma in Buddhist sources, and creating karma is often likened to the planting of seeds in the earth. Some seeds are good and some are bad, and each bears sweet or bitter fruit at the appointed time. So it is with good and bad deeds. The karmic choices we make today will come to 'maturation' (*vipāka*) or bear 'fruit' (*phala*) tomorrow. Sometimes karma will bear fruit in the same lifetime, but other times it may manifest itself many lifetimes in the future. An example of how karma bears fruit in the present life is the way the features of an angry person become progressively distorted and ugly with time (M.3.203–6). Various aspects of the life to come are said to be karmically determined, including the family into which one is born, one's caste or social standing, physical appearance, character and personality. Any karma accumulated but not yet spent is carried forward to the next life, or even many lifetimes ahead. In this sense individuals are said to be 'heirs' to their previous deeds (M. 3.203). The precise manner in which karma operates, and the mechanism that links given acts and their consequences, is a matter of debate among Buddhist schools. The Buddha simply described the process as profound, and as inconceivable (*acinteyya*) to anyone except a Buddha (A.4.77).

It is important to grasp that the doctrine of karma is not the same as determinism. This is the belief that everything that happens to a person is preordained and brought about by fate or destiny. The Buddha made a distinction between karma and deterministic fate (*niyati*) in this sense, and accepted that random events and accidents can happen in life. Not everything need have a karmic cause, and winning the lottery or catching a cold can be simply random events. In the *Aṅguttara Nikāya* (3.61), for instance, the Buddha disagrees with certain of his contemporaries who held the view that 'whatever good, bad, or neutral feeling is experienced, all that is due to some previous action', explaining that certain illnesses, for example, could be attributed to physical causes (the 'humors') rather than the effect of karma.

## *Merit*

Good karma is highly prized by Buddhists, and is often spoken of as 'merit' (*puṇya*, Pāli: *puñña*). Its opposite, bad karma, is referred to as 'demerit' or *pāpa*. A good deal of effort is put into acquiring the former and avoiding the latter. The purpose of acquiring merit is to enjoy happiness in this life and to secure a good rebirth, ideally as a god in one of the heavens. Some Buddhists think of merit as if it were a commodity, like money in a bank account which can be earned and spent. Some even go to the extreme of carrying a notebook in which they record their good and bad deeds and total up their 'balance' every day! This materialistic conception of merit is not one the orthodox teachings would support, since the motivation behind it seems to be largely a selfish one. If a person is motivated to do good deeds simply for personal gain, then one could say the underlying motivation is actually greed, and accordingly not likely to generate much merit. In practice in most cases of this

### Merit transference

Many Buddhists believe that merit can be transferred from one person to another, just like donations can be made to charity. Many rituals and good deeds are preceded by a dedication to the effect that any merit that arises from the act should be directed towards a named recipient or group. This practice of 'merit transference' has the happy result that instead of one's own karmic balance being depleted, as it would in the case of money, it increases as a result of the generous motivation in sharing. It is doubtful to what extent there is canonical authority for notions of this kind, although at least the motivation to share one's merit in a spirit of generosity is karmically wholesome and would lead to the formation of a generous and benevolent character.

kind the motivation is probably a mixed one, partly selfish and partly altruistic, so a limited amount of merit may be produced, but such behavior cannot be said to be acting in accordance with the spirit of Buddhist teachings. In particular it misses the important point that merit is produced as a by-product of doing what is right and should not be sought as an end in itself.

A very common way to earn merit, particularly for the laity, is by supporting and making donations and offerings to the *sangha* or order of monks. This can be done on a daily basis by placing food in the bowls of monks as they pass on their alms round, by providing robes for the monks at the annual Kaṭhina ceremony held at the end of the rainy-season retreat, by listening to sermons and attending religious services, and by donating funds for the upkeep of monasteries and temples. Merit can even be made by congratulating other donors and empathetically rejoicing (*anumodanā*) in their generosity.

## *Western perspectives*

We have explained Buddhist ideas about karma and rebirth at the start of the book because these notions are often puzzling to Western readers who are exposed to different cultural presuppositions about time and history, as alluded to earlier. In particular, many questions often arise concerning the coherency of such notions. For example, it might be asked why, if we are all reborn, do so few people remember previous lives? In part this may have to do with the way we are brought up and taught to think in certain ways. In societies where there is no supporting framework for a belief in reincarnation, such as in the West, memories of previous lives may simply go unrecognized or unacknowledged. When such memories are reported by children they are commonly dismissed by teachers and parents as the product of an overactive imagination. Again, individuals may experience peer-pressure and be unwilling to risk ridicule by reporting experiences that society (and in particular the scientific establishment) does not accept. There is, however, a growing body of evidence from individuals who claim to recall previous lives, many of which it is difficult to account for unless the memories are genuine.

It must be admitted, however, that vivid and detailed recollections of past lives are rare, even in cultures like India and Tibet where rebirth is accepted. The Dalai Lama, for instance, the leader of Tibet's Buddhists, does not claim to recall his previous life in any detail. One explanation sometimes given for this is that death and rebirth are traumatic experiences which tend to erase almost all memories from the upper levels of the mind. The only way to recover them subsequently is by entering altered states of consciousness such as the kind induced by meditation or hypnosis, or to be born with a particular aptitude or gift of recall. However, Buddhists do not regard such questions as of great importance: in their view what matters is not speculation about the past but doing good deeds in the present.

There is also often curiosity among Western students of Buddhism as to how reincarnation can be squared with population statistics, and, in particular, why the earth does not fill up with all the people who die and are reborn. Once again this question is based on certain anthropocentric assumptions about the nature of the cosmos (for example, that there is only one planet in the universe where people live), and overlooks the fact that in each world-system there is thought to be constant transit between the realms of the gods, humans, *asuras*, animals, ghosts and the hells.

Is belief in the six realms an article of faith for Buddhists, and do all Buddhists believe in the possibility of being reborn as an animal? Buddhism has very few dogmas, and the traditional worldview described above is not something in which Buddhists are required to believe. Some may believe in the literal truth of the scriptures (just as some Christians believe in creationism) while other may believe in more modern theories (as other Christians believe in evolution). Although most Buddhists – and in particular those from Asian countries – do accept the traditional teachings, not all do. In particular, many Western Buddhists tend to reject the more 'medieval' elements of the traditional scheme and replace them with notions more congenial to the modern age, perhaps interpreting the six realms as referring to other dimensions of existence, levels of reality, parallel worlds, or simply states of mind. Indeed, some contemporary Buddhists reject the idea of rebirth altogether, although in doing so they seem to cast aside a large body of traditional belief without having much to put in its place. According to the scriptures, the recollection of his own previous lives, and a vision of how other people die and are reborn in accordance with their karma, both formed a key part of the Buddha's enlightenment experience as he sat under the Bodhi tree, as we shall see in the next chapter. It is hard to see how that aspect of the experience can be disentangled from the rest of his 'awakening', and if the texts are mistaken about his vision of previous lives, how can we have faith in their claim that the Buddha gained enlightenment? To reject the belief in rebirth, accordingly, seems to throw the baby out with the bathwater. For most Buddhists, belief in a continued personal existence in some form or other after death seems to remain an important part of their understanding of Buddhist teachings.

So is the aim for Buddhists to move from one life to another in an upward trajectory experiencing greater happiness each time round? In practice this does seem to be a goal many Buddhists – both monks and laymen – would be happy to achieve, but it is not the final solution to suffering that the Buddha left home to seek. As we shall see, the Buddha was dissatisfied with the temporary bliss he attained through meditation and would accept nothing less than a permanent solution to the problem of human suffering. This is because however much good karma one accumulates, it is finite and will eventually expire, not unlike the energy of a spacecraft in a decaying orbit. Sooner or later the good karma that results in a heavenly rebirth will run its course and even the gods will die and be reborn. The solution the Buddha proclaimed was that the answer to the problem of suffering does not lie in a better rebirth in the cycle of reincarnation (*saṃsāra*), and that only nirvana offers a final solution.

## Key points you need to know

- Buddhists believe the universe is infinite in space and time, and undergoes periodic cycles of evolution and destruction known as *kalpas*.
- Time is conceived of as cyclic rather than linear. Individuals live over and over in the endless cycle of rebirth known as *saṃsāra*.
- There are six realms of rebirth: the gods, *asuras*, humans, animals, hungry ghosts, and in hell. None of these is permanent.
- Movement between the six realms of rebirth is determined by karma – the good and bad deeds a person performs in the course of a lifetime.
- The only way to escape from *saṃsāra* is by attaining nirvana. This is the ultimate goal of all Buddhists.

## Discussion questions

1. How does Buddhism understand the nature of the cosmos with reference to a) time and b) space?
2. What are the 'Six Realms of Rebirth' and how are they described in Buddhist teachings?
3. Explain the main features of karma as understood in Buddhism.

## Further reading

Kloetzli, Randy. *Buddhist Cosmology: From Single World System to Pure Land: Science and Theology in the Images of Motion and Light*. Delhi: Motilal Banarsidass, 1983.

McGovern, William Montgomery. *A Manual of Buddhist Philosophy: Cosmology*. Lucknow, India: Oriental Reprinters, 1976.

Obeyesekere, Gananath. *Imagining Karma: Ethical Transformation in Amerindian, Buddhist and Greek Rebirth (Comparative Studies in Religion & Society)*. Berkeley, CA: University of California Press, 2002.

O'Flaherty, Wendy Doniger. *Karma and Rebirth in Classical Indian Traditions*. Berkeley, CA: University of California Press, 1980.

Reichenbach, Bruce R. *The Law Of Karma: A Philosophical Study*. Honolulu, HI: University of Hawaii Press, 1990.

Reynolds, Frank and Mani B. Reynolds. *Three Worlds according to King Ruang: A Thai Buddhist Cosmology*. Berkeley, CA: Asian Humanities Press, 1982.

Sadakata, Akira. *Buddhist Cosmology: Philosophy and Origins*. 1st English ed. Tokyo: Kosei Publishing Company, 1997.

Sankaranarayan, Kalpakam, Kazunobo Matsudu, and Motohiro Yoritomi. *Lokaprajñapti: a Critical Exposition of Buddhist Cosmology*. Mumbai: Somaiya Publications, 2002.

Sunthorn, Na-Rangsi. *The Buddhist Concepts of Karma and Rebirth*. Bangkok: Mahamakut Rajavidyalaya Press, 1976.

# 2 The Buddha

## In this chapter

The problems in uncovering traces of the 'historical Buddha' are similar to those faced in the search for the 'historical Jesus'. While the personality of the founders dominates both religions, relatively little is known about their lives. The earliest sources give us snapshots of the Buddha throughout his career: as child prodigy, family man, student of yoga, philosopher, teacher, and miracle-worker, but there is no biographical narrative that links all of these phases together. Moreover, the earliest texts tend to dwell on certain incidents in the Buddha's life – such as his enlightenment and death – and give little information about others. In the centuries following the Buddha's death, a standard biography was synthesized from the various fragments and stories in circulation, and preserved in literary compositions of high quality. Even the earliest of these accounts are highly embellished and contain hagiographic elements which obscure the historical reality.

## Main topics covered

- The Buddha
- The Buddha's birth
- Renunciation
- Austerities
- Enlightenment
- The first sermon
- The Buddha's last days
- The death of the Buddha

## *The Buddha*

'Buddha' is not a personal name, but a Sanskrit word meaning 'one who has awakened' or 'one who has woken up'. In Buddhism, it is a title given to those enlightened individuals who have fully attained the goal of the religious life. In addition to 'the Buddha', such individuals may also be referred to by their followers in other ways, for example as the Bhagavat, or 'Lord'. Naturally these titles only apply once the individual has achieved the goal, and before then they are known by another term, namely *bodhisattva* (Pāli *bodhisatta*). Literally this means an 'enlightenment being', in the sense of someone 'bound for enlightenment', or a Buddha-in-training. While not particularly important in early Buddhism, the term '*bodhisattva*' became extremely important later on in the movement known as the Mahāyāna, which arose a few centuries after the Buddha's death.

The person we refer to as the Buddha was born just inside the borders of Nepal in a region known as the Terai lowlands. In common with Indian custom he had both a personal name and a clan name. His personal name was Siddhārtha (Pāli: Siddhattha) and his clan name was Gautama (Pāli: Gotama). The people he came from were known as the Śākyas, and for this reason the Buddha is often referred to as Śākyamuni, meaning 'the sage of the Śākyas'. We cannot say exactly when the Buddha was born, since the chronology of the period has yet to be firmly established. Indeed, it is only in the last century or so that archaeologists have discovered concrete proof that the Buddha existed at all. Apart from what the scriptures of Buddhism tell us, there is very little independent evidence of the Buddha's life, and few artefacts survive from the period when he lived and taught.

### The Buddha's life in a nutshell

The traditional accounts of the Buddha's life give us few facts on which to construct a biography, but one widely-accepted chronology of events would be as follows. He was born at a place called Lumbinī in Nepal, and at sixteen married Yaśodharā, who bore him a son called Rāhula ('Fetter'). Some sources say his son was born soon after the marriage, while others suggest his birth came much later at the age of twenty-nine shortly before Siddhārtha renounced the world and became a wandering student seeking religious knowledge. Six years after embarking on this quest he obtained the awakening he sought, and was henceforth known as the Buddha. For the remainder of his life, a total of forty-five years, he traveled throughout the towns and villages of north-east India giving religious teachings. At the age of eighty he succumbed to illness and passed away into the state of nirvana from which he would never more be reborn.

Various dates for the Buddha's life have been proposed by scholars. Commonly, he is said to have lived from 566–486 B.C.E., or from 563–483 B.C.E. The most recent research, however, suggests that these dates are too early and that the Buddha may have lived closer to our own time, perhaps from 490–410 B.C.E., or 480–400 B.C.E. Chronological precision is not really possible since due to the nature of the sources all dates from this period are accurate only to plus or minus ten years.

Buddhist sources tell us that the Buddha came from a royal lineage, and describe the pomp and ceremony of his father's court at great length. This is likely to be something of an exaggeration, since the political system in existence among the Śākyas was not kingship but republicanism. The Buddha's father was most likely the leader of a tribal confederation which decided its affairs in a council of elders. However, the Buddha would very probably have had a privileged aristocratic upbringing, and have benefited from a traditional education studying subjects such as religious law and custom (*dharmaśāstra*), statecraft, grammar, logic, and other arts and sciences. As a member of the *kṣatriya* or warrior caste, the second of the four castes, the Buddha would have been expected to lead a practical life as a man of action, either as a warrior or political leader like his father. The Buddha would thus have been an urbane and educated young man familiar with the customs and manners of the aristocracy and equipped by his upbringing to mingle comfortably with the kings and courtiers he would encounter later on his travels as a wandering teacher. This, along with his own personal charisma, would have a considerable bearing on the spread and reception of the Buddha's teachings during his lifetime.

The few brief facts mentioned in the text box are the kernel of a story which is referred to elusively in the earliest sources in the form of scattered details, but is not found in any one place as a single continuous narrative. For this reason producing a

## Early scriptures

The teachings of the Buddha are recorded in various collections of scripture known as canons. These derive from an oral tradition which goes back to the time of the Buddha, and which was preserved through a method of communal chanting. The only one of these early canons which has been preserved intact is the Pāli Canon, so called because it is written in Pāli, a vernacular language related to Sanskrit and close to that spoken by the Buddha. The Pāli Canon was committed to writing in Sri Lanka in the first century B.C.E. and consists of three divisions known as 'baskets' (*piṭaka*). These are (1) the Discourses (*Sūtra Piṭaka*) or sermons of the Buddha, which are subdivided into five divisions known as *nikāyas*; (2) the Monastic Rule (*Vinaya Piṭaka*), which contains the rules of monastic discipline; and (3) the Scholastic Treatises (*Abhidharma Piṭaka*), a slightly later compilation of scholastic works.

biography of the Buddha is no easy task, and there are large gaps in his life for which little chronological data is available. While the sources preserve his teachings at great length, it does not seem to have occurred to his followers to record the biographical details of his life in detail. The same happened in the case of Jesus, and despite the much greater amount of archaeological and other data available in respect of the ancient Near East it has so far not been possible to recover the 'historical Jesus'. Constructing a biography of a person is a relatively recent literary innovation, and an added complication in the case of India is that individuals are thought to have lived many times, so that the significance of any one life tends to be lost sight of against the background of the others.

Our earliest literary information about the Buddha comes from the Pāli Canon (see text box), but the scattered details preserved there were not placed in chronological order until several centuries after the Buddha's death. The most famous account of the Buddha's life is the *Buddhacarita* ('Acts of the Buddha'), an epic poem composed by Aśvaghoṣa in the second century C.E. more than half a millennium after the events it narrates had transpired. Literary works of this kind are not of much use to the biographer since they contain much hagiography and constantly refer to supernatural beings and phenomena. Aśvaghoṣa's account is comparatively sober in tone, but from the earliest times the sources had intertwined factual and religious details to such an extent that it is now almost impossible to separate them. For example, early sources describe the Buddha as performing miracles such as walking on water and transporting himself across rivers with a wave of his hand. His whole personality is surrounded in mystique down to distinctive physical marks which were thought to be found on his body. These, known as the 'thirty-two marks of a great man', are part of ancient Indian lore and are believed to mark out great heroes and sages. Such individuals have a noble bearing, a melodious voice, and many other unusual and distinctive features.

Artists later depict these details on images and statues of the Buddha. Among some of the most common are a distinctive hairstyle, displaying what is referred to as a 'snail curl' pattern since it is composed of small clumps which curl to the right, a bit like the spiral pattern on the shell of a snail. Another is the *uṣnīśa* or mound on the crown of the head, indicating, perhaps, his great wisdom. A third is a small tuft of hair between the eyes symbolizing his 'third eye' or great spiritual insight. Perhaps surprisingly, the physical form of the Buddha is never seen in works of art in the early centuries after his death, perhaps because the artistic imagination needed time to ponder the best way to depict it. Only with the passage of time, and perhaps at the request of lay patrons who felt the need to express their devotion, did artists begin to represent the Buddha in human form (see also Buddhist Art in Chapter Five). Although many beautiful images were created, however, it is highly unlikely they bear any close likeness to the historical individual they depict, since they are largely based on stylized conventions of the kind just described.

## Sources for the Buddha's life

There is no continuous narrative biography in the early literature, but the most important sources for details of the Buddha's life include:

- The Pāli Canon. Certain *sūtras* provide biographical details, such as the Discourse of the Great Decease (*Mahāparinirvāṇa Sūtra*) which recounts the last few months of the Buddha's life and confirms he was eighty years old when he died.
- The *Mahāvastu* (Great Story), first century C.E. (anonymous)
- The *Lalitavistara* (Graceful Description), first century C.E. (anonymous)
- The *Buddhacarita* or Acts of the Buddha, an epic poem in twenty-eight chapters composed in the second century C.E. by Aśvaghoṣa
- The *Nidānakathā* (Introductory Tale), second or third century C.E. This text forms the introduction to the *Jātaka*, a collection of popular stories about the Buddha's previous lives.
- Other biographies have been composed down the centuries in different languages, including *The Light of Asia* (1879) by the English poet Sir Edwin Arnold.

## *The Buddha's birth*

For Buddhists, four events in the Buddha's life are held to be of key importance: his birth, enlightenment, first sermon, and death. These are the events around which myths and legends cluster, and they are celebrated in rituals throughout the Buddhist world. The sites at which these events took place, moreover, are regarded as especially important places of pilgrimage. The Buddha's birth, like that of Jesus, was foreshadowed by portents and omens. According to the *Nidānakathā*, at his conception Māyā, the Buddha's mother, dreamt that a white baby elephant had entered her side. This was a very auspicious symbol suggesting that this was no ordinary child. Soothsayers were consulted as to the dream and confirmed that the child would be either a great religious teacher, or a mighty king known as a *Cakravartin* ('world-ruler'). The tradition in India was for a pregnant woman to return to her relatives to give birth, and as the time drew nigh Māyā set out from Kapilavastu, the Śākyan capital, to return home. Her journey was interrupted for the child arrived on the way and was born in a delightful grove at a remote spot called Lumbinī. The texts report that the queen gave birth standing up holding on to the branch of a Sāl tree, and that the baby was born from her side without pain. A number of supernatural phenomena accompanied the birth. Many gods had assembled to witness this wonderful event, and they now took the infant, laid him upon the ground, and bathed him in a miraculous shower of water. The ground shook and trembled, registering the importance of what had taken place, and it is said that the new-born baby stood up and took seven steps, looked around in all directions and declared himself to be the 'chief of the world'. He also proclaimed that this was to be his last birth. Clearly, the sources intend us to understand that this was no normal child, but one who was fully conscious and aware from the moment he was born. Sources such as the *Accariyabbhūtadhamma Sutta* (M.3.123) also claim that the Buddha's awareness of these events preceded his conception, and that he had been waiting mindfully and aware all along in the Tuṣita heaven for the time to enter his mother's womb.

The young boy was given the name Siddhārtha (Pāli: Siddhattha), which means 'one who has achieved his aim'. Amid the celebrations the story takes a darker turn as seven days after his birth queen Māyā passes away. The Buddha was then raised by his aunt, Prajāpatī, who subsequently married his father. The sources do not dwell on the effect the loss of his mother would have had on the young child, but clearly this early bereavement must have had an psychological impact of some kind. Perhaps it brought home to the Buddha the fragility of human life and the powerlessness of individuals to control the forces which shape their lives. It may have predisposed him to a pessimistic outlook, and to seeing the world as a place of sorrow and pain, although he does not come across as gloomy or morbid by nature. Little information is given in the Pāli Canon about the Buddha's childhood, although we are given to understand that he wanted for nothing and had a very comfortable life as a resident in the three palaces belonging to his father (A.i.145). He wore fine clothes and fragrances, and spent his days listening to music and being ministered to by servant girls and attendants who were on hand to attend to any requirements. The Buddha is portrayed as quick-witted and with nascent psychic powers and a keen intelligence. Later sources emphasize his father's fear that the prophesy made at his son's birth might come true, and that the Buddha would leave home to become a religious teacher instead of following in his footsteps. His overprotective father therefore cosseted and pampered the young Siddhārtha, shielding him from any unpleasantness that might intrude from the world beyond the palace walls.

## *Renunciation*

Siddhārtha's comfortable home life would soon come to an abrupt end. The events which provoked this and propelled him into a new life outside the palace walls, and eventually to his awakening (*bodhi*), are narrated in the *Ariyapariyesanā Sutta* of the *Aṅguttara Nikāya*, one of the few texts to provide a continuous narrative of part of the Buddha's life. This and other early sources give the impression that the Buddha's decision to leave home was premeditated and the result of a growing realization that the realities of sickness, ageing and death were things against which he was powerless.

What he sought was nirvana – a state beyond birth and death – a mystical goal which many of his contemporaries also sought under various names and descriptions.

According to the *Dīgha Nikāya* (2.151) it was at the age of twenty-nine that the Buddha took the momentous decision to leave home. The same text tells us that this pattern is reproduced in the life of all the Buddhas, who all undergo the same critical experiences. A well-known story recounted in both this source and the later *Nidānakathā* relates the build-up to the decision. The story relates how the Buddha ventured outside his palace on four occasions accompanied by his charioteer. On the first three he visits a park, and his father arranged to have the streets kept clear of disturbing sights such as elderly and sick people, which might provoke a spiritual crisis in his son. Only healthy, smiling people were permitted to line the thoroughfares. Nevertheless, as luck would have it (or, as later sources explain it, through the intervention of the gods) Siddhārtha was confronted by the sight of an old man, a sick man, and a corpse. Siddhārtha asked his charioteer to explain what had befallen these three individuals, and was thunderstruck when he was told that all humanity was vulnerable to ageing, sickness and death. Hurrying back to the palace he pondered what he had learnt. Deeply disturbed at the transient nature of human existence, he ordered his charioteer to take him out a final time. On this trip he encountered a *śramaṇa*, a religious mendicant dressed in an orange robe. Inspired by the thought that he too could embark on a spiritual quest he decided to leave the palace that very night. Taking a last look at his sleeping wife and son he turned his back on family life forever and left to become a homeless wanderer. The Buddha rode out on his white horse, Kanthaka, with his charioteer, Chandaka, holding onto the tail. In order that its hooves should make no sound which might alert the palace guards, the gods – so the later sources inform us – bore both the horse and rider aloft in the air. Once outside the town, Chandaka pleaded with the Buddha to let him accompany him into the forest, but the Buddha refused, and horse and charioteer returned home both full of grief at the loss of their master.

The story of the Buddha's renunciation is probably best read as a parable rather than a narrative of historical events. It is unlikely that an educated and highly intelligent man like the Buddha would have been unaware of the facts of life, despite his privileged upbringing, and what we see described in the story is more likely a dawning realization about the true nature of the human condition. The palace may represent complacency and self-delusion, and its walls the mental barriers we construct to shield ourselves from unpleasant truths. The Buddha as a young prince was 'living in denial', as we might say today, and the four signs were experiences which challenged the cosy picture of the world he had constructed for himself. Eventually, when reality intruded forcefully in the form of the four signs, the tension became so strong that it provoked a kind of existential crisis which shattered his previous model of the world and launched him into a new and unfamiliar way of life. Experiences of this kind are familiar to everyone: although people no longer travel in chariots, the

**Many characters play a part in the drama of the Buddha's life**

The following is a cast list showing the names of the main protagonists:

| | |
|---|---|
| Ānanda | The Buddha's cousin and personal attendant |
| Ārāḍa Kālāma | The Buddha's first teacher |
| Chandaka | The Buddha's charioteer |
| Kanthaka | The Buddha's horse |
| Māra | The Buddhist devil |
| Māyā | The Buddha's mother |
| Prajāpatī | The Buddha's aunt, and Śuddhodana's second wife |
| Rāhula | The Buddha's son |
| Śuddhodhana | The Buddha's father |
| Udraka Rāmaputra | The Buddha's second teacher |
| Yaśodharā | The Buddha's wife |

equivalent of the four signs can still be seen on almost any city journey in the form of hospitals, care homes, cemeteries, and churches, or unpleasant experiences like the sickness and death of family and friends which thrust themselves into our lives and overturn our comfortable equilibrium.

## *Austerities*

Now free of family and social obligations, Siddhārtha became a *śramaṇa*, one of a loose community of homeless mendicants who devoted themselves to self-mortification, the practice of penances, and a range of religious exercises such as yoga and meditation in the hope of attaining mystical knowledge. Siddhārtha was therefore not alone, but a new recruit to an established counter-culture which had existed for many centuries. *Śramaṇas* like Siddhārtha depended on the laity for alms, although many of them wandered far away from towns and villages to live an arduous life of seclusion in the forest.

In the time-honored fashion, Siddhārtha sought out a religious master (*guru*), turning first to a well-known teacher called Ārāḍa Kālāma who showed him a meditational technique which allowed him to enter a profound state of trance. This state, attained through yogic concentration, was known as the 'sphere of nothingness', and was one in which the mind transcended all thought producing a sensation of deep spiritual peace. Siddhārtha was an able student and quickly mastered this practice. So impressed was his teacher that he offered to make his student joint leader of the group. Siddhārtha declined, since he felt that he still had not achieved the goal he sought.

Taking leave of Ārāḍa, Siddhārtha turned to a second teacher of yoga by the name of Udraka Rāmaputra, and once again excelled as a student. Now he was able to attain an even loftier state of trance enigmatically known as the 'sphere of neither-perception-nor-non-perception'. In this state consciousness becomes so subtle that the mind of the meditator no longer registers even the idea of nothingness. Udraka was so impressed that he offered to exchange places with his student and make Siddhārtha his master, but Siddhartha turned down this offer for the same reasons as before. The problem, as he saw it, was that while the experience of these mystical states was good and valuable as far as it went, it was only a temporary escape from life's problems. While a person could abide for hours or perhaps days in such a state, enjoying sensations of bliss and deep spiritual peace, the fundamental problems of suffering, old age and death remained unresolved. However, the Buddha did not discard his new-found knowledge, and later on when he formulated a distinctively Buddhist method of meditation he included these two states within it.

The Buddha next turned his attention to an alternative form of spiritual practice, one well-established in India, based on subjugating the body by sheer force of will. The belief was that by gaining control over the body one could gain control over all appetites and thereby free oneself from desire. By becoming free of desire no new karma would be produced, and so rebirth in *saṃsāra* would come to an end. The practices of self-mortification were also thought to generate a form of mystical

*Figure 2.1* The Buddha performing austerities

energy known as *tapas* (heat) which became the basis of various magical powers when correctly channelled.

The Buddha began by undertaking exercises in breath-control and attempting to suspend the process of respiration for longer and longer periods. Rather than generating spiritual awareness, however, this simply resulted in painful headaches and stomach pains, and the Buddha abandoned the technique. Next he turned his attention to his intake of food, and reduced this to minute amounts, just a spoonful of bean soup a day. Soon he became painfully thin 'with his ribs standing out like the rafters of a tumbledown shack' (M.i.245) and was barely able to maintain the seated meditation posture without falling over. His hair began to fall out and, close to death, he decided this second technique was also a failure and abandoned it.

The Buddha realized that he had taken the path of austerities to its limit: 'Whatever recluses (*śramaṇas*) or brahmins in the past have experienced painful, agonising and intense sensations as the result of their exertions', he tells us, 'this has been the limit, no-one has gone further than I have' (M.i.246). Unfortunately, the path had turned out to be a dead-end, and the Buddha now cast around in his mind wondering if there might be another way to reach enlightenment. Reflecting on his experience this far he may well have contrasted the two earlier phases of his life: as a young man he had enjoyed material comfort and luxury, but this had left him frustrated and unfulfilled. In the second phase, as a *śramaṇa* in the forest, he had gone to the other extreme and deprived himself of all comforts, pushing his mind and body to their limits in the hope of a spiritual breakthrough that never came. He therefore declared his six-year experiment with self-mortification at an end, and adopted a more balanced and moderate lifestyle. He became convinced that the way forward involved a lifestyle that avoided extremes of all kinds and steered a 'middle way' between over-indulgence and extreme self-denial.

Inspired by this new approach the Buddha recalled an incident from his childhood when he had spontaneously entered a state of trance known as the 'first *dhyāna*'. This was a level of trance lower than those he had attained with his two teachers, but which seemed to him to hold greater promise, perhaps because it did not involve the suppression of the intellectual faculties but instead honed them to a new sharpness. At this moment the realization came to him 'that is the path to enlightenment' (M.i.246), and he began to take nourishment once again to build up his strength. When his companions saw the Buddha eating boiled rice and bread they were disgusted and criticized him for living 'luxuriously' and abandoning the ascetic lifestyle.

## Enlightenment

Undeterred, the Buddha returned to the practice of meditation, this time in a more structured program that involved him in passing through four different *dhyānas* or levels of trance. One particular night when seated under a large pipal or banyan tree (*ficus religiosus*) later known as the Bodhi tree, he entered the fourth state of trance, when his mind was most concentrated and purified. In this state he obtained three kinds of 'true knowledge'. In the first watch of the night he obtained the power to see back into his past lives and to recall them in all their detail. In the second watch, he attained the ability to see not just his own lives, but the decease and arising of other beings in accordance with their good and bad karma. In the third watch of the night he attained knowledge of the Four Noble Truths, namely: 'This is suffering ... This is the origin of suffering ... This is the cessation of suffering ... This is the path that leads to the cessation of suffering' (M.i.249). He knew then that all his spiritual defilements (*āśrava*) such as sensual desire and ignorance had been rooted out and destroyed and that he had achieved his goal. He realized that for him 'Birth is destroyed, the holy life has been lived, I have done what needed to be done and rebirth is at an end' (M.i.249).

Later accounts of this night take on a more mythological form, in which the Buddha first of all gains victory over Māra, an evil, fallen divinity not unlike the Christian Satan. Māra is often referred to as the 'evil one' (Skt.: Pāpīyaṃs; Pāli: Pāpimant), and his name literally means 'death'. Māra personifies all that is negative and opposed to the Buddha's teachings. Māra and the Buddha were lifelong opponents because the Buddha's teachings showed the way to liberate humanity from Māra's power. Despite his best efforts, Māra was never able to do much more than cause mischief because the Buddha was too powerful. The Buddha knew, however, that even he would fall victim to Māra one last time when he eventually faced death.

On the night of his enlightenment, the accounts relate how in an effort to prevent the Buddha achieving enlightenment, Māra approached the seated Buddha with his 'army' of evil forces such as greed, hatred, delusion, hunger and thirst, tiredness, and fear and doubt, hoping to break his resolve. When the Buddha did not flinch Māra adopted an alternative strategy and sent his beautiful daughters – Delight (*Ratī*), Discontent (*Aratī*) and Craving (*Tṛṣṇā*) – in an attempt to seduce the Buddha and deflect him from his purpose. When the Buddha proved immune to their charms, Māra recalled his daughters and unleashed a barrage of terrible storms and fearful sights, but none of this made any impression on the Buddha. The Buddha then reached out and touched the earth with his right hand, calling upon the earth-goddess to bear witness to his enlightenment. This gesture (*mudrā*) known as the 'earth-touching gesture' (*bhūmi-sparśa-mudrā*) or the 'conquest of Māra' (*māra-vijaya*) is one of a number of classic poses that were later incorporated into the stylistic repertoire of Buddhist art. When the Buddha made this gesture the earth trembled, and Māra toppled from his great war-elephant and his forces fled in disarray. The Buddha was now the 'enlightened one', and his victory was complete. It is not hard to see this story as an allegory of the psychological battle the Buddha had fought with the negative forces deep within his own mind. To subdue these dark powers is the

### The tale of Barlaam and Josaphat

Barlaam and Josaphat are two Christian saints venerated in both the Greek and Roman churches who were the protagonists of a popular medieval religious tale. Around a century and a half ago it was discovered that the story is based on the legend of the life of the Buddha. The name Josaphat is a corruption of the Sanskrit word *bodhisattva*, a term applied to the Buddha before he became enlightened.

In the Western version of the tale, Josaphat is the son of a king, and on his birth a prediction is made that he will either become a great king or renounce the world to follow a religious calling. His father does all he can to prevent his son following a religious vocation, but on a visit outside the palace one day Josaphat meets Barlaam, an ascetic who gives him religious instruction. Guided by his spiritual mentor Josaphat renounces the world and becomes a great saint. The story thus parallels the life of Siddhārtha Gautama at various points, although the theology is adapted for a Christian context and the theme concerns the notion of salvation through faith. There are Greek, Georgian, and Arabic translations of the legend, but it became most widely known in Europe through a Latin version in the eleventh and twelfth centuries. From the thirteenth to the fifteenth century numerous vernacular versions appeared and new forms of the story were produced in prose, verse and dramatic form.

supreme challenge, and enlightenment cannot be won without courage and firmness of purpose.

The place where the Buddha achieved enlightenment became known as Bodhgayā. Today the site is marked by the Mahābodhi Temple, and is an important center of pilgrimage for Buddhists from all over the world, but in the Buddha's day it was a remote place and the Buddha spent four weeks there in solitary reflection pondering his future plans. He wondered whether he should take up the career of religious teacher, but at first rejected this option when he reflected on how difficult it would be to communicate the nature of his achievement and explain to others how to attain it. His thoughts turned to the ease and comfort of a private life free from the demands of students and followers. The texts report that at this point, the gods – alarmed by the prospect of the Buddha not communicating his *Dharma* (teachings) to anyone – intervened, and the deity Sahampati appealed to the Buddha to proclaim his teachings to the world. Moved by compassion, and realizing that there were individuals who could benefit from hearing his teachings, the Buddha agreed.

## *The first sermon*

But who should the Buddha teach? He became aware, so the texts inform us, by his clairvoyant powers, that his two previous teachers had since passed away, so he set out for the holy city of Benares (now known as Varanasi) on the Ganges, where he knew he would find the five companions who had previously abandoned him when he rejected the practice of austerities. He encountered them in a park set aside for royal deer on the outskirts of Benares. At first they were lukewarm towards him, but soon realized that a profound transformation had taken place in the wandering *śramaṇa* they had known earlier. The Buddha declared that he was now a *Tathāgata* ('one who has attained what is really so') and preached his first sermon, marking the inauguration of his teaching ministry and the beginnings of the religion we now know as Buddhism.

This first sermon is preserved in a scripture called 'Setting in Motion the Wheel of the Dharma' (*Dharmacakra-pravartana Sūtra*). This relatively short text contains the essence of Buddhist doctrine, and begins by speaking of the 'middle way' the Buddha had found between the extremes of self-indulgence and harsh austerity. It then makes reference to the Four Noble Truths he had perceived on the night of his enlightenment: the truth of suffering, the truth of the arising of suffering, the truth of the cessation of suffering, and the truth of the path that leads to the cessation of suffering (these will be explained in the next chapter).

In Buddhism the wheel is a potent symbol. In the title of this sermon the *Dharma* is likened to a wheel because it is without beginning or end, and roams from place to place. The wheel of the *Dharma* is often depicted with either four or eight spokes, representing the Four Noble Truths or the Eightfold Path (the last of the Noble Truths). In iconography, the Buddha is often shown making a wheel-shaped gesture by touching together the thumb and index finger of his left hand. This is known as the *Dharma-cakra-mudrā* ('gesture of the *Dharma* wheel') and calls to mind the first sermon.

On hearing the Buddha speak, one of the five mendicants by the name of Kauṇḍinya immediately grasped the essence of the teaching and became a *śrotāpanna* or 'stream-enterer', a term denoting a relatively advanced stage of spiritual understanding. Kauṇḍinya was said to have attained the '*Dharma*-eye' and to have been freed from all doubt in the Buddha's teachings. This act of transmitting the truth from teacher to disciple is also an important part of 'turning the wheel', and on this day the Buddha initiated a lineage of teachers and students that would carry his doctrines to every part of Asia, and eventually the whole world. Over the course of the next week all four of the other mendicants also attained this state as the Buddha gave further teachings. All five accepted him as their teacher and he ordained them as monks (*bhikṣu*) in a ceremony where he admitted them simply with the words 'Come, monk' (*ehi bhikṣu*). A few weeks later the Buddha delivered a second important sermon on the idea of 'no self' (*anātman*), and on hearing this all five mendicants attained nirvana. Although their understanding was now virtually identical to that of the Buddha they were known not by the title 'Buddha' but as *arhants* (Pāli: *arahants*), meaning 'saints' or 'worthy ones'. This is because the title of Buddha is reserved for those who discover the path to enlightenment through their own efforts rather than by hearing it from another.

News of the Buddha's teachings spread quickly, and before long this small group of five *arhants* had increased to sixty. The Buddha instructed them to spread his teachings out of compassion for the world, just as he had done, thus inaugurating a missionary movement. After the order of monks had been established for five years the Buddha allowed an order of nuns to be founded. At first he was reluctant to permit this, perhaps because it was almost without precedent in India, but on the intercession of his stepmother, Prajāpatī, and his cousin and personal attendant Ānanda, he eventually agreed. Many laymen and women left home and flocked to join these new orders. The male order grew rapidly and flourished, but the female order eventually died out in India and most of South-east Asia in the early centuries C.E., although orders of nuns do survive today in East Asia.

## *The Buddha's last days*

The next biographical details we have of the Buddha relate to a time close to the end of his life. The source is the Discourse of the Great Decease (*Mahāparinirvāṇa Sūtra*), which recounts events in the months before and leading up to the Buddha's eath. The text shows us the Buddha as an old man of eighty, in failing health, but determined to continue giving religious teachings to the end. He is still leading an itinerant lifestyle, perhaps on a last journey to a destination which is never disclosed (although the trajectory could suggest he was traveling to his home town in the north). He frequently calls upon his psychic powers to assist him in controlling illness and pain until such time as he is ready to let go. The nature of his medical condition is not made clear, and the Buddha may have been suffering from a variety of ailments. It is often said that the cause of his death was food-poisoning after eating a meal of pork, but the account in the Discourse of the Great Decease shows the Buddha recovering from this, and his death takes place some time later, apparently due to natural causes.

At this point numerous questions arose. What would happen to the *sangha* after the Buddha died? Who would be his successor? When Ānanda asked him specifically about this, the Buddha replied that he would appoint no successor, since he had never considered himself to be the leader of the *sangha*. Henceforth, he said, the monks should be self-reliant and hold fast to the *Dharma* as their island and refuge, and the *Vinaya* (the monastic rules) as their teacher. The Buddha told his followers to resolve any doubts by checking whatever views they heard against the teachings

## *Vihāras*

The term *vihāra* literally means 'dwelling', one associated particularly with a Buddhist monastery. Originally, when monks and nuns used to wander through the countryside, settling down only during the rainy season, the term was used to designate an individual hut within the rainy-season retreat. Later, with the establishment of permanent dwellings for the monks, the term came to indicate an entire monastery. For this reason, it is customary to refer to monasteries by this generic term, although in some countries, such as Thailand, it is reserved for a shrine hall. In the early period, monks of differing doctrinal affiliations lived side-by-side in the same *vihāra*. This would typically comprise individual cells arranged around a central courtyard very often enclosing a railed Bodhi tree, a shrine room and an ambulatory. As times changed, and the needs of the *sangha* began to reflect growing institutionalization, some *vihāras* became large, complex, and wealthy units with elaborate administrative hierarchies. Some, like Nālandā and Somapuri, developed into universities with many thousands of resident students. The modern Indian state of Bihar takes its name from the Buddhist *vihāras* that were abundant in the region.

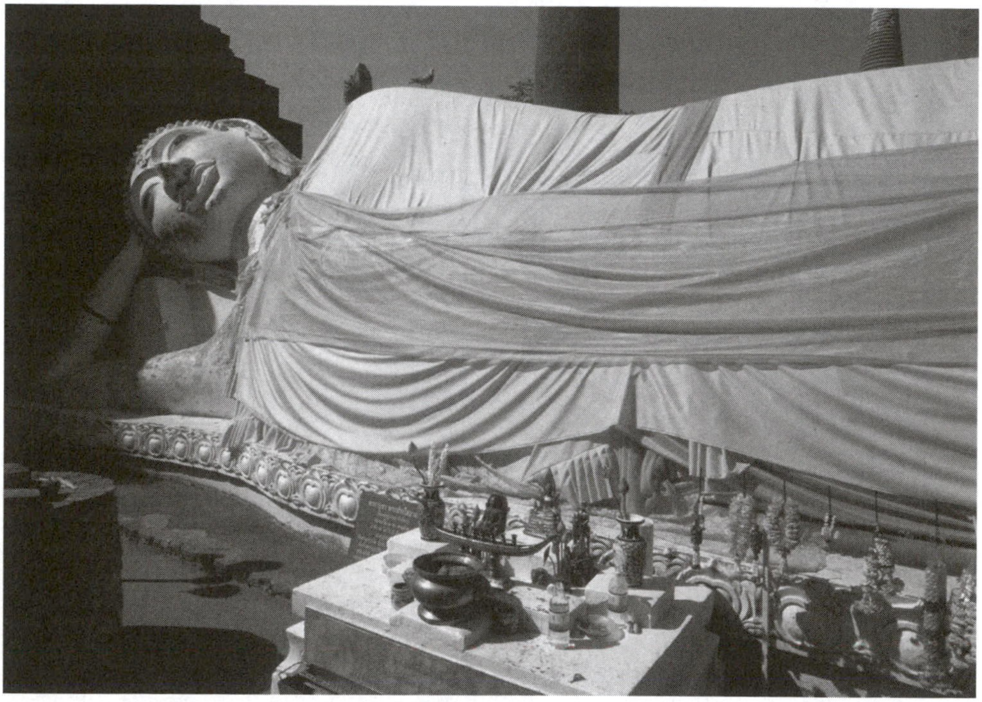

*Figure 2.2* Reclining Buddha, Ayutthaya, Thailand

in the scriptures. This meant there would be no need for a head or patriarch and no central institution charged with determining orthodoxy.

At last the Buddha came to the end of his journey at a remote village by the name of Kuśinagarī, where he lay down between two Sāl trees, the same kind of tree his mother had grasped as she gave birth. The text reports that the trees bloomed, although it was not their season, and that other supernatural phenomena accompanied the Buddha's passing. Numerous gods were said to be in attendance, crowding in to witness the momentous scene. The Buddha instructed that his body should be cremated and his remains placed in a special monument known as a *stūpa* (see Chapter Five) reserved for the Buddhas and World-Rulers (*cakravartins*). In due course his relics would be divided into eight portions, and a *stūpa* built for each. The Buddha recommended the practice of pilgrimage both to *stūpas* and to four of the main sites in his life, those associated with his birth, enlightenment, first sermon, and death. He then directed some words to Ānanda, who was distraught at the passing of the master he had served for a quarter of a century, predicting that Ānanda, who was not yet an *arhant*, would become one soon. Then he called the monks together and invited them to ask any final questions they might have. When none were forthcoming, the Buddha uttered his final words: 'Conditioned things (*saṃskāra*) are subject to decay. Strive diligently (to attain perfection)'.

The Buddha then passed through several levels of meditative trance, before entering nirvana from the fourth *dhyāna*. At last he had attained 'the deathless' (*amṛta*), the goal he had abandoned his home to seek, and would never again be reborn.

## Key points you need to know

- The main details of the Buddha's life are as follows. His name was Siddhārtha Gautama, and he was an Indian prince of the Śākya clan who was born at Lumbinī in present-day Nepal. He married at sixteen, left home at twenty-nine to seek spiritual knowledge, gained enlightenment at thirty-five, taught for forty-five years, and died aged eighty.
- The Buddha's dates are not known with certainty. The current scholarly consensus is that he died between 410–400 B.C.E.
- Almost all we know about the Buddha's life comes from Buddhist texts. There is little corroborating historical evidence from other sources until a century and a half after his death. The Buddha's supermundane nature is emphasized from the earliest times, and as time passes, the accounts of his life become increasingly embellished with tales of miraculous events.
- The Buddha was cremated and his relics were divided up into eight portions and distributed among the local rulers.

## Discussion questions

1. Do you think it will ever be possible to construct a biography of the 'historical Buddha' from the existing sources?
2. To what extent was the concept of the 'middle way' a guiding principle in the Buddha's life?
3. Do the supernatural details in the early sources help or hinder the modern reader in coming to an appreciation of the Buddha as a religious teacher?

## Further reading

Chan Koon San. *Buddhist Pilgrimage* (Adobe ebook, 3.3mb).

Thomas, Edward J. *The Life of the Buddha As Legend and History.* London: Routledge and Kegan Paul, 1949.

Schober, Juliane (ed). *Sacred Biography in the Buddhist Traditions of South and Southeast Asia.* Honolulu: University of Hawaii Press, 1997.

Pye, Michael. *The Buddha.* London: Duckworth, 1979.

Carrithers, Michael. *Buddha: A Very Short Introduction.* Oxford: Oxford University Press, 2001.

Cousins, Lance S. 'The Dating of the Historical Buddha: A Review Article', *Journal of the Royal Asiatic Society,* 6, 1996:57–63.

Reynolds, Frank E. 'The Many Lives of Buddha: A Study of Sacred Biography and Theravāda Tradition', in Donald Capps and Frank E. Reynolds (eds). *The Biographical Process: Studies in the History and Psychology of Religion.* The Hague: Mouton, 1976, 37–61.

Johnston, E.H. *The Buddhacarita or Acts of the Buddha* [translation of Aśvaghoṣa's epic poem]. New Delhi: Motilal Banarsidass, 1972.

# 3 *The* Dharma

## In this chapter

*Dharma* is one of the 'three jewels' (*triratna*) – namely the Buddha, the *Dharma*, and the *Sangha* (the monastic community) – which collectively comprise the essence of the Buddhist religion. *Dharma* denotes the teachings and doctrines set forth by the Buddha, and it is one of the words by which Buddhists refer to their religion. The most fundamental Buddhist doctrines are known as the Four Noble Truths, and these are discussed in this chapter in turn, along with an explanation of the Buddhist theory of causation known as 'dependent origination'. Another important doctrine explained here is 'no self' (*anātman*). This is the Buddhist teaching that has fascinated Westerners more than any other but which has given rise to much misunderstanding. The material in this chapter is important for both the early teachings of Buddhism and the doctrinal developments in later centuries which will be explored in subsequent chapters.

## Main topics covered

- The First Noble Truth: Suffering (*duḥkha*)
- The Second Noble Truth: Arising (*samudaya*)
- Dependent origination (*pratītya-samutpāda*)
- The Third Noble Truth: Cessation (*nirodha*) or nirvana
- The Fourth Noble Truth: the Path (*ārga*)
- Holy persons
- The doctrine of no-self (*anātman*)

## *The Four Noble Truths*

We saw in the last chapter that on the night of his awakening the Buddha apprehended the Four Noble Truths, and that when he gave his first sermon in the deer park at Sarnath he made specific reference to them. His audience consisted of five ascetics

> Monks, it is through not understanding, through not penetrating the Four Noble Truths that this long course of birth and death has been passed through and undergone by me as well as by you. What are these four? They are the noble truth of suffering (*duḥkha*); the noble truth of the origin of suffering; the noble truth of the cessation of suffering; and the noble truth of the way to the cessation of suffering. But now, monks, that these have been realized and penetrated, cut off is the craving for existence, destroyed is that which leads to renewed becoming, and there is no more re-becoming (D.ii.90)

with a background in religious discipline and familiarity with philosophical notions, and the teaching the Buddha gave was of an advanced kind, comparable to a postgraduate class. In other sermons when speaking to ordinary layfolk, the Buddha does not generally mention these points of doctrine, and instead delivers a 'gradual talk' (*anupūrvikā kathā*) in which he encourages the practice of generosity (*dāna*) and morality (*śīla*) as the way to a heavenly rebirth.

The Noble Truths (*ārya-satya*) thus provide a sophisticated and advanced formulation of Buddhist teachings. They form the cornerstone of Buddhist doctrine, and encapsulate the Buddha's understanding of the human predicament and its solution. The Four Truths assert that:

(1) life is suffering.
(2) suffering is caused by craving.
(3) suffering can have an end.
(4) there is a path which leads to the end of suffering.

The Four Truths provide a kind of diagnosis of the ills which affect humanity, and a remedy for the 'sickness' that afflicts all sentient life. The Buddha was often compared to a physician, and his teachings (*Dharma*) to a medicine. The formulation of the Four Truths is like that of a medical examination: first, the condition is diagnosed; second, its cause is sought; third, the physician makes a prognosis for recovery; fourth and finally, a course of treatment is prescribed.

## *The First Noble Truth: Suffering*

The word translated as 'suffering' in the above extract is *duḥkha*. *Duḥkha* is a term with a spectrum of meanings, all denoting circumstances or situations that are in some way unsatisfactory, or not as we would wish them to be. According to context, it can be translated as 'suffering', 'pain', 'ill', 'unsatisfactoriness', 'anguish', 'stress', 'unease', and a range of other synonyms. *Duḥkha* is the opposite of *sukha*, which means 'pleasure', so one of its basic meanings is certainly 'pain'. But just as in English

> This, monks, is the Noble Truth of Suffering (*duḥkha*). Birth is suffering, sickness is suffering, ageing is suffering, death is suffering. Sorrow, grief, pain, unhappiness and despair are suffering. Association with what one dislikes is suffering, being separated from what one likes is suffering. Not to get what one wants is suffering. In short, the five aggregates which are grasped at (*upādāna-skandha*) are suffering (Vin.i.10; S.v.421).

'pain' can refer not just to physical but also to psychological or emotional distress, and also to situations which are bothersome or inconvenient ('it was a pain having to go to work today'), so *duḥkha* can also have a more generalized range of meaning and a more nuanced translation is often required.

Some of the biological aspects of suffering mentioned in the First Noble Truth – such as old age, sickness and death – were things the Buddha himself had seen at first hand on his visits outside the palace with his charioteer. The problem that concerned the Buddha was not just the unwelcome nature of these experiences, but the fact that they would be repeated over and over in life after life, and would happen not just to oneself but to everyone one loved. Individuals are powerless in the face of these circumstances, regardless of what progress is made in science and medicine. Though we may live longer, we will never be immune from the risk of accidents, and death will inevitably separate us again and again from family and friends.

In addition to mentioning the biological aspects of human suffering that the Buddha had himself observed, the First Noble Truth broadens out to include other aspects of suffering as well. There is a reference to psychological states such as 'sorrow' and 'despair', and psychological afflictions like depression can sometimes be more debilitating and difficult to cope with than physical ones.

Next, the Buddha goes on to speak about the emotional pain of being separated from what is dear to one, such as from the things or people one loves, and being forced to endure experiences, places, or situations which one dislikes. This is followed by a reference to the general feeling of frustration that can arise when things don't work out as we planned, and ambitions go unfulfilled. Clearly, this is at several removes from physical pain, but often the effect can be such as to sour our whole outlook on life and leave a lingering and pervasive feeling of disappointment or failure.

Finally, the First Noble Truth ends with a cryptic reference to the 'five aggregates which are grasped at'. This introduces a Buddhist doctrine known as *anātman*, or the 'no-self' teachings, which will be examined further below. This claims that our nature as human beings is constituted in such a way that makes it impossible for us ever to find complete happiness or fulfillment in *saṃsāra*.

The various kinds of suffering identified above are classified by Buddhist sources into three categories. The first of these is '*duḥkha-duḥkha*', which means suffering 'plain and simple', as we might say. This includes all the examples of suffering due to biological causes (birth, sickness, ageing, death) mentioned in the First Noble Truth. Next comes *vipariṇāma-duḥkha*, which means 'suffering due to change'. It is a basic tenet of Buddhist thought that everything that arises will cease – in other words, things are impermanent and constantly changing. Given this fundamental instability we can never know what will come next, and so cannot guarantee that our happiness will endure. The fact that in *saṃsāra* nothing is permanent means that it is impossible to find lasting satisfaction or fulfilment. Finally, the third aspect of suffering is '*duḥkha* as formations' (*saṃskāra-duḥkha*). This kind of suffering arises because everything in *saṃsāra* is made up of component parts, like a package of self-assembly home furniture: you never find a bookcase or a chair in the box, just an assemblage of bits and pieces. Buddhism teaches that the whole world is like this, and that since everything is made up of component parts it will sooner or later be reduced to them. In other words, everything (including us) will fall apart, just like that bookcase we assembled.

Many people approaching Buddhism for the first time find the analysis provided in the First Noble Truth pessimistic and wonder whether the bad news isn't being overdone. The translation of *duḥkha* as 'suffering' helps reinforce this impression, and can make the First Noble Truth sound as if the Buddha believed that human life was constant agony. This is not what he intended, and he was certainly aware from his own comfortable childhood inside the palace that life could have its pleasant moments. Buddhists generally reject the charge of pessimism and claim that their religion is neither optimistic nor pessimistic, but realistic. They point out that few lives are untouched by sorrow, whether caused by physical suffering, psychological

## The Parable of the Traveler

An ancient Indian story recounts how a traveler slips on a precipice and falls over the edge. As he tumbles down he grasps hold of a creeper and manages to stay his fall. At first he feels relieved, but looking down sees that beneath him is a pit of poisonous snakes. To add to his alarm, he notices that two mice, one black and one white, are nibbling away at the creeper he is holding onto. In this moment of despair he sees that honey is trickling down the creeper from a beehive that was overturned when he fell. As it reaches his lips he relishes the sweet taste and exclaims 'Oh, how wonderful is the taste of that honey!'

The story depicts the Buddhist view of the human predicament. We are like the traveler, with death (the pit of snakes) staring us in the face. The black and white mice (night and day) are constantly whittling away at our lifespan. Yet in spite of this dire situation we, like the traveler, are captivated by pleasure (the honey) and forget all about the perils that surround us.

disorders, death, or more existential causes such as frustration, disappointment, and disillusionment. In their view, the First Noble Truth simply 'tells it how it is', and if it sounds negative this is because there is a natural inclination for people to suppress or ignore the unpleasant realities of life.

A Buddhist might also maintain, reverting to the medical analogy which began this section, that there is also a more positive aspect to the First Noble Truth, just as when we go to the doctor to find out what is wrong with us. While it may be unwelcome to be told we have a condition of some kind, it is certainly better to find out and be treated than live in ignorance until the disease is so far advanced that nothing can be done. It takes courage to take the first step, but since we can look forward to good health and happiness when we are well, the message is ultimately one of hope. Those who heed the Buddha's call and take up the religious life, furthermore, are said to experience joy (*prīti*) and happiness, as well as an inner calmness and serenity.

## *The Second Noble Truth: Arising*

If suffering is an inevitable part of life, how does this suffering come about? The Second Noble Truth explains that the cause of suffering is due to craving (*tṛṣṇā*). Just as with *duḥkha*, we have to be careful how we translate the word *tṛṣṇā*. It is quite common to translate this as 'desire', but this can lead to the mistaken idea that Buddhism sees all desire as wrong, and thus to the paradoxical conclusion that we must somehow seek nirvana without desiring it. A common reason for this misunderstanding is that in English 'desire' can be for good things as well as bad things: for example, one can desire to give up smoking, take exercise and eat healthy food (good things); and one can also desire to smoke cigarettes and to eat junk food (bad things). The Sanskrit word *tṛṣṇā*, however, has a more limited semantic range and refers only to negative desires and addictions (another word, '*chanda*', is reserved for good or wholesome desires). For this reason 'craving' is a better translation for *tṛṣṇā*, since it reminds us that the Second Noble Truth is referring to desire that is of an excessive, selfish, or morbid nature, and usually directed towards unwholesome objects or ends. Whereas craving tends to be repetitive, limiting, and cyclic, desire for wholesome things is liberating and enhancing. For example, the desire of a chain-

### The Truth of Arising (*samudaya*)

This, O Monks, is the Truth of the Arising of Suffering. It is this thirst or craving (*tṛṣṇā*) which gives rise to rebirth, which is bound up with passionate delight and which seeks fresh pleasure now here and now there in the form of (1) thirst for sensual pleasure, (2) thirst for existence, and (3) thirst for non-existence.

smoker to give up cigarettes breaks a compulsive habit and enhances the health and quality of life of that person.

Craving is like sticky glue that makes us become attached to things, and once attached we cannot easily let go, as in the case of bad habits that are hard to break. Giving up craving is akin to weaning oneself off an addiction, such as to cigarettes or drugs, and is no easy thing to do. The Buddha's favorite metaphor for craving was fire. In the Fire Sermon (S.iv.19), he said that all our experience was 'ablaze' with desire. Just like fire, craving spreads rapidly from one thing to another and seems to destroy what it feeds on without ever being satisfied. After one cigarette we soon want another, and so it goes on. There is no end to desires of this kind, and the satisfaction they provide is short-lived. The Buddha compared the pleasure gained through satisfying such desires to the temporary relief of scratching a boil.

The Second Noble Truth makes reference to three forms of craving, and the first of these is craving for sensual pleasures (*kāma*). (The word *kāma* is the same word found in the title of the ancient Indian treatise on erotic pleasure, the *Kāma Sūtra*.) Sensual craving (*kāma*) is any kind of desire for gratification that comes by way of the senses, such as the desire to experience pleasurable sensations of touch, taste, smell, sight, or sound. Since Indian psychology includes the mind as one of the senses (thus counting six senses instead of the usual five), this also includes pleasurable fantasies and daydreams (M.i.51). The second kind of craving refers to the desire for existence (*bhava*). This is a kind of instinctual urge, a deep yearning to be, which propels us from one life to another and brings us back again and again to seek new pleasures and experiences. The third aspect of craving is an inverted form of desire, of the kind that drives us not towards things but away from what we do not like. This is desire that manifests itself in a negative way and which seeks to destroy (*vibhava*) rather than possess. Such destructive desires can be directed towards both self and others. When directed towards the ego they manifest themselves in self-harming behavior, and, in extreme cases, suicide. They are typically seen in self-deprecatory remarks and other instances of low self-esteem in which people 'put themselves down'.

In the formulation of the Second Noble Truth *tṛṣṇā* is picked out as the single cause of the arising of suffering. Elsewhere, however, the cause of suffering is said to be threefold in nature, consisting of greed (*rāga*), hatred (*dveṣa*) and delusion (*moha*). Other formulations again, such as in the doctrine of dependent origination (see text box), explain the arising of suffering as a twelvefold chain that includes ignorance as its first link and desire as its sixth. In spite of the different formulations, it is clear that the root problem is a complex involving both cognitive error (such as ignorance or delusion), and inappropriate affective dispositions or emotional responses (such as excessive attachment or aversion). The problem is therefore one which affects both the head and the heart, and needs to be addressed through a program of retraining or therapy which develops insight and understanding as well as eliminating stubborn emotional attachments to unwholesome things.

## Dependent origination (Skt.: *pratītya-samutpāda*; Pāli, *paṭicca-samuppāda*)

The doctrine of dependent origination is a fundamental Buddhist teaching on causation. It holds that all phenomena arise in dependence on causes and conditions, and as a consequence lack intrinsic being of their own. The doctrine is expressed in its simplest form in the Sanskrit phrase *idaṃ sati ayaṃ bhavati* ('when this exists, that arises'), a proposition that can be expressed in the logical form A→B (when condition A exists, effect B arises), or as its negation –A→–B (where condition A does not exist effect B does not arise). The important corollary of this teaching is that there is nothing that comes into being through its own power or volition, and there are therefore no entities or metaphysical realities – such as God or a soul (*ātman*) – that transcend the causal nexus. In this respect the doctrine dovetails with the teaching of no self (*anātman*), discussed later in this chapter. Early sources indicate that the Buddha became enlightened under the Bodhi Tree when he fully realized the profound truth of dependent origination, namely that all phenomena are conditioned (*saṃskṛta*) and arise and cease in a determinate series.

There are various formulations of the doctrine in early sources, but the most common one illustrates the soteriological implications of causality in a series of twelve stages or links (*nidāna*) showing how the problem of suffering (*duḥkha*) and entrapment in *saṃsāra* arises due to craving (*tṛṣṇā*) and ignorance (*avidyā*). The twelve links in the process (often depicted around the rim of the wheel of life or *bhavacakra*) are:

(1) Ignorance (*avidyā*)
(2) Compositional factors (*saṃskāra*)
(3) Consciousness (*vijñāna*)
(4) Name and form (*nāma-rūpa*)
(5) Six sense spheres (*ṣad-āyatana*)
(6) Contact (*sparśa*)
(7) Feelings (*vedanā*)
(8) Craving (*tṛṣṇā*)
(9) Grasping (*upādāna*)
(10) Becoming (*bhava*)
(11) Birth (*jāti*)
(12) Old age and death (*jarā-maraṇa*).

The significance of the individual links is open to interpretation, but one popular understanding is that of the fifth-century commentator Buddhaghosa in terms of which the series extends over three lives. Thus (1)–(2) relate to the previous life, (3)–(7) to the conditioning of the present existence, (8)–(10) to the fruits of the present existence, and (11)–(12) to the life to come. Various later schools came to their own, sometimes radical, understanding of the doctrine. Chief among these is that of the Mādhyamika, for whom dependent origination came to be synonymous with the concept of emptiness (*śūnyatā*), as explained in Chapter Six.

## *The Third Noble Truth: Cessation*

The Third Noble Truth is a corollary of the Second. If craving (*tṛṣṇā*) is the cause of suffering (*duḥkha*), it follows that once craving is removed, suffering will cease. This is exactly what the Third Noble Truth proclaims. This state of being free from suffering is known as nirvana, and is the supreme goal of the Buddhist path. Nirvana literally means 'blowing out', in the way that the flame of a candle is blown out. What is blown out are the three 'fires' (also known as the 'three poisons') of greed, hatred and delusion which are the components of craving. The simplest definition of nirvana is 'the end of greed, hatred, and delusion' (S.38.1). So long as these three 'fires' continue to burn, the individual will remain trapped in *saṃsāra*, going round and round in the wheel of rebirth which is driven by his or her own craving for pleasurable experiences.

Someone who embarks on the Buddhist path seeks to reverse this process. Over the course of many lifetimes, as the negative forces of craving and ignorance are slowly weakened through following Buddhist teachings, an individual can begin to cultivate positive states of mind and to undergo a spiritual transformation in which virtuous qualities come to predominate over negative ones. Such individuals become empowered, growing stronger, freer, and happier as they leave behind negative states such as fear, doubt, worry and anxiety. Eventually they evolve into saints (either as *arhants* or Buddhas) who have developed their capacities far beyond the limits of ordinary folk.

When recounting the story of the Buddha's life it was mentioned that he 'attained nirvana' while seated under the Bodhi tree at the age of thirty-five, and that then he attained 'final' nirvana on his death at the age of eighty. It is important to distinguish clearly these two kinds of nirvana. The first refers to the destruction of greed, hatred, and delusion by a living human being, and denotes essentially an ethical and spiritual transformation. Having achieved nirvana in this sense – often referred to as 'nirvana in this life' or 'nirvana with remainder' (*sopadiśeṣa-nirvāṇa*) since the body continues to exist afterwards – the Buddha lived on for forty-five years giving religious teachings. When he died at the age of eighty he entered 'final nirvana' (*parinirvāṇa*) or 'nirvana without remainder' (*anupādiśeṣa-nirvāṇa*), a discarnate or disembodied state from which he would never more be reborn.

## The Truth of Cessation (*nirodha*)

This, O Monks, is the Truth of the Cessation of Suffering. It is the utter cessation of that craving (*tṛṣṇā*), the withdrawal from it, the renouncing of it, the rejection of it, liberation from it, non-attachment to it.

The first kind of nirvana is relatively easy to understand. Here, we see an outstanding human being, a person displaying qualities of the kind we are familiar with from the biographies of saints, heroes, and role models from various backgrounds. The second kind of nirvana, however, is more problematic, for it is not clear what has happened to the Buddha once his mortal body has been left behind. We know the Buddha will not be reborn, but where has he gone? There is no definitive answer to this question in the early texts. The Buddha said that it was a bit like asking where a flame has gone once the candle is blown out. Of course, it has not actually gone anywhere, all that has happened is that the process of combustion has ceased. Likewise, when craving and ignorance are eliminated rebirth ceases, just like a flame goes out when deprived of oxygen and fuel. The Buddha's point here was that the question about what happens to a Buddha in final nirvana is based on a misconception, and since the question is in some sense misconceived, it is difficult to answer in a straightforward way. However, there are two possibilities at least that can be eliminated. These are known as the 'two extremes', and are the views that final nirvana means a) the total annihilation of the subject, or b) the eternal existence of a personal soul. Both these alternatives give a distorted idea of final nirvana since they presuppose the existence of a self or soul (*ātman*) that is either destroyed or continues to exist after death. As we shall see below, the Buddha's teaching on the nature of the self made no allowance for such an entity, so these explanations of nirvana had to be rejected.

In general, the Buddha was not keen for his followers to explore questions of the above kind, and discouraged speculation about things which could only be known through personal experience. He compared idle speculation about the nature of final nirvana to a man who was out walking one day when he was struck by a stray arrow. The man insisted that he would not have the arrow removed until his curiosity had been satisfied on a number of points, such as the identity of the archer, his name and clan, where he had been standing, and a host of other trivial details (M.i.246). The Buddha urged his followers not to behave like this foolish man and waste their lives in idle speculation when there was a clear need to take urgent practical action to pluck out the arrow of suffering from their bodies.

There is a famous verse which refers to the situation of an enlightened being (*arhant*) after death. The verse reads:

> There exists no measuring of one who has gone out (like a flame). That by which he could be referred to no longer exists for him. When all phenomena (*dharmas*) are removed, then all ways of describing have also been removed.
>
> (*Suttanipāta* v.1076)

This suggests there are no reference points by which an enlightened person can be known after death. In keeping with this, the sources generally speak of nirvana using negative terminology such as 'blowing out', 'cessation', 'the absence of desire', and 'the extinction of thirst', although occasionally more positive terms are encountered, such as 'the auspicious', 'the good', 'purity', 'peace', 'truth', and 'the further shore'. Certain passages seem to suggest that nirvana is a transcendent reality which is 'unborn, unoriginated, uncreated and unformed' (*Udāna* 80), but it is difficult to know how to interpret such statements. Thinkers in some later schools would speculate further on the nature of final nirvana, interpreting it in various ways in the light of their own philosophical views, while others were happy to leave the subject as mysterious and elusive, seeing final nirvana as a transcendent realm whose nature could only be known by those who had experienced it.

## *The Fourth Noble Truth: the Path*

The Fourth Noble Truth – that of the Path or Way (*mārga*) – explains how suffering is to be brought to an end and the transition from *saṃsāra* to nirvana is to be made. The Eightfold Path is known as the 'middle way' because it steers a course between a life of indulgence and one of harsh austerity. It consists of eight factors divided into the three categories of Morality (*śila*), Meditation (*samādhi*), and Wisdom (*prajñā*) (M.i.301).

Let us describe the eight factors briefly.

1. **Right View**, in essence means seeing and accepting the Four Noble Truths. A complete understanding is not envisaged in the preliminary stages, simply an initial acceptance of – and confidence or faith (*śraddhā*) in – the Buddha and his teachings. This initial confidence will be confirmed through personal experience over the course of time, and nothing has to be believed purely as an article of faith. Right View (*samyag-dṛṣṭi*) is also explained in the *Mahācattārīsaka Sutta* in terms of a traditional religious outlook on life involving belief in the moral

### The Truth of the Path (*mārga*)

This, O Monks, is the Truth of the Path which leads to the cessation of suffering. It is this Noble Eightfold Path, which consists of (1) Right View, (2) Right Resolve, (3) Right Speech, (4) Right Action, (5) Right Livelihood, (6) Right Effort, (7) Right Mindfulness, (8) Right Meditation.

## The Noble Eightfold Path

| | |
|---|---|
| 1. Right View<br>2. Right Resolve | WISDOM (*prajñā*) |
| 3. Right Speech<br>4. Right Action<br>5. Right Livelihood | MORALITY (*śīla*) |
| 6. Right Effort<br>7. Right Mindfulness<br>8. Right Meditation | MEDITATION (*samādhi*) |

law of karma, respect for parents and religious teachers, and in the possibility of personal spiritual progress.

2. **Right Resolve** (***samyak-saṃkalpa***) means developing right attitudes such as freedom from desires, friendliness, and compassion. It includes making a serious commitment to attaining a state of contentment (*naiṣkāmya*) and freedom from sensual desires (*kāma*), abandoning hatred (*avyābādha*) and abstaining from causing any injury to others (*ahiṃsā*).
3. **Right Speech** (***samyag-vāc***) means not telling lies, avoiding 'divisive speech' (such as making remarks that can cause enmity among people), avoiding harsh speech (speech which is aggressive or hurtful to others), and frivolous talk (such as gossip and idle chatter).
4. **Right Action** (***samyak-karmanta***) means abstaining from wrongful conduct through the body such as killing, stealing, or behaving inappropriately with respect to sensual pleasures.
5. **Right Livelihood** (***samyag-ājīva***) means not engaging in an occupation which causes harm or suffering to others, whether human or animal. This involves being honest in one's business affairs and not cheating one's customers (M.iii.75). It also involves avoiding certain trades and professions that cause death or harm such as 'trade in weapons, living beings, meat, alcoholic drink, or poison' (A.iii.208).
6. **Right Effort** (***samyag-vyāyāma***) means developing one's mind in a wholesome way by practicing mindfulness and mental cultivation as in meditation. It involves slowly transforming one's mind by replacing negative thoughts with positive and wholesome ones.
7. **Right Mindfulness** (***samyak-smṛti***) means developing constant awareness in four areas: in relation to the body, one's feelings, one's mood or mental state, and one's thoughts. It also involves eliminating negative thought patterns such as the

'five hindrances' (*nīvaraṇa*), namely (desire for sensual pleasure, ill-will, sloth and drowsiness, worry and agitation, and nagging doubts).

8. **Right Meditation (*samyak-samādhi*)** means developing clarity and mental calm by concentrating the mind through meditational exercises. By such practices the practitioner is able to enter states like the four *dhyānas*, the lucid trances which played such an important part in the Buddha's quest for awakening. The various techniques of meditation used to concentrate the mind and integrate the personality will be explained more fully in Chapter Seven.

As noted, the eight factors of the Path fall into three areas, and these can be pictured in the form of a triangle. Morality (*śīla*) forms the baseline and is the foundation of religious practice since without self-discipline and virtuous behavior it is difficult to make progress in any endeavor. Meditation (*samādhi*) denotes the process of calming and self-integration that takes place at the deepest levels of the psyche, while wisdom (*prajñā*) relates to knowledge and understanding of the nature or reality and the ability to see clearly how awakening can be achieved. These three brace and support one another like the sides of a triangle, and each is in constant contact with the other two. Thus just as morality is the foundation for meditation and wisdom, it is also strengthened by them in turn, since inner calm and clear understanding produce a heightened moral sensibility which helps us distinguish more clearly between right and wrong. Meditation boosts the intellectual faculties and makes wisdom stronger and more penetrating, and wisdom supports meditation by making clearer and more intelligible the experience of the meditative states.

It is important to realize that the Noble Eightfold Path is not like a series of stages one passes through on the way to nirvana, in the way that a traveller making a journey might pass through various towns before reaching his destination. The eight factors are not objectives to be reached and then left behind; rather the Path is a continuous program in which the eight factors are developed cumulatively. Another misleading interpretation is to think of the eight factors of the Path as rungs on a ladder which is climbed in order to reach nirvana as a ninth rung at the top. In fact nirvana is not mentioned in the Path at all, the reason being that it is the lived experience of the Path itself that constitutes nirvana. In following the Path one acts like a Buddha, and by acting like a Buddha one progressively becomes one. The Path is essentially a means of self-transformation, a remodeling project or spiritual makeover, which turns the ordinary unenlightened person into a Buddha.

## Holy persons

Not all who practice the Eightfold Path do so at the same level. The sources distinguish various kinds of practitioners who are more or less advanced in their spiritual practice. First of all comes the category of the 'worldly person' (*pṛthagjana*) or non-Buddhist, who does not follow the Path at all. Such people will continue to

> **The four holy persons (*ārya-pudgala*)**
>
> 1. Stream Winner (*śrotāpanna*)
> 2. Once-Returner (*sakṛdāgāmin*)
> 3. Non-Returner (*anāgāmin*)
> 4. *Arhant*

wander in *saṃsāra* until such time as they hear and respond to Buddhist teachings. Next come ordinary Buddhists, who follow a basic form of the Path, in contrast to the more advanced practitioners who follow the 'Noble' (*ārya*) form. The distinction here relates to the degree of insight into Buddhist teachings one possesses. At a higher level come what we might terms the 'saints' of Buddhism, or holy people who are close to nirvana and destined to attain it in the near future.

Four categories of 'holy person' (*ārya-pudgala*) are distinguished, the first being that of the 'stream winner' (*śrotāpanna*). Such a person, through deep meditation on the 'three marks' of suffering (*duḥkha*), impermanence (*anitya*) and 'no-self' (*anātman*), has gained a glimpse of nirvana and has entered the 'stream' that will carry him or her inexorably towards it within seven lives at the most. All of these lives will be as either a human or a god. Next comes the 'once-returner' (*sakṛdāgāmin*), who will return at most one further time to the human world, with any further rebirths taking place in the higher heavens. Third is the 'non-returner' (*anāgāmin*), who will never again be reborn in the human realm.

Having freed himself entirely from craving and hatred, he no longer has any attachment to the realm of sense-desires (*kāma-loka*) and so will not be reborn there, but still lacks sufficient insight to put an end to rebirth. Such a person will be reborn in one of the five 'pure abodes', which are the five highest heavens reserved especially for *anāgāmins*. The last of the four noble persons is the *arhant*, one who has freed himself from any belief in a self (*ātman*), eliminated all ignorance and spiritual defilements, and destroyed all desire for rebirth at any level of existence. For the *arhant* all suffering (*duḥkha*) is at an end, and at death he will attain final nirvana and never more be reborn, like the Buddha.

## *The doctrine of no-self*

Buddhism sees the human subject as made up of two parts, one spiritual (*nāma*), the other material (*rūpa*). In recognizing that there is both a spiritual (*nāma*) and material (*rūpa*) side to human nature the Buddha was not saying anything new in the context of Indian philosophy. He went on, however, to extend the analysis and to define five categories in terms of which human nature can be analyzed. This further analysis is referred to towards the end of the First Noble Truth in the phrase 'the five aggregates which are grasped at (*upādāna-skandha*) are suffering'. This teaching of the five aggregates was elaborated on by the Buddha in his second sermon, the *Anatta-lakkhaṇa Sutta* (Vin.i.13), preached five days after the first. The five aggregates are collectively known as the 'aggregates of attachment' (*upādāna-skandha*) because as the means to pleasurable experiences they are themselves objects of desire or craving (*tṛṣṇā*) and are grasped at in life after life.

Before looking at the five aggregates individually, the important point to note is not so much what the list of the five includes as what it does not. Specifically the doctrine makes no mention of a soul or self, understood as an eternal and immutable spiritual essence. By adopting this position the Buddha set himself apart from the orthodox Indian religious tradition known as Brahmanism, which claimed that each person possessed an eternal soul (*ātman*) which is either part of, or identical with, a metaphysical absolute known as *brahman* (a sort of impersonal godhead). He also rejected the views of other contemporary teachers, such as the Jain leader Mahāvira, who taught that at the core of each individual was an eternal and unchanging spiritual principle known as the *jīva*, or life principle.

The Buddha said he could find no evidence for the existence of either the personal soul (*ātman*) or its cosmic counterpart (*brahman*), and he also rejected the Jain and similar teachings concerning the *jīva*. Instead his approach was practical and empirical, more akin to psychology than theology. He explained human nature as constituted by the five factors much in the way that an automobile is constituted by its wheels, transmission, engine, steering, and chassis. Unlike science, of course, he believed that a person's moral identity survives death and is reborn.

In stating that the five factors of individuality are suffering, however, as he did in the First Noble Truth, the Buddha was pointing out that human nature cannot provide a foundation for permanent happiness because the doctrine of the five aggregates shows that the individual has no real core. Because human beings are made up of these five constantly shifting components it is inevitable that sooner or later suffering will arise, just as an automobile will eventually wear out and break down. Suffering is thus engrained in the very fabric of our being.

## *The five aggregates*

Let us now consider the five aggregates in turn. The first and simplest of the five is form (*rūpa*). Although not exactly equivalent to 'matter' this may be thought of as denoting the physical substance of the body. The second of the five categories is feeling (*vedanā*), and this denotes the capacity to respond affectively to a stimulus. Feelings are classified as pleasant, unpleasant, or neutral, and the most basic kind of feelings are simple sensations of the stimulus–response kind. An example of an unpleasant sensation might be to be pricked by a pin; a pleasant one would be a hot relaxing bath on a cold day. In addition to the capacity for feeling, human beings also

### The five aggregates

1. Material form (*rūpa*)
2. Feelings and sensations (*vedanā*)
3. Perceptions (*saṃjñā*)
4. Mental formations (*saṃskāra*)
5. Consciousness (*vijñāna*)

have the power of perception and conceptual thought, and this constitutes the third category, known as *saṃjñā*. This includes the capacity to discern and discriminate between things, for example to name and distinguish different colors.

The picture sketched so far is abstract and two-dimensional, and lacks any reference to the features which distinguish one person from another. These are the elements which constitute the fourth category. Granted the power to think and feel, individual development will be shaped by personal experiences and reactions to them. From these reactions are built up particular tendencies, traits and habits, and eventually the complex pattern of dispositions which is referred to as 'character'. It is the particular configuration of these traits and characteristics which defines people as the individuals they are. Buddhist commentators drew up long lists of virtues, vices, and other mental factors in order to provide an exhaustive account of this fourth category, which we have called 'mental formations' (*saṃskāra*). A central role here is played by the will or volition (*cetanā*), the mental faculty through which we deliberate and take decisions, and through which karma is produced. Retrospectively, the fourth category is the sum of the karma or moral choices made in previous lives.

The fifth category, *vijñāna*, is usually translated as 'consciousness', but this term can be misleading as a translation since it is usually taken to mean the mental 'stream of consciousness'. The experience of *vijñāna* as a stream of mental awareness, however, is merely one of its many modes. It is better understood as functioning at a deeper level as that which animates an organism. It is by virtue of *vijñāna* that we have bodily sensations, that we see, hear, taste, touch and think. The translation 'sentiency' may be preferable to 'consciousness' since it is not restricted to the mental sphere in quite the same way. *Vijñāna* has an important function in relation to death and rebirth. Following death, *vijñāna* fuses with a new biological form giving rise to a being with a new physical body but a karmic profile carried over from a previous life. Buddhist sources refer to *vijñāna* in this transitional phase as the '*gandharva*'.

According to Buddhism, then, the human subject can be deconstructed into these five aggregates without remainder, and since the five make no reference to an eternal soul Buddhism is said to teach a doctrine of 'no-self' (*anātman*). In terms of this doctrine, the common but fallacious belief in an eternal soul is really a case of mistaken identity whereby one or more of the *skandhas* is mistaken for a soul.

So, in the doctrine of 'no-self' is the Buddha denying that individuals exist or have any unique personality or identity? No, the ego is not denied by this teaching. As explained above, the particular traits and characteristics which go to make up an individual (as when we say 'that was typical of him') are explained as belonging to the fourth *skandha*, the *saṃskāra-skandha*. Here are the found the various tendencies and patterns of behavior which collectively give shape to an individual character. The doctrine of *anātman* is not taking away anything: it is simply recognizing that the concept of an eternal and unchanging soul is redundant, and is not required to explain how human beings function.

## Key points you need to know

- '*Dharma*' means the teachings and doctrines of Buddhism.
- The doctrinal foundations of Buddhism are the Four Noble Truths.
- The Four Noble Truths teach that 1) life is suffering; 2) suffering is caused by craving; 3) suffering can have an end (this is nirvana); 4) the way to nirvana is the Noble Eightfold Path.
- There are two kinds of nirvana: nirvana in this life, and nirvana after death.
- The Noble Eightfold Path has three divisions: Morality, Meditation, and Wisdom.
- Those close to the end of the Path are known as 'holy persons' (*ārya-pudgala*).
- Buddhism analyses the human being into five component parts, known as the 'five aggregates': these are form, feeling, cognition, mental formations, and consciousness.
- According to the doctrine of 'no-self' (*anātman*), there is no permanent, unchanging soul or self apart from the five aggregates

## Discussion questions

1. What is suffering (*duḥkha*) and what causes it?
2. What is *nirvāṇa*, and how is it attained?
3. What did Buddha mean when he taught that there is 'no-self' (*anātman*)?
4. What is the doctrine of 'dependent origination' (*pratītya-samutpāda*) and how important is it in the early teachings?

## Further reading

Sumedho, Ajahn. *The Four Noble Truths*. (Acrobat ebook.) Available from http://www.buddhanet.net/pdf_file/4nobltru.pdf.

Santina, Peter. *Fundamentals of Buddhism*. (Acrobat ebook.) Available from http://www.buddhanet.net/pdf_file/fundbud1.pdf.

Hamilton, Sue. *Identity and Experience: The Constitution of the Human Being according to Early Buddhism*. London: Luzac, 1996.

Johansson, Rune. E. A. *The Psychology of Nirvana*. London: Allen & Unwin, 1999.

Harvey, Peter. *The Selfless Mind: Personality, Consciousness and Nirvana in Early Buddhism*. London: Curzon Press, 1995.

Welbon, Guy R. *The Buddhist Nirvana and its Western Interpreters*. Chicago, IL: University of Chicago Press, 1988.

# 4 *The Buddhist* Sangha

## In this chapter

This chapter defines the various aspects of the Buddhist community and the monastic and ethical codes that govern its behavior. It also highlights some of Buddha's most famous early disciples, as well as the geographic spread of the early Buddhist community.

## Main topics covered

- The *sangha* defined
- The *Vinaya Piṭaka*
- Paracanonical *Vinaya* literature
- Canonical *Vinaya* literature
- Non-canonical *Vinaya* literature
- The laity
- Important disciples in the early *sangha*
- Monks
- Lay disciples
- Royal patrons
- Monastic life
- Geographic dispersal of the early *sangha*

## *The* sangha *defined*

Tradition generally acknowledges that the Buddha spent forty-nine days in the vicinity of the Bodhi tree following his experience of enlightenment. Eventually, he was persuaded to propagate the *Dharma* by a deity known as Brahmā Sahampati, and upon so doing, his first followers were two merchants who became lay disciples. The Buddha moved on to Benares, where he preached his first sermon to five old ascetic friends who had previously wandered around with him for six years practicing

*Figure 4.1* Interior of monastery on Dobongsan, near Seoul, Korea

austerities. As noted above, this initial sermon was followed by a second, and in short order the five ascetics attained nirvana.

The five ascetics requested both preliminary ordination into monkhood (called *pravrajyā*) and full ordination as well (called *upasaṃpadā*). The Buddha accomplished this with a simple exhortation of 'Come, O Monk!' (*ehi bhikṣu*). Thus the monastic order, or *sangha*, was born, and within a short period this monastic community expanded rapidly and enormously.

Despite the fact that the term *sangha* is used today in a more extended and comprehensive fashion than originally, referring to almost any community or group loosely associated with Buddhism, in the time of the Buddha, the term was used in a radically different fashion. The Sanskrit word *sangha* simply connotes a society or company or a number of people living together for a certain purpose. In the midst of many religious *sanghas* in the general wanderers' (*parivrājaka*) community, the Buddha's followers appropriated the term in a rather distinct fashion, one that gave their fledgling community a clear and unique identity. While outsiders may have referred to the Buddha's first disciples as *Śākyaputrīya-śrāmaṇas* or 'mendicants who follow the Buddha', the original community referred to itself as the *bhikṣu-sangha*, or community of monks. Later, when the order of nuns was founded, they became known as the *bhikṣuṇī-sangha*, and the two units were collectively known as the *ubhayato-sangha*, the 'twofold community'. In Theravāda countries, this quite narrow usage of the term *sangha* has remained the predominant meaning of the word, as is pointed out by most modern scholars writing on the Buddhist community. Occasionally, in the early literature, the Buddha uses the term *cāturdisa-saṇgha* or the '*sangha* of the four quarters', but it seems clear from his usage that he still means the monastic *sangha* exclusively.

The dramatic growth of the *sangha* required certain adjustments to be made in the formal ordination procedure for monastics, and over time, the entire process became rather formalized. Monks were allowed to confer both ordinations, and the entire process was preceded by a threefold recitation of the following formula:

> I go to the Buddha for refuge,
> I go to the *Dharma* for refuge,
> I go to the *Sangha* for refuge.

Both the monks' and nuns' communities were charged to wander continually teaching *Dharma*, settling down only during the rainy season when traveling about was simply not practical in India.

Initially, the Buddha's plan for community life worked admirably. Monks and nuns settled down during the rainy season in one of two types of dwelling: (1) a self-constructed hut known as an *āvāsa*, or (2) a donated hut known as an *ārāma*. In each case, furniture and requisites were kept to a bare minimum, and the monastic dweller engaged in serious study and meditation for the roughly three-month period of rain-retreat confinement. As might be anticipated, within a short time after the Buddha's death, the rain retreat became institutionalized, expanding communal needs considerably, and the wandering ideal became largely a fiction in early Buddhism. Large monastic units developed, usually identified as *vihāras*, and often cataloged by their location as 'the *Sangha* of Vaiśālī' or 'the *Sangha* of Śrāvastī', and so forth. Although the movement toward settled, lasting monasteries contradicted Buddha's injunction regarding settled permanent dwelling, it did provide the opportunity for the development of Buddhism as a religious tradition. And it was this social institution that was exported by various rulers in the Buddhist missionary enterprise. In time, the monasteries that developed in diverse Buddhist cultures became formidable units, serving as festival and pilgrimage sites and commanding economic and political, as well as religious respect.

Although the monastic vocation was by no means ascetic, in keeping with the Buddha's insistence on a 'middle path' between asceticism and luxury, it was certainly a serious step that most individuals were not capable of making. As such, Buddhist history records that the Buddha also admitted lay members – male disciples or *upāsikas* and female disciples known as *upāsikās* – into his community, and they eventually became a vital, symbiotic part of that community. Nevertheless, the lay community was initially considered autonomous to, and even distinct from, the monastic community.

## *The* Vinaya Piṭaka

Buddhist scholar Michael Carrithers is quoted to have said, 'No Buddhism without the *Sangha* and no *Sangha* without the Discipline'. In other words, in order to effect the highest level of ethical conduct from the monastic and lay communities, disciplinary codes for each unit were enacted. For the monastic community, this took the form of a portion of the canon known as the *Vinaya Piṭaka*.

The *Vinaya Piṭaka* is that portion of the Buddhist canon regulating the monastic life of the monks and nuns. Properly speaking, though, a consideration of the monastic aspect of Buddhist life must be taken in broad spectrum, focusing not just on that portion of the monastic law which was canonized, but on *Vinaya* literature in general, thus affording us an opportunity to view the developmental process going on within the early Buddhist community in the first few centuries after the the Buddha's death. For convenience, then, we arrive at the following schema:

- Paracanonical *Vinaya* literature
  - *Prātimokṣa Sutra*
  - *Karmavācanā*
- Canonical *Vinaya* literature
  - *Sūtravibhaṅga*
  - *Skandhaka*
  - Appendices
- Non-canonical *Vinaya* literature
  - Commentaries
  - Miscellaneous texts

## *Paracanonical* Vinaya *literature*

### *Prātimokṣa*

The *Prātimokṣa* is an inventory of offences organized into several categories classified according to the gravity of the offence. Many scholars now agree that the *Prātimokṣa*, as a technical term in the Buddhist lexicon, seems to have undergone at least three stages of development: as a simple confession of faith recited by Buddhist monks and nuns at periodic intervals, as a bare monastic code employed as a device insuring proper monastic discipline, and as a monastic liturgy, representing a period of relatively high organization and structure within the *sangha*. We find the following classes of offences within the monks' text:

1. *Pārājika dharmas*: offences requiring expulsion from the *sangha*.
2. *Sanghāvaśeṣa dharmas*: offences involving temporary exclusion from the *sangha* while undergoing a probationary period.

3. *Aniyata dharmas*: undetermined cases (involving sexuality) in which the offender, when observed by a trustworthy female lay follower, may be charged under one of several categories of offences.
4. *Naiḥsargika-Pāyantika dharmas*: offences requiring forfeiture and expiation.
5. *Pāyantika dharmas*: offences requiring simple expiation.
6. *Pratideśanīya dharmas*: offences which should be confessed.
7. *Śaikṣa dharmas*: rules concerning etiquette.
8. *Adhikaraṇa-Śamatha dharmas*: legalistic procedures to be used in settling disputes.

The nuns' text contains only seven categories, the third being excluded. The number of rules cited varies in the texts of the diverse Buddhist schools, ranging from 218 to 263 for the monks and from 279 to 380 for the nuns. When formalized into the *Prātimokṣa Sutra* recited as a confessional at the twice-monthly *Poṣadha* or fast-day ceremony, concurrent with the new and full moon days, three new features were added to the text: a series of verses preceding and following the text, praising the virtuous, disciplined life; an introduction used to call the *sangha* together and instrument the confessional procedure; and an interrogatory formula, recited after each class of offence, aimed at discovery of who was pure and who was not. Thus within a short time after the founder's death, the monks had provided themselves with an organizational tool for implementing purity in the monastic order.

## *Karmavācanā*

The *Karmavācanā* is the functional, legalistic device by which the communal life of the *sangha* is regulated. We might say that what the *Prātimokṣa* represented to the individual monk or nun, the *Karmavācanā* represented to the *sangha*. At least fourteen *Karmavācanas* can be listed:

1. Admission into the order (*pravrajyā*).
2. Full ordination of monks (*upasaṃpadā*).
3. Holding the confession ceremony (*poṣadha*).
4. Holding the invitation ceremony (*pravāraṇā*).
5. Residence obligation during the rainy season (*varṣopagamana*).
6. Use of leather objects (*carman*).
7. Preparation and use of medicines (*bhaiṣajya*).
8. Robe-giving ceremony (*kaṭhina*).
9. Discipline.
10. Daily life of monks.
11. Beds and seats in dwellings (*śayanāsana*).
12. Schisms in the order (*sanghabheda*).
13. Duties of a student and teacher to one another.
14. Rules for nuns.

All of these are handled under a general procedure called *sanghakarma* (literally, 'an act of the *sangha*') arising either by a general requisition or a dispute. To be considered valid, the proper number of competent monks must be assembled, all absentee ballots gathered, and a motion (or *jñapti*) set forth. The motion is then read aloud or proclaimed (this is the *Karmavācanā* or 'announcing the action') and a decision, positive or negative, obtained. On the basis of the decision, democratically elicited, the *sangha* acts as a unified order.

## *Canonical* Vinaya *literature*

### *Sūtravibhaṅga*

The term *Sūtravibhaṅga* is literally translated as 'analysis of a *sūtra*'. Thus the *Sūtravibhaṅga* is a detailed analysis of the offences recorded in the *Prātimokṣa Sutra*. As we should expect, the *Sūtravibhaṅga* has the same general categories of offences as the *Prātimokṣa Sutra*. Regarding each of the *Prātimokṣa* rules, the *Sūtravibhaṅga* has a fourfold structure: (1) a story (or stories) explaining the circumstances under which the rule was pronounced; (2) the *Prātimokṣa* rule; (3) a word-for-word commentary on the rule; and (4) stories indicating mitigating circumstances in which exceptions to the rule or deviations in punishment might be made. In addition to the *Prātimokṣa* offences, several new terms are found in the *Sūtravibhaṅga*: *sthūlātyaya* or grave offence, *duṣkṛta* or light offence, and *durbhāṣita* or offence of improper speech. These new terms were added because by the time the *Sūtravibhaṅga* was compiled, the *Prātimokṣa* had become fixed (that is, closed) with new rules considered inadmissible. To provide the flexibility of a situational ethics, the *Sūtravibhaṅga* expanded necessarily in this direction. Like the *Prātimokṣa*, there is both a monks' and nuns' *Sūtravibhaṅga*.

### *Skandhaka*

The *Skandhaka* contains the regulations pertaining to the organization of the *sangha*. It functions on the basis of the acts and ceremonies dictated by the *Karmavācanās*. We might say that the *Karmavācanās* are to the *Skandhaka* what the *Prātimokṣa* is to the *Sūtravhibhaṅga*. There are twenty sections in the *Skandhaka*, each referred to as a *vastu*:

1. *Pravrajyāvastu*: admission to the *sangha*.
2. *Poṣadhavastu*: the monthly confession ceremony.
3. *Varṣāvastu*: residence during the rainy season.
4. *Pravāraṇāvastu*: the invitation ceremony at the end of the rainy season.
5. *Carmavastu*: use of shoes and leather objects.
6. *Bhaṣajyavastu*: food and medicine for the monks.
7. *Cīvaravastu*: rules concerning clothing.

8. *Kaṭhinavastu*: rules concerning the production and distribution of robes.
9. *Kośambakavastu*: dispute between two groups of monks in Kauśāmbī.
10. *Karmavastu*: lawful monastic procedure.
11. *Pāṇḍulohitakavastu*: measures taken by the *sangha* to correct disciplinary problems.
12. *Pudgalavastu*: ordinary procedures for simple offences.
13. *Pārivāsikavastu*: behavior during the *parivāsa* and *mānatvā* probationary periods.
14. *Poṣadhasthāpanavastu*: prohibiting a monk from participating in the *poṣadha* ceremony.
15. *Śamathavastu*: procedures to settle disputes.
16. *Sanghabhedavastu*: schisms in the *sangha*.
17. *Śayanāsanavastu*: monastic residences.
18. *Ācāravastu*: behavior of the monks (not discussed elsewhere).
19. *Kṣudrakavastu*: miscellaneous, minor matters.
20. *Bhikṣuṇīvastu*: rules specificially for nuns.

In addition to the twenty *vastus*, there is an introductory section discussing the Buddha's genealogy, birth, and life history up to the conversion of Śāriputra and Maudgalyāyana, and also a concluding section covering the Buddha's death, the council of Rājagṛha, the history of the patriarchs, and the council of Vaiṣālī.

## Appendices

Appendices are attached to several of the *Vinayas* as a supplement. They serve two basic functions: providing summaries of the rules found in the *Sūtravibhaṅga* and *Skandhaka*, and providing interesting bits of monastic history.

## *Non-canonical* Vinaya *literature*

Fortunately, a wide variety of *Vinaya* commentaries have come down to us, and their importance need not be stressed here.

## *The laity*

Many Buddhist scholars have pointed out that the basis of Buddhist spiritual life is merit (*puṇya*). For the male and female lay disciples (known as *upāsakas* and *upāsikās*, respectively), this merit could be cultivated in two primary ways. First, they could practice wholesome acts which created the attainment of merit or 'good karma'. But additionally, they could establish the monastic *sangha* as a special 'field of merit' (or *puṇya-kṣetra*). By providing acts of giving (*dāna*) and generosity to the entire monastic community, they enhanced their own spiritual growth while supporting the religious professionals of their faith. In return for their support, the laity received the wise counsel and *Dharma* instruction from the monastic community. It is no surprise, then, that the rigor of disciplinary rules for the monastic community is easily explained in the context of understanding this symbiotic nature of the monastic–lay relationship. Since the monastic vocation required a retreat from worldly life and an eremitic ideal, the individual monk or nun had to remain worthy of the highest respect in order to retain the support of the laity.

For the lay community, ethical conduct was governed by adherence to five vows, generally known as the *pañca-śīla*: (1) to abstain from taking life, (2) to abstain from taking that which is not given, (3) to abstain from sexual misconduct, (4) to abstain from false speech, and (5) to abstain from intoxicating substances. In some variants, this formula was expanded to eight and to ten precepts. Additionally, a number of famous discourses, like the Pāli *Sigālovāda Sutta*, regulate ethical conduct within the various relationships that occur in normal social intercourse. While the major focus of the earliest Buddhist communities, in various Asian Buddhist cultures, was clearly monastic, we will see later in this book that Buddhism's globalization, and spread to Western cultures, yields a profound shift in emphasis from the monastic lifestyle as the normative, ideal pattern for Buddhists to a new and profound accent on the lay lifestyle as the more usual choice for modern Buddhists.

## *Important disciples in the early* sangha

During the time period immediately following the Buddha's attainment of enlightenment, many disciples became an integral part of the early history of the Buddhist community. What follows is a brief mention of some of the most important disciples, classified under the headings of 'Monks', 'Lay disciples', and 'Royal patrons'.

### Monks

**Ānanda.** Ānanda was the Buddha's cousin and was converted to Buddhism during the Buddha's visit to Kapilavastu. During the twentieth year of the Buddha's ministry, he became the Buddha's personal attendant, and remained so for the rest of the Buddha's life. Most notable among his accomplishments were his recitation of all the *sūtras* at the first council after the Buddha's death, and his role in helping to establish the order of nuns (*bhikṣuṇīs*) by coming to the aid of Mahāprajāpatī, who became the first nun.

**Upāli.** Belonging to a barber's family, Upāli also became a monk at Kapilavastu, eventually becoming a master of the *Vinaya*, which he recited in total at the first council.

**Rāhula.** Following his enlightenment, the Buddha eventually returned to Kapilavastu to visit his family. At that time the Buddha's former wife Yaśodharā sent their son Rāhula to receive his birthright. Instead, however, the Buddha ordained the young boy (who was only seven years old at the time) as a novice (*śrāmaṇera*). Rāhula is known as the chief of the novices.

**Śāriputra and Maudgalyāyana.** Śāriputra was originally a follower of a wanderer named Sañjaya. One day he met a novice Buddhist monk named Aśvajit, who expounded to *Dharma* to him. Śāriputra immediately perceived the true meaning of the teaching and became an *arhant*. Śāriputra then recited the *Dharma* to his close friend Maudgalyāyana, who also immediately became enlightened. The two young men became monks, and established themselves as two of the Buddha's closest and wisest disciples. Śāriputra is often associated with the *Abhidharma*, while Maudgalayāyana was known for his miraculous powers.

**Mahākāśyapa.** A very senior and highly disciplined monk, Mahākāśyapa was selected to head the first council, held at Rājagṛha in the first rainy season following the Buddha's death. He is reputed to have selected the 500 monks who attended, and to have personally questioned Ānanda on the *Sūtras* and Upāli on the *Vinaya*.

**Devadatta.** Also related to the Buddha, Devadatta became a monk but, unlike the Buddha's other followers, was a threat to the *sangha* by constantly, toward the end of the Buddha's ministry, trying to usurp leadership of the community. After several unsuccessful attempts to murder the Buddha, Devadatta founded his own order based on more austere religious practices. When his followers eventually left him to return to the Buddha's *sangha*, he coughed up blood and died.

## Lay disciples

**Anāthapiṇḍika.** He was a wealthy banker in Śrāvastī. After becoming a lay disciple, he built a monastery known as Jetavana, where Buddha spent the final twenty-five rainy seasons of his ministry.

**Viśākhā.** She was a banker's daughter. Born into a Buddhist family, she was eventually married into a family who followed a rival religious system. Although instructed by her father-in-law to support this new system and its followers, she rebelled, eventually bringing her father-in-law to Buddhism. She is known for having performed social services for the *sangha*, engaging in activities such as offering daily food for the monks, offering medicine to the sick, and providing robes for the monks.

## Royal patrons

**King Bimbisāra.** Bimbisāra ruled Magadha from his chief city of Rājagṛha. Having become a disciple of the Buddha after hearing a *Dharma* discourse, he built the very first monastery offered to the *sangha*: Veṇuvana Ārāma (literally 'Bamboo Grove Park'). He was responsible for the Buddha's adoption of the twice-monthly confessional meeting known as *poṣadha*. He was eventually caught in a court intrigue involving his son, Prince Ajātaśatru and the murderous Devadatta, and briefly imprisoned before regaining his freedom.

**King Prasenajit.** Unlike King Bimbisāra, Prasenajit, King of Kośala, did not give his unqualified support to the Buddha, although he did offer gifts to the *sangha*. Eventually, though, he became a Buddhist lay disciple and ardent patron of the religion.

## *Monastic life*

During the early history of Buddhism, the *sangha* existed as simply another sect of the community of wanderers known as *parivrājakas*. One custom which seems to have been observed by all these sects was that of suspending the wandering life during the rainy season. The Buddhists used this temporary settling down as a means to cultivate living together in concord, establishing careful rules for the observance of the rainy season (*varṣā*), and thus differentiated themselves from the rest of the wanderers' community by establishing the rudiments of Buddhist monastic life.

Buddhist rainy season settlements were generally of two types: *āvāsas* or dwelling places which were determined, constructed, and kept up by the monks themselves, and ārāmas or parks which were donated and maintained by some wealthy patron. With the *āvāsas* and *ārāmas*, huts called *vihāras* were constructed for monks' residences. Later, when monastic dwellings became more fully developed, the term *vihāra* came to designate the whole monastery. In these residences, monks' accommodations were of the simplest kind. Most monasteries were built on the outskirts of towns and villages, so their close proximity to the town made alms procurement easy but provided enough isolation for the monks to pursue their meditative vocation undisturbed by the hustle and bustle of city life.

The three months of enforced communal living quickly made a profound impact on the Buddhist *sangha*. Various institutions within the *sangha* began to emerge to mold the *sangha* into a cohesive body. The recitation of the code of monastic law (*Prātimokṣa*) was adopted on a twice-monthly basis. The preparation and distribution of robes (*kaṭhina*) took on collective features, eventually becoming a distinct ceremony, as did the 'Invitation' or *Pravāraṇā* held at the end of the rainy-season residence and dealing with purity during the rainy season. Initial and full ordination procedures (*pravrajyā* and *upasaṃpadā*, respectively) were administered by the *sangha* rather than by individual monks.

The monastery as a unit, however, was by definition a self-limiting institution at the outset. At the end of each rainy season the monks were to abandon the settlement and begin wandering once again. Nevertheless, monks did tend to return to the same monastic residence year after year. Eventually, blending motivations of self-preservation and usefulness to their lay communities, monks ceased to wander at all. Thus individual *sanghas* grew up, such as the *Sangha* of Śrāvastī. Gradually, as the wandering life became a fiction, the Buddhists established themselves as a distinct group, bound by the teaching and discipline of the Buddha and committed to their own attainment of nirvana, as well as the spiritual uplift of the laity; but with the rise of distinct *sanghas*, the maintenance of commonality became acute. As each *sangha* became increasingly more individualized and removed geographically from other *sanghas*, the first seed of sectarianism was sown.

## *Geographic dispersal of the* sangha

During Buddha's lifetime, his religion and *sangha* did not spread far. Most of his preaching was conducted in and around the great regions of Magadha and Kośala. Within Magadha three places seem to be most noteworthy. First was the capital city of the region: Rājagṛha. Here Bimbisāra's patronage resulted in the first gift of an *ārāma* to the *sangha*. Also in Magadha, Pāṭaliputra was later to become the stronghold capital of perhaps the greatest king of Indian history, Aśoka. Besides these two cities, on the outskirts of Rājagṛha was Nālandā, later to become the seat of one of the most important early Buddhist universities. Magadha also marks the birthplace of the religion as it was in Bodhgayā that Buddha's enlightenment was attained. In Buddha's early wanderings, he gained his largest group of followers in Magadha. Kośala, ruled by Prasenajit, was most important for its capital of Śrāvastī, where Buddha received his two early patrons Anāthapiṇḍika and Viśākhā, and where he spent the last twenty-five rainy seasons of his ministry. Within the kingdom of Kośala was Kapilavastu, Buddha's home.

To the east of Koúala and north of Magadha were several other kingdoms which, although being strongholds of the *Brāhmaṇical* tradition, felt Buddha's impact: the Licchavis, the Videhas, and the Koliyas, to name a few. Also to the east was the region of Aṅga, mentioned occasionally in the early texts, as is the city of Kauśāmbī. The west and north seem to have been much less frequented by the early Buddhists. Consequently, we can see from the above that during its earliest history, the Buddhist *sangha* spread within some rather closely defined limits. The wide dispersal of Buddhism, both within India and outside its borders, belongs to a period at least several hundred years after the Buddha's death. This expansion, Buddhism's globalization, and the development of the *sangha* in modern Buddhist cultures will be explored elsewhere in this book.

### Key points you need to know

- The Buddhist *sangha* consists of monks, nuns, laymen and laywomen.
- Monks and nuns follow a strict disciplinary code known as the *Vinaya Piṭaka* while the laity follows five basic ethical maxims known as the 'Five Precepts'.
- The *Vinaya Piṭaka* regulates both the individual lives of the monastic *sangha* members and the monastic institution itself.
- The monastic community and the laity are mutually supporting, existing in a symbiotic relationship.
- Within several hundred years of the Buddha's death, the *sangha* spread throughout India and beyond.

## Discussion questions

1. How did the *sangha* originate, and what are the main principles governing the daily lives of monks and nuns?
2. Can Buddhist behavioral codes like the *Vinaya* remain relevant in the modern world? If not, why? If so, how?
3. How does Buddhism envisage the relationship between monastics and the laity?

## Further reading

Dutt, Sukumar. *Buddhist Monks and Monasteries of India: Their History and their Contribution to Indian Culture*. London: George Allen & Unwin, 1962.

Holt, John. *Discipline: The Canonical Buddhism of the Vinayapiṭaka*. Delhi: Motilal Banarsidass, 1981.

Prebish, Charles S. *Buddhist Monastic Discipline: The Sanskrit Pārtimokṣa Sūtras of the Mahāsāṃghikas and Mūlasarvāstivādins*. University Park, PA: Pennsylvania State University Press, 1975.

Wijayaratna, Mohan. *Buddhist Monastic Life According to the Texts of the Theravada Tradition*. Translated by Claude Gangier and Steven Collins. Cambridge: Cambridge University Press, 1990.

# Part II

# Development

# 5 *Buddhism in India*

## In this chapter

This chapter deals with the main developments in Indian Buddhism from the death of the Buddha to the eventual disappearance of Buddhism from India. It explains the formation of the main Indian Buddhist sects and schools and traces the doctrinal differences and scholastic debates between them. These learned discussions culminated in the composition of influential scholastic treatises in the early medieval period which provided the intellectual backbone to Buddhist teachings. The chapter concludes with a discussion of the origins of *Tantra*, the arrival of Islam, and the destruction of the great monastic universities of North India.

## Main topics discussed

- Developments after the death of the Buddha
- Early councils and schools
- The formation of the *Tripiṭaka* or Buddhist Canon
- The Mauryan Empire and Aśoka
- *Stūpas* and the Buddha-image
- Developments in the North-west
- *Tantra*
- Monastic centers

## *Developments after the death of the Buddha*

The history of Buddhism in India extends from the fifth century B.C.E. to the thirteenth century C.E. It lingered on thereafter in isolated pockets but by the fifteenth century Buddhism had virtually disappeared from India, and would never again have the influence and prestige it once held. The modern period saw some revivals, partly inspired by the 'discovery' of Buddhism by Western scholars (see Chapter Eleven for more information on this) and also by conversions among Hindus of low caste who saw the adoption of Buddhism as a way of escaping from their low social status. Such modern developments, however, are a minor blip against a background of centuries of decline.

## *The early period*

Although little is known for certain about the chronology of the early period, and there is still great uncertainty about the precise dates of the Buddha's life as discussed in Chapter Two, we can be reasonably sure that the Buddha lived at the beginning of the Magadhan period (546–324 B.C.E.). At this time north India was divided politically into sixteen 'great states' or *mahājanapadas*, of which Magadha was one. Located south of the Ganges it included much of present-day Bihar in its territory, with its capital first at Rājagṛha and later Pāṭaliputra. The state of Magadha was ruled by King Bimbisāra during most of the Buddha's lifetime and was undergoing rapid growth and expansion as the society changed from an agrarian to a mercantile basis. The king was a devoted follower of the Buddha, and Magadha was the heartland of the early Buddhist movement. Bimbisāra died from mistreatment at the hands of his son and successor, Ajātaśatru, and under Ajātaśatru many of the smaller neighboring states were conquered and assimilated into what eventually became the Magadhan empire.

## *Early councils and schools*

The Buddha died in the eighth year of Ajātaśatru's reign, and shortly after his death the Council of Rājagṛha – often called the 'First Council' – was convened with the objective of establishing a canon or authoritative record of the Buddha's teachings. Tradition has it that the three divisions or 'baskets' (*piṭaka*) of the Buddhist canon (see text box for details) were compiled at this council, although Theravāda accounts mention only two.

At the first council, a senior monk named Kāśyapa was charged with supervising the convocation made up of 500 *arhants*, or enlightened followers. He called upon Ānanda, the Buddha's cousin and personal attendant (who reportedly gained enlightenment during the proceedings of the council) to recite the Buddha's discourses, and on another monk, Upāli to recite the rules of the *Vinaya*. Their utterances were accepted as accurate and decreed as constituting the content of the canon from that time on. Modern research, however, has cast serious doubts on the historicity of the traditional account and in particular the claim that the canon was fixed in the year of the Buddha's death.

The so-called 'Second Council' took place 100 or 110 years after the Council of Rājagṛha and was held at Vaiśālī. It arose out of a dispute concerning monastic

## Buddhist scriptures

The *Tripiṭaka* or 'three baskets' is the name for the Buddhist canon of scriptures. In the form it has come down to us it consists of a threefold collection of sacred texts, namely:

- The *Sūtra Piṭaka* or 'Basket of Discourses' containing the teachings and sermons of the Buddha
- The *Vinaya Piṭaka* or 'Basket of Monastic Discipline' containing the history and rules of the *sangha*
- The *Abhidharma Piṭaka* or 'Basket of Higher Teachings' containing scholastic treatises analyzing the Buddha's teachings.

The tradition that the canon was fixed at the Council of Rājagṛha in the year of the Buddha's death is unlikely to be correct since there is internal evidence of evolution and change within the three collections. The third in particular shows the greatest variation, suggesting that it is the latest of the three. Each of the early schools preserved its own version of the *Tripiṭaka*, and the only one that survives intact is the canon of the Theravāda school known as the Pāli Canon because it is composed in Pāli, a derivative of Sanskrit. By the end of the first century C.E. all the different versions had been committed to writing in a variety of Indian languages and dialects. Only fragments of these originals remain, although longer extracts have survived in Chinese translations. While the early schools regarded the canon as closed, the Mahāyāna believed that it was still open and continued to incorporate new literature for over a thousand years after the death of the Buddha. New *sūtras* and *śāstras* (treatises) were added and given canonical status, with the result that in the Chinese and Tibetan *Tripiṭakas* the threefold structure breaks down.

practices, and in particular the handling of money by monks. One faction, the Vṛjiputrakas (or Vajjians) claimed that this, together with nine other practices, was legitimate. The more orthodox, on the other hand, regarded them as illegal and prohibited by the *Vinaya*. The council, consisting of 700 respected monks under the presidency of Revata, ruled against the Vṛjiputrakas but it is unclear how far their practices were reformed as a result. The need for a council to be convened at this relatively early date shows that serious disagreements were surfacing in the early community, which would soon lead to fragmentation and schism.

Around 350 B.C.E. a further council was held at Pāṭaliputra which was to have a profound effect upon the later tradition. It was at this council, known to modern scholars as the 'Council of Pāṭaliputra', that the 'Great Schism' between the 'Elders' (Sthaviras) and the 'Great Assembly' (Mahāsāṃghikas) occurred. The circumstances surrounding the Third Council are unclear and have been the subject of much debate. An earlier generation of scholars identified one possible cause as five theses put forward by a monk named Mahādeva to the effect that the Buddha was greatly superior to the *arhant*. This was an innovation, since previously Buddhas and *arhants* had been regarded as attaining essentially the same state of enlightenment (*bodhi*). It was thought that the Mahāsāṃghikas accepted Mahādeva's five points and emphasized the Buddha's compassion and supernatural qualities, while the Sthaviras rejected them and held to the notion of the Buddha's nature as essentially human. More recent research by Prebish and Nattier, however, has shown that Mahādeva lived one generation later, thus eliminating his five theses as a possible cause of the split.

A second explanation for the split advanced by earlier scholars was that it was caused by an attempt by the Mahāsāṃghikas to introduce additional rules into the *Vinaya* which the Sthaviras refused to accept. Recent research, however, suggests that this explanation is back to front, and that the division occurred because the Mahāsāṃghikas refused to accept a proposed expansion of the *Vinaya* by the Sthaviras. This council is not recognized by the Theravāda school, which instead speaks of a 'Third Council' as having taken place later under the reign of Aśoka, as we shall see below.

The Mahāsāṃghika school went on to become one of the most successful and influential forms of Buddhism in India, giving rise to several sub-schools in later years such as the Ekavyāvahārika, the Lokottaravāda and the Bahuśrutīya. Since innovations in this school concerning the nature of Buddhas and *bodhisattvas* have several features in common with later Mahāyāna concepts, there is a strong likelihood that members of the Mahāsāṃghika school played a part in the formation of the Mahāyāna before it emerged as a distinct entity.

The Sthaviras claimed to represent older more orthodox teachings that could be traced directly back to the Buddha, and they branded their opponents as heretics, even though the Mahāsāṃghikas appeared to have been the more populous body. The Theravāda school claims direct descent from the Sthaviras but although they share the same name (*Thera* and *Sthavira* being the Pāli and Sanskrit forms of the same word meaning 'elder') there is no historical evidence that the Theravāda school arose as a distinct entity until around two centuries after the Great Schism.

As Buddhism spread throughout India, a diversity of schools developed over the first four hundred years, some based on major doctrinal differences and others merely as regional variants. Retrospectively, various Mahāyāna scholars determined that there were eighteen of these schools, although their accounts of the relationship and differences between them are not consistent. One simple classification, according to Vinītadeva, has the following four major schools with their offshoots: (1) Sthavira, and the Jetavanīyas, Abhayagirivāsins, and the Mahāvihāravāsins; (2)

## Early schools

The four main groupings were:

- Sthaviras
- Mahāsāṃghikas
- Sarvāstivādins
- Vātsīputrīyas

Mahāsāṃghikas, and the Pūrvaśailikas, the Aparaśailikas, the Lokottaravādins and the Prajñaptivādins; (3) Sarvāstivādins, and the Kāśyapīyas, Mahīśāsakas, Dharmaguptakas and the Mūlasarvāstivādins; and 4) Saṃmitīya, and the Kaurukullaka, Avantaka and Vātsīputrīya. These can be further simplified as shown in the accompanying text box.

It should be noted that the concepts of some of these schools, such as the Mahāsāṃghikas, may be regarded as proto-Mahāyāna and recent scholarship notes less of a hiatus between early Mahāyāna and earlier Buddhism than previously thought.

## *The Mauryan empire and Aśoka*

While Buddhist monks were engaged in settling their doctrinal differences, political events in the country were moving at a fast pace. North-west India had been colonized by Alexander the Great, and Magadha had grown first of all into a super-state and then under the Mauryas into an empire. The Mauryan dynasty ruled from 324–184 B.C.E. (bear in mind that the chronology of the period as a whole is uncertain: the date of 184 B.C.E. is simply one of a number of guesses, and some authorities date the start of the dynasty to 313 B.C.E.). The Mauryan dynasty was founded by Candragupta who overthrew the preceding Nanda dynasty and founded a capital at Pāṭaliputra. He defeated the Greek king Seleucus Nikator in 305 B.C.E. and as part of the terms of a marriage treaty in 303 B.C.E. a Greek ambassador known as Megasthenes came to reside at his court. Megasthenes composed a detailed account of contemporary life in India which unfortunately has not survived. Candragupta was succeeded by his son Bindusāra in 297 B.C.E., who extended the empire to include Mysore, and brought much of the subcontinent was under Mauryan control with the exception of Kaliṅga (a region around present-day Orissa on the East coast). Bindusāra died in 272 B.C.E. and was succeeded by his son Aśoka, who was consecrated in 268 B.C.E. (some modern authorities say 277). Aśoka conquered Kaliṅga and consolidated the greatest Indian empire down to the time of the Moguls and the British Raj, covering all but the southern part of the sub-continent. He is regarded by historians as one of the greatest Indian rulers of all time, and is something of a national hero. Various

## Did some early Buddhists believe in a Self?

The Vātsīputrīya school (named after its founder Vātsīputra) was universally condemned by other Buddhists for espousing a 'personhood theory' (*pudgala-vāda*), in some respects similar to the non-Buddhist *ātman* concept. The theory posited the existence of an indescribable something (a kind of pseudo-soul) which was 'neither the same as nor different to' the five aggregates (*skandha*) and that acted as a basis for rebirth and karma. The relationship between the 'person' (*pudgala*) and the *skandhas* was compared to that between fire (the *pudgala*) and its fuel (the *skandhas*). Although the *pudgala-vāda* position was criticized, the problem of explaining karmic continuity in the absence of a permanent self which it was designed to overcome was to persist. Other proposed solutions to this problem devised in India included the storehouse consciousness (*ālaya-vijñāna*) and the embryonic Buddha (*tathāgata-garbha*), discussed in Chapter Six.

Aśokan emblems, such as the lion capital found on his pillars, have been adopted for official use by the modern state of India.

Under the patronage of Aśoka Buddhism prospered as never before. The edicts he ordered to be carved on pillars, rocks and caves throughout his empire provide the first tangible historical evidence of Buddhism. A total of thirty-three inscriptions have been found in various parts of India which provide invaluable historical and chronological information on early Indian Buddhist history. Altogether there are sixteen rock edicts, three minor rock edicts, seven pillar edicts, three minor pillar edicts, two pillar inscriptions, and two cave inscriptions. Publishing imperial decrees in this way was a practice common in the Persian empire, and may have been brought to India by Persian craftsmen fleeing the conquests of Alexander the Great. Aśoka's stone pillars were often crowned with a distinctive lion capital and a large spoked wheel, with a smaller wheel on the base. Both of these are well-known Buddhist symbols: the lion symbolizes the 'lion's roar' with which the Buddha preached his *Dharma*, and the wheel symbolizes both the first sermon in which the Buddha set the 'wheel of the *Dharma*' in motion, as well as the concept of the righteous king or 'wheel-turning monarch' (*cakravartin*), with whom Aśoka clearly identified himself.

The edicts proclaim Aśoka's policy of rule by *Dharma* (righteousness) and his belief in the virtues of kindness, tolerance and upright conduct as the means to the happiness and wellbeing of his subjects both here and in the afterlife. The language of the edicts is Prakrit, the connecting link between the classical language of Sanskrit and the modern Indo-European languages of India, and two different forms of script are used.

From the edicts it can be seen that the content of Aśoka's *Dharma* is essentially that of a lay Buddhist. *Dharma* consists, he tells us, of 'Few sins and many good deeds of kindness, liberality, truthfulness and purity' (Pillar Edict 2). In his edicts Aśoka offers father-like advice to his subjects, commending moral virtues such as peacefulness, piety, religious tolerance, zeal, respect for parents and teachers, courtesy, charity, sense-control, and equanimity. No reference is made to the technical aspects of Buddhist doctrine as expounded in the Four Noble Truths. He relates in Rock Edict thirteen that after his bloody conquest of the Kaliṅga region of north-east India, he repented of his warlike ways and became a lay Buddhist. From then on he attempted to rule according to *Dharma* as a *Dharma-rāja* or 'righteous king' (*cakravartin*). He appointed officers known as 'superintendents of Dharma', (*dharma-mahāmātra*), to propagate religion and went on pilgrimages to religious sites. In the best tradition of Indian kingship, Aśoka supported all creeds and called for religious tolerance.

One of the edicts towards the end of Aśoka's reign, known as the 'schism edict', condemns schism in the *sangha* and speaks of monks being expelled. This seems to confirm accounts in Buddhist chronicles of his involvement in a council held at Pāṭaliputra. This council, reckoned as the 'Third Council' by the Theravāda tradition, took place around 250 B.C.E., and according to events related in the traditional chronicles of Sri Lanka – the *Mahāvaṃsa* and *Dīpavaṃsa* – the king played a leading role. Events centered on a monastery in Pāṭaliputra where certain residents refused to celebrate the fortnightly *poṣadha* (Pāli: *uposatha*) ceremony with colleagues they regarded as lax and unorthodox. Aśoka dispatched an emissary to resolve the matter but he, misunderstanding his orders, had a number of monks executed. Aśoka then intervened and convened a council of one thousand monks under the presidency of a senior and learned monk named Moggaliputta Tissa. Prior to the council, the orthodox teaching of the Buddha was identified as 'Distinctionism' (*vibhajyavāda*), and one by one the monks were questioned and expelled if they deviated from it. It is not known exactly what the 'distinction' in question referred to, but it may have been the Buddha's practice of making a distinction between extremes and emphasizing the importance of the middle way. This interpretation is conjectural, but whatever its precise meaning, the appellation 'distinctionists' seems to have been used as an alternative designation for the Theravāda school. Many of the divergent views expressed at the council are recorded in the *Kathāvatthu*, one of the seven books of the *Abhidharma Piṭaka*. The evidence clearly suggests that by this time sectarian divisions had become well established among the originally unified community.

The edicts also record that Aśoka sent ambassadors to five named kings reigning in the Hellenistic world, which again seems to support the Buddhist tradition that he did much to promote the spread of the religion. He is credited with sending his son Mahinda, himself a monk, to Sri Lanka to establish Buddhism there, as well as sending missionaries to other parts of South-east Asia.

## *The* stūpa

Apart from his edicts, Aśoka left another architectural legacy in the form of monuments known as *stūpas*. A *stūpa* is a hemispherical burial mound commonly containing the remains of an individual of religious importance (for example, a Buddha or senior monk) or an article of religious significance (such as a sacred text). The tradition of building *stūpas* goes back to prehistory, and originally they were just simple mounds of earth like a tumulus marking the tomb of an important person.

Shortly before the Buddha died he gave instructions on how his body should be treated after his death, and his instructions were that a *stūpa* should be built to house his remains (see text box).

According to a legend in the *Aśokāvadāna* ('Tales of Aśoka'), Aśoka built 84,000 *stūpas* throughout his empire. Although this number is clearly a pious exaggeration, the text is probably correct in associating the building of *stūpas* with Aśoka, and

The following passage from the Pāli Canon (D.ii.143) is often taken as the scriptural authority for the *stūpa* cult. It occurs in the Discourse of the Great Decease (*Mahāparinirvāṇa Sūtra*) which recounts the last months of the Buddha's life. The Buddha is here addressing Ānanda, his cousin and personal attendant on the question of how his body should be treated after his death.

> 'As they treat the remains of a King of Kings (*cakravartin*), so, Ānanda, should they treat the remains of the *Tathāgata*. At the four crossroads a cairn (*stūpa*) should be erected to the *Tathāgata*. And whoever shall there place garlands, or perfumes, or paints, or make salutation there, or become in its presence calm in heart, that shall long be to them a profit and a joy. The men, Ānanda, worthy of a cairn are four in number. Which are the four?
>
> A King of Kings (*cakravartin*) is worthy of a cairn.
> A *Tathāgata*, an Awakened One (Buddha), is worthy of a cairn.
> One awakened for himself alone (*Prayekabuddha*) is worthy of a cairn.
> A true disciple (*śrāvaka*) of the *Tathāgata* is worthy of a cairn.
>
> And on account of what circumstance, Ānanda, is a *Tathāgata* (and the other three) worthy of a cairn? At the thought, Ānanda, 'This is the cairn of that Awakened One' [...] the hearts of many shall be made calm and happy; and since they had calmed and satisfied their hearts, they will be reborn after death, when the body has dissolved, in the happy realms of heaven. It is on account of this circumstance, Ānanda, that a *Tathāgata*, an Awakened One [...] is worthy of a cairn.
>
> (trans. T.W. Rhys Davids)

a number of third-century *stūpas* made of brick seem to date back to his time. An inscription recorded on a pillar near the Buddha's birthplace in Lumbinī states that Aśoka expanded an existing *stūpa* on the site, so there is historical evidence for the link between Aśoka and *stūpa*-building.

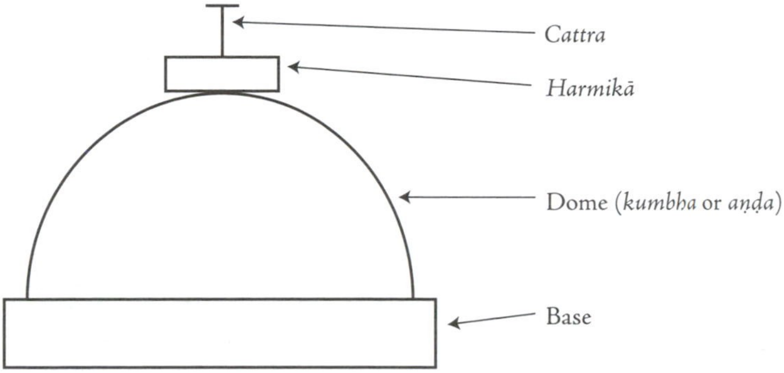


*Figure 5.1* The basic elements of a *stūpa*. To this structure were added an outer railing (*vedikā*, also found around the *harmikā*), entrance gateway (*toraṇa*), circumambulation terrace (*pradakṣinapātha*), reliquary (*bīja*), and parasol (*cattra, htī*) at the top

*Figure 5.2* Small *stūpa* and entrance gate (*toraṇa*), Sāñcī, India

The technique of building and carving using stone was relatively new at this time, and before the Mauryan period wood was the predominant construction material used in India (this is the main reason why so few architectural remains survive from these early times). Once the technique of building with stone had been mastered, masons set about decorating the walls of *stūpas* with Buddhist symbols and scenes from the Buddha's life.

One of the most famous of the early *stūpas* is the one at Sāñcī, on the site of which there is also an Aśokan pillar and edict. Sāñcī is an ancient religious center in present-day Madhya Pradesh near the city of Bhopal in central India, and the site of important architectural remains dating from the third-to-first centuries B.C.E. The most famous of these is the Great *Stūpa*, the oldest part of which dates from the time of Aśoka and which was enlarged and altered continuously down to the beginning of the Christian era. It is fifty-three feet high and is approached through one of four large stone gateways (*toraṇa*) lavishly carved with scenes from the life of the Buddha, animals, plants, and female deities (*yakṣā*). There are two other *stūpas* on the site, the oldest dating from the Śuṅga period (185–72 B.C.E.).

The practice of building *stūpas* accompanied Buddhism as it spread throughout Asia, and the original form evolved under the influence of local architectural styles. To the original solid dome structure a spire was subsequently added, and the final phase of development occurred with the pagoda style of tower found throughout East Asia. Since *stūpas* contain relics or other sacred objects they are thought to be charged with the numinous presence of the Buddha, and often become centers of pilgrimage and popular devotion, as in the case of the Bodnath *stūpa* in Nepal.

## *Buddhist art*

The origins of Buddhist art are to be found in the decoration of the stone railings surrounding *stūpas*. It may be thought surprising that at this early stage there were no representations of the Buddha in human form. Siddhārtha, the Buddha-to-be, is frequently depicted, for example when he leaves home in the 'Great Renunciation', but the post-enlightenment Buddha only appears in the form of symbols, such as a wheel, a tree, or a footprint. Buddha images did not appear until several hundred years after the Buddha's death, probably around the turn of the millennium. This may be explained either as a mark of respect, or as a result of the difficulty of giving aesthetic expression to the mystical post-mortem state the Buddha had attained. One can sympathize with the dilemma of the artist: once the Buddha had entered final nirvana and his body had been cremated, he no longer had a material form, so how was he to be represented? The Buddha had transcended the realm of *saṃsāra* and so the conventional dimensions of time and space no longer applied to him. For several centuries this aesthetic dilemma had no clear solution, until eventually artists, probably under pressure from lay patrons and influenced by the widespread

*Figure 5.3* Frieze representing the Buddha iconically by the symbol of a tree

practice of *bhakti* or devotional practice in Hinduism, found the confidence to depict the Buddha in human form. The earliest images come from two centers, one in the North-west and the other in Mathurā. Among sophisticated believers such images were regarded as symbolic although at the more popular levels of piety a range of attitudes is found, including what often appears as outright devotion to and reverence for the image itself.

For their inspiration artists looked to textual descriptions of the Buddha's appearance, which include a list of somewhat unusual physical characteristics known as the 'thirty-two marks of a great man'. These include descriptions of the head, torso, arms, and the proportion of the limbs, as well as specific bodily marks such as a small mound on the crown of the head (*uṣnīśa*), and a small tuft of hair between the eyes (*ūrṇā*). These features were faithfully reproduced by artists and are widely found in Buddha images in various stylized forms. As the art of depicting the Buddha evolved, many fine examples of Buddha images were produced, with the greatest dating from the Gupta period (320–540 C.E). The artists were often able to capture with great skill the sublime tranquility of the Buddha and express the twofold aspect of his nature as in the world but not of it.

## *The North-west*

After Aśoka's death in 231 B.C.E. Mauryan power declined. The period of the Śuṅgas and Yavanas (187–30 B.C.E.) which followed brought mixed fortunes: in the region of the Ganges Basin Buddhism encountered hostility and persecution under Puṣyamitra Śuṅga, but this period also sees the construction of great *stūpa* complexes such as those at Sāñcī, Bhārhut, and Amarāvatī. In the second century B.C.E. the North and North-west were extensively invaded by Greeks from the former Seleucid satrapies of Bactria and Parthia, as well as by central Asian nomadic tribes, some of whom favored Buddhism. An important Buddhist outpost in the region was Gandhāra, a Buddhist kingdom situated between the lower Kabul Valley in present-day Afghanistan and the Indus river in Pakistan. Gandhāra flourished first under the rule of the Bactrian Greeks from the second century B.C.E. and later under the Śakas and Pahlavas (100 B.C.E.–75 C.E.) who succeeded the Greeks in the North-west. These dynasties in turn were followed by the Kuṣānas (or Kushans), a Scythian tribe from Central Asia who were also supporters and patrons of Buddhism. Gandhāra is famous as a center of Buddhist art, especially sculpture, which was strongly influenced by Hellenic styles. Some of the earliest representations of the Buddha were produced in the region. Gandhāra ceased to exist as an independent kingdom by the seventh century C.E. and the Buddhist presence in the area disappeared soon after.

## Milinda's Questions

Gandhāra forms the background to the famous Pāli work *Milinda's Questions* (*Milindapañha*), which records the conversations between the Bactrian King Milinda (or Menander), and the monk Nāgasena in the first century B.C.E. Milinda is probably a Bactrian king of Śākala in the East Punjab who ruled in the second to first centuries B.C.E. The initial part of the text (also available in Chinese translation) probably dates from the first century C.E., although most of the work was written in Sri Lanka at a later date. Nāgasena makes use of illustrations, similes and metaphors in a lively conversational style to resolve problems and dilemmas in Buddhist doctrine pointed out by the king. The most famous simile is that of the chariot, here used to illustrate the doctrine of no-self (*anātman*). Just as a chariot is simply the sum of its constituent parts, namely the wheels, yoke, axles, and so on, so a human being is said to be simply the sum of the five aggregates (*skandha*). Although individuals bear a name – such as Nāgasena – in the ultimate sense there is no self or essence corresponding to it. Elsewhere the discussions concern questions such as how there can be rebirth in the absence of a self (*ātman*), how there can be moral responsibility without an enduring ego, why the evil prosper and the innocent suffer, and why the scriptures often seem to be in contradiction. At the conclusion of the debate Milinda becomes a Buddhist lay disciple.

## *Abhidharma*

A 'Fourth Council' was convened in this region in the first-to-second centuries C.E. during the reign of Kaniṣka I. The council was dominated by the Sarvāstivādin school and discussed issues of a scholastic nature. These deliberations continued long after the council ended, and in due course evolved into a major Abhidharma treatise known as the *Mahāvibhāṣā* meaning the 'Great Book of Alternatives' or 'Great Book of Options'. The treatise itself was compiled probably during the third century C.E. in Gandhāra under the patronage of King Kaniṣka II. The treatise is a commentary on a fundamental work of Abhidharma, the *Jñānaprasthāna* ('Basis of Knowledge') of Katyāyanīputra, a Sārvāstivādin philosopher. Also known as the *Vibhāṣā*, the text is an encyclopedia of the views of the Vaibhāṣika school and records the views of distinguished teachers of different schools on technical points of doctrine. The *Mahāvibhāṣā* formed the basis of debate between the schools of the Small Vehicle for many centuries, and many shorter treatises such as Vasubandhu's *Abhidharmakośa* were composed to criticize and supplement it.

## *Vasubandhu*

Vasubandhu was one of the most famous natives of the North-west region, probably born during the late fourth century C.E. Later in life he became a follower of the Mahāyāna, as noted in Chapter Six, but here we are concerned mainly with his *Abhidharma* works. Vasubandhu initially studied Sarvāstivādin *Abhidharma* as presented in the *Mahāvibhāṣā* before becoming dissatisfied with those teachings and composing an important summary and critique of the *Mahāvibhāṣā* from the Sautrāntrika viewpoint. The Sarvāstivādins held a distinctive theory of time according to which phenomena (*dharmas*) existed not just in the present but also in the past and future. It is from this belief that they derive their name, which means 'those who hold that everything exists'. In terms of this notion, past, present and future are not separate ontological categories but rather a mode of relationship. *Dharmas*, said the Sarvāstivādins, do not come into and go out of existence on their journey through the 'three times' as they pass from future, to present and past, but always exist and simply undergo a change of position and status relative to one another. One commentator compared this to the way in which a woman can be said to be both a daughter and a mother simultaneously: how she is classified (whether as 'mother' or 'daughter') depends on the context in which her relationship to others is viewed rather than something inherent in her own being. The relationship between past, present and future was thought to be similar and to depend on the position of each with respect to the other, rather than on some basic difference in nature. Abstruse as such questions may sound, Buddhists were forced to wrestle with them due to the implications of basic doctrines such as 'no-self' (*anātman*) in terms of which it is hard to understand how there can be continuity over time in the absence of an enduring subject. For example, if I have no permanent self, what is it that makes me the same person now as I was ten years ago? Theories of the kind just described were an attempt to deal with the complex implications of the basic teachings of the Buddha which were now being worked out, often in response to searching criticisms from non-Buddhist opponents.

In his most famous treatise, the *Abhidharmakośa* or 'Treasury of Abhidharma', Vasubandhu summarizes Sarvāstivādin tenets in about 600 verses grouped in eight chapters. The verses are commented on in the accompanying *bhāṣya* or 'exposition'. The subjects covered include all the main topics of *Abhidharma* philosophy, and a refutation of the views of the rival school of the Vaibhāṣikas is given at many points. This treatise has remained influential down to modern times, being translated into Chinese twice in the sixth and seventh centuries, and also into Tibetan.

## *The rise of the Mahāyāna*

The early centuries of the Christian era saw the rise of the Mahāyāna, a broad-based movement emphasizing inclusivity and an expanded role for the laity. The early understanding of the Buddha was reworked in the new doctrine of his 'three bodies' (*trikāya*), and the figure of the *bodhisattva* came to prominence, replacing the early ideal of the *arhant*. New *sūtras*, purportedly also the word of the Buddha, began to appear, notably the *Prajñāpāramitā* ('Perfection of Wisdom') literature and other profoundly influential texts such as the *Lotus Sūtra*. New philosophical schools, notably the Mādhyamika and the Yogācāra, arose to interpret this material, and in doing so they offered radical reinterpretations of the early teachings. These developments are reviewed in Chapter Six on the Mahāyāna and the reader is referred to that chapter for further information on these points.

## Tantra

A final wave of new literature known as *Tantras* appeared around the seventh century promoting radical forms of practice, including rituals and meditation techniques for accelerating spiritual progress. The form of Buddhism taught in these texts became known as the 'Diamond Vehicle' or Vajrayāna. *Tantra* represents a special path which arose within Mahāyāna Buddhism, which while generally embracing the same aims claimed to provide a rapid means to achieve the goal of enlightenment (*bodhi*) by means of its distinctive techniques. Certain key features can be identified which serve to distinguish it from other forms of Indian Buddhism: it offers an alternative path to enlightenment; its teachings are aimed at lay practitioners in particular, rather than monks and nuns; it recognizes mundane aims and attainments, and often deals with practices which are more magical in character than spiritual; it teaches special types of meditation (*sādhana*) as the path to realization, aimed at transforming the individual into an embodiment of the divine in this lifetime or after a short span of time. Such kinds of meditation make extensive use of various kinds of *maṇḍalas* (circular diagrams), *mudrās* (hand gestures), *mantras* (magic words) and *dhāraṇīs* (spells) as concrete expressions of the nature of reality, and the formation of images of the various deities during meditation by means of creative imagination plays a key role in the process of realization. In *Tantra* there is a proliferation in the number and types of Buddhas and other deities, and great stress is laid upon the importance of the guru or religious preceptor and the necessity of receiving the instructions and appropriate initiations for the *sādhanas* from him. Finally, a spiritual physiology is taught as part of the process of transformation and *Tantra* stresses the importance of the feminine and utilizes various forms of sexual yoga.

The origins of this movement within Buddhism is shrouded in mystery but most modern scholars place the distinct emergence of Tantric Buddhism among circles of adepts based in regions corresponding to present-day Orissa, Bengal, Gujarat and Kashmir. Many elements that make up the doctrines, meditational practices and rituals of *Tantra* can be found considerably earlier both within Buddhism and without. Meditative visualization was known from texts such as the *Pratyutpanna Sūtra* and the *Sukhāvatī-vyūha Sūtra*; *maṇḍalas* can be seen as idealized *stūpas*; *dhāraṇī* texts were in use before the first century C.E., and many Tantric rituals derive from widely practiced ancient rites. These various elements were gradually combined over the centuries until the emergence of recognizable Tantric texts such as the *Mahā-vairocana-abhisaṃbodhi Tantra* in the mid-seventh century which included all the hallmarks of Tantric Buddhism listed above with the exception of sexual yoga. By the end of the seventh century C.E, the *Sarva-tathāgata-tattva-saṃgraha* and other texts had been composed, utilizing the Five Buddha Family system (see text box).

Within a few decades of this, the *Guhyasamāja Tantra* was composed, the first *Tantra* known to contain explicit sexual imagery. This was followed by an explosion in the number of Tantric texts appearing in India both along the lines of the *Guhyasamāja* as well as texts like the *Hevajra Tantra* which makes greater use of sexual yoga, an internal spiritual physiology and emphasizes the role of the feminine to a greater extent. This period also saw the rise of the *mahā-siddhas* or 'great adepts' and the antinomian practices associated with Sahajayāna. This late offshoot of Tantric Buddhism was a simplified form of Tantric practice associated with 'great adepts' like Saraha and others, and later gained popularity in Tibet, especially in the Kagyu school. Tibetan tradition speaks of eighty-four *mahā-siddhas* – colorful and eccentric characters with great magic powers – who transmitted the Tantric teachings from India to Tibet.

With the emerging diversity of Tantric texts, various schemes where used to classify them. Initially, Tantric Buddhism was seen as an alternative path with Mahāyāna and was termed the '*mantra* method' (*mantra-naya*) in contrast to the

## The Five Buddha Family system

This is a fivefold classificatory system for Buddhas, *bodhisattvas* and other divine beings deriving from the middle period Mahāyāna *sūtra* tradition and adopted by the later *Tantras*. Each Family is headed by a particular Buddha endowed with specific qualities. The Families and the Buddhas who head them are the *Tathāgata* Family (*Vairocana*), the *Vajra* Family (*Akṣobhya*), the Jewel Family (*Ratnasaṃbhava*), the Lotus Family (*Amitābha*) and the Action Family (*Amoghasiddhi*). The Five Buddha Family system replaced an earlier Three Buddha Family scheme.

'perfection method' (*pāramitā-naya*). This *mantra* method was subdivided into two groups – *kriyā-tantra*, emphasizing rituals, and *yoga-tantra* emphazing meditative practices – the former group including texts such as the *Subāhu-paripṛcchā* and the *Susiddhikāra*, while the latter included the *Sarva-tathāgata-tattva-saṃgraha* and the *Guhyasamāja*. The *Mahā-vairocana-abhisaṃbodhi* was deemed to share features of both groups and thus was placed in a special dual (*ubhaya*) category. At a later date, this system was revised into the now standard fourfold division of *kriyā-tantra* (action), *caryā-tantra* (performance), *yoga-tantra* (yoga) and *anuttara-yoga-tantra* (supreme yoga). *Anuttara-yoga* itself was further sub-divided into three categories: Father Tantra, Mother Tantra and Non-dual Tantra, although it seems that other naming systems were used such as *mahāyoga*, *anuyoga* and *atiyoga* as still utilized by Tibetans in Nyingma circles.

Although Tantric Buddhism seems likely to have originated outside monastic circles among unorthdox yogins, it was soon introduced into the various great centers of Buddhist learning such as Nālandā, Vikramaśīla, and Ratnagiri. Many of the greatest scholar-monks in India from the eighth century onwards were also renowned as adepts who produced a considerable volume of commentarial literature and independent treatises. Through their influence, Tantric Buddhism became widespread throughout India and neighboring countries. However, although it is known to have been transmitted to Sri Lanka, Burma, Thailand and Indonesia, outside of India Tantric Buddhism achieved its greatest success in Tibet and China, with Shingon as a secondary offshoot in Japan.

## *Monastic centers*

The intellectual vigor of Buddhism during the medieval period attracted large numbers of students to monastic centers of learning. The most famous of these was Nālandā. It was reputed to have been home to ten thousand students with admission being gained through an oral exam at the main gateway. One of the greatest Buddhist monastic universities in India, Nālandā was located between Pāṭaliputra and Rājagṛha in present-day Bihar. It was believed to have been founded by King Śakrāditya of Magadha in the second century C.E. and was later patronized by the Gupta (320–647 C.E.) and Pāla (650–950 C.E.) dynasties. Its enormous size and the quality of its resident teachers attracted students and other visitors from all over the Buddhist world, including the notable Chinese pilgrim monks Xuanzang and Yijing in the seventh century C.E. who both describe it in their travelogues. Ties were also formed with the nascent Buddhist movement in Tibet, resulting in a number of leading Tibetan monks visiting Nālandā and reciprocal visits to Tibet by Indian Buddhist masters.

Through continuing royal patronage, such as that of King Harṣa and the rulers of the Pāla dynasty, other major centers of learning such as Vikramaśīla and Odantapurī also flourished. It was these institutions that produced the last great generation of Indian Buddhist scholars like Śāntarakṣita and Kamalaśīla, who would play a vital role in the transmission of Buddhism to Tibet. A less fortunate consequence of the growth of monastic centers was that monks became increasingly specialized in abstruse doctrines and began to lose touch with the world outside the cloister. Unlike Hinduism, which has always had roots at the village level, Buddhism became concentrated in a few key institutions of higher learning. This proved to be its undoing when Muslim raiding parties began to enter India in increasing numbers from the tenth century. Undefended Buddhist monasteries, often containing valuable treasures, proved irresistible targets to raiders bent on booty in the name of holy war. The Buddhist practice of making images of Buddhas and *bodhisattvas* made them idolaters in the eyes of orthodox Muslims, and many priceless images were destroyed or looted for the precious metals and jewels they contained. (A similar attitude seems to have provoked the destruction of the colossal Buddha statues at Bāmiyān in Afghanistan by the fundamentalist Taleban regime in 2001.) The Turkic general Mahmud Shabuddin Ghorī sacked Nālandā in 1197 and Vikramaśīla in 1203, burning their libraries and destroying priceless literary and artistic treasures. The great library of Nālandā is said to have smouldered for six months afterwards. The site was fully excavated in the twentieth century and now attracts many visitors.

These traumatic events dealt a mortal blow to Buddhism in India, from which it would never recover. There has been a limited revival of Buddhism in India in the twentieth century, due partly to an influx of refugees from Tibet, and to the conversion of the so-called 'Ambedkar Buddhists'. These are followers of Bhimrao Ambedkar (1891–1956), the charismatic leader of the Dalits or outcastes of India. Born into the caste of the Mahar untouchables, Ambedkar converted to Buddhism on 14 October 1956 at Nagpur. Ambedkar regarded Buddhism as the religion most capable of resolving the problems of caste that in his view had plagued India down the centuries. Across India thousands of untouchables followed his example as a protest against their social exclusion, and today almost all the Mahars of Maharashtra regard themselves as Buddhist.

## Key points you need to know

- Following the death of the Buddha the original community fragmented rapidly into numerous sects and schools. In the early centuries there were three important councils: at Rājagṛha, Vaiśālī, and Pāṭaliputra.
- The Buddhist canon is known as the *Tripiṭaka* and according to tradition was fixed at the Council of Rājagṛha in the year of Buddha's death.
- The *Tripiṭaka* has three divisions: 1) the *Sūtra Piṭaka* or 'Basket of Discourses;' (2) the *Vinaya Piṭaka* or 'Basket of Monastic Discipline;' and (3) the *Abhidharma Piṭaka* or 'Basket of Higher Teachings'.
- The 'Great Schism' occurred at the Council of Pāṭaliputra and resulted in a division into two main groups: the Elders (Sthaviras) and the Universal Assembly (Mahāsāṃghikas).
- Under Aśoka's patronage Buddhism prospered in India and missionaries were sent abroad to spread the *Dharma*.
- A *stūpa* is a hemispherical burial mound commonly containing the remains of an individual of religious importance (for example, a Buddha or senior monk) or an article of religious significance (such as a sacred text).
- The first few centuries C.E. witnessed a great age of scholastic debate which resulted in the composition of texts like the Great Book of Options (*Mahāvibhāṣā*) and the Treasury of Metaphysics (*Abhidharmakośa*).
- *Tantra* represents the final phase of Indian Buddhism and Tantric texts begins to appear around the seventh century.
- The great monastic universities like Nālandā and Vikramaśīla were destroyed by Muslim raiding parties by the early thirteenth century, dealing a mortal blow to Indian Buddhism. Buddhism has been virtually extinct in India since the fifteenth century, although a limited revival has taken place in modern times.

## Discussion questions

1. Did the first three councils achieve anything of lasting importance?
2. What contribution did Aśoka make to the development of Buddhism inside and outside India?
3. What is the significance of the *stūpa* in Buddhism?
4. Give an account of the development of the Buddha image in Indian art.
5. Does *Tantra* represent the high point or the low point of Indian Buddhism?

## Further reading

Akira, Hirakawa. *A History of Indian Buddhism*. Honolulu, HI: University of Hawaii Press, 1990.

Cook, Elizabeth. *The Stupa: Sacred Symbol of Enlightenment*. Berkeley, CA: Dharma Press, 1997.

Dasgupta, Shashi Bushan. *An introduction to Tantric Buddhism*. Berkeley, CA: Shambhala, 1974.

Lamotte, Étienne. *History of Indian Buddhism*. Louvain-la-Neuve: Université Catholique de Louvain, Institut Orientaliste, 1988.

Govinda, Lama Anagarika. *Psycho-cosmic Symbolism of the Buddhist Stupa*. Berkeley, CA: Dharma Publishing, 1976.

Nakamura, Hajime. *Indian Buddhism*. New Delhi: Motilal Banarsidass, 1980.

Snodgrass, Adrian. *The Symbolism of the Stupa*. Ithaca, NY: Cornell University, 1985.

White, David Gordon. *Tantra in Practice*. Princeton, NJ: Princeton University Press, 2000.

# 6 *Mahāyāna*

## In this chapter

This chapter documents the development of the Mahāyāna school of Buddhism, highlighting its literature, doctrines, major schools, and prominent thinkers. It considers the most famous celestial Buddhas and *bodhisattvas*, and provides the basis for understanding the forms of Buddhism that developed in Central and East Asia.

## Main topics covered

- Mahāyāna literature
- *Prajñāpāramitā*
- Other Mahāyāna literature
- Mahāyāna doctrines: Buddha-nature, emptiness, *bodhisattvas*, perfection, compassion, skill-in-means
- Celestial Buddhas and *bodhisattvas*
- Mahāyāna schools: Mādhyamika, Yogācāra, Pure Land
- Mahāyāna logicians

## *Introduction*

Mahāyāna is a Sanskrit term denoting a movement in Buddhism begun around 200 B.C.E. in India and identifying itself as the 'Greater Vehicle'. Primarily as a reaction against the highly ecclesiastic, somewhat pedantic, and allegedly self-motivated Buddhism of the time, this new movement emerged as a means of reemphasizing Buddhism as a liberating vehicle for the masses of Buddhist practitioners. In general, it offered a new literature, initially identified as the *Prajñāpāramitā* or 'Perfection of Wisdom' literature, a new theory concerning the nature of Buddhahood, and a new path to a new goal. Drawing much of its philosophical content from the Mahāsāṃghika and Sarvāstivādin schools of early Buddhism, and its notions of community from an overarching emphasis on compassion (*karuṇā*) for all sentient beings, it stressed the emptiness (*śūnyatā*) of all phenomena, the transcendent nature of the Buddha, and the attainment of Buddhahood for all beings by means of a course of practice known as the *bodhisattva* path. While it did not summarily reject early Buddhism, it perceived its overall approach to be inferior, thus the designation of all early Buddhist groups or *nikāyas* as Hīnayāna or 'Lesser Vehicle'. Like its precursor, once established, Mahāyāna began to splinter internally. Within several hundred years, Indian Mahāyāna included the Mādhyamika school founded by Nāgārjuna, the Yogācāra school founded by Asaṅga and Vasubandhu, and the Pure Land tradition. Additionally, Indian Buddhism was shortly joined by a third school, known as Vajrayāna, focusing on the esoteric tradition. As Buddhism spread to China, the overwhelming majority of individual schools that arose were based on Mahāyāna philosophy. It was equally the case as Buddhism moved through Korea and into Japan. As such, Mahāyāna-based Buddhism predominates in East Asia.

## *Mahāyāna literature*

### *Prajñapāramitā*

*Prajñāpāramitā* is a generic term for a series of Mahāyāna texts known as the '*Perfection of Wisdom*' discourses. These texts, the earliest of which date from around 100 B.C.E., represent the first Mahāyāna literature, and are aptly named, due to their special interest in understanding the nature of wisdom or *prajñā*. The foremost scholar of *Prajñāpāramitā* literature, Edward Conze, notes the period of composition of this class of literature to extend for about 1,000 years, divided into four phases: (1) establishment of a basic text representing the initial 'impulse' of the movement, (2) expansion of the basic text, (3) restatement of the basic doctrines into shorter texts and verse summaries, and (4) a period of influence by the Tantric tradition. The oldest text in this category is the '*Perfection of Wisdom Discourse in 8,000 Lines*' (*Aṣṭasāhasrikā-prajñāpāramitā Sūtra*). This text was later expanded into versions of 18,000, 25,000, and eventually, 100,000 verses. It was then shortened into much shorter versions, the two most famous of which are the '*Diamond Sūtra*' (*Vajracchedikā-prajñāpāramitā Sutra*) and the '*Heart Sutra*' (*Hṛdaya-prajñāpāramitā Sutra*). Finally, a series of Tantric texts emerges, one of which is called the '*Perfection of Wisdom in One Letter*'. A large number of commentaries on this class of literature appeared, and both the texts and commentaries alike have been translated into Chinese and Tibetan. The style of the *Prajñāpāramitā* literature is interesting in that it presents an on-going dialogue between the Buddha and a series of disciples at varying stages of personal development. For the most part, those disciples usually associated with the early, so-called Hīnayāna tradition (such as Śāriputra) are generally afforded the lowest position of expression, while those figures identified as *bodhisattvas* (such as Subhūti) are most highly regarded. In other words, the new Mahāyāna path is emphasized at the expense of the older framework. Such is also the case regarding doctrinal issues, with the *Prajñāpāramitā* texts launching an endless diatribe about the inadequacy of the Abhidharma approach and the efficacy of the doctrine of emptiness (*śūnyatā*). Moving out of India rapidly, the *Prajñāpāramitā* literature appears in China as early as 179 C.E. with Lokakṣema's translation of the 8,000 line version.

## Other Mahāyāna literature

### *Vimalakīrti-nirdeśa Sūtra*

One of the most important Mahāyāna texts is the *Vimalakīrti-nirdeśa Sūtra*, a Mahāyāna *sūtra* titled '*Sūtra on the Discourse of Vimalakīrti*'. Frequently quoted, this text relates the story of a famous Buddhist lay disciple named Vimalakīrti who, despite being engaged in wordly activities through his livelihood as a banker, manages to lead an exemplary life as a *bodhisattva*. The story of the *sūtra* focuses on a *Dharma* discourse being delivered by the Buddha in the town of Vaiśālī. The Buddha was surrounded by 8,000 monks and 32,000 *bodhisattvas*, but Vimalakīrti was absent due to an illness. In seeking to learn of Vimalakīrti's condition, the Buddha wants to send any of the disciples so inclined. Each declines due to Vimalakīrti's superior position until the *bodhisattva* Mañjuśrī offers to go, at which point all follow. When queried about his illness, Vimalakīrti offers a response brimming with Mahāyāna philosophy. He attributes his illness to his compassion for the sickness of all sentient beings, noting that he will become cured only when all other sentient beings are cured. What follows is a long discussion on various aspects of Mahāyāna doctrine. Eventually, Vimalakīrti poses the question that provides the highlight of the *sūtra*: he asks how a *bodhisattva* can enter the *Dharma*-door of non-duality? Thirty-one replies follow, each somewhat more insightful and sophisticated than the preceding, but each lacking in complete understanding. When it becomes Mañjuśrī's turn, he simply says 'Good sirs, you have all spoken well. Nevertheless, all your explanations are themselves dualistic. To know no one teaching, to express nothing, to say nothing, to explain nothing, to announce nothing, to indicate nothing, and to designate nothing – that is the entrance into nonduality'. (Thurman: 77) Mañjuśrī then requests Vimalakīrti's answer to his own question. Vimalakīrti's response: complete and total silence. In so doing, he has provided the only perfect answer! Because of the *sūtra*'s high relevance for all of Mahāyāna, it became important in virtually every Buddhist country where Mahāyāna flourished.

## *Laṅkāvatāra Sūtra*

Another important text is the *Laṅkāvatāra Sūtra*, probably written around 400, whose title translates to '*Descent into Lanka*', and whose doctrinal base focuses on the various themes of the Yogācāra school of Buddhism. The context of the *sūtra* is a discourse on Lanka in which the Buddha responds to a series of questions posed to him by a *bodhisattva* named Mahāmati. The text is structured into nine chapters of mostly prose, concluding with an additional verse chapter. It discusses emptiness, the theory of eight-consciousness (*vijñānas*) central to Yogācāra doctrine, five '*dharmas*' culminating in the state of 'suchness' or *tathatā*, a notion of three *svabhāvas* (that is, self-natures) which is contrary to the Mādhyamika idea of two levels of truth, and two forms of the Buddha (eternal and transforming). Perhaps the critical doctrine of the *sūtra* is its statement that the *Tathāgata* (that is, the Buddha) is present in all sentient beings, thus suggesting that all creatures dwell in the 'Womb of the Tathāgata' (called *Tathāgatagarbha*), and presuming the obvious consequence: that Buddhahood is readily available to all. The text outlines the process of attainment whereby consciousness is essentially turned back on its base, reversed upon itself in a process in which all duality and distinctions cease. The *sūtra* had a strong influence on the Chan and Zen traditions.

## *Lotus Sūtra*

This is the familiar, popular title of the *Saddharmapuṇḍarīka Sūtra*, more properly titled in full as '*Sūtra on the Lotus of the Good Teaching*'. It is one of the most popular Mahāyāna discourses, and although it is extremely important in Indian Buddhism, it became even more highly valued in China and Japan, serving as the basis of the Tiantai school of Chinese Buddhism (Japanese: Tendai) and of the school founded by Nichiren. The context of the *sūtra* is a discourse delivered by the Buddha from the famous location known as Vulture's Peak to a huge assembly of disciples of various categories. The main message of the text is that while there are a variety of paths available to disciples (usually identified as three: *śrāvaka* or 'hearer', *pratyeka-buddha* or 'private-buddha', and *bodhisattva* or 'enlightenment being'), there is really only one true vehicle. This 'One Vehicle' Buddhism, or Ekayāna, includes both Hīnayāna and Mahāyāna. This central idea is demonstrated through a series of parables, the most important of which center around a burning house, a blind man, and a prodigal son. Emphasis is also placed on the nature of the *Tathāgata*, developing skill-in-means (*upāya*) or the ability to know how to properly utilize wisdom, and building proper character in the *bodhisattva* (stressing morality, understanding of emptiness, avoidance of doctrinal disputes, and compassion for all beings).

### *Pure Land Sūtras*

The Larger *Sukhāvatīvyūha Sūtra* is a Mahāyāna text important as one of the foundational bases of the Pure Land School of Buddhism. The text of the *sūtra* begins with the Buddha on Vulture's Peak surrounded by a huge retinue of *śrāvakas* (i.e., hearers, disciples) and *bodhisattvas*. Using the premise of instructing Ānanda, the Buddha rehearses the story of a monk Dharmākara who made a series of forty-eight vows under a prior Buddha known as Lokeśvararāja. Dharmākara begins pursuit of the *bodhisattva* path, focusing all his vows on one Buddha-Land. Eventually, Dharmākara is able to actualize his vows, becoming the Buddha Amitābha residing in the Pure Land of Sukhāvatī (the Western Paradise). Rebirth in Sukhāvatī is available to those who (1) make a vow to be reborn there, (2) employ their good merit to do so, and (3) meditate on Amitābha. The *sūtra* ends with a vision of Amitābha. The Smaller *Sukhāvatīvyūha Sūtra* is a Mahāyāna text that is also important as one of the foundational bases of the Pure Land School of Buddhism. As opposed to the larger version of the text, with the Buddha on Vulture's Peak, here the Buddha Amitābha presides over the Pure Land of Sukhāvatī. Birth in the Pure Land is not a result of good works, as in the larger version, and is not even mentioned. The key issue in the smaller text focuses on the metaphor of sound. The sounds present in the Pure Land are to remind one of the Buddha, *Dharma*, and *Sangha*. Additionally, these sounds, and that of Amitābha's name, are prerequisites to meditation. Consequently, they must be repeated if salvation is to be attained

## *Mahāyāna doctrines*

Although Mahāyāna is often cited for the importance of the new literature it created in Buddhism, and for its emphasis on the laity, the ideas and doctrines embodied in that literature were equally important in shaping the later development of the tradition. Most important among the Mahāyāna doctrinal innovations were its new theories about the nature of the Buddha and about reality, as well as its emphasis on the *bodhisattva* as a new ideal type in Buddhism. Concomitant with this new path, was its stress on a series of perfections known as pāramitās, and two of the most important perfections: compassion and skill-in-means.

### Emptiness

The doctrine of 'emptiness' or *śūnyatā* is stressed in many Mahāyāna scriptures, beginning with the *Prajñāpāramitā Sutras*. It goes beyond the early Buddhist position of *anātman* (not-self), stating that even *dharmas*, the momentary building blocks of experiential reality, have no ontological existence in their own right. The doctrine of emptiness thus emphasizes the relational aspect of existence, a presumably proper understanding of the early Buddhist doctrine of dependent origination (*pratītya-*

### Buddha nature

Buddha nature is a Mahāyāna notion that all sentient beings possess an inherently pure nature identical to that of the Buddhas, worldly or cosmic. This Buddha-ness (*tathatā*) is one of the issues that clearly differentiates Mahāyāna from Hīnayāna, for in the latter there is no notion suggesting that all beings can become Buddhas.

*samutpāda*). In this way, emptiness becomes an epistemological tool used to 'unfreeze' the fixed notions of our minds. It is important to understand that *śūnyatā*, utilized in this fashion, is not an ontological state, and that even emptiness is empty. However, it would be incorrect to surmise that the negative terminology associated with the concept is indicative of a subtle nihilism in Mahāyāna. To argue that all *dharmas* are empty does not mean that they do not exist, but rather identifies them as appearances which should not be perceived as objects of grasping. Because the doctrine of emptiness is critical to all Mahāyāna schools of Buddhism, it becomes of paramount importance, not only to the Mādhyamika and Yogācāra schools of Buddhism in India (including all of their respective subdivisions), but to all the Mahāyāna schools across the geographic landscape, ancient and modern. *Śūnyatā* also plays a critical role in all the Vajrayāna schools as well. Consequently, it is probably not unreasonable to cite this doctrine as the single most important Mahāyāna innovation.

In Mahāyāna a number of celestial *bodhisattvas* became extremely important, most notably Avalokiteśvara, Mañjuśrī, Mahāsthāmaprāpta, and Samantabhadra. They served as ideal models for their earthly counterparts by exhibiting extreme compassion and wisdom. The entire Mahāyāna notion of the *bodhisattva* was a clear antithesis to the ideal type in early Buddhism, the *arhant*, whose effort was found by Mahāyānists to be self-centered and ego-based. An enormous literature developed focusing on the *bodhisattva* and the *bodhisattva* path, including such famous texts as the *Bodhisattvabhūmi Sūtra*, *Daśabhūmika Sūtra*, and others. Sometimes, the path of the *bodhisattva* is called the '*Vehicle of the bodhisattva*' or *Bodhisattva-yāna*. It is another means of referring to the Mahāyāna or so-called 'Greater Vehicle' school of Buddhism. Mahāyāna, of course, coined a pejorative phrase to describe the entirety of early Buddhism: 'Hīnayāna' or 'Lesser Vehicle'. Within this Hīnayāna appelation, however, Mahāyāna identified two individual paths: (1) the *Vehicle of the Śrāvaka*, or *Śrāvaka-yāna*, literally 'hearers', the immediate disciples of the Buddha (and their spiritual descendants), and (2) the *Vehicle of the Pratyeka-buddhas*, or *Pratyeka-buddha-yāna*, those who attained enlightenment on their own and who did not embark on a teaching career. In light of the above, it was only logical to also refer to the Mahāyāna path as the *Bodhisattva-yāna*, the '*Vehicle of the bodhisattvas*'.

### *Bodhisattva*

The *bodhisattva* is literally an 'enlightened being', one who has postponed personal salvation in favor of a compassionate effort to save all sentient beings. In early Buddhism the term *bodhisattva* (or *bodhisatta* in Pāli) was used to identify Siddhārtha Gautama, the historical Buddha, and it was assumed that only future historical Buddhas merited this designation prior to their attainment of Buddhahood. In Mahāyāna, this term was given a radical, new interpretation, and used as a designation for anyone aspiring to complete, perfect enlightenment ... to Buddhahood. Motivated by extreme compassion (*karuṇā*), and tempered by the perfection of wisdom (*prajñā*), the *bodhisattva* first completes three basic prerequisites that include generating the thought of enlightenment (*bodhicitta*), undertaking a formal vow to gain complete, perfect enlightenment for the sake of all sentient beings (*praṇidhāna*), and receiving a prediction with regard to future attainment (*vyākaraṇa*). Then, a path known as the *bodhisattva* path, and including ten stages (*bhūmis*), is traversed. This path requires rejection of the personal attainment of nirvana, deliberate rebirth in the cycle of *saṃsāra*, and a sharing of all merit accrued with other sentient beings.

## *Pāramitā*

This is a Sanskrit technical term usually rendered as 'perfection' and applied to a series of practices thought to be essential for spiritual progress. The term *pāramitā* is derived from the Sanskrit prefix *pāram* which generally denotes the other side of something, that is, beyond, and the past participle of a verb meaning 'to go'. Thus, *pāramitā* means 'going to the other side' or 'having gone beyond', and by application 'perfection'. Although the term appears in the literature of various Hīnayāna sects, and is especially important to the Sarvāstivādins, it is in Mahāyāna that the notion of perfection becomes a critical component of Buddhist philosophy and practice. The concept appears early in the *Prajñāpāramitā* literature, emphasizing six *pāramitās*: (1) *dāna* (giving), (2) *śīla* (morality), (3) *kṣānti* (patience), (4) *vīrya* (vigor), (5) *dhyāna* (meditation), and (6) *prajñā* (wisdom). And, of course, the intended ideal emerges: wisdom can be perfected by all beings if certain religious principles are understood and rigorous religious practices are observed. The practices involve traversing the *bodhisattva* path as opposed to the way of the *arhant* in earlier Buddhism. Eventually, four additional perfections were added: (7) *upāya* (skill-in-means), (8) *praṇidhāna* (vow), (9) *bala* (power), and (10) *jñāna* (knowledge). These ten *pāramitās* are correlated with the ten stages of the *bodhisattva* path, each perfection corresponding to a particular stage (*bhūmi*). As a result, a highly ambitious path is outlined which is a guideline for a distinctly Mahāyāna Buddhist practice.

### *Karuṇā*

*Karuṇā* is a Sanskrit technical term meaning 'compassion', and is important in all Buddhist traditions. Considered to be one of the chief attributes of a Buddha, it is among the prime motivating factors in Siddhārtha Gautama's pursuit of enlightenment. In the Hīnayāna sects it finds its highest expression as a member of the fourfold *brahmavihāras* or 'divine abodes'. In the *brahmvihāras* it functions in consonance with love (*maitrī*), sympathetic joy (*muditā*), and equanimity (*upekṣā*) as an expression of the highest ethical standard of pursuit. In Mahāyāna it achieves its fullest development as one of the driving forces in the *bodhisattva*'s religious practice. It is generally linked with wisdom (*prajñā*) in describing the two chief descriptive attributes of the *bodhisattva*. *Karuṇā* is said to be embodied in the *bodhisattva* Avalokiteśvara, who receives much attention in the Chinese and Japanese traditions (as Guanyin and Kwannon, respectively). Compassion is extremely important as the basis of the Pure Land tradition as well.

### *Upāya*

*Upāya* is a Sanskrit technical term literally meaning 'skillful means' or 'skill-in-means'. Although the term is not unheard of in early Buddhism, it is almost always applied to the Mahāyāna tradition, where it is counted as one of the *pāramitās* or 'perfections'. Identified as the seventh perfection, it follows attainment of the perfection of wisdom (*prajñā*). Since one of the critical aspects of Mahāyāna teaching is that *bodhisattvas* must have compassion (*karuṇā*) for all sentient beings, it is logical for Mahāyāna adepts, at a certain stage of development, to know precisely how to apply the wisdom they have experienced. *Upāya* provides that aspect of the teaching. *Upāya* enables the individual who is teaching to find precisely the method of instruction that is appropriate for the person being instructed. Whether a *Dharma* discourse or a shout, meditation instruction or a slap, *upāya* is the skillful means by which a genuine teacher demonstrates the truth of enlightenment.

## *Celestial Buddhas and* bodhisattvas

Many celestial Buddhas permeate the pantheon of Mahāyāna Buddhism. Foremost among them is Amitābha, the Buddha of 'Unlimited Light', said to rule over the Western Paradise of Sukhāvatī. Known in China as Amituo and in Japan as Amida (from the short Sanskrit form Amita), this celestial Buddha is the focus of three major texts of Pure Land Buddhism: the (1) *Larger Sukhāvatīvyūha Sūtra*, (2) *Smaller*

*Sukhāvatīvyūha Sūtra,* and (3) *Amitāyurdhyāna Sūtra.* The legend surrounding Amitābha develops from the story of a monk named Dharmākara who, eons previously, aspired to Buddhahood and made forty-eight vows, each concerning the nature of existence whence he becomes a Buddha. Dharmākara, after countless lifetimes of practice, becomes the Buddha Amitābha. Amitābha is generally conceived of in two ways: (1) as an object of meditation and (2) as the embodiment of compassion. As ruler of the Pure Land of Sukhāvatī, he welcomes all who earnestly wish to be reborn there, requiring only a strong commitment of faith in Amitābha's vows. This faith is expressed by the formula (in Sanskrit): *Namo Amitābhāya Buddhāya, 'Homage to Amitābha Buddha'.* Known in China as the *Nianfo* (*Nanmo Amituofo*) and in Japan as the *Nembutsu* (*Namu Amida Butsu*), its repetition was a necessary ingredient for rebirth in the Pure Land. In fact, Dharmākara's eighteenth vow, often referred to as the most important of all vows, states quite directly that anyone who desires rebirth in the Pure Land need only recite his name or think of this desire ten times, in order to actualize their ambition. Because this tradition relies on faith rather than meditation, it is sometimes referred to as the 'easy way' (*tariki* in Japanese). Amitābha sometimes appears with the *bodhisattvas* Avalokiteśvara and Mahāsthāmaprāpta on his left and right, respectively. He also appears with Bhaiṣajyaguru Buddha, another of the celestial Buddhas. An alternate name for Amitābha is sometimes employed: Amitāyus, literally 'Unlimited Life'.

Another famous celestial Buddha is Akṣobhya, earliest of the non-historical celestial Buddhas. His name literally means 'immovable', and he is said (in the *Vimalakīrti-nirdeśa Sūtra*) to reign over the Eastern Paradise known as Abhirati. His name seems to be first mentioned in the Perfection of Wisdom (*Prajñāpāramitā*) literature, but eventually finds citations in a wide variety of Mahāyāna and Vajrayāna texts. His most usual color is dark blue, but occasionally golden-colored. He usually holds a *vajra* or diamond scepter in his right hand, while making the earth-touching gesture (*bhūmisparśa-mudrā*) with his left. He is often seated on a blue elephant. Legend reports that Akṣobhya, while still a *bodhisattva,* vowed never to manifest anger toward any being, and as a result of his vow, came to rule over the paradise of Abhirati. It is suggested that other practitioners who follow his example will obtain rebirth in Abhirati. While he is prominent in Nepal and Tibet, Akṣobhya is less popular in China and Japan.

Vairocana, yet another celestial Buddha literally means 'Shining Out'. Although he did not become popular until around the seventh century C.E., in Tantric Buddhism he is located at the center of the cosmic *maṇḍala,* surrounded by the other four celestial Buddhas. His symbol is often represented as the *Dharmacakra* or *'Wheel of the Teaching'*, and is sometimes shown making the 'supreme wisdom' *mudrā* in which the right index finger is held by the fingers of the left hand. His is regularly associated with the celestial *bodhisattva* Samantabhadra. Some traditions identify him with the earthly Buddha Krakucchanda, but he is also noted, in the Chinese scholastic tradition, to be the *dharma-kāya* of Śākyamuni Buddha. Vairocana is regarded in some traditions to be the Ādi-Buddha or primordial Buddha. In the iconography, he is depicted as white in color

Perhaps the foremost celestial *bodhisattva* is Mañjuśrī. A prominent *bodhisattva* whose name means 'Sweet Glory', and who is especially important in a number of Mahāyāna *sūtras*. Although present in the *Lotus Sūtra*, he is a primary interlocutor in the *Vimalakīrti-nirdeśa Sūtra* where he, of all the *bodhisattvas* mentioned, comes closest to the brilliance and understanding manifested by Vimalakīrti. A tenth stage *bodhisattva*, he is often shown iconographically holding a lotus which supports a *Prajñāpāramitā* text and a sword, symbolizing the wisdom he manifests in aiding sentient beings. Mañjuśrī is said to appear to people in dreams, and those worshipping him are protected by his power. He is also sometimes referred to as Mañjughoṣa, ('Sweet Voiced'). In Tibetan Buddhism a number of the most prominent figures are considered incarnations of Mañjuśrī.

Maitreya is the name of the future Buddha, literally translated as 'Benevolent One'. Although the notion is present in virtually all the Hīnayāna schools, where they view Maitreya as a *bodhisattva* progressing toward Buddhahood, the notion

*Figure 6.1* The Buddha Maitreya

*Figure 6.2* One-thousand-headed statue of the *bodhisattva* Avalokiteśvara

reaches its apex in Mahāyāna, where Maitreya is depicted as a virtual cult image. He is mentioned in a wide variety of Mahāyāna *sūtras*, and also comes to play a major role in Vajrayāna Buddhism where his heaven is said to represent a Pure Land. He is represented by a detailed and explicit iconography, and is identified as one of the five earthly Buddhas.

*Figure 6.3* Image of Guanyin, Bomunsa Monastery, North Kyongsang, Korea

Finally, Avalokiteśvara is 'The Lord Who Looks Down', one of the most famous and important of the celestial *bodhisattvas* in Mahāyāna Buddhism. Initially, Avalokiteśvara is a minor figure in such texts as the *Vimalakīrti-nirdeśa Sūtra* and *Lotus Sūtra*. His first significant role is in the *Pure Land Sūtras* where he and Mahāsthāmaprāpta serve as the chief attendants to Amitābha Buddha. Presumably, Avalokiteśvara has purified himself for countless ages, and accordingly, is the embodiment of compassion (*karuṇā*) which, along with wisdom (*prajñā*), are the chief attributes expressive of Buddhahood. He aids all people who call upon him in need, helping them with numerous arms of compassion. In art, Avalokiteśvara is represented in a variety of ways, often as a layman with eleven heads, as many as a thousand arms, and a crown with an image of Amitābha in it. He sometimes holds a blue lotus flower in his hand. In China and Japan, Avalokiteśvara was transformed into a female image, known as Guanyin and Kwannon, respectively. In Tibet, he was revered as a patron of the land, known as Chenrezi (*spyan-ras-gzigs*).

## *Mahāyāna schools: Mādhyamika*

Mādhyamika is an Indian Mahāyāna Buddhist school founded by Nāgārjuna, and emphasizing the emptiness (*śūnyatā*) of all components of experiential reality (*dharmas*) as its major doctrine. One of the most important schools of Buddhism across the face of the globe, it had its beginnings in the writings of Nāgārjuna, a second or third century C.E. philosopher, famous for his *Prajñāpāramitā*-inspired logical discourses. The title of the school essentially means 'Middle Way', and it uses as its primary text the *Mūlamādhyamika-kārikās* of Nāgārjuna, a treatise that expounds in great detail about the genuine meaning of dependent origination (*pratītya samutpāda*) and emptiness (*śūnyatā*). Although subscribing to the merits of the *bodhisattva* path, and the efficacy of Mahāyāna ethical maxims, Nāgārjuna and the Mādhyamika school are far more concerned with emphasizing the nature of ultimate reality (*paramārtha-satya*) from the Buddhist perspective. The Mādhyamika philosophy and the development of the school were continued by Nāgārjuna's most immediate successor Āryadeva. The negative dialectic of the school came to be one of its trademarks, and this emphasis was carried on by Buddhapālita (c. 470–550) who headed a Mādhyamika subdivision known as the Prāsaṅgikas. Buddhapālita was rivaled by Bhāvaviveka (c. 490–570 C.E.) who founded another Mādhyamika subdivision known as the Svātantrikas, a group which utilized a positive dialectic. Eventually the school became championed by such important Indian Buddhist figures as Candrakīrti, Śāntideva, Śāntirakṣita, Kamalaśīla, and others. In addition to its enormous influence on Indian Mahāyāna, it became the basis of a Chinese school (Sanlun) and Japanese school (Sanron), as well as providing the philosophical core for much of Tibetan Buddhism.

### The founder: Nāgārjuna

As a philosopher, Nāgārjuna is best known for the Buddhist texts attributed to him. His most famous text is the *Mūlamādhyamika-kārikās* (see below). He is also credited with writing the *Dvādaśa-dvāra Śāstra*, a text discussing the notion of emptiness (*śūnyatā*) in twelve headings; the *Vigrahavyāvartanī*, an attack on the logical school of Nyāya, the *Mahāprajñāpāramitā-upadeśa Śāstra*, a voluminous text extant only in Chinese (but perhaps not written by Nāgārjuna), the *Suhṛllekha* or *'Friendly Epistle'* written to an Indian king, and a large variety of ancillary texts. The basic method utilized by Nāgārjuna is the *reductio ad absurdum* approach in which Nāgārjuna dismantles his opponents on the basis of their own arguments while offering his critics no opportunity to utilize the same approach on his work.

## The basic text: *Mūlamādhyamika-kārikās*

The *Mūlamādhyamika-kārikās* are a Sanskrit text attributed to Nāgārjuna and established as the basis for the Mādhyamika school of Indian Buddhism. The text title literally translates to '*Root Verses on the Middle Way*', and presumably reflects Nāgārjuna's personal description of his philosophical stance. The text itself is divided into twenty-seven very short chapters including a total of about 450 verses. It is a polemical treatise which refutes the views of other Buddhist (particularly Sarvāstivādin and Sautrāntika) and non-Buddhist schools. His method of refutation, the *reductio ad absurdum* argument, called *prasaṅga* in Sanskrit, became the hallmark of the text. Nāgārjuna used this method to defeat his opponents' arguments in terms of their own assumptions. The text insists on a strict application of the notion of emptiness (*śūnyatā*) as an epistemological tool designed to avoid the presumption that any dharma or 'building block of reality' can have a fixed, permanent, own-being (*svabhāva*). Chapter thirteen, verses seven to eight insist that even emptiness is empty, and that an individual who turns emptiness into a viewpoint is 'incurable'. Perhaps the highlight of the text, in which it establishes Mahāyāna's primary philosophical position, is Chapter twenty-four, verse eighteen, in which Nāgārjuna maintains that, 'It is dependent origination (*pratītya-samutpāda*) that we call emptiness'. He goes on to say in the next verse that since no *dharma* exists independently, no *dharma* exists which is not empty. This latter point has enormous implications for Buddhist theory and practice. The importance of the text can, at least in part, be measured by the sizable number of commentaries it provoked, spanning several centuries.

## Major doctrine: emptiness

The underlying theme of all Nāgārjuna's writings is that of emptiness, as established in the *Prajñāpāramitā* tradition. He is a thoroughgoing Mahāyānist in rejecting any notion of own-being (*svabhāva*), continually emphasizing what he calls the 'middle way', and insisting that dependent origination, the Buddha's theory of causality, is the clearest expression of the doctrine of emptiness. Although he was presumably a *bodhisattva* of high attainment, Nāgārjuna says little about this aspect of the Buddhist path, focusing instead on the identity of nirvana and *saṃsāra*, which he maintains to be two forms of the same reality.

## *Mahāyāna schools: Yogācāra*

Yogācāra is an Indian Mahāyāna Buddhist school founded by two brothers, Asaṅga and Vasubandhu, emphasizing the doctrine of *cittamātra* or 'mind only' as the basic mode of knowing and experiencing phenomenal reality. Beginning in the fourth century C.E., the Yogācāra school is so named because it argues for the 'practice of yoga' as the primary means of religious attainment. Its name notwithstanding, the main emphases of the school are predominantly philosophical and psychological. Drawn not only from the writings of Asaṅga (which include primarily the *Mahāyāna-saṃgraha* and the *Abhidharmasamuccaya*) and Vasubandhu (focusing on the *Viṃśatikā* and *Triṃśikā*), the school utilizes a wealth of Mahāyāna texts such as the *Saṃdhinirmocana Sūtra, Laṅkāvatāra Sūtra, Madhyānta-vibhāga*, and others stressing the bold new doctrine of the world of perception as a manifestation of mind. In addition to the primary doctrine of *cittamātra*, the school offers a new theory of eight consciousnesses, adding manas or 'mind' and *ālaya-vijñāna* or 'storehouse consciousness' to the traditional six consciousnesses of earlier Buddhism. For this reason, the school is sometimes called Vijñānavāda (literally 'holders of the doctrine of consciousness'). Although it affirms the traditional Mahāyāna notion of emptiness (*śūnyatā*), it replaces the Mādhyamika school's theory of two levels of truth with 'three natures' including: (1) an imagined or mentally constructed level known as *parikalpita*, (2) a relative reality known as *parantantra*, and (3) ultimate reality known as *parinispanna*. The notion of 'three bodies of the Buddha' also develops within the Yogācāra literature. The practical teaching of the school, including a description of its religious path, is embodied in Asaṅga's text called the *Yogācārabhūmi Śāstra*. The school reached its peak in the middle centuries of the first millennium C.E., as witnessed by its importance at the Nālandā University. The school also became exceedingly important in the development of a number of Chinese and Japanese Buddhist schools as well.

## The founders: Asaṅga and Vasubandhu

Asaṅga was a famous Buddhist who was originally born to a Brahmin family in Puruṣapura (modern Peshawar) sometime in the fourth century C.E. Asaṅga was the eldest of three brothers. He was converted to the Mahīśāsaka school of early Buddhism and became a monk in this tradition. Apparently he received teaching, through a vision, directly from the future Buddha Maitreya who provided him with a series of texts that were collected under the name of *Maitreyanātha*. Quickly converting to Mahāyāna as a result of this interaction, Asaṅga began composing texts in his own name, founded the Yogācāra school of Buddhism, and converted his brother Vasubandhu who, by that time, had developed a reputation as one of the eminent teachers of the Sarvāstivādin school of Buddhism. Asaṅga is identified as the author of the *Mahāyānasaṃgraha, Abhidharmasamuccaya*, and a major commentary on the *Saṃdhinirmocana Sūtra*. Perhaps more influenced by the Sarvāstivāda school of early Buddhism than Nāgārjuna's dialectic, Asaṅga advocated an idealism that sought to synthesize the various aspects of Mahāyāna thought. He developed an eight-membered theory of consciousness, emphasizing a 'storehouse consciousness' or *ālaya-vijñāna* that was a repository for the seeds of past karmic acts, an alternative to Nāgārjuna's notion of two levels of truth resulting in three natures called *svabhāvas*, an emphasis on the practice of the *bodhisattva*, and a doctrine known as the *Tathāgata-garbha* or 'Womb of the Buddha' underscoring the potential for all beings to attain Buddhahood.

Vasubandhu was an Indian Buddhist scholar, of somewhat uncertain history, who is reputed (as noted above) to be the author of the *Abhidharmakośa*, but later a primary figure in the development of the Yocācāra school of Buddhism. General consensus identifies Vasubandhu as the younger brother of Asaṅga, probably born in Puruṣapura in the fourth century C.E. (and quite possibly 320–400 C.E.). He is said to have lived around Kaśmīr and died in Ayodhyā. Originally a member of the Sarvāstivādin school of Buddhism, over time he became critical of its views as established in the *Mahāvibhāṣā*, and composed the *Abhidharmakośa*, literally meaning 'sheath' or 'storehouse' of *Abhidharma*, to critique that position. This text establishes Vasubandhu as a proponent of the philosophy of the Sautrāntika Buddhist school. Apparently later, however, Vasubandhu is converted to the Yogācāra school of Mahāyāna Buddhism by his brother Asaṅga. As a Yogācārin, Vasubandhu is recognized as the author of at least two major texts, the *Viṃśatikā* or '*Twenty Verses*' and the *Triṃśikā* or '*Thirty Verses*'. Each of these texts develops the theory of consciousness-only, critical for Yogācāra philosophy. It is admittedly difficult to reconcile how an individual could embrace so many differing viewpoints, and so passionately, during the course of one lifetime. A possible explanation was voiced by the German scholar Erich Frauwallner who suggested that there were actually two Vasubandhus. He claimed that Vasubandhu the younger lived from 320–380 C.E., was Asaṅga's brother, and was a Mahāyāna philosopher exclusively. According to Frauwallner, Vasuabandhu the elder lived from 400–480 C.E., was a thorough-going Hīnayānist, and the author of the *Abhidharmakośa*. This viewpoint, although interesting, has been rather thoroughly discredited.

## Major doctrines: *Ālayavijñāna*

*Ālayavijñana* is literally translated as 'storehouse consciousness', and is the central concept of the Yogācāra school of Buddhism. In early Buddhism, a theory of six consciousnesses was postulated, each applicable to a particular sense organ. Yogācāra (especially in the writings of Asaṅga and Vasubandhu) added two further items to the list, extending it to eight: (1) *manas*, a subtle mental element which functions by receiving and disposing of data from the other six consciousnesses, and (2) the *ālaya-vijñāna*. This so-called 'storehouse consciousness' receives the seeds (known as *bījas*) of karmic activity and stores them until they ripen and manifest themselves in a process referred to as 'perfuming' (*vāsanā*). In so doing, this consciousness theory of Yogācāra accounts for such mental activity as memory, hard to explain through more traditional theories of consciousness. While the vast majority of seeds that ripen and manifest themselves are 'tainted' (*āsrava-bījas*), resulting in a perception of reality that is delusional, the *ālaya-*

*vijñāna* also contains a number of pure seeds (called *anāsrava-bījas*) that emerge from the deepest layer of the *ālaya* (referred to as the *param-ālaya*). It is the ripening of these pure seeds that establishes the potential for a complete restructuring of experience, known as *āśraya-parāvṛtti* or literally 'a turning over of one's basis', through meditation. Precisely because the *ālaya-vijñāna* functions as a storehouse, it is sometimes referred to as the *Tathāgata-garbha* or the 'Womb of the Tathāgata'.

## Major doctrines: *Trikāya*

The *trikāya* is a Mahāyāna Buddhist concept, literally referring to 'three bodies of the Buddha'. The doctrine, predominantly developed in texts associated with the Yogācāra school of Buddhism (such as the *Laṅkāvatāra Sūtra*), is a reflection of a sophisticated Mahāyāna Buddhology. It argues that Buddha is revealed in a variety of ways to a variety of individuals, each reflective of the individual's particular level of spiritual development. At the lowest level, one encounters the *nirmāṇa-kāya* or 'apparitional body'. This body is depicted as the historical Buddha, visible to ordinary, common worldlings as an inspiration to begin the Mahāyāna Buddhist path. It exists only insofar as it is an apparitional manifestation of ultimate reality. Once on the path, the practitioner, now known as a *bodhisattva*, encounters the Buddha in another form: as *saṃbhoga-kāya* or 'enjoyment body', a subtle-bodied, quasi-material preacher of Mahāyāna scriptures, neither fully human nor fully absolute. At the completion of the path, one attains *dharma-kāya* or '*Dharma* body', the true nature of Buddhahood, ultimate reality itself, an abstract resolution of all dualities, beyond any conceptualization or designation. Thus, the mature notion of the *trikāya* offers three ways of relating to the essential notion of Buddhahood, each reflective of the psychological development of the practitioner, culminating in the proper experience of Buddhahood as ultimate reality itself, empty of any dualities whatsoever.

## *Mahāyāna schools: Pure Land*

The Pure Land school is based on the Mahāyāna Buddhist notion identifying a *Buddha-kṣetra* or 'Buddha-Land' where a celestial Buddha resides. In Mahāyāna cosmology, there are virtually countless Buddhas, and so also there are countless 'Pure Lands' where these Buddhas dwell. By their very nature, these Pure Lands are paradises, resplendent with manifold benefits and beauties, and as such, ideal places for rebirth. Nonetheless, existence even in a Pure Land cannot be considered permanent, and must be viewed as only a more favorable location from which to pursue one's on-going path to salvation. It is, however, an especially important oasis in times of *Dharma* decline when earthly conditions seem not to favor spiritual development and advancement. A number of Pure Lands became quite important in the development of Mahāyāna. Of particular note is the Pure Land of Amitābha

Buddha, known as Sukhāvatī, and praised in a variety of Mahāyāna texts. Pursuit of rebirth in Amitābha's Pure Land developed into a formal Buddhist school which gained a wide following in East Asian Buddhism. It must be noted, though, that other Pure Lands, such as that of the 'Healing Buddha' Bhaiṣajyaguru-Buddha, are mentioned throughout the literature.

## *Mahāyāna logicians*

### Bhāvaviveka (c. 490–570 C.E.)

Bhāvaviveka was a southern Indian Buddhist, also known as Bhavya, who founded the Svātantrika school, one of two divisions of Indian Mādhyamika Buddhism. Bhāvaviveka went to Magadha and studied the works of Nāgārjuna, founder of the Mādhyamika school. He was a slightly junior contemporary of another student of Nāgārjuna's work, Buddhapālita (c. 470–540 C.E.), who utilized Nāgārjuna's well-known negative dialectic to found the Prāsaṅgika school of Mādhyamika. Bhāvaviveka utilized a positive dialectic in opposing Buddhapālita, in a sense countering those critics who thought Buddhism's dialectic of negation to be counterproductive to expressing a positive goal for the religion. He also differed from Buddhapālita on the nature and relationship of the ultimate (*paramārtha*) and the relative (*saṃvṛti*). His writings include a commentary on Nāgārjuna's *Mūlamādhyamika-kārikās* known as the *Prajñāpradīpa*, a refutation of the Yogācāra position known as the *Karatalaratna*, preserved only in the Chinese version as *Zhangzhen lun*, a verse text refuting rival philosophical systems and known as the *Madhyamaka-hṛdaya*, and his own personal commentary on the *Madhyamaka-hṛdaya* referred to as the *Tarkajvālā*. Bhāvaviveka's work was especially formative for the eighth century philosophers Śāntirakṣita and Kamalaśīla who extended his work considerably.

### Candrakīrti (c. 650 C.E.)

Candrakīrti was a Mahāyāna philosopher (c. 650) who championed the Prāsaṅgika school of Mādhyamika. He saw himself as the successor to Buddhapālita, and as such, clearly the rival of Bhāvaviveka's Svātantrika-Mādhyamika school. He argued strongly against the positive dialectic utilized by Bhāvaviveka, and sought to uphold the approach and intent of Nāgārjuna. He is credited with the composition of a number of extremely important philosophical treatises, most notably the *Prasannapadā* or *'Clear Worded'* and the *Madhyamakāvatāra*. In some respects, Candrakīrti was able to move beyond Nāgārjuna because of his formal training in logic, and his ability to utilize the work of Dignāga. His exposition of the two levels of truth, ultimate (*paramārtha-satya*) and worldly (*saṃvṛti-satya*), is extremely important in the Prāsaṅgika school.

## Dharmakīrti (c. 650 C.E.)

Dharmakīrti was an Indian Buddhist logician who was regarded in some circles as the classic, representative Buddhist philosopher. Dharmakīrti studied at Nālandā University, and elaborated on the logic and epistemology set forth by an earlier great Buddhist logician, Dignāga. He is especially well-known for his text called the *Pramāṇavārttika*, purportedly a commentary on Dignāga's *Pramāṇasamuccaya*, but more accurately a reworking and supplement to Dignāga's treatise. In this text, he was especially interested in inference, direct perception, and a general theory of knowledge. Dharmakīrti was also the author of a highly regarded logic text known as the *Nyāyabindu*, and exerted much influence on the later Buddhist logicians.

## Dignāga

Dignāga was an important Buddhist logician responsible for abandoning the old logic of the so-called Nyāya school and founding the New Buddhist Logic. Dignāga lived in the fifth to sixth century of the Common Era (and dates of 400–485 C.E. or 480–540 C.E. are suggested as possibilities), and is best known for his two famous logic treatises: the *Pramāṇasamuccaya* (preserved in Tibetan) and the *Nyāyamukha* (preserved in Chinese). He replaced the five-membered syllogism of the older logic with a new, three-membered variety. He spent much time at Nālandā University, had Dharmakīrti as his chief disciple, and falls under the general approach of Yogācāra idealism.

### Key points you need to know

- Mahāyāna Buddhism began around 200 B.C.E. as a means of emphasizing liberating practices for the mass of Buddhist practitioners.
- Mahāyāna created a rich new Buddhist literature, beginning with the *Prajñāpāramitā Sutras*.
- New concepts emerged, suggesting a radical new interpretation of the nature of the Buddha, a bold new way of understanding phenomenal reality, and a new path (that of the *bodhisattva*) to the goal.
- Within a few centuries, several important Mahāyāna sects developed, each with its own philosophical and soteriological perspective.
- Many important Mahāyāna philosophers helped to develop Mahāyāna's message.
- Mahāyāna philosophies were exported from India throughout Asia.

## Discussion questions

1. How important was the Perfection of Wisdom (*Prajñāpāramita*) literature in the formation of the Mahāyāna?
2. Explain Mahāyāna 'Buddhology' in the light of earlier notions about the nature of the Buddha.
3. What are the stages of the *bodhisattva* path, and how do they employ the various perfections (*pāramitās*)?
4. Why do some scholars consider Nāgārjuna the greatest Buddhist philosopher?
5. How does the Yogācāra theory of consciousness compare to other Buddhist theories of 'mind'?

## Further reading

Conze, Edward. *Buddhist Thought in India: Three Phases of Buddhist Philosophy*. London: George Allen & Unwin, 1962.

Dayal, Har. *The Bodhisattva Doctrine in Buddhist Sanskrit Literature*. London: Routledge and Kegan Paul, 1932.

Nagao, Gadjin. *Mādhyamika and Yogācāra: A Study of Mahāyāna Philosophies*. Albany, NY: State University of New York Press, 1991.

Streng, Frederick. *Emptiness: A Study in Religious Meaning*. Nashville, TN: Abingdom Press, 1967.

Thurman, Robert (trans). *The Holy Teaching of Vimalaktrti*. University Park, PA: Pennsylvania State University Press, 1976.

Williams, Paul. *Mahāyāna Buddhism: The Doctrinal Foundations*. London: Routledge and Kegan Paul, 1989.

# 7 *Meditation*

## In this chapter[1]

This chapter discusses the various meditational systems throughout the Buddhist tradition. It begins with those in early Buddhism, and proceeds through the Mahāyāna tradition. It also considers the Pure Land approach as well as that of Tantric Buddhism. It also briefly considers the Zen approach.

## Main topics covered

- The Practice of Calm
- The Practice of Insight
- The standard structure of Mahāyāna meditation
- Visionary and ecstatic techniques
- Techniques of spontaneity

### *Hīnayāna: introduction*

The canonical collections of Buddhist scripture contain large numbers of texts devoted to meditation. It is clear that the Buddhists felt free to borrow contemplative techniques from other contemporary sects, and also that the early tradition would vary received techniques to suit the capacities of individual meditators. Thus the texts recount how the Buddha himself gave such-and-such a meditation to a particular monk, and an entirely different one to another monk, yet leading them both infallibly to the goal of liberation. Several of these techniques were enshrined in texts of their own, while others were mentioned only casually in the course of other discussions. Two of these techniques, however, became central to the entire contemplative path:

---

1 Stephan V. Beyer is the author of this chapter, which is reproduced by kind permission of The Pennsylvania University Press. 'The Doctrine of Meditation in the Hīnayāna' and 'The Doctrine of Meditation in the Mahāyāna' have been published previously in *Buddhism: A Modern Perspective* edited by Charles S. Prebish.

*Figure 7.1* Wall carving of Buddha meditation posture, Sāñcī, India

the process of withdrawal from sensory input in progressive states of trance (*jhāna*), as set forth, for example, in the *Sāmaññaphala Sutta*, and the process of observation of sensory input in progressive states of mindfulness (*sati*), as in the *Satipaṭṭhāna Sutta*.

The early and rather inchoate mass of material, often overlapping and occasionally contradictory, was given a semblance of order in the various *Abhidharma* schools and received its classical Theravāda formulation at the hands of Buddhaghosa in the fifth century C.E., in his compendious *Visuddhimagga*. By now the two opposite processes of sensory withdrawal and sensory observation had been coordinated as parts of a coherent whole, a standard structure of meditation that would persist in the Mahāyāna, and would be used in both the Chinese and Tibetan academies. Here the process of withdrawal, and the ascent to ever higher levels of abstract trance, was called calming (*samatha*), and was considered to be mental training prerequisite to the mindful observation of events. The mindful observation of events was called insight (*vipassanā*), leading recursively to the trances that finally freed the meditator from the ongoing world-process.

## *The Practice of Calm*

Buddhaghosa lists forty objects of contemplation that may be used in the process of calming the mind. These seem to fall into two classes: those that are involved directly in the induction of trance, and those that function to eliminate distractions and impediments in the contemplative process.

### The ancillary techniques

Meditators may generally be classed into three personality types, according to the predominance in them of lust, hatred, or delusion. These three defilements, when turned to the practice of religion, produce personalities based respectively on faith, intellectuality, or enthusiasm. It is the function of a meditation master to observe the way his disciple walks, stands, eats, and wears his robe, to determine from these clues his basic personality type, and prescribe for him those ancillary meditations that will either counteract his particular defilement or encourage the exercise of the corresponding religious virtue.

#### The Ten Uglinesses and Mindfulness of the Body

To counteract the defilement of lust, the master may prescribe a meditation on ugliness, here referring specifically to the ten stages of decomposition of a corpse, that the meditator may realize the loathsomeness of the body. He meditates upon the swollen purple rotting corpse, and he thinks: 'This body of mine is the same as that one. It will become like that one, and it will not escape'.

Again, the monk may perform mindfulness of the body with himself as the object, looking upon himself as a bag covered with skin and filled with all sorts of filth: 'In this body there is hair, body hair, nails, teeth, skin, flesh, sinews, bones, marrow, kidneys, heart, liver, membranes, spleen, lungs, stomach, bowels, intestines, faeces, bile, phlegm, pus, blood, sweat, fat, tears, grease, saliva, mucus, fluids, and urine'.

Neither of these meditations is designed to lead to the sensory withdrawal of the trance state; rather they function to eliminate the defilement of lust, so that the distractions of lust do not intrude upon the meditator when he turns to the inculcation of the trance. As such, they may be prescribed as preliminary to the trance meditations, or as specific antidotes to lustful distractions as they occur.

#### The Four Immeasurable Contemplations

To counteract the defilement of hatred, the master may prescribe the immeasurable contemplations, also called the abodes of Brahma, since they are held to lead to rebirth in the high heaven of the god. Here the meditator concentrates in turn upon love, compassion, sympathetic joy, and equanimity, diffusing these emotions throughout the four directions and toward all sentient beings.

Love is a feeling of friendship and brotherhood with all beings. But this emotion may easily degenerate into lust, so it is followed by compassion, an awareness of the pitiful state into which these beings have fallen through ignorance. But again this may lead to spiritual pride and a feeling of superiority, so the meditator trains himself in sympathetic joy, that he may share the happiness of others and rejoice in the merits they have accumulated. And finally he achieves a state of equanimity wherein he makes no distinction between friend or enemy, but is even-minded toward all creatures.

Although, technically speaking, these contemplations can lead into the trance states, they are in fact never so used, for the emotions aroused in them remain worldly qualities. They are prescribed to forestall the distractions of hatred in the course of meditation, or to counteract hateful feelings that may tumble into consciousness in the course of the trance itself.

## Mindfulness of Breath

For a meditator who suffers from the defilement of delusion – or enjoys the problematic virtue of enthusiasm – the master may prescribe a calming meditation called mindfulness of the breath. The meditator schools himself to be aware of the motion of his breath as it moves in and out of his body, gradually calming both his body and his mind with a one-pointed concentration upon its soothing motion, thinking: 'Calming my body I shall breathe in ... Calming my body I shall breathe out...'.

This meditation was something of a problem for the commentators on the early texts, for it is part of a larger technique called the foundation of mindfulness, which was held to be a path to nirvana in and of itself. This technique began with mindfulness of breath, and proceeded to mindfulness of the body (as above), and then to mindfulness of the feelings, mindfulness of the thoughts, and finally mindfulness of events. It thus comprised both calm and insight, which the commentators were striving to maintain as separate processes within the structure.

In actual practice, then, the foundation of mindfulness has often been used alone as a special path for contemplatives of an active and imaginative disposition. But as incorporated into the standard structure it is used as an ancillary meditation for excitable individuals, as a preliminary to the trance itself, or as an antidote to the troubling delusions that may appear therein.

### The Six Remembrances

A meditator whose lustful defilements have been transformed into the virtues of faith may be helped in his meditation by the practice of remembrance. Here he thinks repeatedly upon the virtues of the Buddha, the *Dharma*, and the *Sangha*, upon the rewards of morality and charity, and upon the happy state of the gods. Thus he increases his faith in the teachings, and in turn this increase of faith – although not directly leading to sensory withdrawal in the trance-provides him with the necessary motivation and reinforcement for his trance meditations.

### The Mindfulness of Death, the Remembrance of Peace, the Loathsomeness of Food, and the Analysis of the Four Elements

Again, there are ancillary meditations that may be prescribed for one whose defilement of hatred has been transformed into the religious virtue of intellectuality. He may practice the mindfulness of death, wherein he analyzes intellectually the inevitability of his own passing away, or the remembrance of peace, wherein he reflects upon the safety of nirvana amid the torments of this world. In both cases, he uses his intellect – as opposed to faith, as above – to motivate and reinforce his trance meditations. Or such a meditator may use similar intellectual means to counteract the distractions that may occur in his trance. He may contemplate the loathsomeness of food, reflecting upon the disgusting way in which food is prepared and ingested and eliminated, that he may turn away from greed and yearning for sensory pleasures; or he may perform the analysis of the four elements, examining the fact that his beloved body is nothing but an accidental concatenation of earth and water, fire and air.

This catalog of ancillary techniques was a means for the commentators to deal with the mass of different meditations given in the canonical texts. We have noted that they had occasional difficulty in creating a workable scheme, especially where their sources specifically stated that an ancillary discipline in fact led to liberation. But the commentators also show that they possessed a keen insight into human nature, and into the efficacy of auto-therapeutic techniques. Their scheme of ancillary meditations has continued in use to this day, and has been successful in training a wide variety of personalities to pursue the rigors of the trance.

## The trance techniques

Buddhaghosa has thus far dealt with twenty-six of his forty objects of contemplation (ten uglinesses, four immeasurables, and six remembrances, as well as mindfulness of the body, mindfulness of the breath, mindfulness of death, remembrance of peace, loathsomeness of food, and analysis of the four elements). The remaining fourteen objects of contemplation are all involved directly with the induction of the trances, proceeding to even higher levels of abstraction and withdrawal from sensory output.

## The Ten Devices

According to the standard scheme, all these trance states may be achieved through meditation upon a device (*kasiṇa*). Buddhaghosa lists ten of these: earth, water, fire, air, blue, yellow, red, white, light, and space. The earth device, for example, is a circle of earth of even color and texture. The water device may be a round vessel filled with rain water. Or the blue device may be a piece of blue cloth, or a blue painted disc, or a bunch of blue flowers arranged as a round dense mass. This device is then the basis or support for the meditation.

### The Beginning Sign

The meditator erects his device in a quiet and secluded place, and seats himself in the cross-legged posture facing it, first reminding himself of the virtues of meditation and the fact that, in spite of all difficulties, holy men of the past have been able to achieve liberation thereby. He then proceeds to stare at the device, and his mental perception of the object is said to be the beginning sign. And he stares at it some more. And then he stares at it some more.

### The Eidetic Sign

As he sits there staring at the device, he begins to memorize its form, and whether his eyes are open or shut, he clearly sees the object before him, with all its details, exactly as it appears. This memorized and totally accurate picture of the object is called the eidetic sign, and with this eidetic sign as his object he enters into beginning meditation. The meditator should immediately rise from his seat and leave the device, going into his dwelling and concentrating upon his eidetic sign rather than upon the beginning sign (his perception of the object itself). And should he be distracted from his concentration upon this memorized image (as he inevitably is), or should the image simply fade away (as it inevitably does), then he should arise once more, return to the device, and again establish the eidetic sign before returning to his dwelling.

### The Representational Sign

In the course of this frustrating concentration upon the elusive eidetic image, five hindrances tend to arise in the meditator's mind:

1. Lust: images of desired objects appear before him, distracting him from his concentration, or he remembers sensory pleasures of the past.
2. Hatred: he begins to think of people and things he dislikes, and images of past injuries appear in his mind.
3. Sloth and torpor: he falls asleep (this is quite common), or becomes weary and depressed at the mental effort he is making.
4. Remorse and distraction: he becomes extremely sensitized to sensory input and is easily distracted, and becomes so frustrated that he is ready to abandon his attempts.
5. Perplexity and doubt: he is confused at his lack of success, and begins to doubt whether meditation actually works.

But as he focuses upon the eidetic sign, these five hindrances begin to fade. As he gets better and better at concentration, he enters into the meditation of approach for longer and longer periods of time. And in this meditation of approach the eidetic sign itself changes. It becomes the representational sign, a shining and glowing shape that appears before him, no longer a duplicate of the actual device but rather an abstract visual representation of its essence. Thus the earth device is no longer a particular piece of earth, with perhaps a twig here or a leaf there, but rather a shining disc like the rising moon. The representational sign of the water device appears like a mirror in the sky. The blue device is not seen as made of flowers and petals, but appears in its representational sign like a pure, clear, blue gem. And whereas the eidetic sign was fixed and unchanging, the representational sign is infinitely malleable, and may be contracted to a glowing dot or expanded to fill the entire universe. The meditator is thus in a state of approach with the representational sign as his object; the hindrances are suppressed, and he is approaching a state of trance. And as his meditation becomes more and more firm, he enters into the meditation of attainment with the representational sign as his object, and there he abides, for he has 'attained' the first trance.

### The Four Trances

In the first trance, the five hindrances are totally absent, for they have been replaced by the five factors of concentration:

1. Discursive thought: the meditator still engages in linear thinking, and is able to reflect upon his attainment of the trance.
2. Reasoning: he is aware of himself in his situation, and can consider its antecedents and consequences.
3. Enthusiasm: he enjoys the state of trance, is delighted at its attainment after all his struggles, and wishes to continue in such a state.
4. Pleasure: his body and senses are suffused with pleasant feelings.

5. One-pointedness: he is completely concentrated upon the object, and can no longer be distracted.

In the second trace the meditator realizes that discursive thought and reasoning are in themselves distracting, so he eliminates factors 1 and 2. He no longer thinks about his trance state, but simply is in trance, with inner tranquillity and concentration of mind, with the enthusiasm and pleasure that are born of his concentration.

Then the meditator realizes that his enthusiasm for this state is itself distracting, so he eliminates factor 3. He abides in a state of trance wherein there is nothing but pleasure and concentration, and this third trance is said to be the highest state of physical pleasure that can possibly be achieved.

Finally, the meditator realizes that pleasure is distracting, so he eliminates factor 4. He transcends both pleasure and pain, and can no longer be swayed by any worldly temptation. He abides in a state of pure and absolute concentration upon the representational sign, his mind pure and translucent, clear and undefiled, dextrous and supple, firm and unshakeable.

## The Four Formless Realms

Aside from the ten devices, there are now four objects of contemplation remaining in Buddhaghosa's list of forty, and these carry the meditator into even greater sensory withdrawal, into states further and further removed from the realms of form. These are the formless attainments, which render the mind of the meditator ever more pure and supple.

1. The Realm of Infinite Space: here the meditator wearies of the material thing that is the object of his meditation, and wishes to transcend it. He sees that the fourth trance is full of danger, for it takes a material thing as its object. So he takes the representational sign and extends it to the very ends of the universe; and he eliminates the object itself, and concentrates exclusively upon the infinite space that remains.
2. The Realm of Infinite Perception: then the meditator realizes that the trance of infinite space is full of danger, for it is not peaceful, and may slip back into the realm of material things. So he eliminates the infinite space that was the object of his trance, and concentrates exclusively upon the infinite perception that had pervaded it.
3. The Realm of Nothing-At-All: then the meditator realizes that the trance of infinite perception is full of danger, for it is not peaceful, and may slip back into the realm of infinite space. So he eliminates his own infinite perception, and concentrates exclusively upon the nothing-at-all that remains.
4. The Realm of Neither Idea Nor Non-Idea: finally the meditator realizes that the trance of nothing-at-all is full of danger, for it is not peaceful. He thinks, 'It is ideas that are a disease, an abscess, a dagger in the heart'. So he eliminates the idea

even of nothing-at-all, and concentrates exclusively upon peace, and abides in the realm of neither idea nor non-idea.

We may note that the meditator ascended the four trances by eliminating one factor of concentration at a time, until only pure one-pointedness remained. Here the meditator has proceeded from one formless realm to the next by progressively eliminating the object of each formless trance, gaining states of abstraction ever further removed from the phenomenal world.

## *The Practice of Insight*

Buddhaghosa's *Visuddhimagga* is based on a grand scheme of seven purities, of which the last five refer specifically to insight meditation. These seven purities are: purity of virtue, purity of mind, purity of view, purity of overcoming doubt, purity of knowledge and insight into right and wrong paths, purity of knowledge and insight into progress, and purity of knowledge and insight themselves.

### Purity of Virtue

This purity refers to the prior moral training of the meditator, his gradual cutting off of impediments that bind him to the world, and the development of an attitude of moral detachment from worldly things.

### Purity of Mind

The second purity is the state of mental suppleness and clarity, the purity of thought that is achieved through the development of the trance states. Except in special cases (the so-called dry *arhants*), one cannot gain true insight into reality while beset with the prejudices of desire. It is only through the trances and formless attainments that the meditator is able to gain the objectivity of desirelessness. With this objectivity he is ready to turn his mind to the practice of insight, and, no longer blinded by involvement, to see things as they really are.

### Purity of View

The meditator thus begins his training in insight by examining objectively the thirty-two constituents of his own body, or his senses and their objects, or his five aggregates. And with his now pure and supple mind he sees that there is no entity apart from name-and-form, and he realizes that there is neither I nor mine in this concatenation of mind and matter. He sees that sensory experience is as impermanent as the external objects that cause it, and he is freed of all attachment to a self.

## Purity of Overcoming Doubt

Then, like a doctor diagnosing the etiology of a disease, he turns his clear attention upon the source of his mind and body. He realizes that name-and-form come into being through a cause. He sees that his body is caused by ignorance and craving and grasping, projected from past into the present by the action of karma, and when this physical body exists, made up of the four elements, then mental events occur dependent upon the contact of a sensory organ with its corresponding object. Thus he realizes the twelvefold chain of dependent origination, and sees with insight that all things are impermanent, and suffering, and not the self. And thus he is cleansed of all his doubts about the past and present and future.

## Purity of Knowledge and Insight into Right and Wrong Paths

The meditator examines objectively the appearance and disappearance of all the things in the three realms of existence, and perceives their causal inter-relatedness. Each event that passes before his eyes he sees as impermanent, and suffering, and not the self. He gains eighteen great insights, and permanently rejects any notion of finding permanence or happiness or self among conditioned things.

But herein lies danger, for with his budding insight he may be seized by the ten defilements of insight, and give way to excitement and the delusion of progress, thinking he has attained a fruition he has not yet gained. If a meditator has been properly trained by his master, however, he will not fall prey to the seductions of pleasure and magic power he gains here, and will be able to distinguish the right and wrong paths to liberation.

## Purity of Knowledge and Insight into Progress

Having freed himself from the dangers of wrong paths, the meditator continues his systematic and progressive development of insight. Gradually he gains nine knowledges, leading to a culmination of his understanding:

1. Knowledge gained by reflection upon the appearance and disappearance of conditioned things: he completely internalizes his realization of impermanence, and understands that the suffering is not the self, thus seeing everything as it truly is.
2. Knowledge gained by reflection upon the destruction of conditioned things: he sees that every conditioned thing decays and disappears, so he no longer craves for becoming.
3. Knowledge gained by becoming fearful of conditioned things: he sees all things as fearful and full of danger, a trap for the unwary, an empty mirage in the desert to lead him astray.

4. Knowledge gained by reflection upon the danger of conditioned things: he realizes that he is without protection in the midst of things, and turns toward nirvana as safety amid afflictions.
5. Knowledge gained by reflection upon revulsion from conditioned things: he turns his back upon this dangerous world, for he realizes that safety and happiness lie in detachment from things.
6. Knowledge gained by desire for liberation from conditioned things: he no longer clings to any form of worldly existence, and, like a man caught in a trap, seeks only to free himself.
7. Knowledge gained by reflection upon the analysis of conditioned things: with nothing but desire for freedom, he sees all things as calamity and destruction, and analyzes the true nature of things in order to escape from them.
8. Knowledge gained by indifference to conditioned things: as he thus analyzes, he realizes that he need neither fear nor desire any thing, for there is no I or mine anywhere, so he takes no thing as an object of his thought, but turns only to nirvana.
9. Knowledge gained by following the Way: with the culmination of his insight into things, he sets forth to tread the path to nirvana.

## Purity of Knowledge and Insight Themselves

Here the meditator gains knowledge of the four Noble Paths (of the stream-winner, once-returner, nonreturner, and *arhant*). He uses his insight to achieve two further contemplative attainments that bring him to the brink of nirvana itself: the attainment of his fruition and the attainment of the cessation of thought and feeling.

### The attainment of fruition

In this trance state, the meditator takes no thing as the object of his contemplation. He ceases to think upon any thing, and adverts only to nirvana. This is known as freedom of the mind, for it has no 'signs' at all. It is completely transcendent and divorced from the phenomenal. Thus the meditator goes through the series of knowledges gained in his insight meditation. As these knowledges arise in him, he realizes his rebirth as a holy person, with his mind totally fixed on nirvana, and he emerges having gained the fruition of the appropriate Noble Path.

### The attainment of cessation

In this trance state, the meditator takes the final leap from the world, thinking, 'Let me be without thought, and dwell in bliss; here and now let me gain the cessation that is nirvana'. This is the ultimately transcendent experience, and is called nirvana in this very life.

Thus the meditator ascends through all the formless realms, and emerges from each one to realize with his insight that all things therein were impermanent, and suffering, and not the self, and he enters the trance of neither idea nor non-idea, and when one or two moments of thought have passed, he becomes totally without either thought or feeling, and he gains cessation.

This personally experienced nirvana is the final extinction of all defilements. All drunkenness with existence is destroyed, and when the *arhant* dies, he will further gain the final extinction of the aggregates, and never be born again.

The extinction of defilement is called nirvana with remainder, for the *arhant* still has a portion of his life remaining to be lived. At the moment of his death he gains nirvana without remainder, for with the dissolution of his body and the cessation of his last thought he totally transcends the phenomenal. His aggregates are extinct, and he passes into final nirvana.

## *Mahāyāna: introduction*

The Mahāyāna was a complex religious and social phenomenon. It was a religious revitalization movement and a reworking of metaphysics, a revival of archaic contemplative modes and a reordering of religious priorities. The very mood of meditation changed from peace and tranquillity to action and concern, from transcendence to immanence.

We find thus a complex array of meditative techniques generated within the movement, but these tend to fall into three major types: 1. The standard meditative structure inherited from the earlier attempts at systematizing the canonical materials, yet with the twofold process of calm and insight infused with a universalist fervor, making it the vehicle of the new metaphysics and the basis for moral action in the world; 2. The resurgence of older visionary and ecstatic techniques aimed at the construction of alternative realities and the gaining of magic power to control the world of experience; and 3. The development of new techniques of spontaneity to achieve a direct experience of freedom amid the events of public reality.

## *The standard structure of Mahāyāna meditation*

There are many Mahāyāna texts dealing with the inherited contemplative structure, and setting forth the ordered sequence of meditative practice, composed not only in India but also in the academies of China and Tibet. Although the structure remains basically the same (whether in the Chinese *Mohe Zhiguan* of Zhiyi or the Tibetan *Lam-rim chen-mo* of Tsong-kha-pa), there is considerable difference in the working out of details. Here we shall follow the path as it is given by the Indian scholar

Kamalaśīla in his *Bhāvanākrama*, a text that has been used in Tibet since the ninth century as the model for all handbooks on meditation.

## Meditation

Meditation is the ultimate source of wisdom, and is thus central to the entire *bodhisattva* path. The meditator is prepared by his study, so that his meditation will not be erroneous: the fruit of his true meditation will be a clear and manifest knowledge of reality.

## The Practice of Calm

First the meditator must calm his mind, for he cannot know things as they really are with a mind unconcentrated. To this end he takes a contemplative object and focuses upon it one-pointedly, ascending through the four trances and the four formless realms.

The process of calming here is exactly the same as that presented earlier in this chapter. It is true that it is the ontology of the contemplative system that underlies its promise of universal salvation, that it is the wisdom of insight that feeds back into action in the world. But the system still takes as its basis the twofold process of calm as well as insight, for insight arises only in a meditator who has attained the objectivity of detachment, and this objectivity occurs only in a state of calm. This recursive relationship is called the union of calm and insight.

## The Practice of Insight

Kamalaśīla quotes the following verse from the *Laṅkāvatāra Sūtra* as the basic outline for his process of insight: 'He ascends to mind alone, and does not think that external objects really exist. But with reality before him, he transcends mind alone. He transcends non-appearance, and he abides in non-appearance, seeing the Mahāyāna. And in this effortless state, tranquil, made pure by his vows, where nothing appears, there he sees not-self, the highest knowledge'.

The meditator first examines external events: are they really something external to their perception? Or could they be simply the perception itself, as in a dream? He logically analyzes the concept of external things, and discovers that such a concept leads inevitably to ineluctable anomalies. Thus he realizes that there is no such thing as an external object. Every event is a mental event.

The meditator then considers that in the absence of an object there can be no such thing as a subject, and he realizes that reality must be non-dual, with neither subject nor object. Thus, having transcended the notion of an object, he similarly transcends the notion of a subject, and abides in the knowledge of non-duality.

The meditator considers that no event can be caused by itself, nor can it be caused by something other than itself, and he realizes that both subject and object are falsehoods. But if they do not exist, then the knowledge of their non-duality cannot exist either. He transcends the notion that there is such a thing as the knowledge of non-duality, and he abides in the knowledge wherein there is no knowledge of non-duality.

The meditator thus abides in the realization that events neither exist nor non-exist. He enters into the highest reality, a state of meditation wherein he imposes no constructs at all upon experience: he sees all events with the eye of wisdom, and he knows that they have no essence at all.

Thus his calm firmly fixes his mind upon the object, and his insight sees it as it really is. Then the light of knowledge dawns to illuminate the darkness, for the union of calm and insight brings about true understanding, just as his eye sees with the aid of light. This state of meditation is effortless because there is nothing for him to see beyond it, and it is tranquil because he has calmed all the busy work of his mind, which imposed upon reality the constructs of existence and non-existence.

## The return to the world

When the meditator wishes to arise from his contemplative state, he should not yet uncross his legs, but he should think: 'All these events have no essence from the absolute point of view, yet they still exist in conventional reality'. So he awakens his great compassion, and pities the sufferings of those who think that things are real, and thus experience all the sorrows of their delusion. He himself sees reality, and sets forth in great compassion to share his vision with all sentient beings.

Here his means have been made perfect by his wisdom, and all his action in the world is motivated solely by compassion, springing from his hope for the welfare and happiness of others. He realizes the emptiness of things, but he lives amid them for the sake of his suffering children. This is the ultimate religious practice, the union of means and wisdom. He seeks for nothing less than perfect Buddhahood for the sake of all beings, all the while knowing that there is no such thing as Buddhahood, and no such thing as a being.

## The stages on the path

As the *bodhisattva* thus strives, his wisdom and his means growing gradually more perfect, he ascends through five paths to Buddhahood, and treads the ten stages of a *bodhisattva*.

### The path of accumulation

From the moment of his first thought to enlightenment, the *bodhisattva* strives to accumulate a stock of merit and knowledge, acting in the world for the sake of others, and gaining enough skill in meditation that the light of knowledge begins to shine within him.

### The path of preparation

Here the *bodhisattva* practices, with firm conviction that events have no essence at all. And as conviction turns into realization, he passes through four modes of penetration into reality: 1. As the light of knowledge begins to shine, he attains to warmth, or the meditation of the kindling light. 2. As the light of knowledge shines more brightly, he attains to climax, or the meditation of the spreading light. 3. When the light of knowledge shines so brightly that external objects no longer appear and he realizes that nothing exists save mind alone, he gains acceptance, or the meditation of unity. 4. When he reaches the knowledge of nonduality, free of both subject and object, he gains the highest event in the world, the meditation of immediate succession, for he immediately passes into the path of vision and the first *bodhisattva* stage.

### The path of vision

Immediately after the highest event in the world there dawns in him a manifest and transcendent knowledge, and he sees directly the essencelessness of all events. As he ascends to this path of vision, he gains the first of the ten *bodhisattva* stages.

### The path of development

As the meditator gradually develops the vision he has attained, he passes through the remaining nine *bodhisattva* stages, gaining ever greater knowledge and power.

### The path beyond learning

And finally the meditator enters into the diamond-like meditation, and he emerges therefrom as a Buddha. He gains the knowledge that knows everything that can be known, unattached, unhindered, and omniscient. He fulfills all the proper aims of himself and others, and casts aside all the causes of suffering. With a host of magically created bodies he serves the aims of all suffering creatures for as long as the world shall last. He has reached supreme and perfect enlightenment.

### *Visionary and ecstatic techniques*

The enlightenment of the Buddha was a visionary experience, with roots reaching back to the most ancient Vedic literature. There the vision and the word of the Vedic seer opened up the shining realm of the gods to his poetic – and therefore magical – control. Inspired by the drinking of *soma,* the priest homologized the cosmos to the sacred patterns of the sacrifice, and in his ecstasy coerced the gods and the universe itself. There is considerable evidence that *soma* was in fact the psychotropic mushroom *Amanita muscaria*. Even after the secret of *soma* was lost, there remained a tradition of visionary techniques to produce the same glittering vision and the same magical power over the world thus seen. These techniques centered upon the process of visualization, wherein the meditator actually produced an alternative reality for himself: a reality as real (and as unreal) as the one we know, and a reality he could share with others.

### *The Pure Land tradition*

Pure Land texts are often viewed as the products of a Buddhist devotionalism, but they fall also under the category of visionary exercises. This is seen quite clearly, for example, in the *Amitāyurdhyāna Sūtra*. Here is introduced not only the magical *mantra* whose recitation guarantees rebirth in the Western Land of Happiness, but also a series of meditations wherein the meditator in fact creates this paradise for himself. The vision is the magical evocation of the land and of the meditator's own rebirth therein; the word is *Namo Amita Buddha*, recited to this day by millions of the faithful.

### The word

The second element in the meditation is the recitation of the word, the constant repetition of *Namo Amita Buddha*. At every recitation the meditator becomes exempt from the sins that lead to rebirth for eighty million eons. Whoever recites this *mantra* is a white lotus among men. When he dies he will be reborn in the Pure Land, and surely he will gain enlightenment.

### *The* Tantra *tradition*

The same visionary and ecstatic techniques are the basis of the complex contemplations of the *Tantras*. Here the meditator creates a world wherein he himself is the central Buddha, abiding within a divine mansion of knowledge called a *maṇḍala*. Within this new contemplative reality he magically manipulates the powerful sexual symbols of his own transformation, and coerces the attainment of Buddhahood itself.

### The vision

The meditator sits down facing west, and first visualizes the setting sun, until he can see it with his eyes either open or closed. He gazes upon the water, and visualizes the water becoming ice, and the ice becoming crystal, and upon this crystal ground a tower of shining light. He visualizes the land as filled with gold and shining gems, every item so clear that it is ever before his eyes. He visualizes jeweled trees with glittering leaves and flowers, wherein are the mansions of the children of the gods. He visualizes crystal streams and lakes filled with lotus flowers, flowing over beds of gold and diamond sand. And he visualizes the entire Pure Land to be filled with five hundred million jeweled pavilions filled with gods playing heavenly music in praise of the Law.

Then he visualizes the lotus flower with eighty-four thousand petals whereon sits the Buddha of Everlasting Life. He visualizes the form of the Buddha seated upon his lotus throne, and he sees him surrounded by the waters and the trees, as clearly as he sees the palm of his hand. He visualizes every sign of greatness upon the body of the Buddha, shining with dazzling light. He visualizes the beautiful and glittering form of the *bodhisattva* Avalokiteśvara, with his crown and halo and garlands of shining flowers, and the *bodhisattva* Mahāsthāmaprāpta, shining with the light of wisdom and surrounded by multitudes of his retinue. Every single item must appear clearly before the meditator, so bright and detailed that it seems manifestly present to his vision.

And finally he visualizes himself being born in the Western Land of Happiness, seated within a lotus. The lotus had enclosed him, but now it opens up its petals. Rays of light shine upon his body as he opens his eyes and sees the Buddhas and *bodhisattvas* filling the sky!

## The process of generation

Here the meditator first purifies himself of all past sins and erects about the place of contemplation a protective circle that delineates his new divine reality. He dissolves the world of experience into emptiness, and by the process of generation he emerges from the realm of emptiness in the body of the Buddha.

1. From the realm of emptiness, he appears upon the central throne of the *maṇḍala* in the symbolic form of the god, his many hands holding the weapons of power, and in sexual union with his consort. Into this causal deity enter all the Buddhas of the universe. They descend his central channel and emerge into the womb of the consort, whereupon they both melt into Great Bliss. This ball of Bliss is awakened by the song of the gods, and immediately becomes the resultant deity.

*Figure 7.2* Sand *maṇḍala* constructed by the monks of Ganden Shardzay College at Grinnell College, Iowa, 1993

The Buddhas radiate forth from the womb of the consort to take their places as his retinue in the divine mansion of the *maṇḍala*.

2. The meditator then empowers the senses of his new divine body by placing all the deities of the *maṇḍala* upon it, until his body becomes itself the abode of all the Buddhas, and his very senses are rendered divine.
3. The divine Buddha descends upon him from the realm of reality itself and he becomes inseparably united with Buddhahood, taking on the knowledge form of the god.
4. He visualizes that he is then initiated into his divine state by goddesses holding flasks filled with the nectar of the five knowledges, which fills his entire body. Upon the top of his head there appears the *mantra OṂ*, upon his throat *ĀḤ*, and upon his heart *HŪṂ*, and these *mantras* make his body, his speech, and his mind into an unshakeable diamond.

These four steps comprise the process by which he generates himself as the divine Buddha in actuality. Then, initiated as the god, he receives the offerings of a god, visualizing heavenly maidens descending and presenting him with all the worship due a Buddha. And finally he speaks with the divine speech, reciting the *mantra* of the deity, visualizing its syllables circling through his central channel into the womb of his consort, and upward from mouth to mouth, that he may accomplish the four divine functions: pacifying, increasing, subjugating, and destroying.

## The Process of Perfection

In this visionary body he controls the power and enlightenment of the Buddha, and in the process of perfection he plunges himself into the divine understanding of emptiness. He dissolves his body into the Clear Light of emptiness. His *mantra* body disappears, and he emerges from his final contemplation possessed of the knowledge body of Buddhahood.

### *Techniques of spontaneity*

Both the standard structure of meditation and the visionary techniques require great discipline and long training, and in the monastic universities of India they tended to ossify into intellectual rubrics divorced from both experience and action. The final flowering of the Indian Buddhist contemplative genius took place outside the academies, among the crazy long-haired wanderers of the Gupta dynasty and after. Here the search was for a technique that aimed directly at the problem of enlightenment in the world, a way to achieve a liberated mode of action amid the events of public reality, and the techniques are thus basically psychological in orientation. The aim was to achieve spontaneity and freedom, a genuineness of response rather than a controlled apprehension.

### *The* Mahāmudrā *tradition*

This search for spontaneity seems to have been closely associated in many ways with the Tantric tradition, and the term Great Symbol was used as a general term for an entire complex of contemplative techniques. Here the meditator concentrated not upon an external object but rather upon his own thoughts, the very source of his delusion. He watches his thoughts flash by, and he seeks neither to control them nor to fall under their spell. Gradually he learns to let his mind remain in its natural flow. He casts aside all labels, and abandons even the act of attention. His mind is left in its genuine state.

The meditator gains this freedom from his own mind by a number of different practices. He may cut off every thought that occurs, preventing every mental event from coming into manifestation. He may leave his thoughts to do whatever they want, but letting himself no longer be moved by them. Then he alternates these two practices, first cutting off each thought that occurs, then leaving every thought unformed. And finally he realizes that all his practices have themselves been thoughts, and he abandons even his mindfulness, keeping his mind free of all effort and letting it flow naturally and spontaneously in the stream of calm.

Thus he learns to recognize every mental event in its true nature, which is emptiness; by recognizing every thought he is spontaneously freed from every thought. He realizes that every event he experiences is innate and spontaneous, and that every event – being emptiness – is itself enlightenment. He no longer meditates, he no longer thinks, but in his natural and spontaneous flow he lives with his whole being in the magic show we call the world.

## *The Zen tradition*

The same search for the natural and the spontaneous characterizes the Zen tradition as well. The early masters seem to have taught techniques very similar to those of the Great Symbol, but, even more important for their tradition as it developed in China, these masters acted out their spontaneity within the world. Tales of the strange and wonderful actions of the masters became first examples of genuineness to be emulated and then subjects of contemplation in themselves, for they were held to contain the key to truth.

The Zen tradition thus flows in two main streams, which we may label by their more familiar Japanese names. In the Sōtō tradition, the meditator practices just sitting, while in the Rinzai tradition he contemplates upon a *kōan*, a riddle setting forth the inexplicable and genuinely spontaneous deeds of the masters.

Here we find the search for spontaneity carried to its most extreme form. The master shouts at the meditator, beats him, and makes demands upon him that seem cruel and paradoxical. The aim is to break down, as directly as possible, the structures the meditator has erected upon his experience, to eliminate the constructs of existence and non-existence that separate him from his true nature. The master woos and cajoles his students from their established responses, until in despair – in Zen sickness – the meditator suddenly abandons even his mindfulness. He suddenly understands the point, often in a great burst of laughter, and he sees reality.

## *Conclusion*

There is one further point to be made concerning Buddhist contemplative traditions. If we take the process of sensory withdrawal in trance as the structural equivalent of alternative-reality creation, and the process of sensory observation as the structural equivalent of the techniques of spontaneity, we find that Buddhist cultures have almost always tended to erect a tripartite structure of contemplative techniques. Processes for the creation of private realities stand opposed to processes of enlightened participation in the given public reality, and this opposition is mediated in all cases by the standard meditative structure. There is every reason to believe that this tripartite structure in fact defines specifically Buddhist approaches to meditation.

**Key points you need to know**

- Major texts for understanding the meditative tradition of early Buddhism are the *Satipaṭṭhāna Sutta* of the Pāli Canon and Buddhaghosa's *Visuddhimagga*.
- Buddhaghosa lists forty meditational topics in two classes: those that eliminate distractions and impediments to the contemplative process and those that directly induce the trance states.
- The major Mahāyāna meditation texts are the *Bhāvanākrama* of Kamalaśīla in India and the *Mohe Zhiguan* of Zhiyi in China. In Tibet, the most standard text is the *Lam-rim chen-mo* of Tsong-kha-pa.
- Although Mahāyāna emphasizes the practice and calm and insight, as in early Buddhism, it also utilizes visionary and ecstatic techniques as well.
- The Tantric Buddhist tradition adapts the visionary and ecstatic techniques of Mahāyāna by use of various symbols, such as *maṇḍalas* and *mantras*, and by employing techniques of spontaneity through the use of a tradition known as *Mahāmudrā*.
- Zen carries the search for spontaneity to its most extreme form.

## Discussion questions

1. What is the different between calming meditation (*śamatha*) and insight meditation (*vipaśyanā*)?
2. Explain how the system developed by Buddhaghosa takes the practitioner from the unenlightened to the enlightened state.
3. How is the *maṇḍala* used in tantric practice?
4. Compare and contrast the meditational systems of early Buddhism, Mahāyāna, and tantric (or Vajrayāna) Buddhism.
5. Discuss the role of the meditation teacher in the various Buddhist traditions?

## Further reading

Maguire, Jack. *Waking Up: A Week Inside a Zen Monastery*. Woodstock, VT: Skylight Paths Publishing, 2000.

Powers, John. *Introduction to Tibetan Buddhism*. Ithaca, NY: Snow Lion Publications, 1995; pp. 70–85, 219–82.

Sīlānanda, Venerable U. *The Four Foundations of Mindfulness*. Boston, MA: Wisdom Publications, 2002.

Suzuki, Shunryu. *Zen Mind, Beginner's Mind.* Reprint. Tokyo: John Weatherhill, 1973.
Swearer, Donald K. (ed.). *Secrets of the Lotus.* New York: Macmillan, 1971.
Vajirañāṇa, Mahāthera. *Buddhist Meditation in Theory and Practice.* Colombo: M.D. Gunasena & Co., 1962.

*Part III*

# *Buddhism beyond India*

# 8 *Buddhism in South-east Asia*

## In this chapter

South-east Asian Buddhism is the product of a highly complex system of intertwining historical, geographic, political and cultural circumstances. This chapter begins with an overview of the common features of Buddhism in South-east Asia before moving on to look individually at four countries in the region where Buddhism has flourished, namely Sri Lanka, Burma, Thailand, and Vietnam.

## Main topics covered

- Theravāda Buddhism
- General characteristics of Buddhism in the region
- Sri Lanka
- Burma
- Thailand
- Vietnam

## *Theravāda Buddhism*

The form of Buddhism that predominates in the region, particularly in Sri Lanka, Burma, Thailand, Laos, and Cambodia is Theravāda ('the teaching of the elders'). Deriving historically from the Sthavira group of schools that emerged in the third century C.E. in Sri Lanka, Theravāda is the only one of the early Buddhist schools of the Hīnayāna or 'Small Vehicle' to have survived down to modern times. The school itself claims its origins go back to the ancient body of the Elders (Sthaviras) before the separation from the Mahāsāṃghikas, but there is no historical evidence to support this. There are close similarities, however, between the Theravāda and the ancient Vibhajyavādins who were declared by Aśoka to be the orthodox party at the Council of Pāṭaliputra (see Chapter Five). Theravāda Buddhism is characterized by fidelity to the texts of the Pāli Canon, the first complete set of Buddhist scriptures preserved intact in a single canonical language. Its attitude to doctrine and its outlook on social issues is generally conservative, although in modern times monks have come forward to challenge traditional attitudes to politics and on social issues.

## *General characteristics of Buddhism in the region*

According to tradition, Theravāda Buddhism spread initially as the result of missionary activity after being brought to Sri Lanka by Mahinda, the son of Aśoka. From Sri Lanka monks carried the teachings of the Buddha to Burma, Thailand, Laos, and Cambodia, where, compounded with the previous religious practices of the people of those countries, it has produced the now existing local variations of Theravāda Buddhism. Despite these variations, and the fact that the early history of the religion in South-east Asia is even more piecemeal than the foregoing suggests, there are some common features. For example, among the factors that facilitated the spread of Buddhism in the area is the fact that it was adopted by the rulers of the region. These modeled their notion of the Buddhist king or ideal ruler (*cakravartin*) on the Indian emperor Aśoka, who did much to promote the spread of Buddhism. The close association between *sangha* and state in South-east Asia meant that the kings of this region took upon themselves the duty of overseeing the *sangha* of their country to ensure that it conformed to the norms laid down in the *Vinaya*. This interest of the king in the orthodoxy and orthopraxy of his national *sangha* is due to the particular link between *sangha* and kingship that developed in this region as well as in other Theravādin countries. On the one hand, the *sangha* justified the authority of the king, legitimizing the symbols on which his power rested. This was done in several ways, most noticeably through the compilation of historic literary works. On the other hand, the king, who since the lifetime of the Buddha had been the principal sponsor of the *sangha*, not only acquired great merit, but by giving his favor to one or other monastic group (*nikāya*) made sure that none of them became so powerful as to threaten his control.

With the arrival of the colonial powers, the nature of the relationship between political and religious power in the region altered (most notably in Burma) and resulted in the birth of a modern *sangha*, a greater involvement of the laity in religious matters and a strong correlation of religious and national identity. The modern centralized *sangha* is largely a result of the development of the modern nation-state and the consequential centralization of political power. The greater involvement of the laity in all religious matters is due to the fact that the *sangha* had lost in the king its major sponsor and because with the advent of printed texts and increased literacy the teachings of Buddhism had become more accessible.

The involvement of the laity in religious affairs has been mirrored by the social work the monks of this region have been involved in in more recent times. During the last decades of the twentieth century various temples have pioneered development programs geared primarily to the needs of the rural poor. These activities have been at the center of much public debate, raising again the issue of what is appropriate behavior for a monk. The greater interest of the laity in Buddhism has generated a sense of national identity, especially in those countries that came to be under the rule of colonial powers. In Burma, for example, the *sangha* used to be very much under the control of the king. There, a large administrative body ruled over the *sangha* headed by a supreme patriarch (*sangharāja*) appointed by each king in turn. When the British annexed Burma this system collapsed and as a consequence new groups and movements originated within the Burmese *sangha* and communities of lay supporters, which in turn became closely linked to the independence movements. Thailand also saw in the nineteenth century the revival of Buddhism in association with the introduction of social and political reforms. This country, however, had not been colonized. In this case it was the ruling Buddhist dynasty, that of the Chakri kings, that sponsored the revival and the social reforms. The Thai kings had almost divine status, but faced with the modernization movement that threatened to make their existence obsolete, decided to use their traditional role to lead the movement through social reform. The more independent modern South-east Asian *sangha* has also become more openly involved in all sorts of social and political matters. This remains true throughout the region, despite the fact that in more recent times in Laos and Cambodia the political events of the 1970s have severely curtailed the activities of Buddhist monks. In Burma, the monks have alternatively given and denied their support to the various post-war governments.

In addition to the foregoing, three further characteristics of Buddhism in South-east Asia can be noted. The first is the absence of fully ordained nuns, which is due to the fact that their ordination tradition died out in the early centuries C.E. Provisions exist, however, for women to ordain to a level which is intermediate between the Five Precepts (*pañca-śīla*) for a lay Buddhist, and the ten undertaken by the novice (*śrāmaṇerī*). These women, who wear robes, are known in Thailand as *sikkhamat* or *mae chii*, in Sri Lanka as *dasa silmātā*, and in Burma as *thilashin*.

Second is the practice of temporary ordination, a rite of passage into manhood practiced exclusively in the Theravādin countries of South-east Asia. This requires that all men at some point in their life, before their marriage, take ordination and spend some time in a monastery. This custom was not practiced during the lifetime of the Buddha and it is not known when it was introduced in South-east Asia.

The last feature to be mentioned is the co-existence of Buddhist doctrines with local beliefs and practices. One rarely encounters Buddhism in a 'pure' form in South-east Asia, and it usually co-exists alongside a range of village customs and local traditions. As it spread, Buddhism did not attempt to persecute those of other faiths or stamp out indigenous beliefs, and instead sought an accommodation with them whereby each had its own sphere of responsibility. The resulting division of

### The Great Tradition and Little Tradition

The Great Tradition is embodied in Buddhist doctrine and philosophy and is concerned with ultimate questions of human destiny. The Little Tradition, by contrast, centers on mundane matters to do with the practical affairs of everyday life revolving around health, wealth, marriage, children and family life, agriculture and animal husbandry, and averting misfortune. This lower tier of belief is often animistic in character and involves the maintenance of good relations with the spirit world and the various local deities who can bring good or bad fortune. The Nats of Burma (from Sanskrit *nātha*, or 'lord') are one example of a local cult of spirits, but every country and region has its own. A number of anthropological studies have explored the symbiotic relation between the Great and Little Traditions in South-east Asia, some of which are mentioned in the Further Reading for this chapter.

labor is a fascinating blend of what scholars have termed the 'Great Tradition' and the 'Little Tradition'.

From this survey of general characteristics we now turn to the specific features of Buddhism in particular countries.

## *Sri Lanka*

Sri Lanka is the name of the modern state established on the island of Ceylon which lies off the southern tip of India. In Pāli sources the island is known as Tambapaṇṇi-dīpa ('Copper Leaf Island'). This was the first region outside of India to be converted to Buddhism. Buddhism was brought to the island around 240 B.C.E. by the monk Mahinda, son of emperor Aśoka. A monastery known as the Mahāvihāra was built near the capital Anurādhapura, and from there Buddhism spread throughout the island. Anurādhapura, located in the northern part of the country, had been the capital from around the fourth century B.C.E., and as well as being the site of the Mahāvihāra was also the location of other important monasteries such as the Abhayagiri and the Jetavanārāma. It was in Anurādhapura that a cutting from the original Bodhi Tree brought to the island by Mahinda's sister, the nun Sanghamittā, was planted and grew to become what is now popularly believed to be the oldest tree in the world. Sanghamittā also instituted an order of nuns on the island. In the tenth century C.E., because of repeated attacks from India, the capital was moved to Polunnaruwa, although ordinations were still being carried out at Anurādhapura in the thirteenth and fourteenth centuries. The city was finally abandoned as a monastic site after its destruction by the Portuguese, and although it probably remained a pilgrimage center for some time it was not reclaimed from the jungle until the nineteenth century.

The early political history of Sri Lanka was turbulent, and punctuated by frequent invasions by the Damiḷas (Tamils) from India. Out of fear that the Buddha's teachings might be lost the Pāli Canon was committed to writing during the reign of king Vaṭṭagāmaṇi Abhaya (r.29–17 B.C.E.). Around the same time, the king founded the Abhayagiri monastery, which became a rival to the Mahāvihāra. Abhayagiri, also known as the Uttaravihāra, was a major monastic complex which did not become important until a century or two after its foundation. Originally it consisted of a monastery and a *stūpa*, but the latter alone is now standing. According to tradition, on one occasion when the king was fleeing from the Tamils, he came upon the Nigaṇṭha Giri, a Jain ascetic who made insulting remarks about him. The king vowed that if he were returned to the throne he would build a Buddhist monastery on the spot. He fulfilled his vow, and the name of the monastery was a combination of his own name and that of the Nigaṇṭha (Abhaya+Giri). Unlike the Mahāvihāra, or 'Great Monastery', erected earlier during the reign of King Devānaṃpiya Tissa (247–207 B.C.E.) and given to the *sangha*, the Abhayagiri was given to an individual monk. As a result, according to much later sources (on which too much reliance should not be placed) a conflict developed between the monks of the Mahāvihāra and the monks of Abhayagiri allegedly focusing on the issue of whether monks could receive gold or silver, meaning wealth in general, but actually reflecting a struggle for control of Buddhism on the island. Though for quite a long time the fraternities of the two monasteries seem to have lived side by side in amity, when the Abhayagiri monks openly adopted an alternative canonical literature (the heretical *Vaitulya Piṭaka*) the animosity between the monks of the two establishments became very bitter and resulted in the heretical books being burned and the destruction of the Mahāvihāra building. The two communities developed into separate schools, not to be united again for more than a millennium.

Mahāvihāra residents were known as the Theriya school (*Theriya Nikāya*), while Abhayagiri residents were referred to as the Dhammaruci school. Despite some ups and downs in their fortunes, the Dhammarucikas enjoyed favor in Sri Lanka over a long period, with several kings making provisions and donating several monasteries to them. In 1165 a council was held at Anurādhapura and reconciliation between rival schools was achieved. In contrast to the above account from the medieval chronicles, however, there is no actual evidence of any active conflict between the two institutions after the third century C.E. When Anurādhapura was abandoned around the thirteenth century, the history of Abhayagiri essentially ceased.

One of the most famous residents of the island was the great scholar Buddhaghosa, considered to be the greatest of commentators on the Pāli Canon. Although usually dated to the fifth century, recent research suggests he probably lived in the fourth. The hagiographic accounts of his life report that because his speech, like that of the Buddha, was profound and his words spread throughout the world he came to be called Buddhaghosa, literally meaning 'Buddha utterance'. He composed many important works including the encyclopedic Path of Purification (*Visuddhimagga*), a compendium of Theravāda teachings structured according to the three divisions of the Noble Eightfold Path, namely morality (*śīla*), meditation (*samādhi*), and wisdom (*prajñā*). Later tradition ascribes to him an exaggerated number of texts. It is said that while living in India he composed the *Ñāṇodaya* and the *Atthasālinī*, and also began to write a concise commentary (*Parittaṭṭhakathā*) on the *Tripiṭaka*. In order to complete his task, he went to Sri Lanka and studied the Sinhalese commentaries at the Mahāvihāra. According to the Theravādin tradition the commentaries came to Sri Lanka with the first Buddhist missionaries in the third century B.C.E. When his studies ended he wrote the *Visuddhimagga*, and having won the approval of the monks of the Mahāvihāra, he rendered the Sinhalese commentaries into Pāli. When this task was accomplished, Buddhaghosa returned to India. Beside the above-mentioned works Buddhaghosa is credited with composing the *Samantapāsādikā* and the *Kaṅkhāvitaraṇī* commentaries on the *Vinaya Piṭaka*, and the *Manorathapūraṇī* commentary on the *Sūtra Piṭaka*. He is also said to have compiled commentaries on the *Khuddakapāṭha*, the *Sutta Nipāta* and on the *Dhammapada*. Some also ascribe to him the commentary on the *Jātakas* (*Jātakaṭṭhakathā*). In fact the *Vinaya* commentary is probably not his work, and the author of the *Abhidharma* commentary states that he is writing it at the request of Buddhaghosa. It is probably safest to attribute to Buddhaghosa only the *Visuddhimagga* and the commentaries on the four *Nikāyas* or *Āgamas*. The rest is best viewed as the work of the 'school of Buddhaghosa'. Whatever their exact provenance, these works have exerted a major influence upon the doctrine of the Theravāda orthodoxy in Sri Lanka, and the teachings of Theravāda Buddhism as we know them today. Mahāyāna schools also enjoyed popularity around Buddhaghosa's time, but the Theravāda eventually reasserted itself as the dominant tradition.

Due to a combination of political problems and doctrinal disputes, the *sangha* in Sri Lanka fell into decline, and the ordination lineages of both monks and nuns died out. Monks were sent for from the Mon region of present-day Burma, and the male lineage was restored. According to Burmese legend a group of five monks led by the Mon monk Chapata came from Burma to Sri Lanka in about 1180 to study Theravāda Buddhism as practiced at the Mahāvihāra. The group included a prince of Cambodia (possibly the son of Jayavarman VII, the founder of Angkor Wat), another originally from Conjeevaram in South India, and two others from different parts of South-east Asia. This group, later known as the 'Sinhalese Sect', were ordained in Sri Lanka and spent ten years there, thereby becoming elders (*thera*) who could perform ordinations. They returned to Burma in 1190 to establish the Sinhalese form of Theravāda Buddhism. Whether or not the legend is true, it is certain that by the beginning of the thirteenth century the Sinhalese form of Theravāda Buddhism was spreading in South-east Asia. This form of Buddhism, characterized by strict adherence to the *Vinaya*, emphasis on a pure line of succession, and strong links to political authority, has remained a characteristic of the Buddhism of the region down to modern times.

There was further political turmoil in the early modern period when the island was ruled in turn by the Portuguese, the Dutch and the British. Once again the ordination lineage died out and monks had to be sent from Thailand to restart it. Sri Lanka gained independence from the British in 1948, but in modern times has continued to be plagued by political problems and intermittent civil war between the Sinhalese Buddhist majority (numbering over seventy per cent) and the minority Tamil population in the north. At times Buddhist monks have fanned the flames by likening the dispute to a holy war and campaigning for discriminatory constitutional reform. This reached an extreme in 1959 when the prime minister S.W.R.D. Bandaranaike was assassinated by a Buddhist monk who felt his position towards the Tamils was too conciliatory. At the time of writing, after several years of peace the government has been suspended by President Kumaratunga, and the country's political problems show no sign of early resolution.

## *Burma*

Burma is the former and more familiar name of the country now officially known as Myanmar. Buddhism may have been introduced here by one of Aśoka's missions, and it has been present among the native Mon people from the early centuries C.E. The Burmese chronicles claim that Buddhaghosa visited the country and established a tradition of Pāli scholarship. The Pāli name for the Mon country to the south is Rāmañña, and the Sinhalese chronicles relate that when the Sinhalese ordination lineage died out King Vijayabāhu I (1059–1114) of Sri Lanka sent to Rāmañña (lower Burma) for monks to re-establish the *sangha*. From the fifth to the fifteenth century the dominant power in the region was the Khmer empire, in which various forms of Mahāyāna Buddhism were popular. The Khmer was an ancient kingdom roughly corresponding to present-day Cambodia. Though in contact with both India and China, the Khmers favored various forms of Hinduism rather than Buddhism, which did not make any significant headway until the reign of Jayavarman VII, the founder of Angkor Wat in the early twelfth century C.E. There was a presence of Theravāda Buddhism thereafter though the monastic population was decimated under the Khmer Rouge government during the late 1970s and early 1980s. King Anawrahtā (1044–1077) unified Burma by conquering the southern part and gave his allegiance to the Theravāda, although it is likely the Theravāda was dominant even before then. Anawrahtā's capital, Pagān, was sacked by the Mongols in 1287 and the city with its many thousand pagodas and temples was abandoned. The country was not united again until 1752, but soon afterwards was conquered by the British.

*Figure 8.1 Stūpa (chedi)* in Chiangmai, Thailand

The largest monastic sect or *gaing* in Burma is the Thudhamma (Pāli: Sudhamma), Some scholars argue that 'sect' is not the best translation of the term, since the various Burmese *gaings* have not developed separate doctrines and distinguish themselves largely in terms of their different practices. The chief characteristics of a *gaing* are: a distinctive monastic lineage, some form of hierarchical organizational structure, separate rules, rituals and behavioral practices, affiliation across local boundaries, and some recognition by the secular authorities. In historical terms, after the mission of Chapata to Sri Lanka, the Burmese *sangha* at Pagān split into two divisions known as the Purimagana ('earlier going') and Paccagana ('later going'). After the fall of the Pagān dynasty six *gaings* were known to have flourished in the early fourteenth century in the land of the Mons in lower Burma. After a period of reunification, however, the *sangha* in lower Burma declined. Town-dwelling monks began to adopt a distinctive headgear and became influential in the closing decades of the seventeenth century, sparking off a conflict with their forest-dwelling counterparts. A dispute also arose between the so-called *Ton Gaing* and *Yon Gaing*, which centered on the manner of wearing the robe in public, namely whether it should be worn over one shoulder or both. Successive monarchs were drawn into the dispute, which was only resolved in 1782 when King Bodawpaya intervened and restored the orthodox practice favored by the *Yon Gaing* of covering both shoulders. After this the *sangha* remained united for some seven decades until the advent of the Shwegyin Nikāya, a more austere and conservative group which formally separated from the Thudhamma in the mid-nineteenth century. There were nine officially acknowledged *gaings* when then state-sponsored 'Congregation of the *Sangha* of All Orders' was convened in May 1980 in a successful attempt to form a unified *sangha* with a national character. The Thudhamma comprised nearly eighty-nine per cent of all monks in 1980 and outnumbers the Shwegyin by a ratio exceeding twelve to one.

In the second half of the nineteenth century Burma enjoyed a 'golden age' under king Mindon which lasted for twenty-five years from 1852 to 1877. By all accounts an enlightened ruler, Mindon was constantly threatened with the annexation of his country by the British, an event which finally came about in 1886. Prior to this, Mindon moved the capital to Mandalay and took steps to improve the discipline of the *sangha*, which had become lax. He also presided over the 'Fifth Council' between 1868 to 1871 at which all the Theravāda canonical texts were recited and variant manuscripts compared. The final agreed version was engraved on 729 marble slabs, and to commemorate the council Mindon crowned the Shwedagon Pagoda in Rangoon with a new spire.

Burma was part of the British Empire until it was granted independence in 1948 when U Nu became the first Prime Minister. Attempts to develop a form of 'Buddhist Socialism' with Buddhism as the state religion ultimately failed when General Ne Win led a coup in 1962, from which time onwards the country has been ruled by a military junta (SLORC). The regime is not hostile to Buddhism, which remains strong, and eighty-five per cent of the population are Theravāda Buddhists. However, Buddhist pro-democracy advocates, such as Aung San Suu Kyi, winner of the 1991 Nobel Peace Prize, have been placed under house arrest and human rights abuses are commonplace. The country presently remains isolated from the international community.

## *Thailand*

Formerly known as Siam, Thailand became a constitutional democracy in 1932. Buddhism (almost entirely of the Theravāda form) plays a leading role in all aspects of national life, and since the Buddhist Order Act of 1902 has enjoyed constitutional status as the official religion. Under this measure a religious hierarchy was created presided over by a supreme patriarch (*sangharāja*) who is appointed by the king. Because of this link between Buddhism and nationalism, it is traditional for all young men to spend a short period of time as monks, usually during the three-month rainy-season retreat. Most parents would consider it a great honor should their son wish to prolong his stay and take up the religious life on a permanent basis, but for most it is a kind of 'national service' forming a step on the way to an alternative professional career.

*Figure 8.2* Buddha statues in Ayutthaya, Thailand

The Pāli chronicles refer to Thailand as Sāmindavisaya, and speak of a close relationship between it and Sri Lanka dating back to the Middle Ages. The original inhabitants of the region were the Mon, who may have been introduced to Theravāda Buddhism in the early centuries C.E. by missionaries sent from India by Aśoka. Buddhism became firmly established in those areas of the Mon kingdom known as Haripuñjaya and Dvāravatā. From the fifth to the fifteenth century, an important power in the area was the Khmer empire, in which various forms of Hinduism and Mahāyāna Buddhism were also popular. In the eleventh century, missionaries were sent from Burma, and the Thai people arrived in the region having been displaced from China by the Mongols. They found the Theravāda form of Buddhism congenial and it began to displace Mahāyāna forms. Around 1260 the kingdom of Sukhothai became independent from the Khmers and King Rama Khamheng (1275–1317) declared Theravāda the state religion. Sukhothai fell in 1492 and was replaced by the kingdom of Ayudhya, which ruled until 1767. During this time an edition of the Pāli Canon was produced by King Songdharm (r. 1610–1628) and relations between the *sangha* and the crown became closer. Ayodhya was overthrown by Rama I (1782–1809) who founded the Chakri dynasty and devoted himself to the purification of the *sangha*.

One of Rama I's successors – Rama IV, more commonly known as Mongkut (r. 1851–1868) – was himself a monk for twenty-seven years before becoming king. In 1833 Mongkut founded the Thammayut order (Pāli: Dhammayuttika), a reform movement in the Thai *sangha*. The movement, whose name means 'those holding to the Law', advocated stricter compliance with the *Vinaya* in contrast to the mainstream Mahānikai (Pāli: Mahānikāya) order. As abbot of Wat Bovoranives, which became the center of the Thammayut sect, Mongkut laid down strict rules governing ordination, wearing of the monastic robe (over both shoulders instead of just one), and for the conduct of the *kaṭhina* or robe-giving ceremony. He also decreed on becoming king that all monks, including those of the majority Mahānikai (Pāli: Mahānikāya) should henceforth observe the stricter disciplinary practices. Mongkut was concerned to purge Buddhism of its superstitious elements and emphasize its rational aspects so as to make it compatible with science and modern attitudes. The Thammayut movement was instituted in southern Laos around 1850 and Cambodia in 1864 by monks trained in Thailand, and today enjoys the status of official orthodoxy in contemporary Thai Buddhism. Although monks are the main source of religious authority, lay groups have also been established in recent times, and many Thais are pressing for a more modern outlook on the part of the clergy and an updating of the ancient teachings to make them more relevant to the problems of contemporary life.

## Vietnam

By virtue of its geographical location, Vietnam has been exposed to two main forms of Buddhism. The Mahāyāna form predominates in the north, where Chinese influence is strongest, and the Theravāda school is pre-eminent in parts of the south, which has stronger links to the Buddhism of South-east Asia. Historically, Buddhism reached different regions at different times, and its development has been eclectic, often mingling with Taoism and Confucianism. The history of Buddhism in the territory now covered by the modern country of Vietnam dates back at least to the second century C.E. when it was transmitted southward from China to the area then known as Jiaozhou. This territory remained under Chinese hegemony through the tenth century, and while Buddhism certainly existed and probably thrived during that time, later historians tended to discount it as 'Chinese' Buddhism, and concentrated their efforts on the period of independence. Thus, materials relating the history of Buddhism during the period of Chinese dominance are scarce. Sources dating from this period reveal the presence of monastic Buddhism and speak of scripture-chanting, the erection of images, and the miraculous intervention of monks, with little comment, indicating that such things were common enough that the reader needed no explanation. Early records also indicate that the late Han-dynasty governor of Jiaozhou, Shi Yie (Si Nhiep) had a large number of Chinese and central

Asian monks in his entourage. Official Chinese court records speak of eminent and accomplished monks from Jiaozhou who made their way to the northern capitals, showing that there were sufficient resources there for them to receive detailed training in doctrine, scripture, and meditation, and we also have records of foreign monks who settled in Jiaozhou to carry out translation activities. Yijing (635–713 C.E.), a monk who journeyed to India and later wrote an account of other monks who had done the same, mentions that several of them, having taken the southern maritime route either coming or going, stopped off in Jiaozhou. In other words, in some respects Buddhism in Vietnam during this period was simply an extension of Chinese Buddhism, and much of what transpired there reflected developments elsewhere in the empire.

However, there was another strain of Buddhism active in the area at this time. Waves of Indian cultural export had made their way across South-east Asia penetrating as far as Indonesia, and Theravāda forms of Buddhism were among these. Many people in the southern part of Vietnam were more influenced by this form of Buddhism than by Chinese Mahāyāna Buddhism, and so Vietnam came to be the meeting place for the two streams: Mahāyāna going north from India along the Silk Road, down into China, then into Vietnam; and Theravāda going south along the sea coasts through Thailand, Laos, and Cambodia and into Vietnam. Vietnamese Buddhism, as a result, is a unique mixture of Mahāyāna and Theravāda forms.

By the time Vietnam achieved independence from China in the tenth century, Buddhism had been an integral part of the cultural landscape for over eight hundred years. The first emperor of independent Vietnam, Dinh Bo Linh, put together a system of hierarchical ranks for government officials, Buddhist monks, and Taoist priests after ascending to power in 968 C.E. Thereafter, Buddhist monks were part of the national administration, serving the ruler as advisors, rallying the people in times of crisis, and attending to the spiritual needs of the masses.

The Lý Dynasty (1010–1225) was more stable and long-lived than the Dinh and Lê dynasties that preceded it. This dynasty was willing to take in many elements in its task of constructing a national culture and identity, and so many elements of Chinese, Indian, and Cham culture (from the kingdom of Champa which flourished from the sixth to the fifteenth centuries) were included, and many schools of Buddhism were able to exist side-by-side and compete in an open religious marketplace, further facilitating the intermingling of Mahāyāna and Theravāda forms. Archaeological evidence also indicates that Tantric Buddhism had made its way into Vietnam (stelae with *mantras* inscribed on them have been discovered). During this time, Buddhism also became more widely disseminated among the common people, as monks came into villages and 'converted' local deities, ancestors, and cultural heroes to the religion and declared them now 'protectors of the *Dharma*'. This move worked to unify the disparate local cults under the Buddhist umbrella, and aided the unification of the country. In return, the Lý kings supported Buddhism lavishly: giving stipends to eminent monks, erecting and refurbishing temples, and sending envoys to China in search of scriptures. In this way, new developments in Chinese Buddhism were noted in Vietnam, particularly with the importation of Chan 'transmission of the lamp' genre works. This created a dichotomy between an older form of Buddhism that was highly syncretistic and incorporated many elements and practices under its umbrella, and a newer Buddhism that inclined to a purer Chinese nature, centered mostly on Chan (discussed in more detail in Chapter Nine). Chan study and practice became more entrenched under the Tran dynasty (1225–1400), although the older forms also remained vital. A kind of division of labor arose, with Confucianism adjudicating worldly affairs and Buddhism providing the metaphysical and soteriological framework for human life. Many Tran emperors abdicated and retired to Mount Yan Tu to practice Buddhism full-time after a Confucian career as national ruler. Tran rulers also sponsored the establishment of the first actual 'schools' of Buddhism in Vietnam, beginning with the Truc Lam (Bamboo Grove) Chan school founded by the third Tran king. Missionary monks also arrived continuously from China, bringing both the Linji and Caodong schools into Vietnam, and they found a ready audience among the Tran aristocracy. Unfortunately, the surviving literature tends to give only lists of lineages and temples, making it difficult to determine the actual content of teaching and practice. The works that remain show many features reminiscent of the 'Chan of the patriarchs' found in China: encounter dialogues, enlightenment verses, direct transmission of the mind of enlightenment, and so on.

In the fifteenth century, the Vietnamese began to conquer and absorb parts of Cambodia, bringing the religion of the Khmer people into the Vietnamese fold. This strengthened the co-existence between the Vietnamese Chan of the elites alongside the Theravāda teachings and practices of the Cambodians. The country took its current shape during the eighteenth century, and the country's unique blend of schools of Buddhism was fixed from that time. The occupation of the area by the French, in giving the different ethnic groupings of the land a common tongue, facilitated interchange between different forms of Buddhism. In the early twentieth century, Vietnamese culture, like other cultures in East and South-east Asia, had to deal with modernity in the form of science, Western thought, and Marxism. During this time, many educated Vietnamese began abandoning Mahāyāna and Chan Buddhism, which seemed superstitious with all its deities, magical rituals, and practices for gaining rebirth in the Pure Land. They came to favor Theravāda Buddhism, which seemed more pragmatic and this-worldly in comparison. An instrumental figure in this evolution was Le Van Giang, who studied Theravāda meditation with a Cambodian teacher, took the name Ho-Tong, and came back to Vietnam to build the first formally Theravāda temple near Saigon. From this headquarters he began actively disseminating Theravāda Buddhism in the local language, and produced translations of the Pāli scriptures in Vietnamese. The Vietnamese Theravāda Buddhist *sangha* Congregation was formally established in

1957, making what had formerly been a diffuse set of beliefs into a formal school to rival the Chinese-style Chan schools. By 1997, this Congregation had sixty-four temples scattered throughout the country. Buddhist organizations founded in the 1960s include the Unified Buddhist Church of Vietnam, the United Buddhist Association, and the School of Youth for Social Services. The Lam-te lineage of Rinzai Zen introduced in the seventeenth century is today the largest Buddhist order. Under the leadership of the monk Thich Nhat Hanh, well-known in the West as a leading exponent of Engaged Buddhism (the subject of Chapter Twelve), the latter has become a crusading volunteer organization dedicated to improving the lot of rural communities. During the Vietnam War, Buddhist monks were active in efforts to bring hostilities to a close, and many of them immolated themselves publicly to protest the war (see Chapter Thirteen). Others, including Thich Nhat Hanh went abroad to propagate Vietnamese Chan.

## Key points you need to know

- In South-east Asia the Theravāda form of Buddhism predominates, although Mahāyāna Buddhism is influential in parts of Vietnam.
- From Sri Lanka the teachings of the Buddha spread to Burma, Thailand, Laos, Cambodia, and southern parts of Vietnam. They reached the northern part of Vietnam from China,
- Theravāda Buddhism has a history of some 2000 years in the region, and in some places (such as Sri Lanka) slightly more.
- The Pāli Canon was committed to writing in Sri Lanka during the reign of king Vaṭṭagāmaṇi Abhaya (r.29–17 B.C.E.).
- The most famous scholar active in the region was Buddhaghosa, who lived in the fourth century C.E. Originally from India he resided for many years in Sri Lanka and his principal work was the Path of Purification (*Visuddhimagga*).
- Throughout South-east Asia, Buddhism as the 'Great Tradition' exists alongside the 'Little Tradition' of local spirit cults and animistic practices.
- In South-east Asia the *sangha* has often played a political role in advising kings on affairs of state.
- The ordination tradition for nuns died out during the medieval period.
- Temporary ordination is very common in Thailand and it is not uncommon for young men to spend time in a monastery before embarking on a career.
- The head of the *sangha* in Theravāda countries is known as the *sangharāja*, or 'supreme patriarch'.

## Discussion questions

1. What would you say are the main features of Buddhism in South-east Asia? What variations, and what common themes can be identified?
2. What is meant by the 'Great Tradition' and the 'Little Tradition?' Which is the most important? Give an example of a belief or practice associated with the 'Little Tradition'.
3. Of the four countries discussed in this chapter, is there one that seems to you to be the 'odd man out'? Which is it, and why?

## Further Reading

Bischoff, Roger. Buddhism in Myanmar: A Short History. *The Wheel*, No.399/401.

Bunnag, Jane. *Buddhist Monk, Buddhist Layman: A Study of Urban Monastic Organization in Central Thailand*. Cambridge: Cambridge University Press, 1973.

Gombrich, Richard. *Precept and Practice: Traditional Buddhism in the Rural Highlands of Ceylon*. Oxford: Oxford University Press, 1971.

Gombrich, Richard. *Theravāda Buddhism: A Social History from Ancient Benares to Modern Colombo*. London: Routledge, 1988.

Hazra, Kanai Lal. *History of Theravāda Buddhism in South-East Asia: With Special Reference to India and Ceylon*. New Delhi: Munshiram Manoharlal, 1982.

Lester, Robert C. *Theravāda Buddhism in Southeast Asia*. Ann Arbor, MI: University of Michigan Press, 1973.

Reynolds, Frank E. and Mani B. Reynolds. *The Three Worlds according to King Ruang: A Thai Buddhist Cosmology*. Berkeley, CA: Asian Humanities Press, 1982.

Spiro, Melford E. *Buddhism and Society: A Great Tradition and its Buddhist Vicissitudes*. Berkeley, CA: University of California Press, 1982.

Tambiah, Stanley J. *World Conqueror and World Renouncer*. Cambridge: Cambridge University Press, 1976.

# 9 *Buddhism in East Asia*

## In this chapter

This chapter outlines the development of Buddhism in China, Korea, and Japan. It includes historical sketches for each country, a description of the major Buddhist sects in each, and a description of the modern Buddhist tradition in each. The chapter also includes citations of the major figures and prominent Buddhist texts in each culture.

## Main topics covered

- The development of Chinese Buddhist history from the Han Dynasty to modern times
- Chinese Buddhist schools, along with their founders and important texts
- Chinese religious life, including modern Chinese innovations
- The development of Korean Buddhist history from its arrival in the fourth century C.E. to modern times
- Korean Buddhist schools, along with their founders and important texts
- Modern developments in Korean Buddhism
- The development of Japanese Buddhist history from its introduction in the sixth century C.E. to modern times
- Japanese Buddhist schools, along with their founders and important texts
- Recent developments in Japanese Buddhism

## *China: historical sketch*

As early as the first century C.E., Buddhism's presence in Central Asia was clearly visible. Moving north-west out of India from Peshāwār, Buddhism traveled along the trade routes, eventually coming in contact with small communities from the Later Han Dynasty in China that extended into Central Asia along the Silk Route. Many of the families in these communities were both bilingual and bicultural, thus creating an ideal basis for Buddhism to make inroads into China, particularly via entry at Dunhuang.

It is not at all certain whether Buddhism's first entry into China resulted from the fabled account of the Han Emperor Ming's notorious dream in the middle of the first century C.E., or through some other occasion, but there is a clearly historical account of a Chinese emperor practicing Buddhism by the middle of the second century C.E. Additionally, by 148 C.E., a Parthian monk named An Shigao settled in Luoyang to head a team of translators intent on translating Indian Buddhist texts, particularly on meditation, into Chinese. Most of these early translations were of Hīnayāna texts, but the first Mahāyāna missionary, Lokakṣema, worked on a variety of Mahāyāna texts in Luoyang between 168 and 188 C.E.

Despite the fact that the Later Han Dynasty broke apart in the last half of the second century, splitting China into northern and southern parts, the Chinese interest in Buddhism did not diminish. Through the work of innovative figures like Dharmarakṣa, a Chinese-born Buddhist of Scythian lineage, the process of translating Buddhist texts into Chinese continued throughout the Western Jin Dynasty (265–316 C.E.) and the Eastern Jin Dynasty (317–419 C.E.). During this period, monasteries were established, monks ordained, and *sūtras* discussed throughout the south.

Things were not so calm or prosperous in northern China. Under a number of non-Chinese barbarian rulers, nonetheless, Buddhism found favor primarily because it was perceived to be a 'foreign' religion, just as the ruling Huns were largely foreign to China. Eager to take advantage of the monks' knowledge of meditation and the so-called powers derived therefrom, these rulers were sympathetic to Buddhist needs. It was fortuitous for the fledgling Buddhist community that sometime around 310 C.E., a Kuchean monk named Fotudeng apppeared in northern China and gained an influential position in the Later Zhao Dynasty, serving as court advisor for more than two decades and largely protecting the Buddhist effort.

Fotudeng is also known for his two chief disciples, Daoan (312–385 C.E.) and Huiyuan (334–416 C.E.). They encouraged and transacted the translation of a wide variety of Mahāyāna texts, supported a growing Buddhist *sangha* that now included nuns as well as monks, and fostered an intellectual atmosphere that was exciting. Consequently, by the time of the arrival of Kumārajīva (344–413 C.E.), a great Buddhist translator from Kuchea, the Chinese *sangha* was prepared for a new infusion of Buddhist ideas from India. These early Buddhist translators are generally referred to as Buddho-Taoists because they imparted their uniquely Buddhist message through a largely Taoist vocabulary.

By the time of the Northern Wei Dynasty (386–534 C.E.), most of the Buddhist elite had fled south, continuing their literary activity. Under the Northern Wei Dynasty, the *sangha* grew prosperous and highly corrupt, eventually becoming victimized by an extensive Buddhist persecution in 446 C.E. that lasted eight years.

## The anti-Buddhist persecution of 845 C.E.

The high point of Chinese Buddhism occurred during the Tang Dynasty (618–906 C.E.). During this period, monasteries grew and prospered, monks and nuns thrived, and Buddhism was profoundly influential in Chinese culture. Yet by 845 C.E., in the midst of internal political strife, rivalry between the Buddhists and Taoists resulted in the most severe persecution of Buddhism in Chinese history. During a one-year period, virtually all temples were destroyed, monks and nuns were returned to lay life, texts were burned, and metal objects were confiscated and melted down. Although the proscription had but a brief duration, the results were devastating for Chinese Buddhism: the predominantly intellectual schools of Chinese Buddhism disappeared, the economic base of the monasteries was completely devastated, and the libraries (and the literary histories they preserved) were decimated. Even the practice-oriented schools of Chan and Jingtu suffered serious losses, and Buddhism never regained its previous status in Chinese history.

Further, Chinese Buddhism had become highly sectarian with the appearance of a series of 'classical' schools: (1) Jushe, founded by Paramārtha, (2) Sanlun, founded by Kumārajīva, and Faxiang, organized by Xuanzang; 'scholastic' sects: (1) Tiantai, founded by Huisi and (2) Huayan, founded by Dushun; and 'popular' sects: (1) Chan, founded by Bodhidharma and (2) Jingtu, founded by Tanluan. It was not until the Sui Dynasty (589–617 C.E.) that China was reunified and Buddhism consolidated.

Beginning in the eleventh century, there was a strong re-emergence of traditional Chinese religions, and especially so with respect to Confucianism. During the Yuan dynasty that began around 1280, China was under Mongol rule, and as a result, Tibetan Buddhism became a powerful influence in China. Later, under the Ming dynasty (1368–1643), there was a movement toward a unity in the Buddhist schools. Following the revolution of 1911, in which the Manchu dynasty was toppled and the Republic of China established, the Buddhist community lost much of its influence. Although a 'Chinese Buddhist Society' was founded in 1929 by a powerful monk-reformer named Taixu, Buddhism never regained its previous strength. Despite the formation of the Chinese Buddhist Association under the People's Republic of China (in May 1953), the communist government of China effectively truncated the practice of religion in China and closed down all the major Chinese Buddhist monasteries.

## *Chinese Buddhist schools*

The Chinese academic schools of Buddhism were essentially composed of groups of monks who studied and promoted various philosophical ideas that developed within the spectrum of Buddhist thought. They weren't sects in the traditional Western sense of that word, but rather consisted of groups of individuals who believed a set of particular ideas presented the most accurate representation of the truth. In other words, the various Chinese Buddhist schools were attempting to find ways to explain why the Buddhist texts that had made their way to China from India – and especially the various Hīnayāna and Mahāyāna doctrines they espoused – contradicted each other so significantly. Of the ten principal schools of Chinese Buddhism, six (Jushe, Chengshi, Lü, Zhenyan, Sanlun, and Faxiang) were essentially Indian Buddhist schools that had been transplanted to China. Of the remaining four, two (Tiantai and Huayan) were highly scholastic while two others (Chan and Jingtu) were more popular in nature.

### Jushe

The Jushe school was founded by Paramārtha (c. 499–569) in the sixth century, and organized by Xuanzang (c. 596–664). The name is a transliteration of the Sanskrit text known as the *Abhidharmakośa*, thus making this a Chinese version of the Indian Sarvāstivādin *Abhidharma* school. This school emphasized that the elemental building blocks of reality, known as *dharmas*, were real, and therefore presented a realistic view of the Buddhist universe. Although the *Abhidharma* philosophy was an essential part of Chinese Buddhism, this school was never extremely popular in Chinese Buddhism.

### Chengshi

This school is based on an Indian text known as the *Satyasiddhi Śāstra*, written by Harivarman (c. 250–350 C.E.). It was translated into Chinese by the famous Chinese translator Kumārajīva (344–413). Although it was technically a Hīnayāna text, its notions about the emptiness of *dharmas* were very much like those of the Mahāyāna tradition. The text eventually became associated with the Chinese Mādhyamika tradition.

### Lü

This school of Buddhism emerged in the Tang Dynasty of Chinese history and emphasized the *Vinaya* tradition as opposed to doctrinal, philosophical issues. Founded by Daoxuan (596–667), it relied on the Dharmaguptaka *Vinaya*, translated into Chinese by Buddhayaśas and Chu Fo-nien in 412 C.E. as the '*Vinaya in Four Parts*' (*Sifenlü*). This particular *Vinaya* contained 250 rules for monks and 348 rules for nuns, and seems to have been more important in Chinese Buddhism, both Hīnayāna and Mahāyāna, than any of the numerous other complete *Vinayas* possessed by the various Indian Buddhist schools. Although most scholars tend to indicate that this strong emphasis on observance of *Vinaya* reflected Daoxuan's position requiring both monastic discipline and doctrinal teaching in the practice of Chinese Buddhism, they fail to suggest just why the Dharmaguptaka *Vinaya* became the version of choice in China. It might be conjectured that the Dharmaguptaka *Vinaya* is the only Hīnayāna *Vinaya* to include rules governing the method of observance at *stūpas*, a practice which by 600 C.E. was an important aspect of Chinese Buddhism. This school was also the basis for the Japanese *Vinaya* school, known as Ritsu, brought to Japan by Jianzhen in 754 C.E.

## Zhenyan

This was a Buddhist Tantric school, introduced into China during the eighth century. It was probably introduced around 720 C.E. by Śubhākarasiṃha, where it was popular at the Tang Dynasty court. Its name means 'true or efficient word', corresponding to the Sanskrit term '*mantra*', and represents the clearest form of Vajrayāna Buddhism in China. As an independent Buddhist school, it was popular only for a short time, probably no more than two centuries. It was, nonetheless, brought back to Japan by Kūkai (774–835 C.E.), where it was known as the Shingon school.

## Sanlun

Sanlun Buddhism is called the 'Three Treatise School', and is a classical school of Buddhism in China. It was founded by Kumārajīva (344–413 C.E.) based on Nāgārjuna's *Mūlamādhyamika-kārikās* and *Dvādaśa-dvāra Śāstra* as well as *Āryadeva's Śata Śāstra*, hence the name 'Three Treatise School'. It corresponds to the Indian Mādhyamika school of Buddhism. Kumārajīva passed the teaching on to his disciples, especially Daosheng (360–434), Sengchao (374–414), and Senglang (d. 615). Following Kumārajīva's death, a period of decline in Sanlun was experienced, with interest reawakened by Jizang (549–623), considered to be the greatest master of the Sanlun school. After Jizang, the school lost importance in China, but was eventually exported to Japan via a Korean student of Jizang.

## Faxiang

Faxiang is a Chinese Buddhist school organized by Xuanzang (596–664 C.E.) and his disciple Kuiji (632–682 C.E.) from the Shelun school begun by Paramārtha. The school name is a Chinese rendering of the Sanskrit term *dharma-lakṣaṇa* which means '*marks of the dharmas*'. It is based on the writings of Asaṅga and Vasubandhu, and corresponds to the Indian Yogācāra school. The major text of the school is Xuanzang's *Cheng weishi lun* (*Vijñaptimātratā Siddhi* in Sanskrit). Consistent with the basic Yogācāra ideology, the central concept of the school is a development of Vasubandhu's notion that 'everything is ideation only' (*idam sarvam vijñaptimātrakam*). It upholds the theory of eight consciousnesses, with seeds of karmic experiences being stored in the *ālaya-vijñāna* or storehouse consciousness. It classifies all apparently existent reality into 100 *dharmas* organized in five categories, and affirms three levels of truth (as opposed to the Mādhyamika school's notion of two levels). The school did not fare well after Xuanzang and Kuiji, and was severely undermined by the anti-Buddhist persecution of 845 C.E. It was known as the Hossō school in Japanese Buddhism.

## Tiantai

Tiantai is a school of Chinese Buddhism founded by Huisi (515–576 C.E.), organized by Zhiyi (538–597 C.E.), and largely based on the teaching of the *Lotus Sūtra*. The name of the school is taken from the name of the mountain on which Zhiyi exercised: Tiantai Shan. Although Zhiyi actually wrote very little, his teachings were collected and preserved by one of his disciples, Guanding (561–632). These teachings focused primarily on the *Lotus Sūtra* and included three great works: (1) *Miaofa lianhua jing xuanyi* (*Profound Meaning of the Lotus Sūtra*), (2) *Miaofa lianhua jing wenju* (*Commentary on the Lotus Sūtra*), and (3) *Mohe Zhiguan* (*Great Concentration and Insight*). The Tiantai system is explained in five chronological periods. The first, or *Avataṃsaka Sūtra* Period, is said to have lasted only three weeks, and dated from the Buddha's attainment of enlightenment. Because his disciples did not understand his teaching, he began the second period, known as the *Āgama* Period, lasting twelve years, and during which time the Buddha preached his basic but not final or complete teaching. The third, or *Vaipulya* period, lasted eight years and presented the basic Mahāyāna teachings. In the fourth period, known as the *Mahāprajñāpāramitā* period and lasting twenty-two years, he emphasized the doctrine of *śūnyatā*, as taught in the Perfection of Wisdom literature. The fifth and final period, called the *Lotus Sūtra* period, corresponds to the last eight years of the Buddha's life, and here the Buddha taught the doctrine of Ekayāna, that there is really only one vehicle, and that the *Śrāvaka-yāna*, *Pratyeka-buddha-yāna*, and *Bodhisattva-yāna* are only apparent contrasts. Additionally, Tiantai classifies the Buddha's doctrine into two quartets of teachings with the first including (1) sudden doctrine, (2) gradual doctrine, (3) secret doctrine, and (4) indeterminate doctrine. Sudden doctrine was taught in the *Avataṃsaka* period. Gradual doctrine was taught over the second, third, and fourth chronological stages. Secret doctrine and indeterminate doctrine were used when the Buddha taught disciples of differing capacities at the same time. The second quartet of teachings includes (1) *Piṭaka* doctrine, (2) common doctrine, (3) special doctrine, and (4) round or perfect doctrine. In the *Avataṃsaka* period special and round doctrines were taught. The *Āgama* period utilized only the *Piṭaka* doctrine. The *Vaipulya* period utilized all four of these doctrines, and the *Mahāprajñāpāramitā* period employs mostly the round doctrine, but also the common and special doctrines. Only the *Lotus Sūtra* period can be considered totally round and complete.

## Huayan

Huayan is a school of Chinese Buddhism derived from the *Huayan Ching* or *'Flower Ornament Sūtra'* (Sanskrit: *Avataṃsaka Sūtra*) and playing an important role in Tang Dynasty history. The text from which the school takes its origin was presumably translated into Chinese by Buddhabhadra around 420 C.E. The school itself was founded by Dushun (557–640 C.E.) and organized by Fazang (643–712 C.E.). Its fundamental tenet is sometimes referred to as the 'Buddhist teaching of totality' because of the school's emphasis on the interpenetration of all phenomena. This idea is expressed through the doctrine of *Dharma-dhātu* or mutual causality, and the notion that principle (*li*) and phenomena (*shi*) are interdependent. Like other Mahāyāna schools, it affirms the idea of emptiness (*śūnyatā*), identifying the ideal realization as suchness (*tathatā*). Like other Chinese scholastic schools, it did not fare well in the aftermath of the anti-Buddhist persecution of 845 C.E. It was taken to Japan in the eighth century, becoming known as the Kegon school.

## Chan

Chan is a Buddhist school in China whose name is presumably a transliteration of the Sanskrit term *'dhyāna'*, meaning meditation, and thus identifying the major thrust of the school. The Chan school traces its beginnings to Bodhidharma, an Indian meditation master who arrived in north China sometime between 516 and 526 C.E. and is reckoned to be the first Chinese patriarch (and twenty-eighth Indian patriarch) of the school. Bodhidharma passed on his teaching lineage to his disciple Huike, and a line of transmission was thus established in China. The history of the school is not without controversy in that the identity of the sixth patriarch was questioned, with one group arguing for Shenxiu (606–706 C.E.) and another for Huineng (638–713). Eventually Huineng wins out by offering a better poetic response demonstrating his qualifications. Huineng's Chan is thoroughly Mahāyāna, emphasizing emptiness (*śūnyatā*) and the suddenness of the enlightenment experience (*wu*). Eventually, a monastic tradition for Chan emerged based on the rules of Bozhang Huai-hai (720–814) and geared to a Chinese lifestyle that was different from that of Indian Buddhism. During the Tang Dynasty, Chan divided into five 'houses', only two of which survived (eventually merging during the Ming Dynasty): (1) Linji, founded by Linji Yixuan, and (2) Caodong, founded by Dongshan Liangjie (807–869) and Caoshan Benji (840–901). Linji was taken to Japan by Eisai as Rinzai Zen, while Caodong was taken to Japan as Sōtō by Dōgen. Chan practice emphasizes meditation, and, depending on the school, may require enigmatic sayings called *gongan* (*kōan* in Japanese), reflection on which is designed to bring the mind beyond logic to direct experience of reality. Great emphasis is put on the relationship between the master and the disciple, with the master urging the student on through skillful means and great compassion.

## Jingtu

This is the formal title of the 'Pure Land School' in China (corresponding to the Jōdo Shū in Japanese Buddhism). Devotion to Amitābha Buddha was, prior to Huiyuan (344–416 C.E.), an optional practice within Buddhism. Huiyuan established this enterprise as an independent activity, and developed a new Buddhist school around the practice by forming the White Lotus Society in 402 C.E. His disciple Tanluan (476–542) organized the school, and is claimed as the first Chinese patriarch of the Jingtu Zong. They emphasize Amitābha's (shortened to Amita and rendered Amituo in Chinese) vow to cause all faithful beings to be reborn in his paradise, focusing religious practice on repetition of the phrase known as the *Nianfo*: '*Nanmo Amituofo*', literally meaning, '*Homage to Amita Buddha*'. This practice is also used in the Japanese version of the Pure Land school, where it is called the '*Nembutsu*' ('*Namu Amida Butsu*'). Because the school relies on the saving grace of Amitābha Buddha, it is often referred to as the 'easy path', of dependence on outside help (*zili* in Chinese; *tariki* in Japanese). Textually, the school utilizes the *Sukhāvatīvyūha Sūtras* and the *Amitāyurdhyāna Sūtra*. The school was passed down through a succession of masters including Daozhuo (562–645), Shandao (613–681), and Cimin (680–748). Due to its simplicity of practice, it was better able to survive periods of decline (*mo-fa* in Chinese; *mappō* in Japanese), and thus weathered the anti-Buddhist persecution of 845 C.E. better than virtually all other Buddhist schools. It was founded in Japan by Hōnen (1133–1212), where it remains among the most popular Buddhist schools.

## *Chinese Buddhist religious life*

Because Chinese Buddhism has been influenced by indigenous Chinese practices throughout its history, and especially so with respect to Taoist ideals, there are apparent disparities between Indian and Chinese Buddhist life. Unlike their Indian counterparts, Chinese monastics generally did not beg for their food, and were routinely supplied by offerings from lay donors. Moreover, vegetarianism became the normative practice in Chinese monasteries despite the fact that meat-eating is not expressly forbidden by the *Vinaya*. In addition, monasteries often became

### Modern Chinese Buddhist innovations

Although there are few Chinese Buddhist activities on the mainland, in Taiwan a number of far-reaching Buddhist organizations have emerged in the last several decades. Among these are Fo Guang Shan, which has built enormous Buddhist monasteries around the globe through its 'Buddha's Light International Society', and the 'Buddhist Compassion Relief Love and Mercy Foundation' founded in 1966 by a Buddhist nun known as Dharma Master Chen Yen. These organizations have reawakened both the message and visibility of Chinese Buddhism in the modern world.

landholders in their own right, some of which accumulated significant wealth. Family life in Chinese monasteries mirrored traditional Chinese family life, with elaborate tonsure relationships and hierarchies existing in most Chinese monasteries.

The monastic and lay communities were united through a series of festivals and rituals reflecting significant days in the religious calendar. Some of these festivals honored holidays inherited from Indian Buddhism (such as celebrating the Buddha's birthday), while others were distinctly Chinese (such as vegetarian feasts). Because Chinese culture had a significant concern for the afterlife, 'merit books' were kept which provided a basis for other-worldly expectations. And since both the Indian and Chinese Buddhist tradition afforded a significant role to shamanism, Chinese Buddhists were concerned with various deities and non-ordinary forces.

## *Korea: historical sketch*

Prior to the introduction of Buddhism, Shamanism was the earliest form of religion in Korea. Buddhism arrived from China in 372 C.E. with the appearance of the monk Shundao, sent by the ruler of the Ch'in Dynasty to the Koguryŏ court of King Sosurim (371–384 C.E.), which ruled the northern portion of the Korean peninsula. A monastery named Ibullan was built for Shundao, and he was followed by a Serindian monk known as Mālānanda who spread Buddhist teaching to the kingdom of Paekche, in the south-western portion of the peninsula, in 384 C.E. The third of the 'three kingdoms' of Korea, Silla (in south-eastern Korea), was less developed than the other two, and Buddhism was not accepted until 527 C.E., during the reign of King Pŏphŭng. Nevertheless, by the beginning of the sixth century, Buddhism had established its overall position, and the practice of sending monks to China for texts and teachings was widespread. In short order, the Tiantai, Vinaya, Sanlun, Satyasiddhi, Nirvana, and Huayan schools were prevalent.

The Kingdom of Silla conquered Paekche in 663 C.E. and Korguryŏ in 668, establishing the period of Unified Silla (688–935), during which time Buddhism

*Figure 9.1* The Katbaui, an image of Maitreya carved out of a hillside

became a dominant religion in Korea. Chan Buddhism, known as Sŏn in Korea, was introduced from China by the monk Pŏmnang prior to the Silla, and became the most predominant form of monastic Buddhism. During the Silla, five Buddhist schools were established, collectively representing the 'Kyo', or scholastic Buddhist tradition in Korea: the Kyeyul (*Vinaya*) School, Hwaŏm School, Haedong School, Pŏpsang School, and Yŏlban School. Buddhism reached its apex in Korea in the Koryŏ Period (918–1392) through considerable construction projects sponsored by the government. In the tenth century the Buddhist Canon was printed, and a new edition printed in the thirteenth century. In the eleventh century, however, a great Buddhist scholar named Ŭich'ŏn traveled to China, and sought to merge the Sŏn and Kyo traditions into a new school based on Tiantai teachings. Ŭich'ŏn was followed by Chinul (1158–1210), who became one of the greatest reformers of Korean Buddhism. Chinul sought to harmonize the great wisdom found in the Kyo *sūtras* with the deep wisdom and insight brought by the Sŏn meditation practices. Chinul's new order became known as the Chogye Order.

During the Chosŏn or Yi Dynasty (1392–1910) Buddhism suffered as Neo-Confucianism, adopted from China, became normative. Within several hundred years, Buddhism was severely suppressed, losing its state support and witnessing a reduction in the number of monasteries and sects. Eventually the number of sects was reduced to two: a meditation sect and a textual sect. By 1623, monks were barred even from living in the capital, with this proviso remaining in effect until 1895.

In the aftermath of the Chosŏn Dynasty, the Japanese gradually assumed more and more control over Korean life. While the Japanese control over Korea ended following the Second World War, it was not before the two major sects of Korean

*Figure 9.2* Senior monks of the Chogye Order at Chogyesa, Seoul, Korea

Buddhism officially coalesced into one group known as the Chogye sect in 1935. Religious recovery has come slowly to Korea, but recent estimates indicate as many as six million Buddhists practicing their faith in South Korea.

## *Korean Buddhist schools*

The Korean Buddhist tradition developed a rich diversity of Buddhist sectarian traditions, imported initially from China, and enriched by the effort of many Korean scholar-practitioner monks.

### Sŏn

This school was brought to Korea by a monk named Pŏmnang who had studied Chan with the Chinese figure Daoxin (580–651 C.E.), the fourth Chan patriarch. He taught Chan practices in Korea, establishing the Sŏn school. By the ninth century, additional Sŏn lineages were established in Korea and within another century, they became highly organized, eventually founding the 'Nine Mountains Sŏn School', with each of the nine schools residing on the mountain from which each took its name.

## Kyeyul

The Kyeyul or *Vinaya* school was the first of the five (Kyo) scholastic schools to arrive in Korea. This school emphasized the institutional monastic precepts in an attempt to indicate that Buddhism was more than simply meditative practices, or doctrinal ideas, and that the success of Buddhism depended on a morally adept *sangha* of practitioners.

## Hwaŏm

This school was founded by Ŭisang (625–702 C.E.). He traveled to China where he studied with Zhiyan (602–669), the second Chinese patriarch of the Huayan tradition. He returned to Korea in 670 C.E., founding a monastery known as Pusŏk-sa in 676. This temple became the home of the Korean branch of Huayan Buddhism known as the Hwaŏm Order.

## Haedong

This school was based on the teachings of Ŭisang's friend Wŏnhyo. A great scholar, Wŏnhyo emphasized the importance of the *Avataṃsaka Sūtra*, but wanted to find a way to provide a sense of unity among the Korean Buddhist schools. His new school sought to practice *hwa-jaeng* or 'the harmonization of all disputes'.

## Pŏpsang

The fourth scholastic school of the Silla Period was created by Wŏnch'ŭk (613–696 C.E.), a scholar who went to China to study Yogācāra Buddhism in Chang'an. He maintained the traditional Yogācāra approach that all phenomena are mind-based, and that true realization involved transcending the apparent but incorrect distinction between mind and the phenomenal world of objects.

## Yŏlban

The Yŏlban school is called the 'Nirvana School'. It was based on the *Nirvāṇa Sūtra*, and focused on the belief that all beings are endowed with Buddha-nature, an inherent purity that could be realized by engaging in proper Buddhist practice.

Although the above schools predominated in Korean Buddhism, the Chinese version of Tiantai Buddhism existed in Korea, as did Tantric Buddhism. In

## Modern developments in Korean Buddhism

When the Japanese government annexed Korea in August 1910, the Chosŏn Dynasty officially ended. While Buddhism was initially enhanced, allowing monks to travel freely and enter cities for the first time in hundreds of years, the enthusiasm was quickly erased by the Temple Ordinance of 1911, which placed control of all Buddhist activities under the Japanese governor-general. In so doing, the entirety of the Korean *sangha* was targeted for control by the Sōtō Zen school of Japanese Buddhism. Monks were encouraged to marry, resulting in a 1926 ordinance removing formal rules prohibiting marriage for monastics. Eventually, the Kyo and Sŏn schools united into the Chogye Order in 1935. Following World War II, when Korea regained its independence, the *sangha* was once again split between those monks who remained celibate and those who did not. Nearly a decade later, when the government supported a celibate order, violence erupted, and South Korea (in 1962) once again identified two distinct orders: the original and celibate Chogye Order founded in 1935, and a new group known as the T'aego Order with married clergy. A nuns' order has been re-established in South Korea, along with a serious attempt to promote a strong and vibrant Buddhist culture. In addition Korean groups have begun appearing throughout the Western world, emphasizing a lay-oriented form of Sŏn practice.

addition, a modern form of Buddhism known as Wŏn also developed, started in 1924 by Chung-bin Pak (1891–1943), also known as Sot'aesan. Wŏn Buddhism is a 'reformed' school of Buddhism whose religious practice involves worship of a black circle said to represent the *dharma-kāya*. For this reason, it is called the 'round' or 'circular' school. Wŏn Buddhism is not exclusively monastic, as monks are permitted to marry. Since 1953 it has been on the rise in Korea, with over 500,000 disciples and 200 temples by 1975. It has also become popular in many Western countries.

## *Japan: historical sketch*

Japan's indigenous religious tradition is Shintō, generally referred to as the 'way of the gods' (*kami*). Into this environment, Buddhism was introduced in 538 C.E. from Korea, when emissaries were sent bearing Buddha-images and scriptures. Within half a century, the regent, Prince Shōtoku, declared Buddhism to be the state religion. Some sources even compare Shōtoku to the Indian king Aśoka. As such, close ties between the Buddhist *sangha* and secular power were established.

In the Nara Period of Japanese history (710–784 C.E.), an extensive program of temple construction was promoted by Emperor Shōmu. Shōmu's daughter Shōtoku continued efforts favorable to Buddhism. During this period, six academic traditions of Buddhism were imported from China, essentially without modification: (1) Jōjitsu, (2) Kusha, (3) Sanron, (4) Hossō, (5) Ritsu, and (6) Kegon. Study and exegesis of Buddhist texts took place, as well as much emphasis on Buddhist philosophical matters.

By 794 C.E., when the capital was moved to Heian (modern-day Kyōto), Buddhism was ready to blossom in Japan. Consequently, the Heian Period (794–1185) may well be considered the high point in Japanese Buddhist history. Two more important Buddhist schools were imported from China: (1) Tendai, introduced by Saichō (also called Dengyō Daishi) in 805 C.E. and (2) Shingon, introduced by Kūkai (also called Kōbō Daishi) in 816 C.E. Saichō set up a training temple on Mount Hiei, utilizing a twelve-year training period for those monks who came to study and meditate with him. His temple prospered, housing as many as thirty thousand monks. Kūkai, on the other hand, established the headquarters of Shingon on Mount Kōya, about fifty miles from the capital. Emphasizing the arts and drawing on his personal brilliance, disciples flocked to study with Kūkai. Combining his writing and systematizing of Buddhist doctrine with a keen aesthetic sense, Kūkai became a court favorite. At one point, Mount Kōya was home to almost a thousand temples, and Shingon became even more popular than Tendai. Nonetheless, by the end of the Heian Period, both schools became decadent. By the middle of the eleventh century, it was felt that a period of decline of the *Dharma* (known as *mappō*) had befallen Japan.

In the next period of Japanese history, known as the Kamakura Period (1192–1338), rule was conducted by military Shōguns and a warrior class known as samurai. A number of new schools of Buddhism arose in this period, perhaps in response to a shift in power from the capital to the provinces. Local temples were supported, and both power and culture began to suffuse to the peasant class for the first time. The first new school to appear was the Pure Land school (Jōdo Shū), begun by Hōnen (1133–1212). Moved by the notion of *mappō*, Hōnen argued that recitation of the name of Amida would ensure followers of rebirth in the Western Paradise following their death. Hōnen's disciple Shinran (1173–1263) carried this notion one step further by suggesting that one could not earn their way into the Western Paradise, but rather it was Amida's vow to save all beings that produced the desired result. Shinran's innovation was thus referred to as Jōdo Shinshū or the 'True Pure Land' school. Around the same time, a fisherman's son known as Nichiren (1222–1282) founded a new school named after him. Its basic premise was that the truth of Buddhism was to be found in the *Lotus Sūtra*, with all other forms of Buddhism being wrong. For Nichiren, salvation was to be obtained by reciting the name of the *Lotus Sūtra* in the following invocation: *Nam Myōhō Renge Kyō* (*'Homage to the Scripture on the Lotus of the Good Teaching'*) while staring intently at a diagram known as the

*Gohonzon*. His program was fiercely nationalistic, intending to deliver the Japanese people from social and political chaos and ruin. Two major schools of Zen were also introduced during the Kamakura Period. Upon returning (in 1191) from a trip to China, Eisai (1141–1215) began Rinzai Zen in which the primary mode of attaining enlightenment (*satori*) was the use of seemingly nonsensical sayings known as *kōans*, aimed at moving the mind beyond conceptualization to a direct perception of reality. Rinzai was especially successful among the samurai. More popular with the masses was Sōtō Zen, begun by Dōgen (1200–1253) upon his return from China in 1227. In the Sōtō form of Zen, one practices *zazen*, or sitting meditation, with the intention of 'just sitting' (known as *shikantaza*), of manifesting the notion that one already is a Buddha. Because of its simplicity, it was sometimes called 'farmer's Zen'. In any case, the Kamakura Period also witnessed a general development of the arts, and particularly the tea ceremony, Noh theatre productions, and Haiku poetry.

The Ashikaga Period (1333–1573) divided the country among feudal lords, leading to continual turmoil and eventually civil war. Only the Zen monasteries remained peaceful places in this period. The rest of Japanese Buddhism was singularly militant. Buddhist militancy was extinguished by the Shōgun Nobunaga who destroyed the temples on Mount Hiei in 1571, later decimating the Shingon center at Negoro and the Jōdo Shinshō complex in Osaka.

In 1603 Iyeyasu Tokugawa established a military dictatorship that lasted until 1867. This era, known as the Tokugawa Period, marked a period when Japan completely isolated itself from the outside world. Although there was little religious liberty, various Buddhist schools kept their traditions alive with scholarship and similar efforts. Encouraged by Shintō nationalism, the Meiji Restoration began in 1868, lasting up to the Second World War. In the time since 1945, nearly two hundred new sects have arisen in Buddhism, generally referred to as 'new religions' (*shinkō shūkyō*).

## *Japanese Buddhist schools*

As noted above, Buddhist schools were imported to Japan during three major periods of Japanese history: the Nara Period, during which time six scholastic schools were imported; the Heian Period, during which time the Tendai and Shingon schools appeared; and the Kamakura Period, during which time the Pure Land traditions, Zen, and Nichiren appeared. Collectively, the Buddhist schools helped shape Japanese culture, influencing everything from religious life to fine arts and architecture.

### Kusha

The Kusha school is based on the Indian Buddhist text known as the *Abhidharmakośa*, from which the school takes its name. It reflects the teachings of the Chinese Jushe school, offering a detailed analysis of the elements of existence (*dharmas*), which were held to be real. The school was introduced to Japan in 658 C.E. by two monks who had studied with the famous Chinese monk Xuanzang.

## Jōjitsu

This school is named after the Indian Buddhist text to which its name refers: the *Satyasiddha Śāstra*. It is based on the Chinese Chengshi school, and was brought to Japan by a Korean monk named Hyegwan (Ekwan in Japanese), who traveled from Koguryŏ, arrived in Japan in 625 C.E., and settled at Hōryū-ji temple. This school offered a critique of the Kusha school, emphasizing the emptiness (*śūnyatā*) of all elements.

## Sanron

This school is another of six academic traditions of Japanese Buddhism during the Nara Period, imported without substantial modification, from China. It corresponds to the Indian Mādhyamika and Chinese Sanlun schools of Buddhism. The school was brought to Japan in 625 C.E. (along with the Jōjitsu school) by the Korean monk Ekwan, a disciple of Jizang's who lived at Genkō-ji temple. The Sanron school never had the impact on Japan that its counterpart did on China.

## Hossō

This school is the Japanese version of the Chinese Faxiang (Sanskrit: Yogācāra) school of Buddhism. The teachings were introduced to Japan on at least four separate occasions by: (1) Dōshō, who went to China in 653 C.E. and studied under Xuanzang, (2) Chitsū and Chidatsu, who went to China in 658 also studying under Xuanzang, (3) Chihō, Chiran, and Chiyū, who went to China in 703 studying under Zhizhou, and (4) Gembō, who went to China in 716 and studied under Zhizhou. Dōshō's lineage, passed on through the famous monk Gyōgi (668–749), is referred to as the Southern Temple, while Gembō's lineage is called the Northern Temple.

## Ritsu

This is the Japanese *Vinaya* school of Buddhism. It was brought to Japan from China by Jianzhen, a monk of the Lü school, in 754 C.E. He built an ordination platform at Tōdai-ji temple, as well as several other branches. This school adhered to the Dharmaguptaka *Vinaya*, known in Chinese as the '*Vinaya* in Four Parts' (*Sifenlü*). It contained 250 rules for monks and 348 rules for nuns. In the Heian Period (794–1185) the school declined, especially because the Tendai master Saichō eliminated the formal *Vinaya* as too rigorous, retaining only a modified version. It experienced a modest revival during the Kamakura Period (1192–1338), and continues today as a small school.

## Kegon

This school of Japanese Buddhism is derived from the *Kegon-kyō* or '*Flower Ornament Sūtra*' (Sanskrit: *Avataṃsaka Sūtra*; Chinese: *Huayan Ching*) and played a role in the Nara period of Japanese history. Brought to Japan by the Chinese monk Shen-hsiang around 740 C.E., it was avidly promoted by Emperor Shōmu. The main monastery of the school was Tōdai-ji in Nara, where the emperor built a huge statue of the Buddha Vairocana. The emperor's keen interest in Kegon was political as much as religious, and the school was primarily attractive to the elite. With the coming of the Heian Period, the Kegon school lost most of its influence in Japanese Buddhist culture.

## Tendai

This Japanese Buddhist school is equivalent to the Chinese Tiantai, brought to Japan by Saichō (767–822 C.E.) in the eighth century. After building a small monastery on Mount Hiei, Saichō was sent to China to study, focusing essentially on Tiantai, but also including other schools. Upon returning, he consolidated his teaching into the Tendai school. Doctrinally, there is little difference between the Chinese and Japanese versions of the school, and both lay great emphasis on the *Lotus Sūtra* as the primary scripture. A twelve-year training period for Tendai monks was instituted, indicative of the great emphasis the school placed on the moral life. There is also an esoteric aspect to the Tendai school.

## Shingon

This is the esoteric school of Buddhism in Japan, founded by Kūkai (774–835 C.E.). Ordained at twenty, Kūkai traveled to China in 804, studying the Zhenyan-yen or 'True Word' school extensively. Upon his return to Japan in 805, he became head monk at Tōdai-ji, but left to found his own monastery on Mt. Kōya in 816. This monastery became the main center of the Shingon school. Like all schools of Buddhist *Tantra*, the Shingon school emphasizes ritual practices involving *mantras*, *maṇḍalas*, and *mudrās*, as well as various meditational practices. It identifies with Vairocana Buddha, and engages in a variety of initiation (*abhiṣeka*) and empowerment rites.

## Jōdo Shū and Jōdo Shinshū

The Pure Land School (Jōdo Shū) of Japanese Buddhism was founded by Hōnen (1133–1212). Although originally a Tendai monk, Hōnen embraced the Pure Land ideal primarily through the teachings of Shandao and Genshin after having become convinced that the Tendai path was becoming increasingly unworkable as a means for attaining salvation. Of course, Pure Land teachings had been in Japan at least since the time of Ennin (794–864), who had studied it and other traditions while in China, but Hōnen is regarded as the 'founder' of the school in Japan. The textual basis of the school remained the *Larger and Smaller Sukhāvatīvyūha Sūtras*, as well as the *Amitāyurdhyāna Sūtra*, and the religious practice focused on the *Nembutsu*, thus identifying it as an 'other-power' or 'easy path' approach to salvation. For Hōnen, the formula '*Namu Amida Butsu*' was a means of strengthening one's faith in Amida, not merely an expression of trust, and was considered by him an appropriate religious practice in a period of *Dharma* decline (called *mappō* in Japanese Buddhism). Unlike its later offshoot, Jōdo Shinshū, Hōnen's school continued the Buddhist monastic tradition. Hōnen's school was both threatening and alienating to the more formal and established Buddhist schools of the time, resulting in a five-year exile, terminated only one year prior to his death.

The True Pure Land School (Jōdo Shinshū) of Japanese Buddhism was founded by Shinran (1173–1263), and based on the Jōdo Shū of Hōnen (1133–1212) that preceded it. The school is based on the Pure Land texts which emphasize the saving grace of Amida (Sanskrit: Amitābha) Buddha. Shinran's religious practice focuses on the recitation of the formula known as the *Nembutsu*, precisely stated as *Namu Amida Butsu* ('*Homage to Amida Buddha*'). This formula is an expression of complete trust in Amida, recitation of which presumably guarantees the disciple's rebirth in the Pure Land. Since it is Amida's effort that results in the religious advancement of the disciple, this school falls under the designation of *tariki*, the 'other-power' or 'easy path' tradition in Japanese Buddhism. Unlike many other schools of Japanese Buddhism, Jōdo Shinshū is an exclusively lay organization with no formally monastic tradition. Nonetheless, it has an extensive series of temples and functioning clergy. The head of the organization is known as the abbot, located at the main temple, with the position being maintained on a hereditary basis. Today Jōdo Shinshū has two main divisions (Ōtani and Honganji), both having their main centers in Kyoto. Collectively, the school maintains the largest membership of all Japanese Buddhist schools.

## Zen

Zen is a Japanese technical term (short for *Zen-na*) said to be a transliteration of the Chinese term *Chan* or *Channa*, which in turn, is a transliteration of the Sanskrit technical term for meditation or *dhyāna*. It refers to a meditative practice in which one seeks to bring the mind under control as a step in the process of attaining enlightenment. Although a variety of Zen 'schools' developed in Japan, they all emphasize Zen as a teaching that does not depend on sacred texts, that provides the potential for direct realization, that the realization attained is none other than the Buddha nature possessed by each sentient being, and that transmission occurs outside the teaching. This last statement is traced to the apparently initial transmission of the teaching from the Buddha Śākyamuni to Kāśyapa in a silent sermon on Vulture's Peak. In so doing, a lineage was established which is considered unbroken, despite Buddhism's transmission into a large variety of cultures in its 2,500 year history.

The Rinzai Zen school of Buddhism was brought to Japan by Eisai Zenji (1141–1215) and continued the Linji Chan tradition from China by combining meditative practice with the use of *kōans*. Eisai traveled to China first in 1168 and again in 1187, receiving the seal of enlightenment in the Huang-long lineage of the Linji Chan tradition, known in Japan as the Ōryō school. Although this was the first Zen school in Japan, it died out rather quickly, being supplanted by the Rinzai Yōgi school of Zen. The Rinzai Yōgi school has produced a long line of famous masters dating back to the thirteenth century. They paved the way for more recent individuals like Hakuin Zenji (1685–1768). The Rinzai school of Zen, along with Sōtō, is one of two active schools today. It continues to rely on *kōan* practice and strict discipline, and for this reason has become very popular outside Japan.

The Sōtō Zen school of Buddhism was brought to Japan by Dōgen Zenji (1200–1253) and continued the Caodong Chan tradition of China. Originally a student of Eisai (1141–1215), Dōgen went to China in 1223. He experienced enlightenment under the Chan master Tientong Rujing (1163–1228), and received *Dharma* transmission from him. Returning to Japan, he eventually became abbot of Kōshō-ji monastery, and about a decade later founded Daibutsu-ji monastery, later referred to as Eihei-ji, one of the two main monasteries of Sōtō Zen. Although the goal of Sōtō Zen, gaining enlightenment, remains identical to that of Rinzai Zen, the methods of the two main schools of Zen are quite different. Sōtō utilizes a practice known as *shikantaza* or 'just sitting'. It presumes that sitting in meditation itself (i.e., *zazen*) is an expression of Buddha nature. Rinzai combines sitting meditation with the use of *kōans*, enigmatic, riddle-like 'public cases' designed to dramatically push the mind beyond conceptual thought patterns, fostering sudden illumination. Sōtō Zen continues to play a prominent role in modern Japanese Buddhism, and is one of the most popular Zen forms exported outside Japan.

## Nichiren

Nichiren (1222–1282) was the founder of a Japanese Buddhist school named after him and professing the belief that salvation could be attained by reciting the name of the *Lotus Sūtra*. Born into a fisherman's family, Nichiren was ordained at age fifteen, and like many famous Buddhist figures before him, went to study at the Tendai monastic complex on Mount Hiei. While he was critical of the other Buddhist schools of the time, he felt that the Tendai tradition came closest to the true Buddhist message. However, he felt that even this tradition had minimized emphasis on the *Lotus Sūtra*, which he felt was the most important scripture of the school, causing him to leave Mount Hiei in favor of a monastery closer to his home. He set about to personally save Japan from the social and political ruin that he was certain would result from practicing the 'wrong' religion espoused by the traditional Buddhist sects. He even predicted an invasion of Japan. As a result, he professed the notion that the *Lotus Sūtra* was the only Buddhist text suited to religious practice in a time of *Dharma* decline (*mappō*), and that recitation of its title was the means to liberation. The religious practice cultivated by Nichiren involved recitation of the phrase *Nam Myōhō Renge Kyō* or '*Homage to the Scripture of the Lotus of the Good Teaching*', while gazing at a diagram known as the *Gohonzon*, a *maṇḍala*-like form with the above words inscribed on it. His revolutionary notions and approach resulted in his exile,

## Recent developments in Japanese Buddhism

Following Japan's defeat in World War II, religious life changed dramatically. State Shintō, which had been hostile to Japanese Buddhism, was no longer in control. The American occupation provided Japan with a renewed contact with Western culture. The aftermath of the war offered more than just a new secular role for the government, providing an influx of Western political, economic, and intellectual ideas. Formerly Buddhist Sōtō and Rinzai schools, for example, became Komazawa and Hanazono Universities, respectively.

Most significantly, new religions (*shinkō shūkyō*) began to appear and flourish. The most significant of these is Sōka Gakkai, or the 'Society for the Creation of Value', founded by Tsunesabarō Makiguchi in 1938. Based on the teaching of Nichiren, it has promoted a series of profoundly this-worldly goals and personal well-being. More than just a religion, it has developed a political party known as the Kōmeitō, as well as an international organization known as Sōka Gakkai International, with centers in most of the cities of the Western world. Sōka Gakkai is rivaled by another movement, known as Risshō Kōsei-kai, which is also based on the efficacious teaching of the *Lotus Sūtra*. Founded in 1938 by Niwano Nikkyō and Nagamuna Myōkō, it tries to actualize what the school calls the 'seeing self' – identical to the Buddha-nature present in all beings – through societal relationships. Each of these groups has afforded a more equal role to women, offering a more enlightened approach to Buddhism in the modern world.

and he was not allowed to return to Kamakura until 1274, following an attempted Mongol invasion that Nichiren felt vindicated him. A Buddhist school known as the Nichiren-shū grew up around the figure of Nichiren, emphasizing both his emphasis on the efficacy of the *Lotus Sutra* and his extreme sense of Japanese nationalism.

## Key points you need to know

- Although Buddhism was introduced to China in the Han Dynasty, it took centuries to fully acculturate.
- The high point of Chinese Buddhism was the Sui and Tang Dynasties (618–906 C.E.).
- The major Chinese Buddhist schools include: Jushe, Chengshi, Lü, Zhenyan, Sanlun, Faxiang, Tiantai, Huayan, Chan, and Jingtu.
- Buddhism arrived in Korea from China in 373 C.E. and has proceeded intact through many dynasties.
- The major Korean Buddhist schools include: Sŏn, Kyeyul, Hwaŏm, Haedong, Pŏpsang, and Yŏlban.
- Buddhism arrived in Japan from Korea in 538 C.E.
- Many Buddhist schools developed during the Nara Period and the Kamakura Period.
- The major Japanese Buddhist schools include: Kusha, Jōjitsu, Sanron, Hossō, Ritsu, Kegon, Tendai, Shingon, Jōdo and Jōdo Shinshū, Zen, and Nichiren.
- Since 1945 many new religions (*shinkō shūkyō*), many with Buddhist ties, have developed.

## Discussion questions

1. Why were Pure Land and Ch'an Buddhism able to survive the anti-Buddhist persecution of 845 C.E. better than the other Chinese Buddhist schools?
2. Which are the strongest and most successful Buddhist schools in Japan, and how have they achieved that status?
3. How has Korean Buddhism changed in the modern world?

## Further reading

Buswell, Robert. *The Zen Monastic Experience: Buddhist Practice in Contemporary Korea*. Princeton, NJ: Princeton University Press, 1992.

Ch'en, Kenneth. *Buddhism in China: A Historical Survey*. Princeton, NJ: Princeton University Press, 1964.

Ch'en, Kenneth. *The Chinese Transformation of Buddhism*. Princeton, NJ: Princeton University Press, 1974.

Grayson, James Huntley. *Korea: A Religious History*. Oxford: Clarendon Press, 1989.

Kitagawa, Joseph. *Religion in Japanese History*. New York: Columbia University Press, 1966.

Lancaster, Lewis and C. S. Yu (eds). *Introduction to Buddhism in Korea: New Cultural Patterns*. Berkeley, CA: Asian Humanities Press, 1989.

Lopez, Donald, S., Jr. (ed.). *Religions of China in Practice*. Princeton, NJ: Princeton University Press, 1996.

Tanabe, George J., Jr. (ed.). *Religions of Japan in Practice*. Princeton, NJ: Princeton University Press, 1999.

# 10 *Buddhism in Tibet*

## In this chapter

This chapter explores the development of Tibetan Buddhism. It considers the historical development of the tradition, the major schools of Tibetan Buddhism as well as their founders and major texts, famous Buddhist figures and places, *Tantra*, the tradition of the Dalai Lama, and the Tibetan Holocaust.

## Main topics covered

- The historical development of Tibetan Buddhism from the seventh century C.E. up to the present
- The major schools of Tibetan Buddhism: Nyingma, Sakya, Kagyu (and Karma Kagyu), Gelug, Kadampa, and Dzogchen
- Famous Buddhist figures, including Padmasambhava, Atīśa, Tilopa, Nāropa, Marpa, Milarepa, Gampopa, and Tsongkhapa
- *Tantra*, including its basic structure and major texts
- The tradition of the Dalai Lama
- The Chinese annexation of Tibet and its implications for Tibetan Buddhism

## *Historical sketch*

Tibet is sometimes referred to as the 'Land of the Snows', by virtue of its status as the highest country in the world. Situated on about 1.5 million square miles of rigorous and mountainous terrain, it has a population of only about six million people. Located between India and China, it has only minimal resources and few trade routes to connect it with other cultures and economies. Prior to the appearance of Buddhism in Tibet, the pre-Buddhist religion seems to have been a proto-shamanistic tradition known as *Bön*. In this tradition, the central figure was the *bön*, or the individual who cries out to evoke the gods. Two kinds of *Bön* developed in Tibet: White *Bön* and Black *Bön*. The former was a positive tradition, involving suppression of evil spirits

*Figure 10.1* A Tibetan monastery

and the worship of ancient Tibetan deities, while the latter was negative, dealing with black magic and the like. Eventually, many of the *Bön* traditions found their way into Buddhism. John Powers suggested that Buddhism's introduction to Tibet 'is believed to have been accomplished by the efforts of various Buddhas and *bodhisattvas*, who first prepared the populace for the *Dharma* and then assumed human forms in order to propagate it' (Powers, 1995: 221).

Tibet's first historical contact with Buddhism comes in the reign of Songtsen Gampo (Srong-btsan-sgam-po) (616–650 C.E.). Legend suggests that the daughter of King Aṃśuvarman of Nepal married this Tibetan king and established the cult of Tārā. Equally, when the king conquered Chinese border areas, Tibetans went to China to study. And there is a rich history of contact with Central Asian kingdoms such as Khotan and Kuchā. Sometime around 632 C.E., the king sent an emissary to Kaśmīr to establish a script for the Tibetan language.

By the eighth century, King Trisong Detsen (Khri-srong-lDe-brstan) (755–797) established the first Buddhist monastery in Tibet, had Buddhist texts translated from Chinese and Sanskrit, and brought the renowned scholar Śāntarakṣita from Nālandā University to Tibet. He also brought Padmasambhava, an accomplished Tantric master, to Tibet. One Tibetan Buddhist sect, the Nyingma (rNying-ma), claims Padmasambhava as its founder. Precisely because Tibet had contacts with both India and China, there was much controversy, and perhaps even confusion, about Buddhist doctrines and practices.

Eventually, a council was held near Lhasa under the reign of King Trisong Detsen in 792–794. Tibetan Buddhism in the sixth century was complicated by the fact that the king, Songtsen Gampo, was married to both Nepalese and Chinese wives, thus affording a dual input of information and practice relative to Buddhism. Following the completion of the great monastery at Samye (bSam-yas) in 787 C.E., a council was convened there to resolve the differences between the Tantric notions of Padmasambhava, the earlier Indian Buddhist ideals of Śāntarakṣita, and the Chinese viewpoints present. The council took the form of a debate between Śāntarikṣita and a Chinese monk generally called Huashang in the literature. The Chinese monk argued for the notion of 'sudden' enlightenment while Śāntirakṣita argued for 'gradual' enlightenment. Śāntirakṣita also stressed the efficacy of meritorious action which Huashang refuted. The Chinese position was soundly defeated, continuing an Indian basis for the development of Tibetan Buddhism. After the debate, the Chinese participants left the country. As a result of the Indian scholar's victory, Tibetan Buddhism continued to owe its development largely to the Indian tradition.

Despite a short interlude in which Tibetan Buddhism was persecuted under the reign of Lang Darma (gLang-dar-ma) (838–842), the Buddhist tradition prospered in Tibet. Within two hundred years, a great monk-scholar from India named Atīśa arrived in Tibet to infuse new Buddhist understanding into the tradition and to help establish the Tibetan *sangha* on firmer footing. Atīśa's chief disciple Dromdön ('Brom-ston) established the Kadampa (bKa-gdams-pa) school, representing the first Tibetan Buddhist school with a clear historical origin. Later, the Kagyu (bKa-rgyud) school was founded by Marpa (1012–1097), a great Tantric master who had traveled to India for his training. Marpa's lineage was carried on by Milarepa (Mi-la-ras-pa) (1040–1123), a great poet-saint, and Milarepa's disciple Gampopa (sGam-po-pa) (1079–1173) established the first monasteries of this new tradition. Also around this time, the Sakya (Sa-skya) school began (1073), emphasizing scholarship.

The last major school of Tibetan Buddhism, known as Gelug (dGe-lugs), was founded by Tsongkhapa (1357–1419). Modeled on the famous Indian monastic universities, the Gelug school established its own major centers near the capital of Lhasa. Members observed a strict discipline, emphasized both esoteric and exoteric traditions, and distinguished themselves by wearing yellow ceremonial hats (in contrast to the red hats worn by the other sects). Tsongkhapa's third successor was identified as an incarnation of Avalokiteśvara, and was proclaimed the first Dalai Lama, seen as both the religious and political head of Tibetan Buddhism. This lineage continues today, with the fourteenth Dalai Lama having been enthroned in 1950, just prior to the Communist Chinese invasion of Tibet. Over time, Tibetan Buddhism spread to Sikkim, Bhutan, Mongolia, and even into the Soviet Union.

*Figure 10.2* Monastery prayer wheels

## *Major schools of Tibetan Buddhism*

Tibetan Buddhism is best known for its four major schools traced below. They all reflect a Mahāyāna philosophical orientation, and are associated with particular teaching lineages, which are preserved today in the modern world. Each lineage traces its heritage back to particular Indian teachers, and to special practices, yet they all reflect a common Indian Buddhist heritage.

### Nyingma (rNying-ma)

This is the earliest of four major schools of Tibetan Buddhists, literally titled 'Ancient Ones'. The school of Buddhism traces its origin back to the foundation of Buddhism in Tibet in the seventh and eighth centuries. It seems to possess authentic Indian Buddhist teachings brought to Tibet primarily by Padmasambhava. It is perhaps the least political of the Tibetan Buddhist schools. Early in its history, Tibetan Buddhism was persecuted by King Lang Darma (836–842 C.E.). In response to the threat, many of the sacred texts were hidden by Padmasambhava and others for protection and designated *Terma* (*gter-ma*) or 'treasures' to be resurrected at a safer time. Thus, the Nyingma school has the largest corpus of *Terma* literature of any of the four schools. Its religious practice revolves around the Dzogchen (rDzogs-chen) (or *Atiyoga*) technique. Within about a century there was to be something of a renaissance in western and central Tibet, focusing on figures such as Atīśa, Marpa, and others, and radically changing the nature of Tibetan Buddhism, resulting in three new major schools of Buddhism.

## Sakya (Sa-skya)

This school of Tibetan Buddhism was founded by Drokmi ('Brog-mi), taking its name from the monastery he founded in 1073. Drokmi was a contemporary of Atīśa, and studied at Vikramaśīla monastery in India for eight years. In his teaching he emphasized the 'new' *Tantras* of Atīśa and Rinchen Sangpo (Rin-chen bzang-po). The abbots of the monastery founded by Drokmi (and coming from the Khon family) had enormous power during the twelfth and thirteenth centuries, were highly respected for their extensive learning, and were permitted to marry. Drokmi passed on the Sakya lineage to his son, and thereafter it was usual to pass the lineage from uncle to nephew. The school was also especially interested in matters of Buddhist logic. Sakya Paṇḍita established a relationship with Mongolia, and his nephew Chögyel Pakpa (Chos-rGyal 'Phags-pa) (1235–1280) was prelate to Kublai Khan. The school also strongly influenced Tsongkhapa and the Gelugs sect. The school is still prominent in the modern world, both in Asia and the West.

## Kagyu (bKa-rgyud)

This Tibetan Buddhist school traces its origins to Marpa (1012–1097) and is regarded as one of the four primary schools of Tibetan Buddhism. Marpa was a Tibetan Buddhist skilled in Sanskrit who traveled to India, eventually receiving Tantric teaching from Tilopa and Nāropa. Based on the teachings he brought back to Tibet, he laid the ground for the Kagyu school, emphasizing the practice of Mahāmudrā and the 'Six Dharmas of Nāropa'.

The 'Six *Dharmas* of Nāropa' are a set of Vajrayāna doctrines taught to Nāropa by his guru Tilopa. These teachings were in turn transmitted to Marpa, Nāropa's student, who brought them to Tibet where they became an instrumental part of the Kagyu school of Buddhism. The six teachings include: (1) the product of inner heat, (2) experience of one's body as illusory, (3) the dream state, (4) clear light perception, (5) the in-between (rebirth) state, and (6) consciousness transference. When properly practiced, the Six *Dharmas* of Nāropa lead to the attainment of supernormal powers known as *siddhi*.

Marpa passed on his teachings to his closest disciple Milarepa (1040–1123) who became the greatest poet-saint in Tibetan history. Milarepa in turn was the spiritual master of Gampopa (1079–1153) who organized the Kagyu school and founded its first monasteries. Following Gampopa, the school subdivided into four major groups and eight lesser schools. In the Kagyu school, much emphasis is placed on the direct transmission of teaching from spiritual master to spiritual heir.

## Karma-Kagyu (Karma bKa-rgyud)

This important subsect of the Kagyu school of Tibetan Buddhism was founded in the twelfth century by Tüsum Khyenpa (Dus-gSum mKhyen-pa) (1110–1193), known as the first Karmapa. The lineage of the tradition is established through the line of Karmapas that has remained unbroken from the time of the founder. The founder of the school built a number of monasteries, with many of his successors expanding their sphere of influence and the importance of the subsect. They are known as the 'Black Hat' sect because of the black hat, supposedly made of the hair of 10,000,000 *ḍākinīs* (or female demons) worn by the Karmapa on certain ritual occasions. The tradition has produced many famous lamas, including the nineteenth century figure Jamgön Kongtrül ('Jam-mgon Kon-sprul) and the most recent Karmapa Rigpe Dorje (1924–1982), who preserved the lineage during and after the Tibetan Holocaust, establishing a major center in Rumtek, Sikkim.

## Gelug (dGe-lug)

This Tibetan Buddhist school was founded by Tsongkhapa (1357–1419). Tsongkhapa, the founder of the school, not only joined the order as a young boy, and had extensive training in both the exoteric and esoteric Buddhist traditions, but also was profoundly influenced by the Kadampa school. Consequently, the Gelug school that Tsongkhapa founded literally means 'School of the Virtuous', and reflects both an emphasis on the *Vinaya* and systematic study of the doctrinal texts. The school is sometimes referred to as the 'Yellow Hat School' because they rejected the traditional red hat of the prior Buddhist schools in favor of the yellow hat now traditional in their group. They became the most influential of the Tibetan Buddhist schools, and once the line of the Dalai Lamas was established within this school, the Gelug school was afforded political leadership as well. Like all other surviving Tibetan Buddhist schools, they pursue their activity in exile in the aftermath of the Tibetan Holocaust.

## Kadampa (bKa-gdams-pa)

The Kadmapa is a Tibetan Buddhist school founded by Dromdön ('Brom-ston) (1008–1064), chief disciple of Atīśa. Apparently the sect received the name Kadampa because it held to the authoritative word (bKa-gdams) of Atīśa as embodied in the *Bodhipathapradīpa* or *'Lamp for the Way of Enlightenment'*. Dromdön and his

*Figure 10.3* Tibetan monks of the Gelukpa Order wearing ceremonial hats

immediate successors were referred to as the 'earlier' Kadampa, and although they did not survive for very long, their traditions were later adopted by Tsongkhapa. Dromdön eventually founded a monastery which housed Atīśa's relics, and was succeeded there by a series of his own disciples. He established a monastery north of Lhasa which became the main center of the school. The school carried on Atīśa's concern for proper monastic practice and Tantric ritual.

## Dzogchen (rDzogs-chen)

Dzogchen is the *Atiyoga* tradition of meditation brought to Tibet by Padmasambhava and Vimalamitra, and forming the essential practice of the Nyingma school of Buddhism. It was systematized by Longchenpa (kLong-chen-pa) in the fourteenth century. In this system, ultimate reality, referred to as *dharma-kāya*, is personified as the Buddha Samantabhadra. In the simplest sense, Dzogchen aims at the pure awareness of this ultimate reality.

### *Famous Buddhist figures and places*

Tibetan Buddhism has benefited from a long series of remarkable figures who have enhanced its tradition and preserved its heritage, despite sometimes incredibly difficult circumstances. These individuals represent the living embodiment of profound religious experience, began teaching lineages that still exist in the modern world, and defined Buddhist practices that have developed the Tibetan tradition. The most famous of these figures are described below.

## Padmasambhava

Padmasambha was a Tantric Mahāsiddha from Kaśmīr who came to Tibet in the late eighth century and was instrumental in the development of early Tibetan Buddhism. When King Trisong Detsen (755–797 C.E.) wanted to found a Buddhist monastery during his reign, Padmasambhava was invited to Tibet to exorcise the demons of the indigenous *Bön* religion from around the site. This being accomplished, the monastery of Samye was established sometime around 787 C.E., on a site about thirty miles from Lhasa. It is difficult to estimate exactly how long Padmasambhava actually stayed in Tibet, but he had a profound impact on the Buddhist tradition there, generally being regarded as the founder of the Nyingma school of Tibetan Buddhism. He is still revered by this school under the name Guru Rinpoche. During his stay in Tibet, Padmasambhava hid a great many authoritative texts called *Terma* (*gTer-ma*) of the Nyingma school which he expected to be discovered in the future to be expounded upon by appropriately qualified people known as *Tertöns* (*gTer-ston*). Consequently, the school founded by Padmasambhava has the most extensive collection of *Terma* texts of any school of Tibetan Buddhism, including Padmasambhava's biography and the *Tibetan Book of the Dead*.

## Atīśa

Atīśa (982–1054) was a famous Bengali Buddhist scholar who arrived in Tibet in 1042, spending the last years of his life there. Atīśa was invited to Tibet from the monastic university of Vikramaśīla on the basis of his vast knowledge of both the exoteric and esoteric Buddhist teachings. He helped Tibetan Buddhism purify the *sangha*, emphasizing celibacy and strict practice, and continued teaching *Tantra* until his death. His primary writing in this period was the *Bodhipathapradīpa* or '*Lamp for the Way of Enlightenment*'. Atīśa's work also had much influence on later Tibetan Buddhists, especially Tsongkhapa and the Gelug school.

## Tilopa

Tilopa (989–1069) was a great *Mahāsiddha* and teacher of Nāropa. His name literally means 'crusher of sesame', presumably a reflection of his long-time occupation in Bengal, following a long period of collecting esoteric teachings and practices throughout India. Although Tilopa is often described as being quite erratic, appearing only partially clothed, and acting 'crazy', he transmitted the Tantric practices he unified to Nāropa. Under the name of the Six *Dharmas* of Nāropa, these

### *The Tibetan Book of the Dead*

*The Tibetan Book of the Dead*, or *Bardo Thödol* (*Bar-do thos-grol* in Tibetan), is a text attributed to Padmasambhava and belonging to the category of texts identified above as *Terma* (*gTer-ma*). The text elucidates six kinds of 'in-between states' (*bar-do*), or those conditions that result in the forty-nine days between the time one dies and is reborn into a new form: the (1) birth *bardo*, (2) dream *bardo*, (3) meditation *bardo*, (4) experience of death *bardo*, (5) supreme reality *bardo*, and (6) state of becoming *bardo*. The final three *bardos* are linked to the three bodies of the Buddha (*trikāya*). The experience of death *bardo* is associated with the *dharma-kāya* or ultimate body, during which time a white light is manifested. The supreme reality *bardo* is associated with the *saṃbhoga-kāya* or enjoyment body, during which time lights in five colors appear, with each color being associated with a *maṇḍala* representing one of the five 'Buddha families' in Tantric theory. Finally, the state of becoming *bardo* is associated with the *nirmāṇa-kāya* or the apparition body, during which time lesser lights associated with the six states of existence (*bhavacakra*) are manifested. The strong imagery and rituals associated with the text are designed to help the adept attain liberation. A number of English translations of the text are available, beginning with that of W.Y. Evans-Wentz, originally published in 1927.

teachings were taken to Tibet where they were instrumental in the Kagyu school of Tibetan Buddhism.

## Nāropa

Nāropa was a Vajrayāna practitioner and disciple of Tilopa who was instrumental in the development of Tibetan Buddhism through the teachings he imparted to his student Marpa. He was a scholar turned yogi, having abandoned his position at Nālandā University in order to pursue training under Tilopa. It was through Nāropa that Marpa received the *Mahāmudrā* teaching, as well as that set of teachings known as the Six *Dharmas* of Nāropa. As a result of his association with Marpa, Nāropa is regarded as a critical figure in the Kagyu school of Tibetan Buddhism.

## Marpa

Marpa (1012–1097) was an important Tibetan Buddhist regarded as the founder of the Kagyu school of Tibetan Buddhism. As a married householder who was skilled in Sanskrit, Marpa went to India on three occasions in search of *Dharma* instruction.

On his first visit he met a great master named Nāropa under whom he trained for many years at Nālandā. Following a second visit to India, he took Milarepa as his disciple. On his third visit, late in life, Marpa met Nāropa a final time, and also met the famed teacher Atīśa (982–1054) who came to Tibet in 1042. Marpa is credited with bringing the Mahāmudrā teaching to Tibet, as well as the Six *Dharmas* of Nāropa. Sometimes called 'The Translator', the Kagyu school of Tibetan Buddhism begins its lineage with Marpa.

## Milarepa (Mi-Las Ras-pa)

Milarepa (1040–1123), whose name means 'Cotton-Clad Mila', was a famous disciple of Marpa and is regarded as the greatest poet-saint in Tibetan Buddhism. While his early life is interesting, it is overshadowed by those events prior to and after he became Marpa's student. He became Marpa's student in middle age, initially acting only as his servant. Milarepa was subjected to a seemingly enormous number of tests and trials by the master for six years prior to receiving any significant *Dharma* instruction. He eventually received teaching from Marpa, particularly concentrating on the Six *Dharmas* of Nāropa, and became the second patriarch of the Kagyu lineage. Milarepa spent many years living alone in the caves of the Himalayas, only gradually accepting disciples. During this period of solitude, he composed many songs reflecting teaching. These he shared with his closest disciple Gampopa (1079–1153) who organized the Kagyu school and founded its first monasteries.

## Gampopa (sGam-po-pa)

Gampopa (1079–1153) was a disciple of Milarepa, a major figure in the Kagyu lineage of Tibetan Buddhism, credited with beginning the monastic tradition in that lineage. Sometimes called the 'Doctor of Dvag-po', Gampopa became a monk in the Kadamspa lineage at age twenty-six, following the death of his wife. Six years later, he undertook a period of training with Milarepa, acquiring his major teaching (and Dharma transmission) in just over a year. These teachings included the Six *Dharmas* of Nāropa and *Mahāmudrā*. He is famous for his text known as *The Jewel Ornament of Liberation*. Following Gampopa, the Kagyud tradition split into four major groups.

## Tsongkhapa (Tsong-kha-pa)

Tsongkhapa (1357–1419) was an important Tibetan Buddhist who founded the influential Gelug school of Tibetan Buddhism. Born in north-east Tibet, he entered the Buddhist order as a novice during his childhood. He studied in central Tibet, examined all the basic areas of Buddhist scholarship, and was especially fond of both logic and *Vinaya*. Tsongkhapa took full ordination at age twenty-five, and began what was at first a modest teaching career. Within a quarter-century he was a major figure in Lhasa, had moved away from the Kadamspa school and begun the Gelug school or 'School of the Virtuous'. It was so named because Tsongkhapa underscored both an emphasis on *Vinaya* and doctrinal study. Tsongkhapa was regarded as a great scholar, implementing a monastic curriculum that led to a sort of spiritual Ph.D. known as the Geshe degree. His writings fill more than a dozen volumes, includes the voluminous *Lam-rim chen-mo*, an exceedingly important text on the stages of the Buddhist path. The sect he founded continues today, known as the 'Yellow Hat School'. The lineage of the Dalai Lama also was established within the school founded by Tsongkhapa, making the school a political as well as religious force.

## Samye (bSam-yas)

The first Buddhist monastery built in Tibet, probably completed around 787 during the reign of King Trisong Detsen. It is located about thirty miles from Lhasa. Presumably founded by Padmasambhava and Śāntirakṣita, and modeled on the Indian Buddhist temple of Odantapurī in Bengal, a Sarvāstivādin ordination lineage was established at Samye, and it became a lively place for religious discussion and debate. It was the site of a famous debate between Śāntirakṣita's pupil Kamalaśīla and a Chinese monk known as Huashang over the issue of sudden versus gradual enlightenment. In spirited debate, Kamalaśīla successfully defended the Indian position, thus establishing the efficacy of the Indian standpoint for Tibetan Buddhism.

## **Tantra** ***and Tantric texts***

*Tantra* is a technical term, literally meaning 'continuity' or 'thread', and is generally applied to the esoteric school of Buddhism that developed in India, but which quickly spread (especially) to Tibet, China, and Japan. Its origins in India were discussed in Chapter Seven, so here we are concerned mainly with its development in Tibet. The school espoused a doctrinal system that emerged from Mahāyāna philosophy and emphasized techniques of spontaneity centered around the use of *mantras*, *maṇḍalas*, and provocative psychological techniques. It attempted to move beyond all dualities, symbolized especially by the masculine and feminine principles, by their very union. In this system, the masculine principle is identified with skillful means (*upāya*) and the feminine principle with wisdom (*prajñā*). The term is also applied to a class of literature composed of four types: (1) *kriyā-tantra* (2) *caryā-tantra* (3) *yoga-tantra*, and (4) *anuttara-yoga-tantra*. The latter two classes are generally regarded as 'higher' than the previous two, this determination being made by the spiritual development of the practitioner for whom each was intended. In Tibet, the oldest

Buddhist school known as Nyingma further divides *anuttara-yoga-tantra* into three additional categories: (1) *mahāyoga*, (2) *anuyoga*, and (3) *atiyoga*. This later practice is known as *dzogchen*.

*Anuttara-yoga-tantra* is the fourth, and last, of the four classes of Buddhist *Tantra*. In the Tibetan Buddhist canon, the *Tantras* are located in the seventh subdivision of the *Kanjur* (*bKa'-gyur*). They include twenty-two volumes, containing more than three hundred texts. It is the last class of *Tantra*, *anuttara-yoga*, that designates the ideal types called *siddhas* or perfected ones. Philosophically, the *anuttara-yoga-tantra* is based on the Mādhyamika school, emphasizing emptiness (*śūnyatā*), the elimination of all subject-object duality, and the union of wisdom (*prajñā*) and skill-in-means (*upāya*). Religiously, the *anuttara-yoga-tantra* focuses on ritual acts involving meditation, the union of male and female yogic practitioners, eating of sacramental food, and other rites designed to attain powers known as *siddhis*. Two of the most important Buddhist Tantric texts, the *Guhyasamāja-tantra* and the *Hevajra-tantra* belong to this class.

The *Guhyasamāja-tantra* is an important Vajrayāna Buddhist text belonging to the *anuttara-yoga-tantra* class. Along with the *Cakrasaṃvara-tantra*, *Hevajra-tantra*, and *Kālacakra-tantra*, it is included among the most important texts in Tantric literature. It was almost certainly written before 750 C.E., and possibly as early as the sixth century. It is composed of two parts, a *Mūla-tantra* of seventeen sections, and an *Uttara-tantra* comprising the eighteenth section. It is sometimes called the *Tathāgata-guhyaka*. In its meditational framework, it presents a visualization of the Buddha, depicted as Vairocana, and an accompaniment of four female *bodhisattvas*: Locanā, Māmakī, Pāṇḍarā, and Tārā.

All dualities and distinctions are denied in the text, using the term *vajra* or 'diamond' to symbolize ultimate reality. It also offers a unique rendering of the technical term '*bodhicitta*' (usually translated as '*thought of enlightenment*') as the unity of emptiness (*śūnyatā*) and compassion (*karuṇā*).

The *Hevajra-tantra* also is an important Vajrayāna Buddhist text belonging to the *anuttara-yoga-tantra* class. It has been preserved in Sanskrit, Chinese, and Tibetan

> Tārā is one of the most popular deities in Tibetan Buddhism. According to the legends, she was born from tears shed by Avalokiteśvara. Since Avalokiteśvara is associated with compassion, Tārā became his female manifestation. She became exceedingly important in Tibetan Buddhism, where a cult grew up around her worship. She is reputed to have twenty-one forms, varied by color, posture, and the like. She is most often represented as green or white. Many sources refer to her as a Buddha, and she is sometimes called the 'mother of all the Buddhas'. Atīśā (see above) was a lifelong devotee of Tārā.

*Figure 10.4* Images of Tārā

versions, all of which seem to be later than around 700 C.E. It is a complicated text opening with a dialogue between the Buddha as Vajrasattva and a *bodhisattva* named Vajragarbha. Although the text contains much philosophical material, it focuses mainly on religious practice and ritual, described in detail. The text is fraught with seemingly contradictory material, as well as sexual concern, the resolution of which is critical for an accurate understanding of the Vajrayāna path.

The *Kālacakra-tantra* is a text of the *atiyoga* subdivision of the *anuttara-yoga-tantra*, literally meaning '*Wheel of Time*', and considered to be one of the most complex Tantric texts. It was probably introduced to Tibet from India in the eleventh century. It is comprised of three basic parts: (1) a section that considers the physical world and its aspects, including temporal factors, (2) a section that considers the psycho-physical world of the individual, and (3) a section focusing on visualization of the deities. It is still regularly practiced in the Gelug school of Tibetan Buddhism.

## *Tradition of the Dalai Lama*

The Dalai Lama is an honorary title afforded to successive reincarnations of Avalokiteśvara, chosen from within the Gelug school of Tibetan Buddhism, and considered to be both the political and religious leader of Tibet. The lineage started in the Gelug sect begun by Tsongkhapa (1357–1419). Tsongkhapa's nephew was his third successor in the lineage of this school, and was given the honorary title Dalai Lama (dalai bla-ma) by the Mongolian ruler of the time (Altan Khan). It denoted one whose wisdom was as great as the ocean, and elevated the Gelug sect to a political prominence higher than that of the other Tibetan Buddhist sects. With the passing of each Dalai Lama, a new reincarnation (called a *tulku*) is sought after, providing much intrigue in the selection process. Additionally, the histories of the various Dalai Lamas are enormously interesting, demonstrating much complexity and literacy of Tibetan Buddhism. To date, there have been fourteen Dalai Lamas, the current one being Tenzin Gyatso (born in 1935). In 1989 he was awarded the Nobel Peace Prize in recognition of his work in the aftermath of the Tibetan Holocaust. Although based at the Tibetan refugee community in Dharamsala, India, he is a constant world traveller, promoting issues relative to the plight of the Tibetan people and world peace in general.

The Panchen Lama is a title given to the abbot of Tashi Lhunpo Monastery by the fifth Dalai Lama. Just as the Dalai Lama in Tibetan Buddhism is thought to represent an incarnation of Avalokiteśvara, the Panchen Lama (pan-chen bla-ma) is felt to be an incarnation of Amitābha. Originally a religious title only, Panchen Lamas served as representative of the office of Dalai Lama following the death of each, until a new Dalai Lama could be identified.

One controversy surrounding the tradition of the Dalai Lamas involves the formation of a new school of Buddhism called the 'New Kadampa Tradition' by Geshe Kelsang Gyatso. This school contends that the current Dalai Lama (and the Gelug tradition headed by him) has departed from the original teachings of the tradition. The main point of contention between the two schools surrounds the continued veneration of a wrathful protector deity of the Gelug sect known as Dorje Shukden (rDo-rje shug-ldan). Because of this deity's association with sectarian rivalry within the Gelug tradition near the end of the twentieth century, the current Dalai Lama has urged Tibetans to cease their veneration of this deity. By refusing to do so, Geshe Kelsang Gyatso and the New Kadampa Tradition disagrees, and envisions itself as maintaining the tradition of Atīśa and Tsongkhapa. The new group maintains headquarters in the United Kingdom.

## *The Holocaust and thereafter*

Following the Chinese annexation of Tibet, the fourteenth Dalai Lama, Tenzin Gyatso, fled to India in 1959 and established a government in exile, along with many other important Tibetan lamas, *tulkus*, and rinpoches, some of whom were still children. Victimized by a Chinese government that saw Tibetan religion in general and Buddhism in particular as remnants of an old, outdated style of life that was contrary to Maoist communism, and which destroyed most of Tibet's

*Figure 10.5* The Potala Palace, Lhasa, Tibet. The official residence of the Dalai Lama

magnificent monasteries – executing many monks and nuns in the process – the only hope for Tibetan Buddhists to preserve their ancient tradition was to flee. Refugee centers were established in India, Nepal, Bhutan, Sikkim, and elsewhere, eventually allowing Tibetan Buddhism to begin to re-establish itself in exile. Despite the fact that religious persecution was lessened in the final two decades of the twentieth century, Tibetan Buddhism remains strictly regulated in Tibet. Nonetheless, having attracted many sympathizers and Western adherents in the last half-century, Tibetan Buddhism remains highly visible on the world scene.

## Key points you need to know

- Buddhism was introduced to Tibet from India during the reign of Songtsen Gampo (616–650 C.E.).
- Within 150 years the first Buddhist monastery at Samye was established.
- By 1500 C.E. the four 'great' schools of Nyingma, Kagyu, Sakya, and Gelug had been established.
- Tibetan Buddhism has produced a long series of remarkable figures, beginning with Padmasambhava and continuing up to the present day.
- The Tibetan Buddhist Vajrayāna tradition is defined by its reliance on complicated Tantric texts and practices.
- The lineage of Dalai Lamas began with the nephew of Tsongkhapa, and continues with the current Dalai Lama, Tenzin Gyatso (b. 1935) being the fourteenth in the lineage.
- Tibetan Buddhism lives in exile following the Chinese annexation of Tibet nearly a half-century ago.

## Discussion questions

1. Discuss the sectarian traditions in Tibetan Buddhism in terms of their histories, doctrines, practices, and lineages.
2. What are the four traditional types of *tantra*?
3. What are *mantras* and how do they work?
4. Choose any three famous figures in Tibetan Buddhist history and explain why their role is critical to the development of Tibetan Buddhism.

## Further reading

Lopez, Donald S., Jr. (ed.). *Religions of Tibet in Practice*. Princeton, NJ: Princeton University Press, 1997.

Powers, John. *An Introduction to Tibetan Buddhism*. Ithaca, NY: Snow Lion Publications, 1995.

Powers, John. *A Concise Encyclopedia of Buddhism*. Oxford: Oneworld Publications, 2000.

Samuel, Geoffrey. *Civilized Shamans: Buddhism in Tibetan Societies*. Washington, DC: Smithsonian Institution Press, 1993.

Thurman, Robert. *Essential Tibetan Buddhism*. San Francisco, CA: Harper San Francisco, 1995.

Tucci, Giuseppe. *The Religions of Tibet*. Berkeley, CA: University of California Press, 1980)

Willis, Jan D. *Feminine Ground: Essays on Women and Tibet*. Ithaca, NY: Snow Lion, 1987.

# *Part IV*

# *Modernity*

# 11 *Buddhism in the Western world*

## In this chapter

This chapter explores Buddhism's globalization in general and spread into the Western world in particular. Utilizing the United States as a case in point, it describes the historical progression of the various Asian Buddhist traditions into North America. It also considers the specific issues that impact on Buddhism's development outside of its Asian homeland.

## Main topics covered

- Buddhism's Western presence in historical perspective
- Globalization: Europe, Australia/New Zealand, North and South America
- America as a case study
- Developmental issues in American Buddhism

### *Buddhism's Western presence in historical perspective*

In many respects, Buddhism's spread to regions beyond the Asian landmass is historically new. Of particular interest is how the teachings and practices of Buddhism found new homes in foreign lands. At the risk of being overly general, a marked feature of the spread of Buddhism in Asia seems to have been its 'top-down' introduction. Kings and rulers adopted Buddhism, invited monks, and established Buddhism as the state religion. The state support of Buddhist monasteries and its residents functioned to further centralize power and at the same time to introduce a culture that was often valued as superior to one's own.

Immediately, however, as a striking counter-example, an informed reader will think of China in the first centuries of the Common Era. In the first and second centuries Buddhist monks and scholars were not invited and not welcomed. Rather, the educated ruling Han elite devalued Buddhist teachings as 'foreign', and even barbarous, constituting a threat to the ideal of a harmonious political and social order. The monastic way of life seemed incompatible with Chinese ideals of filial piety, this-wordly pragmatism and the importance of productive work. Certainly the newly emergent Mahāyāna Buddhism with its ideal of the *bodhisattva* – who could be a lay Buddhist, active in this world – and the evolving blend of Confucian, Daoist and Buddhist elements soften the critique. Nevertheless, Buddhism remained in a state of risky co-existence during most of its first half-millennium on Chinese soil.

Compared to the histories of Buddhism's spread, acculturation, and indigenization in the variety of Asian countries, what is new and different about Buddhism in the West? Only a few points can be listed here. Strikingly, Buddhism has not been established as state religion in any Western country, and nowhere has it enjoyed the lavish patronage it enjoyed at times in South, South-east, East, and Central/Inner Asia. Additionally, Buddhist teachings and practices were not introduced from a top-down approach, but commenced their diffusion from below, often championed by powerless, economically disadvantaged people. Buddhism has spread, and is spreading, as a ferment in the various Western societies. Initial results of this 'Awakening of the West', as the British writer Stephen Batchelor titled his important narrative of the encounter of Buddhism and Western culture, are recognizable in the arts, in the steadily increasing number of converts and Buddhist institutions, and in the growing recognition of Buddhist groups as participants and partners in the multi-religious composition of Western societies.

Furthermore, Buddhism in Asia reached the so-called 'ordinary' people, the masses, by the absorption of and blending with local cultural features and ritual practices. The diffusion of Buddhist teachings and worldviews to the non-elite, lower strata of society developed through practice by way of ritual and performance. It was through its abundant use of folk religious, shamanic aspects and practices that Buddhism gained a lasting grounding and impact in the larger segment of society. The Western diffusion generally lacks this trajectory of magical/shamanic practices. Most Western Buddhists, with the important exception of Asian Buddhist immigrants, have not engaged in this folk religious or popular Buddhist aspect. Rather, they praise Buddhism as rational and scientific, grounded on reason and individual experience. However disenchanted and rationalized Western converts might understand and interpret Buddhism, just as in Asia, the dissemination of Buddhist concepts to a broader clientele took place no sooner than when the practical and this-wordly elements (called the 'integration of Buddhism') became emphasized. Although it may not have involved the performance of magical/shamanic rituals, the practice-based features of meditation and liturgy seem to have enabled Buddhism's rapidly increasing diffusion since the 1960s.

Whereas we note here both similarities and differences, we would like to highlight three further characteristics. First, in Asia, it generally took many centuries until an acculturated, regionalized form of Buddhism evolved. Thus, in China it was no sooner than the Sui and Tang Dynasties (589–906 C.E.) that indigenous forms of

Chinese Buddhist traditions – such as Chinese Pure Land, Tiantai, Chan – evolved. In addition, it took approximately 500 years from the arrival of Buddhism in Japan for its own indigenous schools to develop (in the Kamakura period). In contrast, in the West, attempts to create adapted, regionalized forms of Buddhism seem to occur at a much faster pace. During the last three or four decades, in only Buddhism's second century of Western presence, Western Buddhists have proposed vigorous endeavors to form a 'Western', 'European', or 'American Buddhism'. Whatever premature or mature state these new shapes have taken already, the proclamation of such innovative, non-Asian derived forms mirrors the self-consciousness and ambitious attempts of Western Buddhists. It certainly is no risk to forecast that in the twenty-first century independent, Western forms and schools of Buddhism will develop and prosper on a much larger scale.

Second, the development of Western Buddhist forms is a recent phenomenon. These new schools and lineages additionally pluralize the spectrum of Buddhist schools and traditions present in Western countries. This plurality and diversity constitutes a marked characteristic of Buddhism in the West. In Asia, one usually will find one yāna or major tradition in a country, be it Theravāda in South and Southeast Asia, Mahāyāna in China and East Asia, or Vajrayāna in Central and Inner Asia. In the West, however, all these different yānas have appeared in one country or region; perhaps even in one city, be it Los Angeles, London, Berlin, or Sydney. Traditions hitherto separated by thousands of miles in Asia have become neighbors in the West. The process of getting to know each other has started. And it seems that a co-operation and mutual recognition of the specific interpretations and practices flow with more ease in Western than Eastern settings. Some Western Buddhists have even been quick to speak of a Buddhist 'ecumenicism', a term borrowed from mainly Protestant Christian movements of the twentieth century. Finally, related to academic interests and research, the past and present spread of Buddhism to Western regions enables us to scrupulously investigate the progress of diffusion, processes of settlement and growth, as well as the strategies utilized to adapt to the new, socio-culturally foreign contexts. We are now able to rely on a variety of different sources, and to apply different methodological approaches in order to scrutinize the lives of individual Buddhists in Western countries as well as, for example, to follow up in detail the developments of institutionalization, fragmentation, or the dissolution of a specific Buddhist group or school. In contrast, research on Buddhism's spread to new regions and cultures in Asia – at least a millennium ago – often simply lacks the account of detailed data and information we are now able to gather for the past and current spread of Buddhism in the West. The Asian material more often than not is fragmentary, incomplete, and led by specific interests and polemics. At times it is simply coincidental or even accidental. A detailed account of how Buddhist traditions and their proponents gained a footing in a new, religiously different culture and society in Asia most often can be sketched only for time periods ranging from several decades to centuries. Analyses from an ethnographical or sociology of religion point of view, as have most fruitfully been carried out for Buddhist institutions and developments in Western contexts in recent years, are hard to trace for Buddhism's spread throughout Asia. The long-standing, textual orientation so characteristic for Buddhist Studies has prevented many scholars from using methods other than that of philology.

## *The West and globalization*

It is now very common in Buddhist literature to find the expression 'Buddhism in the West'. It should be clarified that we do not perceive 'the West' as a homogeneous whole which provides similar socio-political, cultural, and legal settings in the various countries considered. Quite the contrary. Instead, in a pragmatic view, the notion of 'the West' is used to denote non-Asian industrialized nation-states where Buddhist teachings and practices, Buddhist people and ideas, have become established. Here, 'the West' can be taken as an abbreviation for Canada, the United States of America, Brazil, the various states of Europe, South Africa, Australia and New Zealand. Without going into detail, as previous chapters have done, it is in these non-Asian countries that we have a strong and sufficient knowledge of Buddhist activities past and present. Although there are brief accounts of Buddhists and Buddhist activities in, for example, Mexico, Peru, the Caribbean, Ghana, or Israel, the available data so far is much too scarce and occasional to provide reliable accounts. Hopefully, further regional histories will be available in the near future, both as Buddhism continues to spread and academic research keeps extending its scope of interest.

Viewed from an Asian perspective, Buddhist people, ideas, and practices have not traveled to 'the West' only. In the same way, they have migrated Eastward. In the nineteenth century, workers from Japan or China came to South and North America; and in the second half of the twentieth century emigrants and refugees from Korea, Hong Kong and South-east Asia headed for Canada and the United States. Perceived from the Asian landmass, Buddhism has gone both ways, to the West and the East.

In the period of globalization distances appear to be measured only by the amount of jet lag encountered. Numerous scholars, including historian of religion Ninian Smart, have spoken of the 'Global Period of world history', which commenced with the 1960s. Transcontinental travel and the spread of Buddhist concepts, texts, and teachers had occurred a century ago. However, the tremendously improved modes of transportation now available enable an intensity of communication previously unknown. Aided by postmodern technology, especially including telecommunications and the Internet, formerly distant poles and far away regions have become virtual neighbors in the global web. In this global period, the maintenance of close links with both the (mainly) Asian home country and the various globally spread 'overseas' centers of a Buddhist tradition takes place with a historically unprecedented scope and speed. Up to now, however, scholars researching Buddhist traditions and organizations have only rarely applied theories of globalization and transnationalism to the worldwide spread of Buddhism. In this introduction, we shall provide only one hint of this important analytical perspective.

An obvious feature of the process of globalization is the geographic spread of Buddhist ideas, practices, and people to new, non-Asian regions and countries. This spread continues with other traditions coming from Asian countries to the West, as witnessed by recently founded orders from Taiwan and Thailand (such as the Fo Guang Shan order and the Dhammakaya Foundation, respectively). During the last two decades, this diffusion process has been augmented by the initial steps of newly emergent Western Buddhist organizations gaining a foothold on a global scale (e.g., the British-founded Friends of the Western Buddhist Order or the Diamond Sangha founded by Robert Aitken).

This descriptive level deserves a closer look. The globalization of Buddhism does not refer to a spread from the center to the periphery only, that is from Asia to Western countries. Globalization also encompasses the emergence of new centers with regionalized Buddhist interpretations and practices. The creation of consciously labeled Western Buddhist forms is a development within this overall process of globalization. In other words, Buddhism spreading globally encounters 'local transformation'. The global becomes particularized and socio-culturally particular. As a consequence, the globalization of Buddhism encompasses a dissolving of the Asian center(s) as the main and only agent of authority and the emergence of a variety of different authority centers spread across various continents. We hold that by the end of the twentieth century we had entered a period in which the globalization of Buddhism has truly begun in that a multi- or polycentric form is emerging step-by-step. Buddhist networks and organizations have become comfortable operating on a global scale. Centers of Buddhist authority and legitimacy can be found in eastern and western as well as in southern and northern regions of the globe. The study of the impact of the globalization process and the emergence of new voices within the generalized Buddhist tradition certainly deserves further attention.

## *A case in point: America*

Although it is now rather common to refer to Oriental influences in the writings of such prominent American literary figures as Henry David Thoreau, Ralph Waldo Emerson, and Walt Whitman, and to point to the impact of the Theosophists on the Oriental movement in America, the more specific beginnings of Buddhism in America can be traced to the Chinese immigrants who began to appear on the West Coast in the 1840s. Prior to the discovery of gold at Sutter's Mill, the number of Chinese immigrants was small, but with the news of the golden wealth in the land, the figure increased exponentially. Rick Fields, author of *How the Swans Came to the Lake: A Narrative History of Buddhism in America,* has suggested that by 1852, 20,000 Chinese were present in California, and within a decade, nearly one-tenth of the California population was Chinese. In the Chinese temples that dotted that California coastline, and began to appear in the Chinatown section of San Francisco, the religious practice was an eclectic blend of Buddhism, Taoism, and Confucianism, and although there were a number of Buddhist priests in residence, a distinctly Chinese Buddhism on the North American continent did not develop until much later.

The Japanese presence in America developed more slowly than the Chinese, but had much greater impact. By 1890, when the Chinese presence was already quite apparent, the Japanese population was barely 2,000. The World Parliament of Religions, however, held in conjunction with the Chicago World's Fair in 1893, radically changed the entire landscape for Japanese Buddhism in America. Among the participants at the parliament was Shaku Sōen, who was to return to America a decade later and promote the school of Rinzai Zen (one of the two major branches of Japanese Zen Buddhism). Sōen returned to America in 1905, lecturing in several cities, and establishing a basic ground for the entry of Zen. Upon his return to Japan in 1906, three of his students were selected to promote the Rinzai lineage in America.

The first of Sōen's students, Nyōgen Senzaki, came to California in the first decade of the twentieth century, but delayed his teaching mission until 1922. Sōen's second disciple, Shaku Sōkatsu, lived in America from 1906–1908, and again from 1909–1910, but eventually returned to Japan without having made much impact. By far Sōen's most noted disciple, and the man who made the most impact on the early growth of Buddhism in America, was Daisetz Teitaro Suzuki. Suzuki worked for Open Court Publishing Company in LaSalle, Illinois, from 1897–1909, but returned to Japan to pursue a career in Buddhist Studies. He visited America again from 1936 until the beginning of World War II, and eventually returned for a final time from 1950–1958, lecturing frequently in American universities and cities.

Nonetheless, the Rinzai lineage was not the only one to develop in America. The Sōtō tradition (the other major branch of Japanese Zen) began to appear in America in the 1950s. By the mid-1950s, Soyu Matsuoka Rōshi had established the Chicago Buddhist Temple, and Shunryu Suzuki Rōshi arrived in San Francisco in 1959, founding the San Francisco Zen Center shortly thereafter. The Dharma successors to Suzuki Rōshi have continued the Sōtō lineage, while other teachers in this lineage (including one of the few female rōshis, Jiyu Kennett) have also appeared.

In addition to the traditional forms of Rinzai and Sōtō Zen, still another form of Zen has appeared in America, one that attempts to harmonize the major doctrines and practices of each school into a unified whole. This movement owes its American origins to Sogaku Harada, although he never visited the United States himself.

Proponents of this approach included Taizan Maezumi Rōshi (arriving in 1956), Hakuun Yasutani Rōshi (who visited the United States first in 1962, and then regularly until his death in 1973), and Philip Kapleau, an American by birth who first learned about Japanese religion and culture while serving as a court reporter in 1946 during the War Crimes Trials held in Tokyo. Maezumi Rōshi and Kapleau Rōshi have been enormously successful. Maezumi Rōshi established the Zen Center of Los Angeles, where he resided until his death in 1995. He left a dozen *Dharma* heirs, many of whom have developed their own vital, creative communities. Kapleau Rōshi too was quite successful, having built a stable Zen community in Rochester, New York that was notable for its attempt to develop an American style for Zen practice, and which recently celebrated its thirtieth anniversary. Also significant, and worth mentioning are Robert Aitken Rōshi, who founded the Diamond Sangha in Hawaii in 1959, Eidō Shimano Rōshi, who first came to the United States as a translator for Yasutani Rōshi, and Joshu Sasaki Rōshi, who founded the Cimarron Zen Center in Los Angeles in 1966 and the Mt. Baldy Zen Center five years later.

Zen was surely not the only Japanese Buddhist tradition to make an appearance in America before the turn of the twentieth century. In 1898 two Japanese missionaries, Shuei Sonoda and Kakuryo Nishijima, were sent to San Francisco to establish the Buddhist Mission of North America, an organization associated with a Pure Land school of Japanese Buddhism. Although seriously hampered by the Japanese Immigration Exclusion Act of 1924, by 1931, thirty-three main temples were active. With the outbreak of World War II, more than 100,000 Japanese Americans (more than half of which were Buddhist and two-thirds American born) were relocated to internment camps. In 1944, the name Buddhist Mission of North America was changed to Buddhist Churches of America. With headquarters in San Francisco, this Buddhist organization remains one of the most stable Buddhist communities in North America.

In the 1960s, another form of Japanese Buddhism appeared on the American landscape. It was known as Nichiren Shōshū of America, and by 1974, it boasted 258 chapters and over 200,000 members (although these figures were highly suspect). This group grew out of the Sōka Gakkai movement in Japan, a non-meditative form of Buddhism that based its teachings on the thirteenth century figure Nichiren (1222–1282) and his emphasis on the doctrines and practices focusing on or deriving from the famous *Lotus Sūtra*. Brought to this country by Masayasa Sadanaga (who changed his name to George Williams), the organization set up headquarters in Santa Monica, where it began an active program of proselytizing. Although the group has recently splintered, and is now called Soka Gakkai-USA, it remains a formidable Buddhist presence in America, having become extremely popular among European American and African American Buddhists.

The Chinese are once again making their presence visible in American Buddhism. Although not nearly so visible as the Japanese Buddhist groups, several Chinese

Buddhist organizations have appeared in the last half-century. Perhaps the most notable of these is a largely monastic group originally known as the Sino-American Buddhist Association which, until his recent death, was under the direction of a venerable monk named Hsüan-Hua. Established in 1959, this organization has developed a huge monastery in Talmadge, California known as the 'City of Ten Thousand Buddhas', which serves as the headquarters of what is now identified as the Dharma Realm Buddhist Association. Of even larger size (and quite possibly importance) is the Hsi Lai Temple outside Los Angeles, founded in 1978, and now offering a wide variety of Buddhist teachings and services. Other Chinese Buddhist groups can be found in virtually every major metropolitan area. There are approximately 125 Chinese Buddhist organizations in the United States, more than half of which are in California and one-fifth of which are in New York. The religious practice of the Chinese Buddhist groups in America is largely an eclectic combination of various Buddhist schools, combining Chan, *Vinaya*, Tiantai, *Tantra*, and Pure Land practices. Most of these practices are Mahāyāna-based, and a similar kind of approach is followed by the Vietnamese Buddhist groups that have begun to appear in urban areas, largely as a result of a large influx of Vietnamese immigrants following the termination of the United States' involvement in Vietnam. To some degree, this eclectic approach can also be seen in the various Korean Buddhist groups that began appearing in the United States in the latter half of the twentieth century.

The Buddhist culture to enter America most recently is the Tibetan. Although a few Buddhist groups appeared in the West prior to 1960, the majority came after the Tibetan Holocaust, during which the Communist Chinese made every effort to extinguish religion in Tibet. Following an immediate exile in India, Bhutan, Nepal, and Sikkim, the diaspora has widened, with many Tibetans seeking to reestablish their sacred lineages on American soil. Communities from each of the four major Tibetan sects can now be found in America, with those founded by Tarthang Tulku and Chögyam Trungpa Rinpoche being especially popular and visible. The Tibetan groups are the most colorful of all the Buddhist groups now prospering in America, possessing a rich tradition of Buddhist art and a powerful psychological approach to mental health. They continue to grow rapidly, being very attractive to Euro-American Buddhists. It is no wonder, then, that they quote the thousand-year-old saying attributed to the sage Padmasambhava to explain their rapid growth: 'When the iron bird flies, and horses run on wheels, the Tibetan people will be scattered like ants across the World, and the *Dharma* will come to the land of the Red Man'.

The final sectarian tradition to be considered is that of the Theravāda, which permeated South Asia following the missionary tradition of the Indian King Aśoka in the third century B.C.E., and which continues today. Until quite recently, most Theravāda groups in the United States were similar to the Buddhist Vihara Society in Washington, D.C., an organization founded in 1965 under the direction of the Venerable Bope Vinita from Sri Lanka, and appealing to the large diplomatic community in the nation's capital. Now, however, as many Buddhists from Laos, Cambodia, Thailand, and Burma have migrated to the United States to escape the economic and political uncertainty of the native homes, there is a vigorous new infusion of Theravāda Buddhism into America. Temples are springing up in major cities, as these immigrant groups have tended to settle in ethic communities not unlike the Chinese and Japanese communities of the early decades of the twentieth century.

## *Developmental issues in American Buddhism*

Outlining the historical details of the Buddhist movement in America tells but a small part of the story, for the growth of American Buddhism is far more than its history. Rather, it presents a struggle to acculturate and accommodate on the part of a religious tradition that initially appeared to be wholly foreign to the American mindset. It is important to realize that two different groups were primarily responsible for Buddhism's earliest growth in America. On the one hand, Buddhism is the native religion of a significant number of Asian immigrants. On the other hand, it became the religion, or at least the subject of serious personal interest, for an ever-increasing group of (mostly) Euro-Americans who embraced Buddhism primarily out of intellectual attraction and interest in spiritual practice. This latter circumstance has created its own Buddhist subculture that is literate, urban, upwardly mobile, perhaps even elite in its life orientation. The above bifurcation makes even the issue of Buddhist identity and membership a very murky problem, further exacerbated with confusion about various Buddhist positions on ethical issues, sexuality, gender roles, and the like. This developmental pattern, and the issues associated with it, needs to be explored alongside a careful consideration of each of the Buddhist traditions now present on American soil.

Thomas Tweed's important and influential book *The American Encounter with Buddhism 1844-1912: Victorian Culture and the Limits of Dissent* suggests a variety of reasons for late-Victorian America's fascination with Buddhism. Clearly, there was a growing dissatisfaction with the answers provided by the traditional religions of the time, and apologists, like Paul Carus for example, were quick to suggest that imported Asian religions might well offer more satisfactory answers to the religious needs of Americans. Additionally, several Asian teachers, such as Anagarika Dharmapala and D.T. Suzuki had sufficient personal charisma to advance that cause. On the other hand, few Asian Buddhist teachers took up residence in America, and the two primary Buddhist organizations – the American Maha Bodhi Society and the Dharma Sangha of the Buddha – were institutionally weak. Tweed notes well that while Buddhist sympathizers resonated favorably with the mid-Victorian period's emphasis on optimism and activism as important cultural values, on the whole,

Buddhism's presumed characterization as pessimistic and passive made a much more compelling argument for its detractors. Coupled with the serious lack of accurate textual translations, Tweed's insightful postscript suggests that most Victorians, however disillusioned they may have been, looked elsewhere for potential resolutions to their spiritual crises. That American Buddhism in the late twentieth century seemed to be far more extensive than it had at the end of the previous century, and far more visible in American culture, suggests that many of Tweed's postulates for the failure of Victorian Buddhism in America had been remedied. And indeed they have; especially so in the last half of the century.

By 1970, virtually the full extent of Asian Buddhist sects was represented in America, and there was a plethora of Asian Buddhist teachers in permanent residence in the growing number of American Buddhist centers. The growth of these centers has been so utterly staggering in the second half of the twentieth century that in 1988 Don Morreale was able to catalog nearly 350 pages of listings for these groups in *Buddhist America: Centers, Retreats, Practices*. A new edition called *The Complete Guide to Buddhist America* was published in 1998. Web-based catalogs are also available. Dozens of *rōshis*, along with their *Dharma*-heirs, many Tibetan *tulkus*, Chinese monks and nuns, and an increasing number of Theravāda monks from various South and South-east Asian cultures are now visibly active on American soil. The presence of a growing number of Asian Buddhist teachers in America has been complemented and augmented by regular visits from global Buddhist leaders such as the Dalai Lama and Thich Nhat Hanh.

Further, these Asian Buddhist teachers, and the gradually increasing number of American Buddhist masters, are beginning to establish an institutional foundation that is stable, solid, and even ecumenical in nature. In 1987 a conference on 'World Buddhism in North America' was held at the University of Michigan during which a 'Statement of Consensus' was promulgated (a) 'to create the conditions necessary for tolerance and understanding among Buddhists and non-Buddhists alike', (b) 'to initiate a dialogue among Buddhists in North America in order to further mutual understanding, growth in understanding, and co-operation', (c) 'to increase our sense of community by recognizing and understanding our differences as well as our common beliefs and practices', and (d) 'to cultivate thoughts and actions of friendliness towards others, whether they accept our beliefs or not, and in so doing approach the world as the proper field of *Dharma*, not as a sphere of conduct irreconcilable with the practice of *Dharma*'. Geographically-organized organizations, like the Sangha Council of Southern California and associations of the students of famous Buddhist masters, such as the White Plum Asanga linking the *Dharma*-heirs of Taizan Maezumi Rōshi, are now becoming commonplace in the American Buddhist movement.

The availability of accurate primary and secondary literature has expanded almost exponentially in the latter half of the twentieth century. Several university presses, such as the State University Press of New York, University of Hawaii Press, University of California Press, and Princeton University Press have been leaders in publishing scholarly books devoted to the study of Buddhism, and a variety of trade publishers has emerged as well, such as Snow Lion and Wisdom Publications, that emphasize Buddhism specifically. Reliable translations of the entire Pāli Canon are now readily available throughout the world, and a project to publish translations of the entire Chinese Buddhist canon is currently underway, sponsored by the Bukkyo Dendo Kyokai. This translation endeavor represents a significant step forward in the American Buddhist movement because it requires extensive language training in Sanskrit, Pāli, Chinese, Japanese, and Tibetan. This training is usually, although not exclusively, obtained in American universities. As of 1994, nearly two dozen North American universities could boast at least two full-time faculty devoted to the academic discipline of Buddhist Studies, and nearly 150 academic scholars of Buddhism are located on the North American continent, many of whom can best be identified as 'scholar-practitioners'. Moreover, the American Buddhist movement is aided by the presence of a growing number of individuals who have traveled to Asia for extensive training and then returned to the United States to share their approach with Americans. One of the most successful enterprises of this kind is the Insight Meditation Center in Barre, Massachusetts, initially guided by Joseph Goldstein, Jack Kornfield, Sharon Salzberg and Christina Feldman, each of whom received extensive vipassanā training in Asia.

Certainly, the issue of social and religious anomie is no less critical in the latter years of the twentieth century than it was in the previous century. A quick perusal of Theodore Roszak's *The Making of a Counter-Culture*, Harvey Cox's *The Secular City*, or Peter Berger's *Sacred Canopy: Elements of a Sociological Theory of Religion* show how the pervasive influence of secularism and pluralism, as noted above, created the same kind of religious crisis as witnessed prior to the World Parliament of Religions, held in Chicago in 1893. Roszak even argued that the counter-culture of the 1960s was 'essentially an exploration of the politics of consciousness' (1969: 156). However, the counter-culture of the twentieth century differed from that of the preceding century in that it was no longer either passive or pessimistic, and this was clearly obvious in the American Buddhist movement.

Quite apart from issues relating to the specificity with which American Buddhist life is manifested (lay versus monastic ideals; urban versus rural lifestyle), a distinct and unique application of Buddhist ethics, formerly known as 'socially engaged Buddhism', but now commonly called simply 'engaged Buddhism', is emerging that demonstrates in dramatic fashion both the active and optimistic approach of today's American Buddhism. The overarching approach of engaged Buddhism is clearly portrayed in Christopher Queen's useful book *Engaged Buddhism in the West*, and summarized extremely well in Kenneth Kraft's introduction to his edited volume *Inner Peace, World Peace*. Organizations like the Buddhist Peace Fellowship, founded in 1978, aggressively demonstrate how to strike a careful balance between meditational training and political activism. Their task in bringing this activism and optimism to the American Buddhist public is aided by a strong new Buddhist journalism in America that has fostered exciting publications such as *Tricycle: The Buddhist Review*, the *Shambhala Sun*, *Turning Wheel: Journal of the Buddhist Peace Fellowship*, and many publications of individual Buddhist centers. Additionally, the useful and productive development of the Internet has allowed American Buddhism to expand its sphere of influence to a *sangha* not necessarily limited to a given geographic space. The electronic *Journal of Global Buddhism*, for example, has created links to literally hundreds of American Buddhist *sanghas* across the totality of North America.

### Key points you need to know

- For the first time in history, all Buddhist traditions and sectarian divisions may be present in one country at the same time.
- Many Asian Buddhist organizations are aggressively exporting their form of Buddhism throughout the world.
- Some Buddhist traditions are being actively imported by Western cultures.
- Western teachers are now replacing Asian teachers in Western countries, and women teachers are appearing in parity with male teachers.
- There are many conflicts between Asian immigrant and American convert communities.
- Western Buddhist communities are significantly more democratic than their Asian Buddhist counterparts.
- Meditation is generally favored by convert Buddhists while other practices are predominant in Asian immigrant communities.

## Discussion questions

1. Which Buddhist traditions are most popular in the West?
2. How can we determine whether Buddhism has been transplanted into rather than onto Western soil?
3. Compare and contrast the various Buddhist practices employed in Western Buddhist communities. Which ones are most likely to succeed, and why?
4. To what extent does Buddhism's success in the West depend on the development of a broadly-based ecumenical movement?
5. What do you think the future holds for Buddhism as all religions begin periods of major globalization?

## Further reading

Prebish, Charles S. *Luminous Passage: The Practice and Study of Buddhism in America*. Berkeley, CA: University of California Press, 1999.

Prebish, Charles S. and Martin Baumann (eds). *Westward Dharma: Buddhism Beyond Asia*. Berkeley, CA: The University of California Press, 2002.

Prebish, Charles S. and Kenneth Tanaka (eds). *The Faces of Buddhism in America*. Berkeley, CA: University of California Press, 1998.

Queen, Christopher S. (ed.). *Engaged Buddhism in the West*. Boston, MA: Wisdom Publications, 2000.

Roszak, Theodor. *The Making of a Counter Culture*. Garden City, NY: Anchor Books, 1969.

Seager, Richard H. *Buddhism in America*. New York: Columbia University Press, 2000.

Williams, Duncan Ryūken and Christopher S. Queen (eds). *American Buddhism: Methods and Findings in Recent Scholarship*. Richmond: Curzon Press, 1999.

# 12 *Socially engaged Buddhism*

## In this chapter

This chapter describes a new movement in Buddhism known as 'socially engaged Buddhism'. It has become so important in modern Buddhism worldwide that one Buddhist scholar has argued that it has become a new 'vehicle', joining the previously identified three vehicles of Buddhism (Hīnayāna, Mahāyāna, and Vajrayāna). This chapter outlines the main features of this new movement and presents a case study of the Buddhist Peace Fellowship, one of the largest activist groups in Buddhism. It concludes with an exposition of and critical reflection on two issues of importance to engaged Buddhism – human rights and ecology.

## Main topics covered

- What is socially engaged Buddhism?
- The Buddhist Peace Fellowship
- Engaged Buddhism: old or new?
- Human rights
- Ecology

### *What is socially engaged Buddhism?*

Not long before Dr. Martin Luther King was assassinated, he nominated the Vietnamese monk Thich Nhat Hanh (mentioned in Chapter Eight) for the Nobel Peace Prize. The emergence of what has come to be known as 'socially engaged Buddhism' or increasingly as 'engaged Buddhism', owes both its existence and visibility to Thich Nhat Hanh. This does not mean to say that Buddhism had never been socially active in its early history, but rather that Buddhism is often perceived to be individual and passive in its approach to human social problems. This viewpoint may have been the one promoted by the earliest Western scholars who, in the nineteenth

*Figure 12.1* The Great *Stūpa* at Swayambunath, Kathmandu, Nepal

century, tended to focus on Buddhist texts which seemed almost world-rejecting. By contrast, more than a century later, and utilizing not only Buddhist values, but also American and European forms of social protest and active social involvement, socially engaged Buddhists have aggressively employed boycotts, hospice work, tax resistance, ecological programs, voter mobilization, prison reforms, letter-writing campaigns, and a host of other techniques to actively project Buddhist moral values into our dialogue with our planet and each other.

The term 'socially engaged Buddhism' derives from the French words 'engagé' and 'l'engagement', but Nhat Hanh was actually using this phrase as a cover-term for three Vietnamese ideas emphasizing 1) awareness in daily life, 2) social service, and 3) social activism. This acknowledgment of the three Vietnamese bases for socially engaged Buddhism is important because it captures not only the association of the term with social, political, economic, and ecological issues, but also a general sense of involving the ordinary lives of families, communities, and their inter-relationship. In other words, while socially engaged Buddhism applies to human rights issues such as anti-violence and environmental concerns, it also impacts the lives of individual Buddhists living 'in the world'.

The interest in socially engaged Buddhism has been so great that in 1986 Arnold Kotler founded Parallax Press in Berkeley in order to publish and distribute information relevant to the movement. Although the staple product of Parallax Press remains the many books written by Thich Nhat Hanh, it also boasts a wide range of authors and editors, including Allan Hunt Badiner, Catherine Ingram, Claude Whitmyer, Joanna Macy, Stephen Batchelor, Susan Murcott, Maha Ghosananda, Sulak Sivaraksa, and the Dalai Lama. Moreover, the press also serves as a resource center for information on retreats, public lectures, and other issues relative to socially engaged Buddhism. Parallax Press is by no means the only publishing outlet for work on socially engaged Buddhism, but it is the most visible and accessible.

One modern Buddhist writer – Christopher Queen – has suggested that there are four different 'styles' of Buddhist ethics. The first is called 'The Ethics of Discipline', in which the conduct caused by mental impurities fueled by the 'three poisons' of Buddhism – greed, hatred, and delusion – are combated by observing the five vows of the laity. Here the focus is on the individual Buddhist practitioner. Then there is 'The Ethics of Virtue', in which the individual's relationship comes more clearly into focus by engaging in such practices as loving kindness, compassion, joy, and equanimity. This marks a shift from observing strict rules to following a more internally enforced ethical framework. Third, there is 'The Ethics of Altruism', in which service to others predominates. Finally, there is the comprehensive 'Ethics of Engagement', in which the three previous prescriptions for daily living are applied to the overall concern for a better society, and this means creating new social institutions and relationships. Such an approach involves, as Queen maintains, awareness, identification of the self and the world, and a profound call to action.

It is with that in mind that a number of socially engaged Buddhist activists have worked to extend the traditional principles of morality into a program of Buddhist social ethics. In this the work of Thich Nhat Hanh is paramount. Critical to the attempt is the notion of extending the traditional five vows of the laity in accord with a supplementary series of fourteen precepts (see text box) constructed by Nhat Hanh as part of the Tiep Hien Order, or 'Order of Interbeing', a community of activist-practitioners founded in 1964.

Perhaps the greatest challenge for socially engaged Buddhism in the West is organizational. It is far less developed in its organizational patterns and strategies than its Christian or Jewish counterparts. As such, it is still learning from the many experiments in interfaith dialogue, such as the Society for Buddhist-Christian Studies. Nevertheless, an inspiring array of activities can now be found in the records of the individual Buddhist communities who are actively pursuing socially engaged Buddhist programmes. These activities are highlighted in the many books on the subject, such as Christopher Queen's, *Engaged Buddhism in the West*, which vividly feature such projects as the San Francisco Zen Center's hospice volunteer program, the Hartford Zen Center's Maitri AIDS Hospice, the Upaya Community's 'Being with Dying' program, Zen Mountain Monastery's meditation program in the New York state prisons, and many others.

**The fourteen precepts of the 'Order of Interbeing'**

1. Do not be idolatrous about or bound to any doctrine, theory, or ideology, even a Buddhist one.
2. Do not think the knowledge you presently possess is changeless absolute truth.
3. Do not force others to adopt your views, whether by authority, threat, money, propaganda, or even education.
4. Do not avoid contact with suffering or close your eyes to suffering.
5. Do not accumulate wealth while millions remain hungry.
6. Do not maintain anger or hatred.
7. Do not lose yourself in distraction, inwardly or outwardly.
8. Do not utter words that can create discord or cause your community to split apart.
9. Do not say untruthful things for the sake of personal advantage or to impress people.
10. Do not use the Buddhist community for personal gain or profit, or transform your community into a political party.
11. Do not live with a vocation that is harmful to humans or nature.
12. Do not kill. Do not let others kill.
13. Possess nothing that should belong to others.
14. Do not mistreat your body.

## *The Buddhist Peace Fellowship*

Although many Buddhist communities, from the major sectarian traditions have extensive programs in various aspects of socially engaged Buddhism, none offers as comprehensive a program as that of the Buddhist Peace Fellowship based in Berkeley, California. Working with individual Buddhist communities from virtually all the Buddhist traditions, it has sponsored an impressive number of programs in its short twenty-year history. The Buddhist Peace Fellowship began in 1978 in Hawaii at the Maui Zendo as a project jointly founded by Robert and Anne Aitken, Nelson Foster, and a few of their Zen friends. Within a short time, this first American expression of socially engaged Buddhism was joined by a rather eclectic collection of *Dharma* friends that included beat poet Gary Snyder, academic scholar Alfred Bloom, Buddhist activist Joanna Macy, ex-Theravāda monk Jack Kornfield, and a number of other American convert practitioners. From the very beginning, the group was highly ecumenical in nature; most of the members of the infant Buddhist Peace Fellowship (BPF) lived in Hawaii or the San Francisco Bay Area, and in those pre-Internet days it took a year to build the membership roll to fifty. In order to maintain a connected sense of networking, the group began a newsletter, largely facilitated by Nelson Foster, which eventually grew into a formal quarterly journal called *Turning Wheel* (see below). By the end of the 1980s, the group membership had grown to several hundred members and the organization had moved its base of operations to Berkeley, but more importantly, it had actively campaigned for human rights in Bangladesh, Vietnam, and Cambodia, and also worked to free imprisoned monks who belonged to Vietnam's Unified Buddhist Church. Shortly thereafter, the BPF hired a part-time co-ordinator and began forming its first member chapters. Editorial responsibility for the newsletter passed to Fred Eppsteiner and later to Arnie Kotler. The organization also became a vehicle for beginning to document some of the rapid growth in American Buddhist communities.

In 1983, the BPF (along with the San Francisco Zen Center) sponsored its first retreat for Western Buddhists at Zen Mountain Center (at Tassajara Hot Springs). Longer BPF co-sponsored tours took place in 1985, 1987, and 1989. Eventually, near the end of the decade, Thich Nhat Hanh's lay community in the West shared office space in Berkeley with the BPF and the growing Parallax Press.

The BPF is a totally non-denominational Buddhist group that describes itself as being composed of 'meditating activists'. It offers a simple, fivefold statement of purpose, shown in the text box below.

There is no need to maintain active status in any Buddhist organization in order to be a member of the BPF, and membership is available for an inexpensive yearly fee, which supports the work of the group and entitles members to a subscription to *Turning Wheel*.

As of this writing, the BPF has thirty-six chapters spread across the United States. It also has affiliates in Australia, Bangladesh, Canada, Germany, India, Japan, Ladakh, Mexico, Nepal, Thailand, and the United Kingdom. The membership base

### The five aims of the Buddhist Peace Fellowship

To make clear public witness to Buddhist practice and interdependence as a way of peace and protection for all beings.

To raise peace, environmental, feminist, and social justice concerns among North American Buddhists.

To bring a Buddhist perspective of non-duality to contemporary social action and environmental movements.

To encourage the practice of non-violence based on the rich resources of traditional Buddhist and Western spiritual teachings.

To offer avenues for dialogue and exchange among the diverse North American and world *sanghas*.

of the BPF is largely among the American convert Buddhist population, but the BPF works extensively with ethnic Buddhists and people of color who adopt Buddhism as BPF members try to move beyond any residual ethnic or racial insensitivities.

The BPF 'seeks to awaken peace where there is conflict, bring insight to institutionalized ignorance, promote communication and co-operation among *sanghas*, and in the spirit of wisdom, compassion, and harmony, offer practical help wherever possible'. In view of this mission statement, the BPF can work with almost any Buddhist community or *Dharma* center, and with Christian and Jewish groups as well. In addition to its peace efforts in the United States, focusing largely on weapons control and non-violence, the BPF has focused its outreach program on the international effort to promote peace in Asia. A major part of that effort concentrated on trying to bring about the release of Aung San Suu Kyi after years of 'house arrest' in Burma, and on acquiring low-interest loans for right-livelihood projects with Tibetan exile communities living in India and Nepal.

This international work of the BPF is organized as part of their allied association with the International Network of Engaged Buddhists (INEB), organized in February 1989 in Thailand by peace activist Sulak Sivraksa and others. The INEB has groups in more than thirty countries working toward the advancement of socially engaged Buddhism in an atmosphere of inter-Buddhist and inter-religious co-operation, attempting to support 'grassroots *Dharma* activism around the world'.

Up to now, the major areas of INEB interest have been human rights, non-violence, the environment, women's issues, alternative education, and the integration of spirituality and activism. During its first seven years of existence, the INEB promoted these issues by holding an annual winter conference, and now schedules these conferences in alternating years. Their vision and strategy is clear enough:

1. Creating a variety of working groups to explore ways in which Buddhism can be applied in the search for new global paradigms.
2. Furthering INEB's resources to disseminate information on urgent action and human rights campaigns, training workshops, and for our understanding of this interdependent world.
3. Helping to develop workshops and qualified trainers at the grassroots level in various countries and regions.

The INEB works closely with another of Sulak Sivaraksa's programs, founded in Thailand in 1995, and known as the Spirit in Education Movement (SEM). This program promotes alternative, experiential education that addresses issues such as deep ecology, consumerism, and so forth. In addition, the INEB runs an information network, and has developed an extensive publishing programme for the production of books and pamphlets. To stimulate a continually fresh flow of ideas, the INEB began a project known as 'Think *Sangha*', which in 1992 emerged out of a small circle of activists called the Buddhism and Social Analysis Group that sought to network with many scholar-activists in producing Buddhist models for effective social action. Functioning like a think tank, but based on a Buddhist community model, this group has held international meetings as a vehicle for calling attention to its attempt to integrate Buddhist moral values into real-world activities in a way that moves beyond theoretical models. Their vision of community is forthrightly stated, too: 'Our sense of "sangha" is a community of people who interact, challenge, and support one another in the spirit of transformation'.

The most challenging program of the BPF is its 'Buddhist Alliance for Social Engagement' project (BASE). It is based upon its supporters trying to actualize the *bodhisattva*'s vow to save all beings through an active agenda of social and personal transformation. BASE involves six-month cycles of either part-time or full-time commitment. The program started in the Bay Area, but has now spread to other locations. To some degree, the BASE program of training, meditation, and service mirrors the life of a Buddhist monk or nun in Asia, but reflects the American Buddhist preference for a non-monastic lifestyle. BASE participants may enroll full-time (working thirty hours per week in a placement, and thus becoming eligible for financial support), part-time (working fifteen hours per week in a placement while they maintain their regular, outside employment), or on a 'job as placement' basis (for those who are already engaged in social action work, and who participate in the training component of the BASE program).

The BASE program focuses on four major components: (a) social action; (b) retreat and training; (c) commitment; and (d) community. The social action component involves fifteen to thirty hours of work each week in a service or social justice organization. Organizers of the program try to match candidates' skills, backgrounds, and interests closely with the organization of placement. So far, placements have involved hospice work with the Zen Hospice Project, support work at the Women's Cancer Resource Center, working at a local San Francisco health clinic for homeless persons, providing assistance to Bay Area anti-nuclear and environmental groups, and working in one of the urban community garden projects in the Bay Area. The core of the BASE program is its retreat and training component.

## BASE training revolves around:

1. Comprehensive study of the roots of engaged Buddhism and its current manifestations.
2. General *Dharma* teachings and practice.
3. Applications of Buddhist practice to the daily experience of social action.
4. Buddhist-based group dynamics.

The retreat aspect of the program includes:

1. Twice-weekly gathering of meditation/study/discussion on issues of socially engaged Buddhism.
2. Monthly retreats (1–5 days).
3. Opportunity for dialogue and study with activists and thinkers.
4. Mentorship with local Buddhist activists providing ongoing spiritual guidance and support.

The commitment component requires each BASE participant to make a full six-month obligation to the program, during which time the volunteer will work diligently at *Dharma* study, Buddhist practice, and social action. Finally, the community component provides a contextual basis in which to frame the above three aspects of the program. In this aspect of the BASE program, all participants are linked to the entire Bay Area Buddhist community, construed as broadly as possible.

Like many American Buddhist communities, the BPF publishes a journal, known as *Turning Wheel*, as noted above. It is published quarterly, with individual issues corresponding to the seasons. The journal is organized into three primary parts. The first presents a series of 'regular departments', which includes letters; Buddhist readings; columns on ecology; Buddhist activists in history; family practice; news from the chapters; announcements and classifieds; and a director's report. The second is the heart of the journal, and includes a series of articles on a particular theme. Thematic issues have focused on sexual misconduct, home and homelessness, family, hatred, cities, health and health care, and weapons. The third section features book reviews on topics of interest to the BPF. Books can range from the critically important *Engaged Buddhist Reader*, edited by Arnold Kotler, to the pleasant but highly pertinent *That's Funny, You Don't Look Buddhist: On Being a Faithful Jew and a Passionate Buddhist*, by Sylvia Boorstein. The journal also publishes occasional pieces of art and poems. Although it can hardly rival more popular Buddhist publications, having a circulation of only about 6,000, it is one of the most balanced and even-handed Buddhist publications in print. It cuts across tradition and sectarian barriers in its attempt to stimulate useful dialogue and social activism. The BPF also maintain an Internet Discussion Group (bpf-ineb) which addresses all aspects of socially engaged Buddhism.

By any standards, the Buddhist Peace Fellowship is a most unusual Buddhist community. It owes allegiance to no one teacher or tradition, draws freely from the Theravāda, Mahāyāna, and Vajrayāna schools of Buddhism, emphasizes free choice of Buddhist lifestyle, and has no elaborate Dharma centers or temples which function as a home base of operations. In fact, its national headquarters is located on the outskirts of a Berkeley schoolyard. Any first-time visitor would be shocked upon entering its cramped and humble quarters. It is perhaps best to identify the site as a creative application of efficient space management. Yet, to spend one more word on the national headquarters of the BPF would entirely miss the point of the remarkable work marshaled by this selfless group of Buddhist activists. With the help of just a little up-to-date information exchange technology, a powerful impact for peace is made from this tiny office. And in so doing, the BPF is effective in demonstrating the full extent of what a non-traditional Buddhist community can accomplish when wisdom and compassion are combined with healthy doses of energy and motivation.

## *Engaged Buddhism: old or new?*

Opinion is currently divided on to what extent engaged Buddhism is a 'new' form of Buddhism, forged by modernity in response to contemporary concerns, and to what extent it exhibits continuity with traditional Buddhism. Thich Nhat Hanh has stated that Buddhists have always been socially engaged, and so a socially engaged Buddhism is 'nothing new'. Supporters of this view stress that the characterization of Buddhism as 'world-renouncing' is a caricature and point to the concept of the *bodhisattva* in which selfless service to others is the supreme ideal. They also portray the Buddha himself as a social activist who chose to reform society by founding a *sangha* rather than a kingdom.

Others claim that while social ideals may have been latent in Buddhist teachings they were never actualized until modern times, and therefore engaged Buddhism constitutes a sufficient departure from tradition to merit recognition as a new movement in much the same way that Mahāyāna Buddhism came to be regarded as novel and distinctive. Arguments purporting to demonstrate both continuity and discontinuity with the past are commonly heard, and often make reference to particular historical examples where Buddhism was seen to be more (or less) 'engaged'.

Some commentators claim that Christianity has played a part in the emergence of engaged Buddhism, and see its concern with social reform as inspired more by liberal Protestant notions of social service and activism than Buddhist teachings. Others draw a parallel with the 'liberation theology' movement in Latin America and other parts of the Third World. In the recent book *Action Dharma* (2003: 253), James Deitrick describes this supposed mingling of cultural values as 'the infusion of Euro-American thought into the veins of Buddhist Asia'. The arguments go back and forth, but while it is fair to say that there is continuity at the level of values between ancient and modern Buddhism, there is undeniably discontinuity at the level of issues. The kinds of issues which occupy socially engaged Buddhists are essentially of a contemporary nature and there is little evidence of concern for these matters in traditional scriptures. To conclude the chapter we will discuss two questions which are of concern to engaged Buddhism – human rights and ecology

– in order to illustrate the approaches engaged Buddhist writers have adopted and the difficulties they face.

## *Human rights*

Political events in the course of this century have pushed the issue of human rights to the top of the Buddhist agenda. The Chinese invasion of Tibet, the bitter ethnic conflict in Sri Lanka, and the experience of dictatorship in countries such as Burma have all provided Buddhism with first-hand experience of human rights violations. When discussing such cases, leading Asian and Western Buddhists routinely express their concern about social injustice in the vocabulary of human rights, but few stop to ask how far this language is appropriate for Buddhism, and how well the Western concept of human rights fits into the general framework of Buddhist teachings.

The concept of rights is extremely important in Western discussions of social, political and ethical issues. Slogans such as the 'right to choose', 'the right to life', and (in the context of euthanasia) the 'right to die', are the common currency of contemporary debate, as we will see in the following chapter. The concept of a right emerged in the West as the result of a particular combination of social, political, and intellectual developments which have not been repeated elsewhere. From the Enlightenment in the eighteenth century, rights have occupied center-stage in legal and political discourse, and provide a supple and flexible language in terms of which individuals may express their claims to justice. A right may be defined as an exercisable power vested in an individual. This power may be thought of as a benefit or entitlement, which allows the right-holder to impose a claim upon others or to remain immune from demands which others seek to impose.

Contemporary human rights charters typically set out a list of basic rights which are held to be possessed by all human beings without distinction as to race or creed. Many Buddhists subscribe to such Charters, and Buddhist leaders such as the Dalai Lama can often be heard endorsing the principles these charters embody. None of the rights mentioned in the thirty-nine articles of the Universal Declaration of Human Rights proclaimed by the General Assembly of the United Nations in 1948 would seem to be in conflict with Buddhist teachings. Certain of these rights, indeed, seem to be foreshadowed in Buddhist sources: for example, a right not to be held in slavery can be found in the canonical prohibition on trade in living beings (A.iii.208). It is also arguable that other human rights are implicit in the Buddhist precepts. The right not to be killed or tortured, for example, may be thought of as implicit in the First Precept.

A major problem for proponents of Buddhist human rights, however, is that traditional sources have little to say about the kinds of questions which are now regarded as human rights issues. There is no word in early Buddhist sources corresponding to the notion of 'rights' in the way understood in the West. If Buddhism has no word for and hence apparently no concept of rights, how appropriate is it for Buddhists to use the language of rights when discussing moral issues?

A Buddhist may wish to argue that the discourse of rights is not inappropriate for Buddhism because rights and duties are related. Buddhist sources speak more about duties than rights, but a right can be regarded as the converse of a duty. If A has a duty to B, then B stands in the position of beneficiary and has a right to whatever benefit flows from the performance of his duty on the part of A. Although rights are not explicitly mentioned in Buddhist sources, it may be thought that they are implicit in the notion of *Dharmic* duties. For example, if a king has a duty to rule justly, then it can be said that citizens have a 'right' to fair treatment. At a more general level, if everyone has a duty not to take life, then living creatures have a right to life; if everyone has a duty not to steal, then everyone has a right not to be unjustly deprived of their property. Thus it might be argued that the concept of rights is implicit in *Dharma*, and that rights and duties are like separate windows onto the common good of justice.

A line of argument of the kind just sketched may be the beginnings of a justification for an engaged Buddhist doctrine of rights. However, Buddhism must show not only that it can engage in 'rights talk' but also that the rights it claims to defend have a genuine basis in Buddhist doctrine. How might it do this? It might begin by pointing out that human rights are closely tied to the notion of human dignity. Many human rights charters, in fact, explicitly derive the former from the latter. In many religions human dignity is said to derive from the fact that human beings are created in the image of God. Buddhism, of course, makes no such theological claim. This makes it difficult to see what the source of human dignity might be, but if it is not to be sought at a theological level presumably it must be sought at a human one. For Buddhism, it seems that human dignity flows from the capacity of human beings to gain enlightenment, as demonstrated by the historical figure of the Buddha and the saints of the Buddhist tradition. A Buddha is a living celebration of human potential, and it is in the profound knowledge and compassion which he exemplifies – qualities which all human beings can emulate – that human dignity is rooted. Buddhism teaches that we are all potential Buddhas (some Mahāyāna schools express this by saying that all beings possess the 'Buddha-nature' or the seed of enlightenment). By virtue of this common potential for enlightenment, all individuals are worthy of respect, and justice therefore demands that the rights of each individual must be protected.

Not all Buddhists, however, are happy with the Western terminology used above. Phrases such as 'human dignity' are not found in Buddhist literature and sound alien to their ears. The emphasis on the role of the individuals as the primary bearer of rights also seems egocentric and out of keeping with Buddhist teachings on interrelatedness and interdependency. Instead, some contemporary writers have sought to ground a Buddhist doctrine of human rights on notions which have a more authentic

Buddhist pedigree, such as compassion (*karuṇā*), and the doctrine of dependent origination (*pratītya-samutpāda*). It remains to be seen how successful these attempts will be, and whether in time the foundations can be laid for a specifically Buddhist doctrine of human rights to emerge. An intellectual underpinning of some kind seem necessary if engaged Buddhists are to continue to ground calls for respect for human rights in Buddhist teachings.

## *Ecology*

Another issue of concern to engaged Buddhists is ecology. Buddhism is seen by many in the movement as being 'environmentally friendly', and a contrast is often drawn between Buddhism's attitude to the natural world and that of Christianity. According to the account of creation in the Book of Genesis, the world was created by God, and man was appointed as his steward with dominion over it. Writers such as Lynn White have seen this belief as fostering the view that nature exists purely for man's enjoyment, thereby leading inexorably to the exploitation of natural resources, the rise of consumer societies, and ultimately to the present ecological crisis. Buddhism, by contrast, as we saw in the *Aggañña Sutta* discussed in Chapter One, teaches that mankind and the natural world evolved together and that the moral status of human beings has a profound effect on the environment. But is it anachronistic to read environmental concern (or the lack of it) into these creation stories, and to what extent do texts such as the *Aggañña Sutta* demonstrate a serious interest in ecology on the part of ancient Buddhism?

Many volumes have been written by engaged Buddhists seeking to demonstrate the environmental credentials of Buddhism. Three particularly influential books were *Buddhism and Ecology*, edited by Martine Batchelor and Kerry Brown; *Dharma Gaia*, edited by Allan Hunt Badiner; and *Buddhism and Ecology: The Interconnection of Dharma and Deeds* (referred to below as *Dharma and Deeds*), edited by Mary Evelyn Tucker and Duncan Ryūken Williams. The essays in these volumes borrow various ideas from Buddhism and apply them to current environmental problems. They also draw on a wide range of examples, from ancient Theravāda to the modern West, and make frequent reference to ancient Buddhist thinkers like Nāgārjuna, medieval Japanese poets such as Bashō and Chan-jan, socially engaged Thai Buddhists such as Buddhadāsa Bhikkhu, and leading contemporary figures such as the Dalai Lama.

An essay that expresses both social and political concerns is A.T. Ariyaratne and Joanna Macy's introduction to the Sarvodaya movement in Sri Lanka. Sarvodaya is a movement that promotes self-reliance among the local population as well as the decentralization of power. Importance is given to controlling the pollution that has blighted nature and, metaphorically, human wisdom. The essay expresses the powerful nature of the movement in the shift of power from a central to local base, and this movement is spoken of as a Buddhist initiative. Macy, at one point in the essay claims

Sarvodaya as 'a philosophy of development based on indigenous religious tradition, that is, on the *Dharma*' (p.83). Although the founder of Sarvodaya, A.T. Ariyaratne, clearly has a visionary approach to contemporary problems, it is not entirely clear how much Sarvodaya owes to Buddhism. Critics have suggested, for example, that the movement is more inspired by Gandhian ideals than by Buddhism. It has been said that the concept of the voluntary communal work groups which underpin the movement is 'neither uniquely Buddhist nor uniquely Sri Lankan'.

Some of the writings touch upon the economic, social and political dimensions of the environment from a Buddhist perspective. In *Dharma Gaia*, for instance, Stephen Batchelor's essay entitled 'Buddhist Economics Reconsidered' suggests the adoption of new terms and values for a Buddhist economic theory. He writes that a Buddhist economics must be based on the concept of non-duality in such a way that the separation between agent, act and object becomes conceptual. For this to happen the foundation must be emptiness (*śūnyatā*), which the author understands as the view of things and minds as non-separate. The economics would also have to consider the Buddhist acceptance of reality as 'acentric', or that that no one thing occupies a central place as compared to others.

The literature also reveals a good deal of interest in animal welfare. Christopher Key Chapple's essay in *Dharma and Deeds* interprets the *Jātakas* as simple moral tales containing a strong environmental message due to their reference to animals. He points out that animals are included in the six categories of beings of Buddhist cosmology, as we saw in Chapter One. That animals can be seen as potential humans in the *Jātakas* appears to make the boundary between animals and humans much more fluid than it is in the West. Duncan Ryūken Williams's essay in the same volume discusses the Hojo-e ceremony of releasing captured wildlife into its natural habitat in medieval Japan. It would seem, however, that what began as a compassionate action towards animals soon became politicized and corrupted and was no longer sympathetic toward animals. This ceremony is often quoted as an example of Buddhist environmentalism, but this example makes the author cautious and he warns against the idealization of Buddhist practices.

In *Dharma Gaia*, William Lafleur mentions Zhanran, a thinker of the Tiantai School, who spoke of the enlightenment of grass and trees. Lafleur draws the conclusion that some later schools such as Zen, Huayan and Tiantai were able to establish, through Mahāyāna universalism and the logic of interdependence, that Buddhahood is shared by all *sattva*, that is, by all beings and phenomena. While this seems a promising basis for ecology, much work remains to be done to turn it into a fully-fledged theory.

It is noticeable that ecological writings contain in them some reference to Buddhist doctrines such as no-self (*anātman*), emptiness (*śūnyavāda*), dependent origination (*pratītya-samutpāda*), karma and others. These doctrines are linked to the promotion of environmental protection, but for the most part it remains to be demonstrated how such a connection can be established. Interdependence in particular has come under attack as a foundation for environmental ethics: where environmental ethics typically wishes to prove the inherent value of all parts of the natural world, interdependence seeks quite the opposite, seeing entities as lacking intrinsic nature and deriving their value from a relationship to other things.

Meditation is commonly seen as a resource that supports eco-Buddhism, and there are many references to the environmental crisis as being essentially a spiritual crisis. Buddhism is seen by engaged Buddhists as having the necessary resources for addressing this problem. In *Dharma and Deeds*, Ruben Habito's essay on Zen practice strives to prove that Zen teachings support the well-being of the earth. It might be thought that Zen's preoccupation with the 'within' and the 'present' excludes the 'without' and the 'past/future'. However the author rules this out as untrue, for Zen meditation leads to the deepening of mindfulness as well as the awakening of the true self and its realization in ordinary life. This actually helps us to overcome the dichotomy of seeing ourselves as other and, therefore, cultivates a true ecological attitude. Martin Pitt's essay, 'The Pebble and the Tide' in *Dharma Gaia*, also stresses the point that meditation is at the heart of true ecological awareness. In the same section is Suzanne Head's very moving essay. Head describes her direct experience of wilderness when on a retreat to re-establish a healthy relationship with the earth. The focus here is on different ways to reconnect with nature, such as different sorts of meditations, mindful verses or *gāthās*, *haiku* poetry, or simply an attitude of gratitude towards the earth. Much importance is given to such practices, but it perhaps needs to be reiterated that the Buddha at no stage specifically suggested any of the above exercises as a means of gaining environmental awareness; they were all, rather, a way of calming the mind in preparation for the final goal of nirvana. That ecological awareness results from meditation, thus, remains an incidental consequence rather than a primary one.

Apart from meditation, practice and the concern about how to translate the teachings into action occupy an important place. Buddhist nature activists and observers try to understand the issues involved and the success of the ventures undertaken. The essays concerned with practices cover diverse attitudes seen in India, Japan, America, Vietnam and Thailand. Helena Norberg-Hodge's essay, 'May a Hundred Plants Grow From One Seed', in *Buddhism and Ecology* looks at the traditional ecological tradition of Ladakh in India, which she finds is attuned to climatic conditions where frugality is a way of life. The monastery occupies an important position and is involved in community life. However, she points out that the situation has changed since the introduction of modernity. The author is now actively involved in promoting sustainable development projects for Ladakh. This essay has an anthropological character and the way of life projected may be more dependent on culture and climate than on Buddhism.

The nature of the monastic community in Thailand and its role in reducing environment-related problems is often discussed in engaged Buddhist literature. In this context, the practice of the ordination of trees by Thai monks can be mentioned. A typical case was when a group of so-called 'ecology monks' wrapped monks' robes around a number of large trees in a rain forest threatened by the construction of a dam. An adapted monastic ordination ceremony was also performed as a consciousness-raising exercise to draw attention to environmental destruction. That this is a Buddhist practice at all, however, is controversial and has led to the expulsion of many monks from the more traditional *sanghas*, which casts doubt on the authenticity of this environmental practice as genuinely Buddhist. Elsewhere in the Buddhist world Yokoyama's essay explores the harmony in nature as extolled by various Japanese Buddhist schools, and concludes by saying that he sees the potential in Japan to develop an environmentally protective way of life. A problem for this line of argument is that Japan in fact has a poor record on environmental conservation.

In conclusion we must pose the question 'How Buddhist is engaged Buddhism?'. Stephanie Kaza ends her essay 'American Buddhist Response to the Land' in *Dharma and Deeds* (p. 244) with an important comment: 'At this point it is unclear whether ecological practices are primarily motivated by Buddhist tradition or by American environmentalism'. There seems to be a questioning here of the very foundations of American ecoBuddhism, by an American Buddhist herself. The emphasis, indeed, seems to be on how the tradition has been interpreted by renowned American environmentalists and brings to mind Ian Harris's comment that 'Much that masquerades under the label of eco-Buddhism [...] on analysis, turns out to be an uneasy partnership between Spinozism, New Age Religiosity and highly selective Buddhism' (see Further reading). It is clear that engaged Buddhism has achieved a great deal in practical and organizational terms in a short space of time, but it still faces the challenge of demonstrating that its beliefs, practices and values are a genuine expression of Buddhist religiosity.

## Note

Pragati Sahni has given permission for material which comes from her 2003 D.Phil. thesis, 'Environmental Ethics in Early Buddhism', to be reproduced in this chapter.

**Key points you need to know**

- Socially engaged Buddhism has become the leading activist approach for social causes in Buddhism throughout the world.
- Thich Nhat Hanh has created an organization called the 'Order of Interbeing', with fourteen basic precepts for moral action.
- In the United States, the Buddhist Peace Fellowship is the most active socially engaged Buddhist organization.
- The Buddhist Peace Fellowship runs, or is part of, two major activist programs: the Buddhist Alliance for Social Engagement (BASE) and the International Network of Engaged Buddhists (INEB).
- Political developments in many Buddhist countries have made the issue of human rights vitally important for Buddhists, but an authentically Buddhist doctrine of human rights has not yet emerged.
- Environmental issues are of great importance to engaged Buddhists, yet many such issues of contemporary concern are barely mentioned in the ancient scriptures.
- Critics suggest that engaged Buddhism owes more to Western than Buddhist values, and many Buddhists argue that Buddhism should develop its own response to contemporary problems rather than adopting Western ones.

## Discussion questions

1. Do you think socially engaged Buddhism is sufficiently distinctive to be recognized as a new 'vehicle' (*yāna*)?
2. To what extent do groups like the Buddhist Peace Fellowship represent a new kind of Western *sangha*?
3. Do you think engaged Buddhism has anything to contribute to contemporary social and political issues such as human rights and ecology?

## Further reading

Ariyaratne, A.T. and Macy, Joanna. 'The Island of Temple and Tank. Sarvodaya: Self-help in Sri Lanka' in Martine Batchelor and Kerry Brown (eds) *Buddhism and Ecology*. London: Cassell, 1992.

Badiner, Allan Hunt. *Dharma Gaia*. Berkeley, CA: Parallax Press, 1990.

Harris, Ian. 'Causation and Telos: The Problem of Buddhist Environmental Ethics'. *Journal of Buddhist Ethics*. Vol. 1 (1994): 45–56.

Harris, Ian. 'Getting to Grips with Buddhist Environmentalism: A Provisional Typology'. *Journal of Buddhist Ethics*. Vol. 2 (1995): 173–190.

Kraft, Kenneth. *Inner Peace, World Peace: Essays on Buddhism and Non-violence*. Albany, NY: State University of New York, 1992.

Queen, Christopher. *Engaged Buddhism in the West*. Boston, MA: Wisdom Publications, 2000.

Queen, Christopher, Charles Prebish and Damien Keown. *Action Dharma: New Studies in Engaged Buddhism*. London: RoutledgeCurzon, 2003.

Tucker, Mary Evelyn, and Duncan Ryūken Williams. *Buddhism and Ecology: The Interconnection of Dharma and Deeds*. Cambridge, MA: Harvard University Press, 1997.

Online Conference on Buddhism and Human Rights. *Journal of Buddhist Ethics*, October 1995, available online at http://jbe.gold.ac.uk.

Online Conference on Socially Engaged Buddhism. *Journal of Buddhist Ethics*, April 2000, available online at http://jbe.gold.ac.uk.

# 13 *Ethics*

## In this chapter

Buddhism is widely admired for its moral values, particularly its emphasis on non-violence, tolerance and compassion. Its ethical teachings are also distinctive by virtue of the doctrine of karma, which was explained in Chapter One and so will not be discussed again here. Instead this chapter first of all explores the foundations of Buddhist ethics before considering one of the most controversial issues of modern times – war and terrorism.

## Main topics covered

- *Dharma* as moral foundation
- Buddhist precepts and virtues
- Monastic ethics
- *Ahiṃsā*
- Skillful means
- War and terrorism

## **Dharma** *as moral foundation*

The ultimate basis for Buddhist morality is *Dharma*. We explored the meaning of this term in Chapter One, and saw that it embodies the notion of a cosmic order underlying both the laws of nature (such as gravity and causation) and also the moral laws which regulate human conduct (such as karma). Buddhists, accordingly, see morality as embedded in the nature of things and believe that someone who leads a moral life is in harmony with the cosmic order and as a result can expect to prosper and flourish. Those who live immorally, on the other hand, and pursue a course contrary to the requirements of *Dharma*, can expect only unhappiness and misfortune as a result.

In his first sermon, when the Buddha 'turned the wheel of the *Dharma*', he made reference to the Fourth Noble Truth, setting out the Path that leads to nirvana. This Path, as we saw in Chapter Three, is a threefold one consisting of morality (*śīla*), meditation (*samādhi*), and wisdom (*prajñā*). We see from this that morality is integral to the religious life, and since the sources always list the three components in the same order we can conclude that morality is the forerunner and prerequisite for the other two.

Because of the underlying belief in *Dharma*, Buddhist schools tend to share a common core of moral teachings, virtues, and precepts. While there are differences in emphasis – for example, the Mahāyāna emphasizes compassion (*karuṇā*) to a greater degree than the Theravāda – we find a broadly similar set of precepts and virtues set out in different schools. Perhaps the most striking exception to the general pattern is in *Tantra*, where, in certain restricted circumstances, conventional moral teachings appear to be inverted as part of esoteric religious training. By and large, however, lay Buddhists around the world would recognize the Five Precepts as the basis of their moral practice, while Buddhist monks and nuns would regard the *Vinaya* (in its different recensions) as a binding code of conduct. Moral teachings such as the 'Golden Rule' (which in the Buddhist version counsels us not to do to others anything we would not like them to do to ourselves) are also universally admired and expounded. For example, the *Dhammapada* states: 'All tremble at violence, all fear death. Comparing oneself with others one should neither kill nor cause to kill'. (v.129)

## *Buddhist precepts*

There are five main sets of precepts in Buddhism:
1. The Five Precepts (*pañca-śīla*).
2. The Eight Precepts (*aṣṭāṅga-śīla*).
3. The Ten Precepts (*daśa-śīla*).
4. The Ten Good Paths of Action (*daśa-kuśala-karmapatha*).
5. The Monastic Disciplinary Code (*prātimokṣa*).

The most widely observed of these codes is the first, the Five Precepts for laymen. These five are supplemented by additional precepts according to the status of the practitioner or to suit particular ceremonial occasions. The fifth precept, against taking intoxicants, for example, is thought to be particularly relevant for layfolk, while the Eight and Ten Precepts, which supplement the basic five with additional restrictions such as on the time when meals may be taken, are commonly adopted as additional commitments on holy days (*poṣadha*). The disciplinary code (*prātimokṣa*) contained in the *Vinaya* is a set of over two hundred rules (the exact number varies between schools) which sets out in detail the regulations for communal monastic life.

### The Five Precepts

This is the most widely-known list of precepts in Buddhism, comparable in influence to the Ten Commandments of Christianity. The Five Precepts are undertaken as voluntary commitments in the ceremony of 'taking refuge' when a person becomes a Buddhist. They are as follows:

(1) I undertake the precept to refrain from harming living creatures.
(2) I undertake the precept to refrain from taking what has not been given.
(3) I undertake the precept to refrain from sexual immorality.
(4) I undertake the precept to refrain from speaking falsely.
(5) I undertake the precept to refrain from taking intoxicants.

As is common in traditional societies, in India moral teachings are usually expressed in the form of duties rather than rights. These duties are often thought of as linked to a person's social status (such as the caste to which they belong) or their profession or occupation. Ultimately, however, all moral obligations have their foundation in *Dharma*, and there are certain basic requirements of *Dharma* that all must respect, regardless of their social standing or occupation. In Buddhism, these basic requirements of morality are expressed in the form of precepts, and on becoming a Buddhist a person participates in a ceremony known as 'going for refuge' in which he or she formally 'takes the precepts' – in other words, gives a voluntary undertaking to respect and observe them. Interestingly, those becoming Buddhists are not called up to make any avowal of faith in particular beliefs or doctrines, which suggests that in Buddhism moral conduct is seen as more important than dogmas or creeds.

## *Monastic ethics*

As noted in Chapter Four, the life of a Buddhist monk or nun is regulated by the *Vinaya*. The *Vinaya* contains information on the origins of the *sangha*, the early councils, disputes over matters of monastic conduct, and also recounts how the traditions of the order arose. The *Vinaya* also includes a code of over 200 rules for monks (the exact number varies between 218 and 263 depending on the school) known as the *prātimokṣa*. There is a separate code of rules for nuns which is stricter in some respects, and contains from 279 to 380 rules. While many of these rules are of an ethical nature, a large number deal with matters such as diet, clothing, dwellings, furniture, and personal possessions. The rules are arranged in eight sections in decreasing order of seriousness.

The *Vinaya* is in some ways comparable to the Rule of St. Benedict, a code of conduct introduced in the sixth century and still followed today by Christian monks of the Benedictine Order. The Buddhist *Vinaya* predates this by almost a thousand years, and is also more extensive, containing a good deal of background material explaining how each rule came to be introduced, and detailing exceptions and modifications that were made due to new circumstances over the course of time. In these accounts, the Buddha is depicted as laying down the individual rules, although it is clear that a number of them date from after his death.

Sections of the *Vinaya* are a bit like the transcript of a court hearing, or the shorthand notes a scribe might have made when recording the essential points of each case and the verdict handed down. The style is terse and legalistic, but commentators subsequently added their reflections and conjectures to cast light on obscure points (a modern commentary on the rules is available online). These writings mark the beginnings of a legal tradition which takes the early moral teachings as its basis and seeks to develop principles of jurisprudence to resolve questions of guilt and innocence when monks were thought to have infringed the rules. The monastic precepts of the *Vinaya* can therefore be seen as a combination of moral precepts with additional regulations designed to encourage self-discipline, and to ensure the smooth running of monastic communities which were rapidly increasing in size. Of key importance was the public face of the *sangha* and its status in the eyes of the lay community: a *sangha* riven with dissent and lax in discipline would bring the teachings of the Buddha into disrepute, and jeopardize the economic support of the laity on which the monasteries depended for their survival. In this respect, the twice-monthly *poṣadha* ceremony at which all the resident monks assemble to hear the rules recited functions as a public affirmation of the collective moral purity of the monastic community.

## Virtues

To be seen to be following the rules and observing the precepts is an important aspect of moral practice but there is an internal dimension to ethics which is also important. Buddhist teachings place great emphasis on the cultivation of good qualities known as virtues. These are habits or patterns of behavior which are thought to be morally exemplary, such as courage, honesty, and generosity. An individual who develops these qualities to the point where they become second nature is regarded as a person of integrity who can serve as a role model for others. Those people who risk their lives for others, who tell the truth and refuse to compromise on basic principles, or who act unselfishly and put the interests of others before their own, are rightly regarded as heroes and worthy of respect and admiration. Such good qualities become so integrated into the personality of these individuals that they are almost incapable of acting otherwise. To attain a state of such natural and spontaneous goodness is the goal of Buddhist ethics.

The three most basic Buddhist virtues – which we may call the 'cardinal virtues' of Buddhism – are known as non-greed (*arāga*), non-hatred (*adveṣa*), and non-delusion (*amoha*). These are the opposite of the three 'roots of evil' (*akuśala-mūla*) or 'three poisons' namely greed, hatred, and delusion, which are depicted at the center of the *bhavacakra* or wheel of life as we saw in Chapter One. If we wanted to use more familiar terminology to characterize the three cardinal virtues we could label the first one as unselfishness, generosity or liberality. Basically it means abandoning attachment and thinking of others rather than of oneself. The second could be called benevolence, since it is presupposes an attitude of goodwill towards all beings and a disposition to seek their welfare. Non-delusion means wisdom or understanding, particularly with respect to important principles such as the Four Noble Truths of Buddhism.

From the three core or cardinal virtues many others spring. One of the most important of these is compassion (*karuṇā*). This was discussed in Chapter Six in the context of Mahāyāna Buddhism. The list of the Six Perfections (*pāramita*) provides a convenient tabulation of the virtues of a *bodhisattva*, namely generosity (*dāna*), morality (*śīla*), patience (*kṣānti*), perseverance (*vīrya*), meditation (*samādhi*), and wisdom (*prajñā*). Buddhist sources constantly stress the importance of virtues of these kinds and encourage people to cultivate them if they wish to become saints (*arhants*), *bodhisattvas* or Buddhas. Given this emphasis on the virtues in Buddhist practice, there is a growing consensus among scholars today, that Buddhist ethics is best classified as a form of 'virtue ethics'.

## Dāna

*Dāna* literally means 'giving', and denotes the virtue of generosity. As noted above, this is the first of the 'Six Perfections' of a *bodhisattva*, so in an important sense marks the beginning of the religious path, a path along which a selfish person can make little progress. Those who join the monastic community give everything away as a condition of entry, and as religious teachers and exemplars give of their time in teaching and performing good works. In this respect they give the gift of the *Dharma*, which is said to be the highest of all gifts. In economic terms, *dāna* is a virtue which is of particular importance to the laity, since the laity provides everything the *sangha* needs, including robes, food, medicine, and the land and buildings for the monastery. In the countries of South Asia where Theravāda Buddhism is practiced, cloth for the robes is donated in the *kaṭhina* ceremony that takes place after the retreat during the rainy season. This emphasis on generosity is widespread in Buddhist cultures, and stinginess or niggardliness is seen as a particularly negative quality. At all levels of society generous actions are praised and applauded, and a generous heart is thought of as a sign of spiritual maturity. This is because the generous person is less wrapped up in his or her egocentric concerns, and accordingly is more alive to the needs of others. Renunciation and detachment also come more easily to someone of a generous nature.

Buddhist literature provides accounts of exemplary generosity and many Theravāda sources praise it. Throughout South Asia the story of Prince Vessantara, the hero of the *Vessantara Jātaka,* is very well-known. Vessantara was a prince who gave away his entire kingdom, then – as if this was not enough – proceeded to give away even his wife Maddī and their young children as slaves! Fortunately, the story has a happy ending, and generous acts are always thought to lead to good karmic consequences. Typically, generosity is said to produce much wealth, and to lead to a heavenly rebirth.

More heroic sacrifices are made by *bodhisattvas* who give away limbs or sacrifice their entire bodies to save starving animals. A story in the *Jātakamāla*, a fourth-century collection of stories composed by Āryasūra, tells how the Buddha in a previous life threw himself over a cliff in order to feed a starving tigress, so moved was he by compassion for the suffering of the animal and her young cubs. In East Asia the practice of burning off fingers or limbs arose as an act of sacrifice dedicated to the welfare of all sentient beings. In more recent times, during the Vietnam war, a number of Buddhist monks such as Thich Qang Duc burned themselves alive as

*Figure 13.1* Wall mural depicting the sufferings of the hungry ghost (*preta*) realm, Haedongsa Monastery, Andong, Korea.

*Figure 13.2* Wall painting at Ajaṇṭā depicting a scene from the *Vessantara Jātaka* in which Vessantara announces his intention to depart from the palace and the palace women react with horror.

an act of protest. These deeds were seen by some as a modern example of the more extreme kinds of *dāna* just described, although it must be said that opinion among Buddhists is divided on the wisdom and justification for such acts of mutilation and suicide.

## Ahiṃsā

*Ahiṃsā* is the virtue of non-violence, or non-harming. In modern times it has been closely associated with Gandhi and his policy of non-violent protest which achieved great success against the British during the struggle for Indian independence. It is largely because of its emphasis on *ahiṃsā* that Buddhism is widely regarded as non-violent and peace-loving. Buddhist countries have not been exempt from war and conflict, as we shall see below, but there is a strong pressure to seek peaceful solutions to problems rather than resorting to violence.

The origins of *ahiṃsā* in ancient times seem to be lie among the unorthodox *śramaṇa* groups such as Jains and Buddhists, although the principle increasingly

## Teachings on *Dāna*

These five are a virtuous person's gifts. Which five? A virtuous person gives a gift with a sense of conviction. A virtuous person gives a gift attentively. A virtuous person gives a gift in season. A virtuous person gives a gift with an empathetic heart. A virtuous person gives a gift without adversely affecting himself or others. Having given a gift with a sense of conviction, he – wherever the result of that gift ripens – is rich, with much wealth, with many possessions. And he is well-built, handsome, extremely inspiring, endowed with a lotus-like complexion. Having given a gift attentively, he – wherever the result of that gift ripens – is rich, with much wealth, with many possessions. And his children, wives, slaves, servants, and workers listen carefully to him, lend him their ears, and serve him with understanding hearts. Having given a gift in season, he – wherever the result of that gift ripens – is rich, with much wealth, with many possessions. And his goals are fulfilled in season. Having given a gift with an empathetic heart, he – wherever the result of that gift ripens – is rich, with much wealth, with many possessions. And his mind inclines to the enjoyment of the five strings of lavish sensuality. Having given a gift without adversely affecting himself or others, he – wherever the result of that gift ripens – is rich, with much wealth, with many possessions. And not from anywhere does destruction come to his property – whether from fire, from water, from kings, from thieves, or from hateful heirs. These five are a virtuous person's gifts.

From the *Sappurisadāna Sutta* ('The Discourse on the Gifts of a Virtuous Person'), translated from the Pāli by Thanissaro Bhikkhu (slightly amended).

came to influence the orthodox Brahmanical tradition. One orthodox practice the *śramaṇa* schools objected to was the sacrifice of animals, which was rejected by Jains and Buddhists as cruel and barbaric. As a reaction to their criticism, blood sacrifices began to be replaced by symbolic offerings such as fruit, vegetables, and milk. As a moral principle, *ahiṃsā* involves more than just opposition to animal sacrifices. Despite the negative formulation of the term ('non-harming') it also has positive implications in terms of the way one views and behaves towards living creatures generally. It involves, for example, treating all living creatures with kindness and respect born out of a concern for their well-being. As such it comes closer to what in the West is termed 'respect for life', or the 'sanctity of life'. Philosophers who have championed this cause, such as Albert Schweitzer (1875–1965) who received the 1952 Nobel Peace Prize, believed that reverence for life – by which he meant respect for every manifestation of life – was the highest ethical principle.

In ancient India, it was the Jains who followed this principle most strictly. They believed it was wrong to destroy any form of life, however small, and took precautions such as wearing masks to avoid breathing in tiny insects. Buddhist monks followed this example to some degree, and were permitted to carry a water-strainer to remove tiny creatures from their drinking-water. They also refrained from traveling during the rainy season, partly because the rains brought forth innumerable species of insects which could be crushed underfoot by the traveller. Buddhism, however, took the view that *ahiṃsā* imposes the more limited moral obligation to refrain only from the intentional taking of life: in other words, no bad karma results from accidentally treading on an ant, but if one does it deliberately with the intention of causing death or harm, it is a bad act. Buddhist texts place much emphasis on cultivating feelings of concern (*dayā*) and sympathy (*anukampā*) for living creatures, based on the realization that all dislike pain and suffering just as much as oneself.

Due to the importance of *ahiṃsā*, many Buddhists, and in particular followers of the Mahāyāna from East Asia, have embraced vegetarianism as a way of life. The Buddha himself was not a vegetarian, and did not require his followers to give up eating meat (in fact, he opposed an attempt to make vegetarianism compulsory for monks). Many Buddhists in South Asia are not vegetarian, although professions involved in the slaughter of animals (such as that of butcher) are looked down on.

## *Compassion*

Compassion (*karuṇā*) is a virtue that is highly valued in all schools of Buddhism, but in particular by the Mahāyāna. As part of its sweeping reinterpretation of early teachings, the Mahāyāna introduced a new emphasis in ethics. The figure of the *bodhisattva* and the practice of the Six Perfections (*pāramitā*) came to occupy center-stage, and earlier schools were criticized for an alleged selfishness and lack of concern for others. Mahāyāna literature proclaims the importance of compassion (*karuṇā*) on almost every page, and at times raises compassion to the status of a supreme virtue, claiming that it eclipses all others, even wisdom (*prajñā*). The Mahāyāna also frequently berates Hīnayāna schools for an alleged selfishness and lack of compassion, a criticism which is to a certain extent overstated.

Compassion is certainly not absent in early Buddhism, where it is found as the second of the four *Brahma-vihāras*, the 'Divine Abidings' or 'Sublime States'. These are four dispositions cultivated particularly in meditation, consisting of loving kindness (*mettā*), compassion (*karuṇā*), sympathetic joy (*muditā*) and equanimity (*upekkhā*). The practice of these virtues involves radiating these qualities outwards, starting with oneself and then extending their scope to include family and friends, neighbors, the local community, and finally the entire universe. Thus the practice of compassion is not absent from the early path, although it would be fair to say it received much greater emphasis in the Mahāyāna. As far as other ethical teachings go, however, the Mahāyāna largely adopted the formulations of the earlier tradition: monks and nuns, for instance, continued to follow the *Vinayas* of the early schools, while the laity followed the Five Precepts.

In Mahāyāna Buddhism, the attribute of compassion is particularly associated with the great *bodhisattva* Avalokiteśvara ('the one who looks down from on high'). Avalokiteśvara is first mentioned in the *Lotus Sūtra* (c. first century C.E.) and remains a minor figure until his cult became popular in Tibet many centuries later. In Tibetan iconography he is depicted as having many heads and up to a thousand arms, symbolizing his vigilance and readiness to help those in need. In China, Avalokiteśvara assumed a female form, and is widely revered under the name Guanyin (Jap.: Kwannon). In whatever form he appears, Avalokiteśvara is appealed to by those in need or danger across the Buddhist world.

## *Skillful means*

The concept of 'skillful means' (*upāya-kauśalya*) is of considerable importance in Mahāyāna Buddhism and is expounded at an early date in texts such as the *Upāya-kauśalya Sūtra*, the *Lotus Sūtra*, and the *Vimalakīrti-nirdeśa Sūtra*. In chapter two of the *Lotus Sūtra*, the Buddha introduces the doctrine of skillful means and demonstrates by the use of parables throughout the text why it is necessary for him to make use of stratagems and devices. The text depicts him as a wise man or kindly father whose words his foolish children refuse to heed. To encourage them to follow his advice he has recourse to 'skillful means', realizing that this is the only way to bring the ignorant and deluded into the path to liberation. Although this involves a certain degree of duplicity, such as telling lies, the Buddha is exonerated from all blame since his only motivation is compassionate concern for all beings.

The notion of skillful means has its roots in the Buddha's skill as a teacher, and his ability to adapt his message to suit the audience he was addressing. For instance, in his discussions with Brahmins, the Buddha would frequently make reference to their customs and traditions as a way of elucidating some aspect of his own teachings. The Mahāyāna develops this idea by suggesting that the Buddha's teaching in its entirety is essentially a provisional means to bring beings to enlightenment (*bodhi*) and that the teachings which he gives may vary: what may be appropriate at one time may not be so at another. The concept is used by the Mahāyāna to justify innovations in doctrine, and to portray the Buddha's early teachings as limited and restricted by the lesser spiritual capacity of his early followers. In the Mahāyāna, skillful means comes to be a legitimate method to be employed by Buddhas and *bodhisattvas* whenever the benefit of beings warrants it. Spurred on by their great compassion (*mahākaruṇā*), *bodhisattvas* are seen in some sources (such as the *Upāya-kauśalya Sūtra*) breaking the precepts and committing actions that would otherwise attract moral censure. The assumption underlying the doctrine is that all teachings are in any case provisional and that once liberation is attained it will be seen that Buddhism as a body of philosophical doctrines and moral precepts was only of use as a means to reach the final goal, in the way a raft is used for crossing a river but is then discarded.

There is a certain amount of ambiguity surrounding the interpretation of skilful means in the context of ethics. It is not always clear whether the immoral behavior on the part of *bodhisattvas* depicted in some texts is intended as a model for imitation, or simply as an example of the great compassion of which *bodhisattvas* are capable. Just as other stories such as that of Prince Vessantara, and the *bodhisattva* and the tigress (see above), depict the protagonists as capable of superhuman self-sacrifice, but are probably best not taken literally as examples we should follow to the letter, the examples of skillful means we see in Mahāyāna literature are perhaps best understood as idealizing the virtue of compassion without necessarily seeking to encourage ordinary people to rush out and perform immoral deeds.

## *War and terrorism*

Buddhist teachings are strongly opposed to violence, regarding it as the product of mental states associated with greed (*rāga*), hatred (*dveṣa*) and delusion (*moha*). Aggression is thought to be fuelled by the erroneous belief in a self (*ātman*) and the desire to protect that self from harm. This strong notion of a self and what pertains to it (such as 'my possessions', 'my country', 'my race') produces a sharp sense of bifurcation leading to suspicion and hostility towards what is 'alien' or 'other'. The aim of Buddhist teachings is to dissolve this sense of self, and with it the fear and hostility that causes conflict to break out.

A virtue which is important in this context is patience (*kṣānti*), since a lack of tolerance or forbearance is often the cause of violent disputes. There are many stories which exemplify the practice of patience, such as the *Khantivādi Jātaka*. In this tale *Khantivādi*, an ascetic, displays forbearance in not becoming angry even when his limbs are hacked off one by one on the orders of a king. The practice of patience depends on equanimity (*upekkhā*) or even-mindedness towards all persons, whether friends or enemies. It is pointed out that those who are now are enemies, were almost certainly in another life our friends, so no person will remain an enemy for ever.

When the early sources speak of war, they condemn it almost without exception on the ground that war involves killing, and killing is a breach of the First Precept. It matters little whether the war being fought is an offensive or defensive one, for in either case the loss of life will ensue. In marked contrast to the view of Islam about the fate of warriors who die in a holy war, the Buddha expresses the view (Sn.iv.308–11) that soldiers who die in battle go not to a special paradise but to a special hell, since at the moment of death their minds were bent on killing. Some texts affirm that even killing in self-defence, or in defence of family or friends, is wrongful, and in general an attitude of non-resistance in the face of violence is commended. The commentary to the *Dhammapada* relates how on one occasion when the Buddha's kinsmen, the Śākyas, were under attack, they allowed themselves to be slaughtered rather than break the First Precept. Other examples in the *Jātakas* and elsewhere speak of princes and kings who renounced their thrones rather than resorting to violence to defend their kingdoms.

Buddhists often point to the example of the emperor Aśoka as an example of how rulers should govern by peaceful means. As noted in Chapter Five, Aśoka ruled over a great empire in India in the third century B.C.E., the largest to be seen in India until the British Raj. Eight years after his coronation, Aśoka's ordered his armies to attack Kaliṅga, a region on the East coast that had managed to resist him. The campaign was bloody and the casualties were high. Throughout his reign, Aśoka proclaimed numerous edicts which he ordered to be carved on stone throughout his kingdom, and in the fourteenth rock edict he states that in the Kaliṅga campaign 150,000 people were deported, 100,000 were killed in battle, and many more died due to the associated turmoil. He speaks of his distress at the suffering or ordinary decent people ('Brahmins, ascetics, and householders of different religions') who are injured, killed, or separated from their loved ones. The loss of life in the war horrified Aśoka and led to a complete change of heart, as a result of which he renounced the use of military campaigns and resolved to rule henceforth by *Dharma*, stating that 'Conquest by Dharma is the best conquest'.

Not all Buddhist rulers, however, have followed the pacifist example of Aśoka. In the early history of Sri Lanka, numerous battles were fought between the Sinhalese and Tamils invaders from India. The Sinhalese king Duṭṭhagāmaṇi (first century B.C.E.) is regarded as a national hero because he defeated the Tamil general Eḷāra, a victory commemorated in the *Mahāvaṃsa*, one of the traditional Sinhalese chronicles dating to the fifth or sixth centuries C.E. and narrating the history of the island. The chronicle depicts the conflict as a kind of 'holy war' between Buddhists and Hindus, and glorifies the Buddhist victory. It narrates how after his victory Duṭṭhagāmaṇi felt remorse (just as Aśoka had done) but was reassured by enlightened monks (*arhants*) that in defending the *Dharma* he had done nothing that was not in accordance with Buddhist precepts.

In the modern period, Buddhist monks have often made outspoken attacks on their opponents, calling for them to be eradicated by the use of force. In the 1970s, the Thai monk Kittivuḍḍho, a strong opponent of communism, made repeated calls in public statements for communists to be exterminated. He claimed that this was a religious duty and was necessary to protect the Thai nation, its monarchy, and the national religion (Buddhism). In his view killing some five thousand communists was a price worth paying to ensure the well-being of forty-two million Thais.

South Asia is not the only region of the Buddhist world where wars have been fought. During certain historical periods parts of East Asia have been almost a continual battleground, and Buddhism has been caught up and often actively involved as a participant in acts of violence. In medieval Japan, Buddhist monasteries became large landholding institutions and employed warrior-monks (*sōhei*) to defend their lands and to threaten their enemies. Battles were fought between one Buddhist sect and another, as well as against military rulers (*shōgun*) and the imperial court. Many samurai warriors found the beliefs and practices of Zen Buddhism fitted very well with their martial code, since they trained the mind to a high state of alertness and enabled them to remain focused and disciplined on the battlefield. Martial arts such as swordsmanship and archery were strongly influenced by Zen principles, and the philosophical doctrine of non-duality or emptiness (*śūnyatā*) provided a fitting ideology to accompany the suspension of moral norms which many believed appropriate in times of chaos and social upheaval.

This militarism was also in evidence in the modern period, in which Buddhist groups have actively supported Japanese nationalism. The Zen and Pure Land schools gave financial support during the war with China from 1937–1945, and in World War II most Buddhist schools (the notable exception being Sōka Gakkai) supported the Japanese campaign against the allies. Many well-known Zen masters were enthusiastic advocates of the war, and Zen monasteries held services for Japanese suicide pilots before their missions. However, the modern period has also brought forth strong opposition to the use of military force in Japan. The Nipponzan Myōhōji sect was founded by Nichidatsu Fujii in 1947 in the aftermath of the nuclear bombs dropped on Nagasaki and Hiroshima. An offshoot of Nichiren Buddhism, the group works to promote pacifism and oppose the use of nuclear weapons, and has built over sixty *stūpas* or 'peace pagodas' in Japan, as well as five in India and two each in Sri Lanka, the UK and the USA. Sōka Gakkai International, under the leadership of its president Daisaku Ikeda, has been active in the pursuit of its aim of 'Working for peace by opposing all forms of violence'. A third group active on this front is the Rissho Kosei-kai which established the Niwano Peace Foundation in 1978 in order to 'contribute to the realization of world peace'.

## *Terrorism*

Closely related to the moral dilemma of war is the problem of how to deal with terrorism. First of all, how do we define the term? As is often pointed out, groups which are seen by some as terrorists are regarded by others as liberators. The African National Congress, which came to form the government of South Africa, had in 1987 been declared a terrorist organization by Britain and the USA. The word 'terrorist' was coined during the French Revolution by those who saw themselves as acting with justification to overthrow a corrupt regime. Nowadays, however, few groups would call themselves terrorists, preferring to use other labels such as guerrillas, 'freedom fighters', or 'holy warriors'.

According to the Wordnet online dictionary at Princeton University, terrorism is defined as 'the calculated use of violence (or threat of violence) against civilians in order to attain goals that are political or religious or ideological in nature; this is done through intimidation or coercion or instilling fear'. What distinguishes terrorism from war is mainly two things. First, in terrorism violence is used primarily against civilians rather than against enemy troops; and second, terrorist groups do not constitute a legitimate political authority which is empowered to declare war and launch attacks against a hostile power.

In today's world, terrorist attacks are increasingly common. One of the most destructive of these was the attack on the World Trade Center in New York on 11 September 2001 by the Al-Qaeda organization, which has since been linked to bombings in Tunisia, Pakistan, Yemen, Kuwait, Bali, Moscow, Mombasa, and London. In the aftermath of the '9/11' atrocity, President Bush led a coalition of nations that sent troops to Afghanistan and subsequently to Iraq as part of Operation 'Iraqi Freedom' in March 2003. At the time of writing (July 2005) the war is over but the social, political and material infrastructure of Iraq has been largely destroyed, and there is little sign of public order being restored in the face of continuing suicide bombings. The Iraqi dictator Saddam Hussein has been captured, but Osama bin-Laden, the leader of Al-Qaeda, remains at large.

In the circumstances described above, terrorism led to war. Was there a way to avoid this outcome, or is the only way to deal with terrorist outrages by fighting fire with fire? Opinion around the world continues to be divided. Protest marches were organized by groups opposed to the war, and many Buddhist organizations participated. Buddhist leaders who have spoken publicly on the question of the war in Iraq have tended to make three main points. The first is to emphasize the need to fully understand the causes which led to '9/11' taking place. Making reference to the doctrine of dependent origination (*pratītya-samutpāda*) they point out that events do not arise at random but are the product of complex interactions at many levels. Until the circumstances that led to the attack are understood and dealt with, no lasting solution is possible. The second point is that responding to force with force is wrong. The words of the *Dhammapada* are relevant here:

> He abused me, he struck me, he overpowered me, he robbed me. Those who harbor such thoughts do not still their hatred. (v.3)
>
> Hatred is never appeased by hatred. By non-hatred alone is hatred appeased. This is an eternal truth. (v.5)

Buddhist teachings suggest that violence rarely leads to a solution, but only to further violence and a cycle of retaliation which pushes the two sides further and further apart. The third point often made is that there is a need for reflection and self-criticism concerning the part we ourselves may have played, whether directly or indirectly, in provoking the conflict. After the 11 September attack, the Vietnamese monk and engaged Buddhist leader Thich Nhat Hanh expressed the view that

### A Buddhist on terrorism

Aung San Suu Kyi is the leader of the Burmese democracy movement and winner of the 1991 Nobel Peace Prize. She expressed the following view on terrorism.

> You know, I am a Buddhist. As a Buddhist, the answer is very simple and clear. That is, compassion and mercy is the real panacea. I am sure that, when we have compassion and mercy in our heart, we can overcome not only terrorism but also many other evil things that are plaguing the world.

America would have been better off resorting to dialogue than military force. For him the key question was 'Why would anyone hate us enough to do that?'. His answer was 'If we are able to listen, they will tell us'.

Whether or not pacifism is a realistic option in today's increasingly violent world, and whether it can provide the basis for law and order and an effective criminal justice system are questions that are being widely debated. The Buddhist view that force should not be used even in self-defence is one that some people will find difficult to accept. However, Buddhist groups and other pacifist organizations believe there are non-violent alternatives to the use of force in most situations. It has been wisely said that 'pacifism does not mean passivism', and perhaps if the resources that have been spent on war had been put into working for peace many of the world's most intractable disputes would either not have arisen or been solved long ago.

## Discussion questions

1. What is the place of ethics in Buddhism, and what are the most important Buddhist virtues and moral values?
2. Is there any significant difference between monastic and lay ethics?
3. In what way are the ethics of a *bodhisattva* thought to be superior by Mahāyāna Buddhists?
4. Does the doctrine of 'skillful means' maintain that 'the end justifies the means'?
5. How should Buddhists respond to terrorist atrocities like 9/11?

## Key points you need to know

- Buddhist ethical teachings are based upon a concept of *Dharma* or 'Natural Law'.
- Morality (*śīla*) is part of the Noble Eightfold Path and integral to the practice of *Dharma*.
- Buddhism is classified as a form of virtue ethics. Key virtues include *ahiṃsā* (non-harming), generosity (*dāna*), and compassion (*karuṇā*).
- Buddhist laymen and laywomen follow the Five Precepts. Monks have their own special rules of conduct in the *Prātimokṣa* code in the *Vinaya*.
- Given the strong emphasis on non-violence and respect for life Buddhists tend to be pacifists. Historically, however, Buddhists have often supported military campaigns and participated in warfare directly.
- Buddhist responses to terrorism suggest that the causes of the situation should be thoroughly investigated, that hatred should be met with patience and compassion, and that we should be willing to accept responsibility for any part we played in causing the problem to arise.

## Further reading

Bodhi, Bhikkhu. 'Dana, the practice of giving'. Available online http://www.accesstoinsight.org/lib/authors/various/wheel367.html

Bodhi, Bhikkhu. 'Nourishing the Roots. Essays on Buddhist Ethics'. Available online http://www.accesstoinsight.org/lib/authors/bodhi/wheel259.html

Harvey, Peter. *An Introduction to Buddhist Ethic Foundations, Values and Issues*. Cambridge: Cambridge University Press, 2000.

Hershock, Peter. 'From Vulnerability to Virtuosity: Buddhist Reflections on Responding to Terrorism and Tragedy'. *Journal of Buddhist Ethics*. Vol. 10 (2003): 23–38.

Keown, Damien (ed.). *Contemporary Buddhist Ethics*. London: Curzon Press, 2000.

Keown, Damien. *Buddhist Ethics: A Very Short Introduction*. Oxford: Oxford University Press, 2005.

Saddhatissa, Hammalawa. *Buddhist Ethics*. Boston: Wisdom Publications, 1997.

Sizemore, Russell F. and Swearer, Donald K. (eds). *Ethics, Wealth and Salvation: A Study in Buddhist Social Ethics*. Columbia: University of South Carolina Press, 1990.

Victoria, Brian. *Zen at War*. New York and Tokyo: Weatherhill, 1997.

Wijayaratna, Mohan. *Buddhist Monastic Life According to the Texts of the Theravāda Tradition*. Cambridge: Cambridge University Press, 1990.

# 14 *Reflections on the nature and study of Buddhism*

## In this chapter

This chapter reflects upon the work we have done in this volume, beginning with assumptions made about the study of Buddhism. The chapter begins with the development of Buddhist Studies as an academic discipline. It examines the early researchers in Europe and America, as well as the current, modern developments in the discipline. It also highlights the role of 'scholar-practitioners' in current Buddhist Studies and the impact of technology on the discipline.

## Main topics covered

- European antecedents to the study of Buddhism
- Early Buddhist Studies in America
- Current Buddhist Studies
- Scholar-practitioners in Buddhist Studies
- The role of technology in Buddhist Studies

### *European antecedents to the study of Buddhism*

We turn now from questions concerning the nature of Buddhism to the history of its study. Recently, an important volume entitled *Curators of the Buddha: The Study of Buddhism under Colonialism* has attracted much attention. It was the topic of an entire panel at the 1995 annual meeting of the American Academy of Religion and the subject of an interesting review article by Jan Nattier. The book, however, was not the first attempt to contextualize and comment upon the discipline of Buddhist Studies in the West. Although there was very little reliable information in the West pertaining to Buddhism prior to the nineteenth century, Henri de Lubac's *La Rencontre du bouddhisme et l'occident*, published in 1952, was especially useful in summarizing this early literature. One can find such landmark works as Simon de la Loubère's *Du Royaume de Siam*, published in 1691, but it was not until the early

*Figure 14.1* Buddha statue at Big Buddha Beach, Ko Samui, Thailand

nineteenth century, with the appearance of Michel François Ozeray's *Recherches sur Buddhou* (1817), that the picture began to brighten. Soon, the pioneering efforts of Henry Thomas Colebrooke, Brian Houghton Hodgson, Alexander Csoma de Körös, and Eugène Burnouf, followed by their intellectual heirs, brought the reliable study of Buddhism to Europe.

To a large extent, the early interest in Buddhism was philological, converging on the increasing availability of Sanskrit and Pāli manuscripts that were appearing on the European continent. Perhaps the most thorough examination of this development was Russell Webb's *Pāli Buddhist Studies in the West*, serialized in the now-defunct journal *Pāli Buddhist Review*, and which systematically reviewed the developments of Pāli and Buddhist Studies in virtually all European countries, as well as Canada and the United States. Also worthy of note is William Peiris's *The Western Contribution to Buddhism*, which contains much historical detail and interesting character sketches of the early scholars of Buddhism. Jan W. de Jong's *A Brief History of Buddhist Studies in Europe and America* also offers valuable information, although America is virtually absent from the volume despite its title.

Perhaps the only conclusion that might be drawn from the above, insofar as conclusions are possible, is that several distinctions appear obvious from an examination of the above sources. First, geographic associations seem to identify at least two 'schools' of Buddhology: the Anglo-German and Franco-Belgian. The former (and older) was led by Thomas W. Rhys Davids and Hermann Oldenberg, while the latter included primarily Louis de La Vallée Poussin, Jean Przyluski, Sylvain Lévi, Paul Demiéville, and Étienne Lamotte. To these schools, Edward Conze, quite reasonably, adds a third: the Leningrad school, including Fedor Stcherbatsky, Otto Rosenberg, and E. Obermiller. The Anglo-German school almost exclusively emphasized the Pāli literary tradition, while the Franco-Belgian school utilized the Sanskritic materials, along with their corresponding translations and commentaries in Chinese and Tibetan. The Leningrad school is clearly closer to the Franco-Belgian school than the Anglo-German. These are general classifications, but they nonetheless capture the style of the traditions as they have been maintained over the last century.

## *Early Buddhist Studies in America*

Thomas Tweed's *The American Encounter with Buddhism 1844–1912: Victorian Culture and the Limits of Dissent* is a wonderful and complete introduction to the early pioneers of the American Buddhist movement. For those unwilling to wade through more than 200 pages of Tweed's meticulous prose, a pleasant narrative can be found in Rick Fields's chapter on 'The Restless Pioneers' in *How the Swans Came to the Lake*. Unfortunately, there are no such books or chapters documenting the development of the academic study of Buddhist Studies in America – the largest venue of the discipline – and the existence of such work remains a desideratum. As a result, we can only sketch a very short overview of Buddhist Studies in America.

Although some might consider Eugène Burnouf the founding father of Buddhist Studies as a discipline, in the United States, the beginning of Buddhist Studies seems inextricably bound to three primary individuals: Paul Carus, Henry Clarke Warren, and Charles Rockwell Lanman. Carus arrived in America in the 1880s with a Ph.D. from Tübingen, eventually becoming the editor of *Open Court* journal and later of Open Court Publishing Company. Although he wrote more than a dozen books of his own, including the still widely read *The Gospel of Buddhism* (1894), Carus is probably best known for bringing D.T. Suzuki to America and employing him at Open Court for many years.

Henry Clarke Warren and Charles Rockwell Lanman were more scholarly in their approach than Carus, and worked diligently to establish the Buddhist literary tradition in America. Lanman had studied Sanskrit under William Dwight Whitney, earning his doctorate in 1875 before moving on to Johns Hopkins University, and eventually becoming Professor of Sanskrit at Harvard University in 1880. Warren, though horribly deformed as a result of a childhood accident, had studied Sanskrit with Lanman at Johns Hopkins, and followed his learned master back to Harvard, where the two struck up an alliance that culminated in the creation of a new publication series known as 'The Harvard Oriental Series'. Hendrik Kern's edition of the *Jātakamālā*, or collection of Buddhist birth stories, was the first edition, with Warren's famous *Buddhism in Translations* becoming the third volume in 1896.

Following Warren's death in 1899, and with Lanman moving on to other studies in the Indic tradition, the development of Buddhist Studies was left to others. One of these early trail-blazers was Eugene Watson Burlingame, who had studied with Lanman at Harvard before shifting to Yale, where he worked industriously on a variety of Pāli texts. By 1921 he had published a three-volume translation of the *Dhammapada* commentary in the Harvard Oriental Series. Burlingame was followed by W.Y. Evans-Wentz, a 1907 Stanford graduate, who studied extensively in Europe, and is best known for his collaborative compiling of the translations of his teacher, Kazi Dawa-Sandup. Their translation of the *Tibetan Book of the Dead*, although unreliable and now entirely superseded, became extremely popular. By the time of Evans-Wentz's death in 1965, a new group of Buddhological scholars had developed on the American scene, including such committed scholars as Winston King, Richard Gard, and Kenneth K.S. Ch'en.

Despite the work of these early educators, it was not until after 1960 that Buddhist Studies began to emerge as a significant discipline in the American university system and publishing industry. During the Vietnam War years and immediately thereafter, Buddhist Studies was to enjoy a so-called 'boom', largely through the efforts of such leading professors as Richard Hugh Robinson of the University of Wisconsin, Masatoshi Nagatomi of Harvard University, and Alex Wayman of Columbia University. No doubt there were many reasons for the increased development of Buddhist Studies, not the least of which were the increase in Area Studies Programs in American universities; growing government interest in things Asian; the immense social anomie that permeated American culture in the 1960s; and the growing dissatisfaction with (and perhaps rejection of) traditional religion. During the 1960s, a formal graduate program was instituted at the University of Wisconsin, offering both an M.A. and a Ph.D. in Buddhist Studies. Interdisciplinary programs emphasizing the study of Buddhism were soon available at Berkeley and Columbia as well. As other programs arose, such as the program at the Center for the Study of World Religions at Harvard University, and the history of religions program at the University of Chicago, it became possible to gain sophisticated training in all aspects of the Buddhist tradition, and in all Buddhist canonical languages as well. As a result, a new generation of young Buddhologists was born, appearing rapidly on the campuses of many American universities, and rivalling their overseas peers in both training and insight.

This picture of expanding American Buddhology is perhaps not so rosy as one might think, rapid growth notwithstanding. As interest grew, funding for graduate education did not keep pace, and would-be Buddhologists no longer had the luxury of being able to spend six or eight or even ten fully-funded years in preparation for the Ph.D. As a result, the breadth and scope of their training was compromised, resulting in an accelerated urgency for specialization. The consequence was that very few new Buddhologists were appearing with the complete philological training and geographical comprehensiveness of their teachers. Thus, it became usual to find individuals focusing on one tradition, such as Indian or Tibetan or Chinese or Japanese Buddhism, but rarely all of the traditions. And if the distinctions that characterize the Anglo-German, Franco-Belgian, and Leningrad schools, mentioned above, are accurate, the 'American' school is equally divided within itself.

## *Current Buddhist Studies in America*

More than twenty years ago, an article on recent Buddhist literature entitled 'Buddhist Studies American-Style: A Shot in the Dark', was published, explaining at the outset that the conjured image of Inspector Clouseau 'falling through banisters, walking into walls, crashing out of windows, and somehow miraculously getting the job done with the assistance of his loyal Oriental servant', was not an accidental choice on the author's part; that Buddhist Studies in America was just as erratic as poor Clouseau. However, it had only been two years since the American Buddhist Studies community had formed a Buddhism Group (now a Section) in the American Academy of Religion, and it was not unreasonable to expect that its early efforts were a bit helter-skelter.

Lately, Buddhist Studies has begun to engage in the useful process of self-reflection, and the results of that inquiry are fruitful and inspiring. In Winter 1995, the *Journal of the International Association of Buddhist Studies* devoted an entire issue to the topic of Buddhist Studies as an academic discipline, providing the occasion for scholars to reflect on various aspects of the field. José Cabezón, a Buddhist scholar and former Tibetan lama, summarized the critical question:

> Although the academic study of Buddhism is much older than the International Association of Buddhist Studies and the journal to which it gave rise, the founding of the latter, which represents a significant – perhaps pivotal – step in the institutionalization of the field, is something that occurred less than twenty years ago. Nonetheless, whether a true discipline or not – whether or not Buddhist Studies has already achieved disciplinary status, whether it is proto-disciplinary or superdisciplinary – there is an apparent integrity to Buddhist Studies that at the very least calls for an analysis of the field in holistic terms.

In another interesting article entitled 'The Ghost at the Table: On the Study of Buddhism and the Study of Religion', Malcolm David Eckel wrote in his conclusion:

> It is not just students who are attracted to religious studies because they 'want to know what it is to be human and humane, and intuit that religion deals with such things'. There are at least a few scholars of Buddhism who feel the same way. For me the biggest unsettled question in the study of Buddhism is not whether Buddhism is religious or even whether the study of Buddhism is religious; it is whether scholars in this field can find a voice that does justice to their own religious concerns and can demonstrate to the academy why their kind of knowledge is worth having.

In a recent issue of *Tricycle: The Buddhist Review*, Duncan Ryuken Williams, an ordained Sōtō Zen priest and university professor, compiled a short list of institutions which offer graduate study in Buddhism. Although Williams' listing included the expected sorts of categories (Most Comprehensive Programs, Institutions with Strength in Indo-Tibetan Buddhist Studies, and so forth), he also included a category called Practitioner-friendly Institutions, indicating yet another aspect to the current study of the Buddhist tradition: the 'scholar-practitioner'.

## *Scholar-practitioners in Buddhist Studies*

Virtually everyone who begins an academic career in Buddhist Studies eventually pores through Étienne Lamotte's exciting volume *Histoire de Bouddhisme Indien des origines à l'ère Śaka*, either in the original French or in Sara Webb-Boin's admirable English translation. That Lamotte was a Catholic priest seems not to have influenced either his understanding of, or respect for, the Buddhist tradition, although he did worry a bit from time to time about the reaction of the Vatican to his work. Edward Conze (1979: 43), arguably one of the most colorful Buddhist scholars of the twentieth century, once remarked: 'When I last saw him, he had risen to the rank of Monseigneur and worried about how his *Histoire* had been received at the Vatican. "Mon professeur, do you think they will regard the book as hérétique?" They obviously did not. His religious views showed the delightful mixture of absurdity and rationality which is one of the hallmarks of a true believer'. Although there have been only a few scholarly studies chronicling the academic investigation of Buddhism by Western researchers, and fewer still of the academic discipline known as Buddhist Studies, until quite recently, the issue of the religious affiliation of the researcher has not been part of the mix. Almost exclusively, the founding mothers and founding fathers of Buddhist Studies in the West have had personal religious commitments entirely separate from Buddhism. Now, however, it is quite ordinary for individuals teaching Buddhist Studies in universities throughout the world to be 'scholar-practitioners', involved in the practices associated with various Buddhist traditions and sects. Georges Dreyfus's new book *The Sound of Two Hands Clapping: The Education of a Tibetan Buddhist Monk*, for example, traces his monastic career through many years of study in Tibetan Buddhist monasteries in India. Nevertheless, it is not always easy for academics to reveal their religious orientation in an environment that is not uniformly supportive of such choices.

Stories reflecting the study/practice dichotomy in Buddhism are abundant in both the primary and secondary literature on the subject. Walpola Rahula's *History of Buddhism in Ceylon* provides a good summary of the issue. During the first century B.C.E., in the midst of potential foreign invasion and a severe famine, Sri Lankan monks feared that the Buddhist *Tripiṭaka*, preserved only in oral tradition, might be lost. Thus the scriptures were committed to writing for the first time. Nonetheless, in the aftermath of the entire dilemma, a new question arose: What is the basis of the 'Teaching' (that is, *Śāsana*) – learning or practice? A clear difference of opinion resulted in the development of two groups: the Dhammakathikas, who claimed that learning was the basis of the *Śāsana*, and the Paṃsukūlikas, who argued for practice as the basis. The Dhammakathikas apparently won out.

The two vocations described above came to be known as *gantha-dhura*, or the 'vocation of books', and *vipassanā-dhura*, or the 'vocation of meditation', with the former being regarded as the superior training (because surely meditation would not be possible if the teachings were lost). Moreover, not the least characteristic of these two divisions was that the *vipassanā-dhura* monks began to live in the forest, where they could best pursue their vocation undisturbed, while the *gantha-dhura* monks began to dwell in villages and towns. As such, the *gantha-dhura* monks began to play a significant role in Buddhist education. It would probably not be going too far in referring to the *gantha-dhura* monks as 'scholar-monks'. Why is this distinction so important? It is significant for at least two reasons. First, and most obviously, it reveals why the tradition of study in Buddhism, so long minimized in popular and scholarly investigations of the Buddhist tradition, has such an impact on that same tradition, and has resulted in the rapid development of Buddhist schools and institutes of higher learning in the latter quarter of the twentieth century. Furthermore, it explains why the Buddhist movement has encouraged a high level of 'Buddhist literacy' among its practitioners. However, it also highlights the fact that the global Buddhist movement has been almost exclusively a lay movement. While many leaders of various Buddhist groups may have had formal monastic training (irrespective of whether they continue to lead monastic lifestyles), the vast majority of their disciples have not. Thus the educational model on which modern global Buddhists pattern their behavior is contrary to the traditional Asian Buddhist archetype. It is, in fact, the converse of the traditional model. As such, at least with regard to Buddhist study and education, there is a leadership gap in this global Buddhist community, one largely not filled by a *sangha* of 'scholar-monks'.

What has been the response to the educational leadership gap on the part of Buddhist communities? Again, the explanation is twofold. On the one hand, there is a movement in some Buddhist communities to identify those individuals within the community itself who are best suited, and best trained, to serve the educational needs of the community, and confer appropriate authority in these individuals in a formal way. Recently, Sakyong Mipham Rinpoche, son of Chögyam Trungpa and now head of the Shambhala International community, declared nine community members 'Acharyas', an Indian Buddhist designation for a respected teacher. These individuals, one of whom holds a Ph.D. degree from the University of Chicago with specialization in Buddhism, were authorized to take on enhanced teaching and leadership roles in their community and beyond.

Earlier in this chapter, reference was made to the recently published volume *Curators of the Buddha: The Study of Buddhism under Colonialism*. In her review article, after praising Lopez for his frankness and willingness, as an American Buddhologist, to discuss his own encounter with Buddhism, Jan Nattier (1997: 480) concluded by saying, 'If there are difficulties here, they are not with the keen and self-critical eye with which Lopez reflects on his own experience as a student of Buddhism but with the degree to which he generalizes from that experience to characterize prevailing attitudes in the Buddhist Studies field at large'. Whether these generalizations are correct or not remains to be seen. At least the question has now moved beyond Father Lamotte's concern with being 'hérétique'.

## *The role of technology in Buddhist Studies*

Until quite recently, introductory books on Buddhism did not include a single word about the role of computer technology in the development of Buddhist Studies. The earliest formal interest in the application of computer technology to Buddhism seems to have occurred when the International Association of Buddhist Studies formed a Committee on Buddhist Studies and Computers at its 1983 meeting in Tokyo. Jamie Hubbard, in an amusing and highly significant article called 'Upping the Ante: budstud@millenium.end.edu', pointed out: 'The three major aspects of computer technology that most visibly have taken over older technologies are word processing, electronic communication, and the development of large-scale archives of both text and visual materials'. Hubbard went on to relate his first experiences with IndraNet, an online discussion forum sponsored by the International Association of Buddhist Studies in the mid-1980s and co-managed by Hubbard and Bruce Burrill with equipment donated by Burrill. Apart from a small bevy of faithful participants, there was little interest in the forum and it died a largely unnoticed death within two years. Nonetheless, of the three impact-items cited by Hubbard, it was clearly electronic communication that was to have the most important and continuing consequences for the discipline of Buddhist Studies.

Early in the 1990s, a profusion of online discussion forums (or e-mail discussion lists), similar in nature to the one described above, began to proliferate and thrive on the Internet. Although these forums were global in scope, the vast majority of subscribers and participants were from North America. One of the very first of these was 'Buddhist'. Although the traffic on the list was often frenetic, with messages that were sometimes delivered as late as six months after they were composed, it was an exciting beginning. Because the list was unmoderated, and most often concerned with various aspects of Buddhist practice and popular issues within modern Buddhism, the number of postings eventually became sufficiently unwieldy that the owner decided to bequeath the list to a new owner-manager, and the list was moved to McGill University in Canada.

During one of the periods in which the 'Buddhist' list had broken down, Richard Hayes, a professor on the Faculty of Religious Studies at McGill University, surveyed a number of subscribers to the list and discovered that many of these individuals favored beginning a separate list that was not only restricted to academic discussions of Buddhism but moderated as well. In collaboration with James Cocks, who worked in the computer center at the University of Louisville, a new discussion forum called 'Buddha-L' was created, initially monitored by Cocks under guidelines composed by Hayes. The forum considered scholarly discussions of virtually all aspects of Buddhism, as well issues related to teaching Buddhism at the university level, and occasional postings of employment opportunities in academe. Hayes confessed that, because of the narrow, academic nature of the forum, his expectation was for a small but dedicated number of subscribers. Within a year, however, the group had over one thousand subscribers. In addition to the above groups, a number of other discussion groups built an early but substantial following among Buddhists on the Internet. Perhaps the best known of these additional groups is 'ZenBuddhism-L', founded in August 1993 at the Australian National University by Dr. T. Matthew Ciolek, Head of the Internet Publications Bureau of the Research School of Pacific & Asian Studies at the Australian National University.

In February 1992, an electronic Buddhist archive was established by the Coombs Computing Unit of the Australian National University. Under the direction of T. Matthew Ciolek, it was positioned as a subsection of the Coombspapers FTP Social Sciences/Asian Studies research archive which had been initiated several months earlier. It contained over 320 original documents in ASCII (plain text) format, including bibliographies, biographies, directories, Buddhist electronic texts, poetry, and the like. It also offered a unique collection of previously unpublished transcripts of teachings and sermons by many famous twentieth century Zen masters such as Robert Aitken Rōshi, Taizan Maezumi Rōshi, Hakuun Yasutani Rōshi, and others.

E-mail discussion forums and Buddhist databases were not the only form of early Buddhist activity on the Internet. As early as 1993, the first electronic Buddhist journal made its appearance. Called *Gassho*, it was edited by its founder, Barry Kapke, who operated it and other enterprises under a broad, umbrella-like organization known as DharmaNet International, founded in 1991. According to Kapke, it was published 'as a service to the international Buddhist community, inclusive of all Buddhist traditions'. Kapke used the past tense in the above description because *Gassho* went on hiatus following the May/June 1994 issue. Quite simply, its rapid growth exceeded the capability of its entirely volunteer staff to keep up. Just as a new issue was nearly completed for December 1996, both Kapke's home computer and its Internet server crashed, resulting in a loss of all materials for that issue. While no new issues have followed this devastating loss, it was clear from the first issue (available in both online and hardcopy versions), in November-December 1993, that *Gassho* presented a vision of a new kind of Buddhist community. Its masthead referred to it as an 'Electronic Journal of DharmaNet International and the Global Online Sangha'. Gassho notwithstanding, another online electronic journal would eventually provide the occasion for an immensely rapid, and continued, growth in electronic Buddhist Studies by exploiting yet another electronic medium for the dissemination of information: the World Wide Web.

The *Journal of Buddhist Ethics* was born in July 1994. It was originally planned as a traditional, hard-copy scholarly journal by its editors, who quickly learned that potential publishers had little interest in a highly specialized, purely academic journal that was not likely to turn a profit. One of the co-editors, Damien Keown, suggested publishing the journal online, where there would be no expenses, and where the journal could provide a useful service to its constituent community, however tiny it might be. Once a technical editor was added to the staff, plans rapidly moved ahead, making the journal available via the World Wide Web, as well as through FTP and Gopher retrieval. The journal went 'online' on 1 July 1994 with no articles, but with a WWW page outlining the aims of the journal and listing its editorial board members. It advertised its presence on a small number of electronic newsgroups, and within a week had one hundred subscribers. The journal's first 'Call for Papers' was made after Labor Day, and by the end of 1994, it had over four hundred subscribers in twenty-six countries. It currently has over six thousand subscribers in more than fifty countries.

Along with other new features, added to the journal's basic emphasis on scholarly articles devoted to Buddhist ethics, the journal began a new section called Global Resources for Buddhist Studies. Rather quickly, the editors discovered that many communities of Buddhist practitioners began requesting that links to their own developing World Wide Web pages be listed with the *Journal of Buddhist Ethics*. In other words, it became clear that the World Wide Web in general was indeed growing immensely and quickly, furnishing a unique opportunity for communication that Buddhist communities had never known before. Although it was by no means unique in its establishment of a jumping-off point for the exploration of additional

Buddhist resources of all kinds on the Web, along with DharmaNet International and the WWW Virtual Libraries at the Australian National University, and a newer Buddhist Gateway known as the Buddhist Resource File, the *Journal of Buddhist Ethics* provided a new way of thinking about Buddhist communities, one that augmented Gary Ray's cyber-*sangha* and Barry Kapke's global online *sangha*.

More recently, and with an exceedingly more sophisticated technology, major Buddhist Studies sites have been created throughout the world, many prompted by the groundbreaking work of Charles Muller in Japan. These sites provide such items as Buddhist texts in their original languages, constantly updated Buddhist dictionaries, and a wide variety of electronic tools – such as Unicode fonts – for worldwide information exchange in Buddhist Studies. Coupled with the global reach of Buddhist Studies professional societies such as the International Association of Buddhist Studies and the United Kingdom Association of Buddhist Studies, and international forums for virtually instant communication (like the H-Buddhism online community of scholars created by Charles Muller), the discipline of Buddhist Studies begins the twenty-first century with a vision unimagined even a quarter-century earlier.

## Key points you need to know

- The mainstream of Buddhist Studies began in Europe in the middle of the nineteenth century through the pioneering works of Eugène Burnouf, Brian Houghton Hodgson, and others.
- Three schools known as the Anglo-German, Franco-Belgian, and Leningrad schools developed.
- Much of the early work in Buddhist Studies was philological, focusing on texts and translations of basic Pāli and Sanskrit texts. Only later did disciplinary studies in sociology, anthropology, and other areas develop in Buddhist Studies.
- In modern Buddhist Studies, many of the investigators are Buddhists themselves, spanning all the various traditions and sectarian affiliations.
- In current Buddhist Studies, rapid developments in information exchange technology have radically redefined the discipline, and the way Buddhism is promoted and investigated.

## Discussion questions

1. Trace the development of Buddhist Studies as an academic discipline from its beginnings to the present time.
2. Compare and contrast European and American contributions to the study of Buddhism.
3. How will the recent and future advances in information exchange technology change the discipline of Buddhist Studies?

## Further reading

Cabezón, José. 'Buddhist Studies as a Discipline and the Role of Theory'. *Journal of the International Association of Buddhist Studies*. Vol. 18, no. 2 (Winter 1995): 231–68.

Conze, Edward. *The Memoirs of a Modern Gnostic*, part 2. Sherborne, England: Samizdat Publishing Company, 1979.

De Jong, Jan Willem. *A Brief History of Buddhist Studies in Europe and America*. 2nd rev. ed. Bibliotheca Indo-Buddhica, no. 33. Delhi: Sri Satguru, 1987.

Eckel, Malcolm David. 'The Ghost at the Table: On the Study of Buddhism and the Study of Religion'. *Journal of the American Academy of Religion*. Vol. 62, no. 4 (Winter 1994): 1085–110.

Gómez, Luis. 'Unspoken Paradigms: Meanderings through the Metaphors of a Field'. *Journal of the International Association of Buddhist Studies*. Vol. 18, no. 2 (Winter 1995): 183–230.

Hubbard, Jamie. 'Upping the Ante: budstud@millenium.end.edu'. *Journal of the International Association of Buddhist Studies*. Vol. 18, no. 2 (Winter 1995): 309–22.

Lopez, Donald S., Jr (ed.). *Curators of the Buddha*. Chicago, IL: University of Chicago Press, 1995.

Nattier, Jan. 'Buddhist Studies in the Post Colonial Age'. *Journal of the American Academy of Religion*. Vol. 65, no. 2 (Summer 1997): 480.

Peiris, William. *The Western Contribution to Buddhism*. Delhi: Motilal Banarsidass, 1973.

Prebish, Charles. 'The Academic Study of Buddhism in the United States: A Current Analysis'. *Religion*. Vol. 24, no. 3 (July 1994): 271–8.

Prebish, Charles. 'Buddhist Studies American Style: A Shot in the Dark'. *Religious Studies Review*. Vol. 9, no. 4 (October 1983): 323–30.

# *Appendix I*

## *Chronology of Buddhist history*

| | |
|---|---|
| Prior to 6th Century b.c.e. | Vedic Period in India (c. 1500–1000) |
| | Composition of the *Brāmaṇas* (c. 1000–800) |
| | Composition of Early *Upaniṣads* (c. 800–500) |
| 6th Century b.c.e. | Life of Laozi |
| | Life of Confucius (552–479) |
| 5th Century b.c.e. | Life of the Buddha Śākyamuni (c. 485–405) |
| | Reign of Bimbisāra (c. 465–413) |
| | Council of Rājagṛha (c. 405) |
| 4th Century b.c.e. | Alexander the Great in India (c. 327–325) |
| | Reign of Chandragupta Maurya (322–298) |
| | Megasthenese at court of Candragupta (303) |
| | Second Buddhist council at Vaiśālī (c. 305) |
| | Beginning of Buddhist sectarianism |
| 3rd Century b.c.e. | Reign of Indian King Aśoka (272–231) |
| | Third Buddhist council at Pāṭaliputra (250) |
| | Aśoka's missionary Mahinda introduces Buddhism to Sri Lanka (247) |
| 2nd Century b.c.e. | Beginning of Mahāyāna Buddhism (c. 200) |
| | Beginning of composition of *Prajñāpāramitā* literature |
| | *Stūpa* construction at Sañcī (c. 200–000) |
| | An Shigao arrives in China and establishes first translation bureau (148) |
| 1st Century b.c.e. | Reign of Duṭṭhagāmaṇi Abhaya in Sri Lanka (101–77) |
| | Abhayagiri monastery founded in Sri Lanka (c. 100–000) |
| | Pāli Canon written down in Sri Lanka (29–17) |

| | |
|---|---|
| 1ST CENTURY C.E. | Reign of King Kaniṣka in India |
| | Fourth Buddhist council at Kaśmīr (c. 100) |
| | Composition of *Lotus Sūtra* and other Buddhist texts |
| | Buddhism enters Central Asia and China |
| 2ND CENTURY C.E. | Life of Indian Buddhist philosopher Nāgārjuna |
| 3RD CENTURY C.E. | Expansion of Buddhism to Burma, Cambodia, Laos, Vietnam, and Indonesia |
| 4TH CENTURY C.E. | Life of Indian Buddhist philosophers Asaṅga and Vasubandhu |
| | Development of Vajrayāna Buddhism in India |
| | Translation of Buddhist texts into Chinese by Kumārajīva (344–413), Huiyuan (334–416), and others |
| | Gupta Dynasty in India, Buddhist philosophy and art flourish (350–650) |
| | Buddhism enters Korea in 372 |
| 5TH CENTURY C.E. | Nālandā University founded in India |
| | Life of Buddhist philosopher Buddhaghosa in Sri Lanka (c. 400–500) |
| | Chinese pilgrim Faxien visits India (399–414) |
| 6TH CENTURY C.E. | Life of Paramārtha (499–599) |
| | Bodhidharma arrives in China from India (c. 520) |
| | Sui Dynasty in Chinese History (589–17); beginning of golden age of Chinese Buddhism |
| | Development of Tiantai, Huayan, Pure Land, and Chan Schools of Chinese Buddhism |
| | Life of Zhiyi (538–597) |
| | Buddhism enters Japan from Korea (552) |
| | Prince Shotoku sponsors Buddhism in Japan (572–621) |
| | Buddhism flourishing in Indonesia |
| 7TH CENTURY C.E. | First diffusion of Buddhism in Tibet (c. 600) |
| | Life of Dharmakīrti; flourishing of logic and epistemology (c. 600) |
| | Tang Dynasty in Chinese history (618–907) |
| | Life of Wŏnhyo (617–686); foundation of 'unitive Buddhism' in Korea |
| | Life of Songtsen Gampo (618–650); establishment of Buddhism in Tibet |
| | Life of Ŭisang; introduction of Hwaŏm (Huayan) into Korea (625–702) |

| | |
|---|---|
| | Chinese pilgrim Xuanzang visits India (629–645) |
| | Life of Huineng (638–713); Northern/Southern schools controversy |
| | Pala Dynasty in India (650–950) |
| | Unified Silla Period in Korea (668–918); Buddhism flourishes |
| | Chinese pilgrim Yijing travels to India (671–695) |
| 8TH CENTURY C.E. | Life of Padmasambhava (c. 700) |
| | Northern/Southern schools controversy in Japan (c. 700) |
| | Esoteric school (Zhenyan Zong) develops in China (c. 700) |
| | Construction of Borobudur (c. 700–800) |
| | Mahāyāna and Tantric Buddhism flourish in India (700–1100); consolidation of school of logic and epistemology |
| | Nara Period in Japanese history (710–784) |
| | Academic schools (Jōjitsu, Kusha, Sanron, Hossō, Ritsu, and Kegon) proliferate in Japan |
| | Great debate between Tibetan and Chinese Buddhist schools Council of Lhasa in Tibet (742) |
| | rNying-ma-pa School of Tibet Buddhism begins |
| | First Tibetan monastery at Samye |
| | Life of Saichō (767–822); founding of Tendai school |
| | Life of Kūkai (774–835); founding of Shingon school |
| | Heian Period in Japanese history (794–1185) |
| 9TH CENTURY C.E. | Founding of Vikramaśīla monastery in Tibet (c. 800) |
| | Reign of Lang Dharma (836–842) and suppression of Buddhism in Tibet |
| | Great Buddhist persecution in China (845) |
| 10TH CENTURY C.E. | Sung dynasty in China (960–1279) |
| | Koryŏ period in Korea (978–1392) |
| | First complete printing of Chinese Buddhist canon (Szechuan edition) in 983 |
| | Atīśa (982–1054) arrives in Tibet from India (1042) |
| 11TH CENTURY C.E. | Life of Mar-pa (1012–1097) and origins of Kagyu |
| | School of Tibetan Buddhism |
| | Life of Naropa (1016–1100) |
| | King Anawrahtā unifies Burma and gives allegiance to Theravāda Buddhism (1040–1077) |

| | |
|---|---|
| | Life of Mi-la ras-pa (1040–1123); becomes greatest poet and most popular saint in Tibetan Buddhism |
| | Life of Ŭichŏn (1055–1101) |
| | Sakya order of Tibetan Buddhism begins (1073) |
| | Life of Gampopa (1079–1153) |
| | Revival of Theravāda Buddhism in Sri Lanka and Burma |
| | Decline of Buddhism in India |
| 12th Century c.e. | Construction of Angkor Wat (c. 1100) |
| | Theravāda Buddhism established in Burma |
| | Life of Hōnen (1133–1212); founds Jōdo-shū in Japan |
| | Life of Eisai (1141–1215); founds Rinzai Zen School of Japanese Buddhism |
| | Life of Chinul (1158–1210); Chogye order founded; development of Sŏn in Korea |
| | Life of Shinran (1173–1262); founds Jōdo Shinshū in Japan |
| | Kamakura Period in Japan (1185–1392) |
| | Nālānda University sacked by Mahmud Ghorī (1197) |
| 13th Century c.e. | Buddhism disappears from north India. Traces linger in the south (c. 1200) |
| | Printing of *Tripiṭaka Koreana* (c. 1200) |
| | Life of Dōgen (1200–1253) founds Sōtō Zen School in Japan |
| | Life of Nichiren (1222–1282) founds school of Japanese Buddhism named after him |
| | Life of Ippen (1239–1289); foundation of Jishū school |
| | Sakya Paṇḍita converts Mongols to Buddhism (1244) |
| | Theravāda declared state religion of kingdom of Sukhothai (Thailand) (c. 1260) |
| | Life of Butön (1290–1364); collects and edits Tibetan Buddhist Canon |
| 14th Century c.e. | Life of Tsongkhapa (1357–1419); Gelukpa order founded in Tibet |
| | Theravāda Buddhism declared state religion of Thailand (1360) |
| | Ming dynasty in China (1368–1644) |
| | Ch'osŏn period in Korea; Buddhism suppressed |
| | Laos and Cambodia become Theravāda |
| 15th Century c.e. | Tibetan Kanjur printed in China |
| 16th Century c.e. | Office of Dalai Lama instituted by Mongols |

| | |
|---|---|
| 17TH CENTURY C.E. | Life of Dalai Lama V and beginning of rule of Tibet by Dalai Lamas |
| | Control of Japanese Buddhism by Tokugawa Shōgunate (1603–1867) |
| | Life of Bashō; Buddhist influence on *haiku* and the arts in Japan |
| 18TH CENTURY C.E. | Colonial occupation of Sri Lanka, Burma, Laos, Cambodia, and Vietnam; Western domination of South and South-east Asia |
| | Mongolian Buddhist canon translated from Tibetan (1749) |
| 19TH CENTURY C.E. | Beginning of the academic study of Buddhism by Western scholars (c. 1800) |
| | Royal Asiatic Society founded (1823) |
| | Reign of Rama IV in Thailand; reform of Thai *sangha* (1851–1868) |
| | First Buddhist temple founded in the United States, in San Francisco (1853) |
| | Meiji Restoration in Japanese history (1868), marking end of military rule |
| | Life of Nishida Kitarō, founder of Kyoto school (1870–1945) |
| | New religions begin to emerge in Japanese Buddhism |
| | Fifth great Buddhist council in Mandalay |
| | Theosophical Society founded (1875) |
| | Publication of Sir Edwin Arnold's *The Light of Asia* (1879) |
| | Pāli Text Society founded in England by T.W. Rhys Davids (1881) |
| | Mahabodhi Society founded by Anagārika Dharmapāla (1891) |
| | Life of B. Ambedkar, conversion of untouchables in India (1891–1956) |
| | Buddhist Churches of America founded (1899) |
| 20TH CENTURY C.E. | *Taishō Shinshū Daizōkyō* edition of Chinese Buddhist Canon printed in Tokyo (1924–1929) |
| | The Buddhist Society founded in London (1924) |
| | Wŏn Buddhism founded in Korea (1924) |
| | Nichiren Shōshū Soka Gakkai formally established (1937) |
| | Rosshō Koseikai founded (1938) |

| | |
|---|---|
| | People's Liberation Army enters Tibet (1950) |
| | World Fellowship of Buddhists founded (1950) |
| | Sixth great Buddhist council at Rangoon (1954–1956) |
| | Dalai Lama flees Tibet to India (1959) |
| | Friends of the Western Buddhist Order founded (1967) |
| | Development of Engaged Buddhism (1970) |
| | Vajradhatu Foundation founded (1973) |
| | International Association of Buddhist Studies founded (1976) |
| | International Network of Engaged Buddhists founded (1989) |
| | United Kingdom Association of Buddhist Studies founded (1995) |
| 21ST CENTURY C.E. | Destruction of standing Buddha statues at Bāmiyān by Taliban regime (2001) |

# *Appendix II*

Main topics covered

- The Pāli Canon
- The Chinese Canon
- The Tibetan Canon
- The Buddhist Scriptures

## *The Pāli Canon*

The Pāli Canon is the complete scripture collection of the Theravāda school. As such, it is the only complete set of scriptures for any Hīnayāna sect, preserved in the language of its composition. It is often called the *Tripiṭaka* or 'Three Baskets' because it includes the *Vinaya Piṭaka* or 'Basket of Discipline', the *Sutta Piṭaka* or 'Basket of Discourses', and the *Abhidhamma Piṭaka* or 'Basket of Higher Teachings'. There is an especially good summary of the Pāli Canon on pp. 265–76 of *The History of Buddhist Thought* (2nd edition. New York: Barnes and Noble, 1963) by Edward J. Thomas.

### I. *Vinaya Piṭaka* ('Basket of Discipline')

A. *Suttavibhaṅga* ('Analysis of Rules'): Rules of the *Pātimokkha* code with commentarial explanations.
  *Mahāvibhaṅga* ('Great Section'): 227 rules for monks.
  *Bhikkhunī-vibhaṅga* ('Division for Nuns'): 311 rules for nuns.

B. *Khandhaka* ('Sections'): Chapters relative to the organization of the *sangha*.
  1. *Mahāvagga* ('Great Group'): Regulations for ordination, *Uposatha* (Observance) Day, rainy-season retreat, clothing, food, medicine, and procedures relative to the *sangha*'s operation.

2. *Cullavagga* ('Small Group'): Regulations for judicial matters, requisites, schisms, travel, ordination and instruction of nuns, history of the first and second councils.

C. *Parivāra* ('Supplement'): Summaries and classifications of the *Vinaya* rules.

## II. *Sutta Piṭaka* ('Basket of Discourses')

A. *Dīgha Nikāya* ('Collection of Long Discourses'): 34 *suttas*.
B. *Majjhima Nikāya* ('Collection of Middle Length Discourses'): 152 *suttas*.
C. *Saṃyutta Nikāya* ('Collection of Connected Discourses'): 56 groups of *suttas*, grouped according to subject matter.
D. *Aṅguttara Nikāya* ('Collection of Item-More Discourses'): Discourses grouped according to the number of items in an ascending list.
E. *Khuddaka Nikāya* ('Collection of Little Texts')
1. *Khuddaka-pāṭha* ('Collection of Little Readings'): Short *suttas* for recitation.
2. *Dhammapada* ('Verses on *Dhamma*'): Collection of 423 verses, in many cases concerned with ethical maxims.
3. *Udāna* ('Verses of Uplift'): 80 solemn utterances spoken by Buddha.
4. *Itivuttaka* ('Thus it is Said'): 112 short *suttas*.
5. *Sutta-nipāta* ('Group of *Suttas*'): 70 verse *suttas* containing legendary material.
6. *Vimāna-vatthu* ('Stories of Heavenly Mansions'): *Suttas* concerning heavenly rebirths.
7. *Peta-vatthu* ('Stories of the Departed'): 51 poems on unfortunate rebirths.
8. *Thera-gāthā* ('Verses of the Male Elders'): Verses attributed to 264 male disciples of Buddha.
9. *Therī-gāthā* ('Verses of the Female Elders'): Verses attributed to about 100 female disciples of Buddha.
10. *Jātaka* ('Birth Stories'): 547 stories of the previous lives of the Buddha.
11. *Niddesa* ('Exposition'): Commentary on portions of the *Sutta-nipāta*.
12. *Paṭisambhidā-magga* ('Way of Analysis'): An *Abdhidhamma*-style discussion of doctrinal points.
13. *Apadāna* ('Stories'): Verse stories of lives and former lives of various monks and nuns.
14. *Buddhavaṃsa* ('Lineage of the Buddhas'): History of 24 previous Buddhas.
15. *Cariyā-piṭaka* ('Basket of Conduct'): *Jātaka* stories emphasizing a *bodhisattva*'s practice of the perfections.

## III. *Abhidhamma Piṭaka* ('Basket of Higher Teachings')

A. *Dhammasaṅgaṇī* ('Enumeration of *Dhammas*'): Discussion of mental and bodily factors, with reference to ethical issues.
B. *Vibhaṅga* ('Analysis'): Continued analysis of various doctrinal categories.
C. *Dhātu-kathā* ('Discussion of Elements'): Ordering of various factors under a variety of major categories.
D. *Puggala-paññatti* ('Designation of Human Types'): Classification of individuals according to a variety of traits.
E. *Kathā-vatthu* ('Subjects of Discussion'): Polemical treatise concerning doctrines disputed by rival schools.
F. *Yamaka* ('Book of Pairs'): Pairs of questions addressing basic categories.
G. *Paṭṭhāna* ('Book of Relations'): Analysis of causality in 24 groups.

## *The Chinese Canon*

The Chinese Buddhist Canon is called the Decang Jing or 'Great Scripture Store'. The first complete printing of the 'Three Baskets' or *Tripiṭaka* was completed in 983 C.E., and known as the Shuben or Szechuan edition. It included 1076 texts in 480 cases. A number of other editions of the Chinese Canon were made thereafter. The now-standard modern edition of this work is known as the *Taishō Shinshū Daizōkyō*, published in Tokyo between 1924 and 1929. It contains 55 volumes containing 2184 texts, along with a supplement of 45 additional volumes. A fine chapter entitled 'The Chinese *Tripiṭaka*' can be found on pp. 365–86 of *Buddhism in China* (Princeton, NJ: Princeton University Press, 1964) by Kenneth K.S. Ch'en.

I. *Āgama* Section: Volumes 1–2, 151 texts. Contains the equivalent of the first four Pāli *Nikāyas* and a portion of the fifth *Nikāya*.
II. Story Section: Volumes 3–4, 68 texts. Contains the *Jātaka* stories.
III. *Prajñāpāramitā* Section: Volumes 5–8, 42 texts. Contains the perfection of wisdom literature.
IV. *Saddharmapuṇḍarīka* Section: Volume 9, 16 texts. Contains three versions of the *Lotus Sūtra* and some additional material.
V. *Avataṃsaka* Section: Volumes 9–10, 31 texts. Contains material on the *Flower Garland Sūtra*.
VI. *Ratnakūṭa* Section: Volumes 11–12, 64 texts. Contains material on a group of 49 texts, some of which are extremely early Mahāyāna treatises.
VII. *Mahāparinirvāṇa* Section: Volume 12, 23 texts. Contains the Mahāyāna version of the conclusion of Buddha's life.
VIII. Great Assembly Section: Volume 13, 28 texts. Collection of Mahāyāna *sūtras*, beginning with the '*Great Assembly Sūtra*'.

IX. *Sūtra*-Collection Section: Volumes 14–17, 423 texts. Collection of miscellaneous (primarily Mahāyāna) *sūtras*.
X. *Tantra* Section: Volumes 18–21, 572 texts. Contains Vajrayāna *Sūtras* and Tantric materials.
XI. *Vinaya* Section: Volumes 22–24, 86 texts. Contain the disciplinary texts of a variety of Hīnayāna schools as well as texts on *bodhisattva* discipline.
XII. Commentaries on *Sūtras*: Volumes 24–26, 31 texts. Commentaries by Indian authors on the *Āgamas* and Mahāyāna *Sūtras*.
XIII. *Abhidharma* Section: Volumes 26–29, 28 texts. Translations of Sarvāstivādin, Dharmaguptaka, and Sautrāntika *Abhidharma* texts.
XIV. Mādhyamika Section: Volume 30, 15 texts. Contains texts of this important school of Mahāyāna Buddhist thought.
XV. Yogācāra Section: Volumes 30–31, 49 texts. Contains texts of this important school of Mahāyāna Buddhist Thought.
XVI. Collection of Treatises: Volume 32, 65 texts. Miscellaneous works on logic and other matters.
XVII. Commentaries on the *Sūtras*: Volumes 33–39. Commentaries by Chinese authors.
XVIII. Commentaries on the *Vinaya*: Volume 40. Commentaries by Chinese authors.
XIX. Commentaries on the *Śāstras*: Volumes 40–44. Commentaries by Chinese authors.
XX. Chinese Sectarian Writings: Volumes 44–48.
XXI. History and Biography: Volumes 49–52, 95 texts.
XXII. Encyclopedias and Dictionaries: Volumes 53–54, 16 texts.
XXIII. Non-Buddhist Doctrines: Volume 54, 8 texts. Contains materials on Hinduism, Manichean, and Nestorian Christian writing.
XXIV. Catalogs: Volume 55, 40 texts. Catalogs of the Chinese Canon, starting with that of Sengyou (published 515 C.E.).

## *The Tibetan Canon*

The Tibetan Canon consists of two parts: (1) the *bKa'-gyur* ('Translation of the Word of the Buddha'), pronounced *Kanjur*, and (2) the *bStan-'gyur* ('Translation of Teachings'), pronounced *Tenjur*. Because this latter collection contains works attributed to individuals other than the Buddha, it is considered only semi-canonical. The first printing of the Kanjur occurred not in Tibet, but in China (Peking), being completed in 1411. The first Tibetan edition of the canon was at sNar-thang (pronounced Narthang) with the *Kanjur* appearing in 1731, followed by the *Tenjur* in 1742. Other famous editions of the canon were printed at Derge and Cone. Almost fifty years ago, Kenneth K.S. Ch'en provided a short article on the Tibetan Canon titled 'The Tibetan *Tripiṭaka*', published in the *Harvard Journal of Asiatic Studies*, 9, 2 (June, 1946), pp. 53–62, that is still quite useful today.

## I. *bKa'-gyur* (*Kanjur*): Translation of the Word of the Buddha; 98 volumes according to the sNar-thang (Narthang) edition.

A. *Vinaya*: 13 Volumes.
B. *Prajñāpāramitā*: 21 Volumes.
C. *Avataṃsaka*: 6 Volumes.
D. *Ratnakūṭa*: 6 Volumes.
E. *Sūtra*: 30 Volumes. 270 texts, 75 per cent of which are Mahāyāna, 25 per cent Hīnayāna.
F. *Tantra*: 22 Volumes. Contains more than 300 texts.

## II. *bStan-'gyur* (*Tenjur*): Translation of Teachings; 224 volumes (3,626 texts) according to the Peking edition.

A. *Stotras* ('Hymns of Praise'): 1 volume; 64 texts.
B. Commentaries on the *Tantras*: 86 volumes; 3055 texts.
C. Commentaries on the *Sūtras*: 137 volumes; 567 texts.
    1. *Prajñāpāramitā* Commentaries, 16 volumes.
    2. Mādhyamika Treatises, 17 volumes.
    3. Yogācāra Treatises, 29 volumes.
    4. *Abhidharma*, 8 volumes.
    5. Miscellaneous Texts, 4 volumes.
    6. *Vinaya* Commentaries, 16 volumes.
    7. Tales and Dramas, 4 volumes.
    8. Technical Treatises: 43 volumes.
        a. Logic: 21 volumes.
        b. Grammar: 1 volume.
        c. Lexicography and Poetics: 1 volume.
        d. Medicine: 5 volumes.
        e. Chemistry and Miscellaneous: 1 volume.
        f. Supplements: 14 Volumes.

# Glossary

*Abhidharma* (P. *Abhidhamma*) – 'That which is above *Dharma*', or 'That which represents superior *Dharma*'. That portion of Buddhist literature dealing with abstruse philosophy or psychological matters.

*Abhidharmakośa* – A philosophical treatise written by Vasubandhu, covering almost all of the philosophical topics espoused in the Sarvāstivādin *Abhidharma*, and offering many refutations of Vaibhāṣika viewpoints.

*Abhidharma Piṭaka* (P. *Abhidhamma Piṭaka*) – The third 'basket' of the Buddhist canon.

*Āgama* – A traditional or canonical text, corresponding to the *Nikāyas* of the Pāli *Sutta Piṭaka*. Included are the *Dīrghāgama*, *Madhyamāgama*, *Ekottarāgama*, *Saṃyuktāgama*, and *Kṣudrakāgama*.

Ajātaśatru – Bimbisāra's son who imprisoned his father as a result of his (i.e., Ajātaśatru's) involvement with Devadatta. Later he relented and expressed faith in the Buddha (after one of Devadatta's unsuccessful attempts to murder the Buddha).

Ājñāta Kauṇḍinya – One of the five ascetics who practiced austerities with Siddhārtha Gautama. Upon hearing the Buddha's first sermon, Kauṇḍinya became enlightened, and accordingly received ordination as the first monk (*bhikṣu*).

Akṣobhya – One of the five celestial Buddhas, and the first to be mentioned in the *Aṣṭasāhasrikā-prajñāpāramitā Sūtra*.

*ālaya-vijñāna* – 'Storehouse consciousness'; a receptacle for the various dispositions and habit-energies of the other consciousnesses. The 'seeds' planted here, according to the Yogācārins, provide some connection between past, present, and future experiences.

Amita (Jap. Amida; Ch. Amituo) – The abbreviation of Amitābha, the Buddha of the Western Paradise, and the object of devotion in Pure Land Buddhism.

Amitābha – The Buddha of 'Eternal Light'; presiding over the Western Paradise.

Amitāyus – The Buddha of 'Eternal Life'; another name for the celestial Buddha presiding over the Western Paradise.

Ānanda – Siddhārtha Gautama's cousin who became his favorite disciple and personal attendant. He is said to have recited all of the Buddha's sermons at the first council (held at Rājagṛha), and was instrumental in establishing the order of nuns (*bhikṣuṇīs*).

Anāthapiṇḍika – A wealthy banker of Śrāvastī in Kośala who, as a lay disciple (*upāsaka*), built and donated Jetavana monastery to the *sangha*. It was here that Buddha spent many rainy seasons.

*Anātmalākṣaṇa Sūtra* – The 'Discourse on the Marks of the Not-Self'; the Buddha's second sermon to the five ascetics near Banaras, discussing the self, impermanence, and suffering.

*anātman* – 'Not self'; that doctrine of the Buddha which contradicts the Hindu notion of a pure, eternal, subtle self (*ātman*). The doctrine, intended to eliminate attachment, later became problematic in terms of Buddhist explanations of rebirth.

*Aṅguttara Nikāya* (Skt. *Ekottarāgama*) – 'Collection of Discourses Treating Enumerations Classed in Ascending Order'; the fourth section in the *Sutta Piṭaka* of the Pāli Canon.

*anitya* – 'Impermanence'; that Buddhist doctrine which states that all things originate, have duration, and decay. This notion of constant flux or impermanence forms the second of the Buddha's 'three marks of existence' (*tri-lakṣaṇa*).

An Shigao – A Parthian who settled at Lo-yang in 148 C.E. and headed a team of monks, mainly from *Nikāya* sects, which translated works on meditation and breathing exercises.

Anurādhapura – Ancient capital of Sri Lanka, founded by King Devānaṃpiyatissa (250–210 B.C.E.).

Ārāḍa Kālāma – The first teacher under whom Siddhārtha Gautama studied in his quest for enlightenment. He taught the experience of the state of the 'sphere of nothingness'. The future Buddha found the experience lacking, turned down an offer of co-teachership, and searched for another teacher.

*ārāma* – A park which was donated to the *sangha* and maintained by a wealthy donor, designated for use by the monks during the rainy season.

*arhant* – Either a 'worthy one' or 'slayer of the foe', depending on the applied etymology; the final stage in the *Nikāya* Buddhist stages of sanctification; one who has attained enlightenment.

Āryadeva – Nāgārjuna's closest pupil whose work supplemented that of his master. He wrote the *Śata Śāstra*, a Mādhyamika work.

*ārya pudgalas* – Literally, 'noble persons'; a class name which denotes those who have gained entry into the *ārya sangha* or group of 'spiritually elect persons'.

*ārya satyas* – The 'Four Noble Truths'; the basic doctrine of the Buddha's teaching. At the very heart of his teaching, this doctrine states that (1) all life is suffering (*duḥkha*), (2) there is a cause to the suffering (*samudaya*), (3) there is a cessation of suffering (*nirodha*), and (4) there is a path to the cessation of suffering (*aṣṭāṅgika mārga*). This teaching formed the core of the Buddha's first sermon, the *Dharmacakrapravartana Sūtra*.

Āsaṅga – Originally trained in the Mahīśāsaka school of early Buddhism, he left his tradition and was a major force in the establishment of the Yogācāra school of Buddhism. In addition to supposedly receiving a vision of the future Buddha Maitreya, in which several Yogācāra texts were supposedly dictated to him, Asaṅga wrote several books in his own right, and finally converted his brother Vasubandhu.

Aśoka – The third emperor of the Mauryan Dynasty in India, he brought India together under his rule. According to Buddhist legends, he became a lay disciple (*upāsaka*), and took up a policy of Dharma-conquest. Author of an extensive missionary movement, it is also said that the famous 'Third Council' was held during his reign. Aśoka became the model for many other rulers who sought to govern in accordance with the *Dharma*.

*Aśokāvadāna* – A Buddhist text which became perhaps the main source of many stories surrounding King Aśoka.

*āsravas* – Literally 'outflows'; these impurities, consisting of sensual desire, desire for continued existence, false views, and ignorance, must be destroyed to experience enlightenment. Much of Buddhist practice aims at totally uprooting them.

*aṣṭāṅgika mārga* – The 'Eightfold Path'; which is the fourth of the Noble Truths, being an eight-membered guide to practice culminating in the realization of enlightenment. It is organized around the triple training (*tri-śikṣā*) of morality (*śīla*), concentration (*samādhi*), and wisdom (*prajñā*).

*Aṣṭasāhasrikā-prajñāpāramitā Sūtra* – The '*8,000-line Sūtra on the Perfection of Wisdom*'; the earliest, and perhaps basic, Mahāyāna text. It was translated in Chinese around 179 C.E.

Aśvaghoṣa – A Buddhist poet, probably contemporary with King Kaniṣka, who composed the *Buddhacarita* or '*Acts of the Buddha*'.

Atīśa – An Indian scholar (982–1054) who arrived in Tibet in 1042. He was a critical factor in the renaissance of Buddhism in Tibet, with his chief disciple Dromdön ('Brom-ston), founding the Kadampa (bKa-gdams-pa) sect.

*ātman* – In Hinduism, the 'self' or 'soul'; that which is pure, subtle, and eternal, which transmigrates from life to life, carries karmic residues, and is of like essence with the absolute.

*Avadānaśataka* – A Sarvāstivādin collection of legendary stories (*avadānas*) probably composed around the time of King Kaniṣka.

Avalokiteśvara (Ch. Kuan-yin; Jap. Kannon) – A *bodhisattva* who gradually assumed a greater importance in Buddhism, finally arriving at a position in which his image was found along with the Buddha's, or even standing alone as the sole recipient of reverence. Referred to frequently in Mahāyāna texts, he is one of the most important celestial *bodhisattvas*.

*āvāsa* – Dwelling places, staked out, constructed, and kept up by the monks for use during the annual rainy-season retreat.

*Avataṃsaka Sūtra* – The '*Flower Ornament Sūtra*'; a Mahāyāna text which has an extensive portrayal of the *bodhisattva's* search for enlightenment, and offered a view of existence as one of complete identity and interdependence.

*Bhāvanākrama* – A textbook on meditation, written by the Indian scholar Kamalaśīla, and which has been used as a model for all meditation books in Tibet since the ninth century.

Bhāvaviveka – A Mādhyamika adherent who lived around 400 C.E. One of his texts, the *Nikāyabhedavibhaṅgavyākhyāna*, provides important information on the early sectarian movement in Indian Buddhism. He is also known as Bhavya.

*bhikṣu* – This is the technical word for a Buddhist monk or religious professional, as opposed to the layman. In addition to taking a more severe vow with regard to practice, the monk usually lived in the confines of a monastery, having devoted his life to the practice of Buddhism.

*bhikṣuṇī* – This is the female counterpart to the monk. See *bhikṣu*, above.

*bhūmi* – Literally 'earth'; but usually meaning 'stage' in Buddhist usage. The ten stages on the path of the *bodhisattva* are referred to as *bhūmis*, and are the subject of separate discourses: the *Bodhisattvabhūmi* and *Daśabhūmika*.

*bīja* – Literally 'seeds'; which, according to Yogācāra, are planted in the *ālaya-vijñāna*. They carry the various dispositions and habit-energies and, if 'pollinated', give rise to a wrong view of the world.

Bimbisāra – A king, contemporary with the Buddha, who ruled Magadha from his capital in Rājagṛha. He donated the first monastery to the *sangha*, Veṇuvana *ārāma*, and was somewhat responsible for the Buddhists' adoption of the *Poṣadha* ceremony.

Bodhgayā – The traditional birthplace of Buddhism, marking the spot at which the Buddha attained enlightenment.

*bodhi* – Literally 'enlightenment', or that complete and perfect state of awakening experienced by the Buddha.

*bodhicitta* – The 'thought of enlightenment'. It is with this initial step that the *bodhisattva* begins the path to complete, perfect enlightenment.

Bodhidharma – The first patriarch of Chan Buddhism. Said to have come to China around 520 C.E., it is from Bodhidharma that the Chan lineage begins with his transmission of the *Laṅkāvatāra Sūtra*.

*bodhisattva* – A 'Buddha to be' or 'enlightenment being'. Before becoming a Buddha, Siddhārtha Gautama was held to be a *bodhisattva*, generally taken to mean a future Buddha. Whereas the *Nikāya* Buddhist sects hold there to be but one *bodhisattva* – Siddhārtha – the Mahāyānists adopt this concept as the ideal type around which to model religious practice. In Mahāyāna, the *bodhisattva* (which now can be any person) holds off entering final *nirvāṇa* out of compassion, and attempts to lead all sentient beings to complete, perfect enlightenment.

*Bodhisattvabhūmi* – A text outlining the ten stages (*bhūmis*) to be practiced by the *bodhisattva*.

*Bodhisattva-yāna* – The '*Bodhisattva* Vehicle', or vehicle of those who seek the salvation of all sentient beings. The concept is found, for example, in the *Saddharmapuṇḍarīka Sūtra*.

Bodhi Tree – The 'Tree of Awakening'; that tree under which Siddhārtha Gautama resolved to sit until he attained complete, perfect enlightenment. Branches of the tree were sent to various parts of the Buddhist world after the Buddha's death.

Bozhang Huai-hai – Chinese Chan monk (720–814 C.E.) who drew up a monastic constitution which was more detailed and, in some respects, contrary to the *Vinaya*.

Buddha – The 'Awakened One'; title given to Siddhārtha Gautama after he achieved complete, perfect enlightenment under the Bodhi Tree.

*Buddhacarita* – Literally, '*Acts of the Buddha*'; a non-canonical legend of the life of the Buddha, a portion of which remains in Sanskrit and is attributed to the poet Aśvaghoṣa.

Buddhaghosa – Probably the greatest of all Theravāda exegetical writers. Coming from South India to Sri Lanka in the fourth or fifth century C.E., his classic *Visuddhimagga* or '*Path of Purity*' and his numerous commentaries establish him in virtually all aspects of Buddhism.

Buddha-yāna – Literally 'Buddha Vehicle'; the one sole vehicle by which the Buddha teaches the *Dharma*. This concept is found in the *Saddharmapuṇḍarīka Sūtra*.

Burnouf, Eugène – French scholar who worked on manuscripts collected by Brian Houghton Hodgson. His translation of the *Lotus Sūtra* was published posthumously in 1852. He is sometimes referred to as 'the father of Buddhist Studies'.

Butön (Bu-ston) – Tibetan historian living from 1290–1364 who collected and edited Tibetan scriptures.

*caitya* – A religious monument or *stūpa* in which the relics of the Buddha or another famous saint are housed.

*cakravartin* – Literally 'turner of the wheel (of the law)'. It was predicted that Siddhārtha Gautama would become a *cakravartin*, either in the political or religious sense. It may also mean he who dwells or abides in the *cakra* (i.e., the *maṇḍala* or land), equally applying to the Buddha.

*cetanā* – Volition or intention. The motivational impulse that creates *karma*.

Chan – Chan is a Chinese transliteration of the Sanskrit term *dhyā(na)*. It is a Mahāyāna Buddhist school said to have been brought to China by Bodhidharma (usually regarded as the twenty-eighth Indian patriarch) around 520 C.E. It emphasizes rigorous meditation and a disdain for the 'trappings' of religion, and gave rise to Zen in Japan.

*citta* – 'Mind'; one of many words used by Buddhists to denote the mental sphere. Due to its variable character and the general inconsistency in the use of the term, it became a prime target for *Abhidharma* analysis.

*cittamātra* – Literally, 'mind-only'; this concept appears in several Buddhist texts, among them the *Laṅkāvatāra Sūtra*, and represents a response to the problem of what exists if all subjects and objects are devoid of ego and are only imagined. It has frequently been used as a synonym for Yogācāra or Vijñānavāda.

*daimoku* – A formula used by Nichiren Buddhists to attain salvation with the word '*nam myōhō renge kyō*' ('Hail to the Scripture of the Lotus of the True Teaching').

Dalai Lama – The official political head of Tibetan Buddhism. The title, coined by the Mongols, is bestowed on that person thought to be the incarnation of the *bodhisattva* Avalokiteśvara.

*dāna* – Literally 'charity' or 'giving'; one of the six perfections (*pāramitās*). For the lay person, it includes the giving of food, clothing, etc., to the monastic members of the community. For the monk or nun, it includes giving advice, teaching, etc., to the laity.

Daoan – An eminent Buddhist monk in China, living from 312–385 C.E., who condemned the expression of Buddhism in Taoist terms.

*Daśabhūmika Sūtra* – A Mahāyāna text that sets out, in detail, the ten stages of the *bodhisattva* path.

Devadatta – The Buddha's cousin who tried to usurp leadership of the *sangha* by attempting to murder the Buddha. After several unsuccessful attempts, he founded his own order, but when his followers returned to the Buddha, he spit up blood and died.

Devānaṃpiyatissa – King who ruled Sri Lanka from about 250–210 B.C.E. It is said that in 247 B.C.E. he sent emissaries to King Aśoka requesting friendship.

*Dhammapada* – '*Stanzas on the Teaching*'; second book of the *Khuddaka Nikāya* of the *Sutta Piṭaka* of the Pāli Canon.

*Dharma* – The teaching or doctrine of the Buddha. *Dharma* is said to include all the Buddha's sermons and doctrinal pronouncements.

*dharmas* – An *Abhidharma* technical term, used to denote experiential moments, i.e., the building blocks of existence. Thus to analyze existence one must simply break it down into its experiential moments. Various Buddhist schools posited differing numbers of *dharmas*. It is also used in the psychological sense to signify mental states.

*Dharmacakrapravartana Sūtra* – *'Discourse on the Turning of the Wheel of the Law'*; the Buddha's first sermon to the five ascetics in Banaras. Here he preached the futility of the extremes of luxury seeking and asceticism, and outlined the Four Noble Truths.

Dharmākara – In the *Larger Sukāvatīvyūha Sūtra*, a monk who hears the *Dharma* from the Buddha Lokeśvararāja. He takes a series of forty-six vows aimed at establishing a pure land. Ultimately, Dharmākara reveals himself to Amitābha, and the discourse ends with a magnificent vision of this Buddha.

*Dharmakāya* – Literally 'Body of *Dharma*'. In earliest Buddhism this was likely to mean the body of the Buddha's doctrine. After the Buddha's death it was given a metaphysical interpretation by the Sarvāstivādins. When incorporated into the Mahāyānist doctrine of the 'Three Bodies of the Buddha' (*trikāya*), *Dharmakāya* is elevated to the 'Body of Essence' or Buddhahood itself. It is that ultimate reality which can only be perceived by a Buddha.

Dharmakīrti – A great Buddhist logician of the seventh century C.E. whose major writings include the *Nyāyabindu* and *Pramāṇavārttika*.

*dharmatā* – Literally 'nature'; it is used in the *Laṅkāvatāra Sūtra* as the pure state from which the Buddha issues. It is often used in Yogācāra texts.

*dhātu* – Used in two primary contexts, *dhātu* refers to the *Abhidharma* classification of existence into eighteen 'realms', or, in the cosmological sense, to a plane of existence inhabited usually by one consonant with the plane. The three usual cosmological realms are the 'realm of desire' (*kāma-dhātu*), 'form realm' (*rūpa-dhātu*), and the 'formless realm' (*ārupya-dhātu*).

*dhyāna* – Technical term used to denote the states experienced in meditation. In traditional *Nikāya* Buddhism, as outlined in many sources, these are held to be fourfold.

*Diamond Sūtra* – English name for the *Vajracchedikā Sūtra*.

*Dīgha Nikāya* (Skt. *Dīrghāgama*) – *'Collection of Long Discourses'*; the first section of the *Sutta Piṭaka* of the Pāli Canon.

Dignāga – Famous Buddhist logician of the fourth to fifth century C.E., whose writings include the *Pramāṇasamuccaya*, *Nyāyamukha*, and *Hetucakra*.

*Dīpavaṃsa* – Literally, the *'Island Chronicle'*. Along with the *Mahāvaṃsa*, it provides much information on the history of Buddhism in Sri Lanka.

*Divyāvadāna* – Sarvāstivādin text containing much material aimed at popularizing Buddhism, in addition to much *Vinaya*-based material.

Dōgen – Japanese Buddhist (1200–1253) who went to China to study and was responsible for establishing Sōtō Zen (based on the Caodong branch of Chan teaching).

*dṛṣṭi* – Technically speaking, the term means 'views', but this was usually interpreted in Buddhism to mean 'false views', namely those views which maintained positions heretical to Buddhism.

*duḥkha* – 'Suffering'; the first of the Four Noble Truths points out the transciency of all mental and physical pleasures. Thus we find a statement that all life is characterized by suffering.

Dunhuang – Place marking the entrance to China from Central Asia. Buddhism is likely to have made initial impact here, as many cave-temples, wall paintings, and valuable manuscripts have been retrieved from Dunhuang.

Dushun – Chinese Buddhist (557–640 C.E.) who founded the Huayan school of Chinese Buddhism.

Eisai – Japanese Buddhist (1141–1215) who went to China to study and who was responsible for establishing Rinzai Zen, based on the Linji branch of Chan.

Faxian – Chinese pilgrim who traveled to India (399–414 CE). Upon returning to China, he translated many Buddhist texts into Chinese.

Faxiang – School of Buddhism in China organized by Xuanzang (596–664 C.E.) and his disciple Kuiji (632–682 C.E.) out of Shelun. It corresponds to Indian Yogācāra.

Fazang – Chinese Buddhist (643–712 C.E.) who organized the Huayan school of Buddhism on the basis of Dushun's (557–640 C.E.) teaching.

Gampopa (sGam-po-pa) – Important Tibetan Buddhist (1079–1153) who received the lineage of the Kagyupa (bKa-rgyud-pa) school from Milarepa.

Gandhāra – An early locale of the Sarvāstivādin school of Buddhism. Later it is known for its beautiful artwork.

Gautama – Formal name of the clan into which Siddhārtha, later to become the Buddha, was born.

Gelug (de-Gelugs) – Sect of Tibetan Buddhism founded by Tsongkhapa (1357–1419), based on the lineage of Atīśa's Kadampa sect. They are known as the 'yellow hat' sect.

Genshin – Japanese Pure Land Buddhist (942–1017 C.E.) who wrote *Ōjōyōshū*. Due to his personal charisma, he played a major role in the growth of the Amida cult of Buddhism in Japan.

*gohonzon* – In Nichiren Buddhism and Sōka Gakkai, a picture containing the formula *nam myōhō renge kyō*, along with the names of various Buddhas and *bodhisattvas*. The devotee gazes at the *gohonzon* during chanting.

*Guanyin Jing* – The '*Sūtra on Avalokiteśvara*'; the twenty-fourth chapter of the *Saddharmapuṇḍarīka Sūtra*, circulating independently, and dealing with this celestial *bodhisattva*.

Gyōgi – A Hossō Buddhist monk who did much to increase the prestige of the Japanese *sangha* by performing many acts of charity for the common people. He was a trusted advisor to the Emperor Shōmu, and was later called Gyōgi *bosatsu* (*bodhisattva*).

Hakuin – Japanese Zen Buddhist monk (1685–1768) who strongly exemplified the very finest ideals of compassion during the stagnant and degenerate Tokugawa Period.

*Heart Sūtra* – English name for the *Hṛdaya Sūtra*.

Heian Period – Period in Japanese history from 794–1192 C.E. which was probably the high water-mark for Japanese Buddhism.

*Hekigan Roku* – The '*Blue Cliff Records*'; Japanese translation of the *Biyan Lu*.

*Hetucakra* – Buddhist logic text written by Dignāga. It literally means '*Wheel of Justifications*'.

*Hevajra Tantra* – One of the most important of all the Buddhist tantric texts. The Indian tantric master Ratnākaraśānti taught it to the Tibetans.

Hīnayāna – Literally 'Lesser Vehicle'; a pejorative name given to the early (and conservative) schools of Buddhism by the newly emergent Mahāyāna ('Great Vehicle'). It designates the traditional eighteen schools that supposedly arose between the first and fourth centuries following the Buddha's *parinirvāṇa*. It is no longer considered appropriate to use this term, and has been replaced by the designation 'Nikāya Buddhism'.

Hōnen – Japanese Buddhist (1133–1212 C.E.) who was responsible for founding the Jōdo Shū or Pure Land school of Buddhism in Japan.

Hossō – One of the six academic traditions of Japanese 'Nara' Buddhism which had been imported, without substantial modification, from China. It corresponds to the Indian Yogācāra.

Huayan – School of Buddhism in China, based on the *Huayan Jing* (Skt. *Avataṃsaka Sūtra*) or '*Flower Ornament Sūtra*'. It was founded by Dushun (557–640 C.E.) and organized by Fazang (643–712 C.E.).

Huineng – Chinese Buddhist monk of the Southern Chan school who became the Sixth Patriarch after a long and bitter controversy with his rival Shenxiu of Northern Chan. The *Platform Sūtra* of the Sixth Patriarch is attributed to Huineng.

Huisi – Chinese Buddhist (515–576 C.E.) who founded the Tiantai school of Buddhism in China, which was later organized by Zhiyi.

Huiyuan – Chinese Buddhist (334–416 C.E.) who founded the Jingtu (Pure Land) school of Buddhism in China, which was later organized by Tanluan (476–542 C.E.).

Ikeda, Daisaku – The third and present leader of the Sōka Gakkai school of Buddhism.

*Jātaka* – Literally '*Birth Story*'; a collection of 550 tales which tell of the Buddha's previous lives as a *bodhisattva*. It forms the tenth book of the *Khuddaka Nikāya* of the *Sutta Piṭaka* of the Pāli Canon. Most of the stories are in fact extra-canonical.

Jetavana – 'Grove of Prince Jeta', a monastery built for the Buddha by Anāthapiṇḍika and located in Śrāvastī. In the fourth century C.E., a monastery was built in Sri Lanka which carried the same name.

*jhāna* – The Pāli counterpart of the Sanskrit technical term *dhyāna*. See *dhyāna*, above.

Jina – Literally 'Conqueror'; a title applied to Siddhārtha Gautama after he attained complete, perfect enlightenment. It is said that he conquered the *āsravas* or 'outflows'.

Jingtu – 'The field which purifies' or 'Pure Land'; the Pure Land school of Buddhism in China, founded by Huiyuan and organized by Tanluan, and emphasizing faith and devotion as the way to salvation.

*jñāna* – Knowledge, in an intuitive sense. It is the tenth perfection (*pāramitā*) and arises in the tenth *bodhisattva* stage, that of Dharmamegha, or 'The Cloud of Dharma'. *Jñāna* is a direct knowing of things as they really are.

Jōdo Shinshū – The 'True Pure Land' school of Buddhism in Japan, founded by Shinran. In some respects it is based on both Chinese Jingtu and Hōnen's Jōdo Shū. It emphasizes, in radical fashion, the saving grace of Amida.

Jōdo Shū – The 'Pure Land' school of Buddhism in Japan, founded by Hōnen. Based on Chinese Jungtu, it emphasizes faith and devotion to Amida, as well as the repetition of Amida's name in the formula *Namu Amida butsu*.

Jushe – School of Buddhism in China founded by Paramārtha (499–569 C.E.) and organized by Xuanzang (596–664 C.E.). It corresponds to the Indian *Abhidharma* school.

Kadampa (bKa-gdam-pa) – Tibetan Buddhist sect founded by Dromdön ('Brom-ston), based on the teachings of his teacher Atīśa.

Kagyu (bKa-rgyud) – Tibetan Buddhist sect tracing its origins to Marpa (1012–1099), who studied under Nāropa and learned the cycle of the *Cakrasamvara Tantra*.

Kamakura Period – Period in Japan which began in 1192 with a shift of the ruling power from the Heian court to a group of samurai. Civil power was to remain in the hands of the military until the Meiji Restoration in 1867.

Kamalaśīla – Indian Buddhist of the eighth century who wrote the *Bhāvanākrama*, was a great scholar, and defended the official Tibetan doctrine against the Chinese notion of instant enlightenment.

*kami* – Deities in Japanese Shintō.

Kaniṣka – Kushan emperor who reunified India around the turn of the Common Era, and was sympathetic to Buddhism. Much Buddhist learning went on during his reign, one which he perhaps fancied as modeled after Aśoka.

*Kanjur* – Literally 'Translation of Buddha Word'; that portion of the Tibetan Buddhist Canon containing what is thought to be the Buddha's authoritative teaching.

*karma* – 'Action' or 'deed' in Sanskrit. The moral law of causality which states that what a person does in this life will have an effect in later rebirths. It is closely related to *cetanā*.

*karuṇā* – Literally 'compassion'; the primary force behind the action of the *bodhisattva*. It is this compassion which leads the *bodhisattva* to make vows to save all sentient beings before entering *nirvāṇa*.

Kāśyapa – A leading disciple of the Buddha. He is said to have presided over the first Buddhist council at Rājagṛha. Chan also refers to a Mahākāśyapa as the second patriarch in India (the Buddha being the first).

*Kathāvatthu* – *'Subjects of Discussion'*; one of the *Abhidhamma* books in the *Abhidhamma Piṭaka* of the Pāli Canon. These 'subjects' were apparently discussed in the Third Council, held at Pāṭaliputra during Aśoka's reign.

Kegon – One of the six academic traditions of Japanese 'Nara' Buddhism which had been imported, without substantial modification, from China. It corresponds to the Indian Avataṃsaka and Chinese Huayan schools.

Khmer – An ancient kingdom in the region of Cambodia.

*Khuddaka Nikāya* – The fifth section of the *Sutta Piṭaka* of the Pāli Canon, containing fifteen miscellaneous or 'minor' texts.

*kleśa* – 'Defilement'; both moral and intellectual, which must be overcome in order to attain enlightenment.

*kōan* – Literally 'public records' or authenticated cases of dialogue of Zen masters. These seemingly insoluble and confusing statements, sometimes resembling riddles, were aimed at bringing the student to the full realization of enlightenment.

Kōbō Daishi – A posthumous title given to Kūkai, the Japanese Buddhist responsible for establishing Shingon Buddhism in the ninth century.

Koryŏ Period – Period in Korea (918–1392) in which Buddhism in Korea reached the height of its importance.

*kṣaṇa* – Literally 'moment'; that concept in Buddhism that states all things to be of momentary duration. In the formalized doctrine of 'momentariness' (*kṣaṇikatva*), we find things to have an origin (*utpatti*), duration (*sthiti*), and decay (*vināśa*).

*kṣānti* – 'Patience' or 'forbearance'; the third of the perfections (*pāramitās*) practiced by a *bodhisattva*.

Kūkai – Chinese Buddhist who went to China to study and returned to introduce Chinese Zhenyan or *tantra* into Japan under the name of Shingon. The esoteric school of Buddhism emphasized *mantras*, *maṇḍalas*, and the like. From its introduction in the ninth century onward, it was very popular. Kūkai was posthumously named Kōbō Daishi.

Kumārajīva – Great Buddhist translator, from Kucha, who lived from 344 to 413 C.E. With the aid of royal patronage, he made much headway translating Indian Buddhist texts into Chinese (from the time of his arrival in China in 401 C.E.). He is said to have founded the Sanlun school of Chinese Buddhism, based on Nāgārjuna's teachings.

Kuśinagara – The place where the Buddha entered *parinirvāṇa*.

Kūya – Japanese Buddhist (903–972 C.E.) who, through personal charisma, fostered the growth of the Amida cult in Japan.

Kyoto – The capital of Japan immediately after the Nara Period. It was formerly called Heian.

*lakṣaṇa* – Literally 'mark'; the doctrine of the three marks of existence, that is, not-self (*anātman*), impermanence (*anitya*), and suffering (*duḥkha*). It is said to be one of the cardinal teachings of the Buddha.

*Lalitavistara* – The '*Detailed Account of the Sports (of the Buddha)*'; a non-canonical legend of the life of the Buddha, usually associated with the Sarvāstivādin school.

Lamotte, Étienne (1903–1983) – Modern Buddhologist working in Louvain, and author of the classic *Histoire du Bouddhisme Indien des Origins à l'ère Śaka*, as well as translator of many important Buddhist texts. He is considered one of the greatest scholars of Buddhist Studies.

*Lam-rim chen-mo* – Major Tibetan text on meditation, written by Tsongkhapa.

*Laṅkāvatāra Sūtra* – '*Sūtra on the Descent into Laṅkā*'; a Mahāyānist text emphasizing the doctrines of mind-only (*citta-mātra*), the three *svabhāvas*, and the *ālaya-vijñāna*. Although problematic to classify, it does have many Yogācāra affinities.

Lhasa – City in Tibet where Atīśa spent most of his time. It remained of primary importance to Tibetan Buddhists up to the time of the takeover by the Communist Chinese.

Linji Yixuan – Founder of one of the major divisons (Linji Chan) of Chinese Chan Buddhism.

*loka* – Literally 'world'. In Buddhist cosmology one of two usual distinctions: the receptacle world (*bhājanaloka*) and the world of beings (*sattvaloka*).

Lokakṣema – An Indo-Scythian who arrived in China between 166–188 C.E. and represented Mahāyāna viewpoints.

*lokaprajñapti* – The term, literally meaning 'world teachings', or 'worldly designations', is the nearest equivalent to the English word cosmology.

*Lotus Sūtra* – English equivalent for the *Saddharmapuṇḍarīka Sūtra*.

*Lu* – Chinese word for *Vinaya*. A school of Buddhism emerged in China whose primary concern was the study and teaching of the *Vinaya* texts.

Mādhyamika – A Mahāyāna Buddhist school, founded by Nāgārjuna, which purported to represent (as the title indicates) 'the middle way'.

Magadha – Kingdom in India ruled by Bimbisāra (and his descendants) from its capital of Rājagṛha. It was perhaps the most forceful and viable kingdom during the Buddha's lifetime.

*mahābheda* – Literally 'great schism'. This refers to the first split in Buddhism, resulting in the separation of the Sthaviras and Mahāsāṃghikas.

Mahākāśyapa – Disciple of Śākyamuni reagarded by Chinese Chan as the second Indian patriarch. See Kāśyapa above.

*mahāmudrā* – Literally 'great symbol'; a general term for a complex system of Tibetan meditative techniques aimed at spontaneity.

Mahāprajāpatī – The sister of Queen Māyā, who married King Śuddhodana after her sister's death and served as foster mother to Siddhārtha Gautama. She later became the first Buddhist nun.

Mahāsāṃghika – One of the first Buddhist sects. Its name means 'Great Assembly', reflecting the fact that it was the 'majority party' at the time of the split. Scholars initially believed this group to be progressive, liberal, and lax with respect to discipline, but this presumption has proved to be false.

*mahāsattva*–A term which means 'Great Being', which is another descriptive phrase applied to those on the *bodhisattva* path.

*Mahāvaṃsa* – The '*Great Chronicle*' of Sri Lanka, written by King Mahānāma in the fifth century C.E. It contains much information on the history of Buddhism in Sri Lanka, as well as providing some information on Indian Buddhism. It is a companion volume to the *Dīpavaṃsa*.

*Mahāvastu* – The '*Great Account*', a non-canonical legend of the life of the Buddha, written in Buddhist Sanskrit, and belonging to the Mahāsāṃghika-Lokottaravādin school.

*Mahāvibhāṣā* – A later Sarvāstivādin Abhidharma text whose title means '*The Great (Book of) Options*'. It resulted from a huge gathering of monks, convened by King Kaniṣka.

Mahāvihāra – A great monastic institution in Sri Lanka, built during the reign of Devānaṃpiyatissa in Mahāmeghavana park, and housing a branch of the Bodhi Tree.

Mahāyāna – Literally, the 'Great Vehicle'; a school of Buddhism which arose gradually several hundred years after the Buddha's *parinirvāṇa*. More liberal socially and more speculative philosophically than the traditional, orthodox Buddhists of the time, the new group emphasized the *bodhisattva path*, the concepts of emptiness (*śūnyatā*), three bodies of the Buddha (*trikāya*), and 'suchness' (*tathatā*), as well as sparking a new creative drive in the production of Buddhist literature.

Mahinda – Son of King Aśoka who led a mission to Sri Lanka, thus establishing Buddhism on the island kingdom.

Maitreya – The future Buddha. Legend suggests that he dictated many of the Yogācāra texts to Asaṅga, and these are listed under the name Maitreyanātha.

*Majjhima Nikāya* – *'Collection of Middle Length Sayings'*; the second section of the *Sutta Piṭaka* of the Pāli Canon.

Makiguchi, Tsunesaburō – Founder of the Sōka Gakkai school of Buddhism in Japan.

*manas* – One of many terms in the Buddhist vocabulary used to represent mind, and as such, of prime interest for *Abhidharma* theorists. Yogācāra Buddhism later tried to differentiate between the terms *manas*, *citta*, and *vijñāna*, which were often used synonymously in other Buddhist schools.

*maṇḍala* – In tantric Buddhism, a diagram or symbolic representation in which the meditator creates a world wherein he is the central Buddha. The *maṇḍala* thus becomes the entire universe, replete with Buddhas, deities, and the like.

Mañjuśrī – A *bodhisattva*, gradually gaining importance in Buddhism, to the point where his image was often found along with that of the Buddha, or in some cases, standing alone as the sole recipient of reverence. He is one of the prime interlocutors in the *Vimalakīrtinirdeśa Sūtra*.

*mantra* – In tantric Buddhism, a 'tool for thinking' (in Anagarika Govinda's words) which uses the symbolic power in sounds as a means for directly experiencing things as they really are.

*mappō* – 'Latter-Day Dharma'; a Japanese term denoting that period of time in which the Buddha's teachings have fallen into decay.

Māra – Derived from a Sanskrit verb which means 'to die'; this is the name of a demon who tempted the Buddha with his three daughters (Discontent, Delight, and Desire). He also suggested to the Buddha at the end of the latter's life, that he enter *parinirvāṇa*.

*mārga* – The 'path' leading to the cessation of suffering. The fourth Noble Truth is often referred to as the *mārga*.

Marpa (Mar-pa) – Tibetan Buddhist who was the father of the Kagyupa (bKa-rgyud-pa) lineage. He went to India, studied with Nāropa, and returned to Tibet where he eventually passed on the lineage to Milarepa.

Maudgalyāyana – One of Buddha's chief early disciples. Converted to Buddhism shortly after his friend Śāriputtra, he was reputed to be very adept in magical powers.

Mauryan Dynasty – One of the most famous dynasties in India, beginning with Candragupta Maurya (around 320 B.C.E., and which continued with his son Bindusāra and grandson Aśoka.

Māyā – The wife of King Śuddhodana and mother of Siddhārtha Gautama. She died seven days after the birth of her son.

Meiji Restoration – That movement (1867) which marked the end of the military control of Japan by the samurai.

Milarepa (Mi-la ras-pa) – The chief disciple of Marpa. After much tribulation, he received the teaching from Marpa and became one of the most revered persons in the history of Tibetan Buddhism.

*Milindapañha* – The '*Questions of King Milinda*'; a non-canonical Pāli text recording the conversations of the Bactrian King Menander and the Buddhist monk Nāgasena. It is a valuable compendium of Theravāda doctrine.

Moggaliputta Tissa – Buddhist monk chosen to preside over the Third Council, held in Aśoka's capital city of Pāṭaliputra.

*Mūlamādhyamika-kārikās* – The '*Middle Stanzas*' of Nāgārjuna, representing his chief work and which reflects his doctrinal position. It is regarded as one of the greatest, and most perplexing, of all Buddhist documents. It is the basis of the Buddhist school attributed to Nāgārjuna.

*Mumonkan* – '*The Gateless Barrier*', a Japanese translation of a famous Chinese Buddhist text.

Nāgārjuna – Buddhist philosopher who probably lived in the second or third century C.E. and founded the Mādhyamika school of Buddhism. He was a clever dialectician, a mystic of high attainment, and among the very greatest of Buddhist thinkers.

Nāgasena – Learned Buddhist monk whose conversations with the Bactrian King Menander are recorded in the *Milindapañha*.

Nālandā – City on the outskirts of Rājagṛha which became the seat of one of the most important Buddhist universities.

*Nam Myōhō Renge Kyō* – Literally 'Hail to the Scripture of the Lotus of the True Teaching' or simply 'Homage to the *Lotus Sūtra*'. Nichiren Buddhists repeat this formula in the hopes of high attainment.

*Namo Amida Buddha* – 'Homage to Amida Buddha', a formula used by Pure Land Buddhists throughout the world as a means of offering devotion to Amitābha, thus hoping to gain rebirth in his Western Paradise. In Chinese this practice is called *nianfo*; in Japanese *nembutsu*.

Nara – Period in Japanese history so named because the capital was Nara. Established in 710 C.E., it survived until 794 C.E. when the capital was moved to Heian (modern-day Kyoto).

Nāropa – An Indian scholar who turned yogin. He received teaching from Tilopa after much difficulty. Nāropa later served as Marpa's guru.

*nibbāna* – Pāli equivalent of the Sanskrit term *nirvāṇa*.

Nichiren – Japanese Buddhist (1222–1282) who founded a school of Buddhism bearing his name. After originally studying Tendai Buddhism, he was not satisfied with Buddhist methods, but was convinced about the efficacy of the *Lotus Sūtra*, and developed a practice based on this text.

*Nikāya* – 'Collection'; that title applied to the various parts of the *Sutta Piṭaka* of the Pāli Canon, so named because they are collections of various kinds of sermons.

It also means a 'group' and is used to designate sectarian groups in the early Indian Buddhist tradition.

*Nirmāṇakāya* – The 'Apparition Body'; that term used by Mahāyānists to signify the historical Buddha. It is the first of the 'Three Bodies of the Buddha', the others being *Sambhogakāya* and *Dharmakāya*.

*nirodha* – Literally 'cessation'; the third Noble Truth, stating that there can be a cessation to suffering.

*nirvāṇa* – Literally 'blowing out'; in Buddhism the goal of religious practice. The texts are very enigmatic on the topic of *nirvāṇa*. It is obviously that which needs to be experienced to be understood.

Nyingmapa (rNying-ma-pa) – School of Tibetan Buddhism whose name literally means 'ancient ones'. They trace their lineage back to the foundation of Buddhism in Tibet. They seem to possess authentic Indian teachings and have tended to be less political than other Tibetan schools.

*Ōjōyōshū* – '*Compendium on the Essence of Rebirth*', written by the Japanese Buddhist Genshin, it vividly contrasts the miseries of hell with the joys of the Pure Land.

Pāli Canon – The *Tripiṭaka* of the Theravāda school of Buddhism.

*pañcaśīla* – The five rules of moral conduct which Buddhist lay disciples observe. They include not to kill, lie, steal, take intoxicants, or engage in illicit sexual activities.

*pāramitā* – The traditional six (and sometimes ten) 'perfections' engaged in by the *bodhisattva* on the path to complete, perfect enlightenment. They include giving (*dāna*), morality (*śīla*), patience (*kṣānti*), vigor (*vīrya*), meditation (*samādhi*), and wisdom (*prajña*).

*parinirvāṇa* – The final 'blowing out' or that which describes the Buddha's experience at the moment of his death.

Pāṭaliputra – Capital of Magadha during the reign of King Aśoka. It was the scene of Aśoka's Third Council.

*Poṣadha* (P. *Uposatha*) – A twice-monthly meeting where monastics recite the *Prātimokṣa Sūtra*, confess any offences, and transact monastic business. It was instituted at King Bimbisāra's suggestion.

*prajñā* – Literally 'wisdom'; it is the sixth of the perfections (*pāramitās*) and is applied, generally, as a description of a section of the Eightfold Path (Right View and Right Resolve).

*Prajñāpāramitā Sūtras* – The '*Perfection of Wisdom Discourses*'; that class of Buddhist scriptures which mark the rise of Mahāyāna Buddhism. The *sūtras* often feature the Buddha's famous disciples as interlocutors. The texts frequently contrast mundane and ultimate reality, using emptiness (*śūnyatā*) as a striking epistemological tool.

*Pramāṇavāda* – Sanskrit term often used to indicate the science of logic.

*praṇidhāna* – The 'vow' taken by the Buddha and all *bodhisattvas*. The vow emphasizes saving all sentient beings by leading them to complete, perfect enlightenment.

*prasaṅga* – The Sanskrit term for the *reductio ad absurdum* argumentation technique used by Nāgārjuna in debating his opponents.

*Prātimokṣa Sūtra* – A para-canonical code of monastic offences which is recited twice monthly at the *Poṣadha* ceremony and represents the primary tool for the enforcement of monastic discipline.

*pratītya-samutpāda* – Literally 'dependent origination'; the Buddhist chain of causation emphasizing the relational aspect of all elements of existence. It is depicted as a twelve-spoked wheel, operating according to the formula 'because of this, that becomes', and so forth.

*pratyekabuddha* – A 'private' or 'solitary' Buddha. The term applies to those attaining enlightenment on their own and not going into the world to preach the path.

*pravrajyā* – Initial 'going forth' into the monastic order; contrasted with full ordination (*upasaṃpadā*).

*preta* – A 'hungry ghost'; one of the six destinies (*gatis*) into which one may be reborn. Knowing no peace, one in this realm is destined to constantly wander around searching for tiny bits of food.

Pudgalavāda – The 'Personalist' school of early Buddhism. This is a generic name for a number of early Buddhist schools which argued that a *pudgala* or 'person' migrates from life to life. Most other Buddhist school branded this group as heretical.

*puṇyakarma* – Literally 'auspicious karma'; it usually refers to that stock of past good karma built up by those on the path to enlightenment.

*Pure Land Sūtras* – That body of literature dealing with discourses on the Pure Land of Amitābha, and consisting primarily of three texts: *The Larger Sukhāvatīvyūha Sūtra*, *The Smaller Sukhāvatīvyūha Sūtra*, and the *Amitāyurdhyāna Sūtra*.

Rāhula – The Buddha's only son whose name means 'fetter', and who became a monk at age seven, later becoming the chief of all novices.

Rājagṛha – During the Buddha's lifetime, the capital of Magadha. It was the location of the first Buddhist monastery, and the site of the first Buddhist council following the Buddha's *parinirvāṇa*.

Revata – In the tradition of the second Buddhist council at Vaiśālī, Revata was a well-respected monk who supported Yaśas in his stand against the *vṛjiputraka bhikṣus* on the famous ten, presumably illicit, points.

Rhys Davids, Thomas William (1843–1922) – Founder of the Pali Text Society in 1881, he was the most forceful figure in the editing and translating of the texts of the Theravāda school of Buddhism. He is regarded as a major 'superstar' of Buddhology.

*Rinzai* (Ch. *Linji*) – Japanese branch of Zen Buddhism derived from the *Linji* branch of Chinese Chan Buddhism. Brought to Japan by Eisai, it emphasizes the use of *kōans* and the doctrine of subitism.

Ritsu – One of the six academic traditions of Japanese 'Nara' Buddhism which had been imported, without substantial modification, from China. It is the *Vinaya* school.

Robinson, Richard Hugh (1926–1970) – Founder of the Buddhist Studies program at the University of Wisconsin in 1961. Before his untimely death in 1970, he was regarded as the foremost Buddhologist in North America.

*rūpa* – One of the five *skandhas*, dealing with those elements in the realm of 'form'. Since *rūpa* deals with the physical or form realm, it was of primary importance to Abhidharmists' analyses of existence.

*Rūpakāya* – In early Buddhism, a designation for the 'Form Body' of the Buddha, indicating his existence as a human being.

*Saddharmapuṇḍarīka Sūtra* – *'Sūtra on the Lotus of the True Teaching'*; a Mahāyānist *sūtra* which combated early Buddhist doctrines as partial, shallow, and selfish, and which presented a new view of the Buddha as eternal.

Saichō – Buddhist monk in Japan who brought Tiantai Buddhism from China to Japan (calling it Tendai in Japan) in the ninth century. He was posthumously given the name Dengyō Daishi.

Śākya – Tribe living in the foothills of the Himalayas, ruled over by King Śuddhodana and Queen Māyā, unto which the future Buddha is born.

Śākyamuni – An epithet used to describe Siddhārtha Gautama, the historical Buddha, and meaning 'sage of the Śākya (tribe)'.

Sakyapa (Sa-skya-pa) – Tibetan sect of Buddhism founded by Drokmi ('Brog-mi), taking its name from the monastery he founded in 1073 C.E.

*samādhi* – Literally 'concentration' or 'meditation'; the concentration of the mind on a single object with the resulting one-pointedness of mind. It also refers to three steps of the Eightfold Path (Right Effort, Mindfulness, Meditation). It is also the fifth perfection (*pāramitā*).

*Samantapāsādikā* – A voluminous Pāli commentary on the entire *Vinaya Piṭaka*.

*samatha* – Literally 'calming down'; that portion of the Buddhist meditation program aimed at quieting the mind as a prerequisite to the careful observation of events called *vipassanā* or 'insight'. The two practices are part and parcel of the meditational schema outlined in Buddhaghosa's *Visuddhimagga*.

*Sambhogakāya* – According to Mahāyāna, the second of the three bodies of the Buddha. This body, literally meaning 'Enjoyment Body' or 'Reward Body' is the preacher of the Mahāyāna *sūtras* and is seen by those on the *bodhisattva* path.

*saṃjñā* – 'Perception'; the third of the five *skandhas*. It determines the characteristics of an object without placing a 'tag' or 'label' on the object itself.

*saṃsāra* – The cycle of perpetual flux, a term used to designate the entire cycle of transmigration. It is frequently contrasted to *nirvāṇa*.

*saṃskāra* – The fourth *skandha*, literally meaning 'mental constituents' or 'mental formations'. It denotes the volitional aspects of the individual and 'puts the mind in action'.

*samudaya* – The Sanskrit term for the second of the Noble Truths, that of cause. This Noble Truth emphasizes that there is a cause for suffering, centered around the various forms of craving.

*Saṃyutta Nikāya* – The '*Collection of Grouped Discourses*'; the third section of the *Sutta Piṭaka* of the Pāli Canon.

*sangha* – A Sanskrit word meaning 'group', and the generally accepted designation for the Buddhist Order. It is the third in the *triratna* or 'Three Jewels'.

*sanghabheda* – Literally 'schism in the *sangha*'; a term usually applied to the splitting up of sects.

Sanlun – The 'Three Treatise School', a classical school of Buddhism in China. It was founded by Kumarajīva (344–413 C.E.) and organized by Daosheng (360–434 C.E.), and corresponds to the Indian Mādhyamika school of Buddhism. The three treatises referred to are Nāgārjuna's *Mādhyamika Śāstra*, the *Dvadaśadvara*, and the *Śata Śāstra* of Āryadeva.

Sanron – One of the six academic traditions of Japanese 'Nara' Buddhism which had been imported, without substantial modification, from China. It corresponds to the Indian Mādhyamika and Chinese Sanlun schools of Buddhism.

Śāriputra – One of the Buddha's chief early disciples who is said to have gained enlightenment simply by hearing a versified summary of the Buddha's teaching. He is said to have been very learned in the *Abhidharma*, and several *Abhidharma* texts of various schools bear his name.

Sārnāth – Famous place outside of which (in the Deer Park) the Buddha preached his first sermon to the five ascetics.

Sarvagāmin – In the tradition surrounding the second Buddhist council, this figure was an elder monk of Vaiśālī, said to have had Ānanda as his teacher. After being questioned by Śāṇavāsin concerning the disputed ten points, the council convened.

Sarvāstivāda – 'Holders of the Doctrine that All Is'; an important sect of early Buddhism. They became one of the most influential of the early Buddhist sects, and endured as long as Indian Buddhism itself.

Śāsana – A descriptive word meaning 'Teaching' and used to denote the Buddhist religion.

*śāstra* – Literally a 'book' or 'treatise'; usually applied to philosophical Buddhist texts which argued various points of interest in Buddhist philosophy.

*sati* – The Pāli technical term for 'mindfulness'. The basis of Buddhist meditation seems to rest on the 'setting up of mindfulness'.

*Satipaṭṭhāna Sutta* – A *sutta* of the Pāli Canon (No. 10 in the *Majjhima Nikāya*, No. 22 in the *Dīgha Nikāya*) which outlines the essentials of Buddhist meditation. It deals with the 'setting up of mindfulness'.

*satori* – Japanese technical term for enlightenment.

*shakubuku* – Literally 'smash and flatten'; an early technique of Sōka Gakkai Buddhism. It is an aggressive, persistent, sometimes violent conversion tactic meant to wear down one's resistance by constant religious assault.

Shandao – Chinese patriarch (613–681 C.E.) of the Jingtu school of Buddhism.

Shenxiu – Chinese Buddhist monk (600–706 C.E.) of the Northern Chan school who was identified as the Sixth Patriarch but had his title removed by an imperial decision and properly awarded to his rival Huineng of Southern Chan.

*shikantaza* – 'Aiming at nothing except sitting' or 'just sitting'; a practice used by Sōtō Zen to 'stop the mind' in the present moment by merely sitting.

Shingon – School of Buddhism introduced into Japan by Kūkai (later named Kōbō Daishi). It is based on Zhenyan, the Chinese tantric tradition, emphasizing Vairocana as the cosmic Buddha.

Shinran – Japanese Buddhist (1173–1262) who was a former disciple of Hōnen, but broke from traditional Jōdo Shū and formed his own school called Jōdo Shinshū (the 'True Pure Land' school).

Shintō – The native religion of Japan, existing before the entry of Buddhism. Throughout Japanese history, there has been much mutual influencing between the two groups.

Shōtoku – Prince Regent in Japan (d. 621 C.E.) who was responsible for the early growth and development of Buddhism in Japan. He was perhaps a counterpart of the Indian King Aśoka.

Shundao – Monk who brought Buddhism to Korea from China around 373 C.E.

Siddhārtha – 'He whose aim will be accomplished'; the name given to Gautama after the prediction by a sage that he would become either a universal monarch or a Buddha.

*śīla* – Broadly defined to mean 'morality' or 'ethical propriety' (although there is no truly good English equivalent). It seems to be an internally enforced ethical guideline. The stages of Right Speech, Action, and Livelihood on the Eightfold Path are often called, collectively, *śīla*; and it is also the second perfection (*pāramitā*).

*skandha* – Literally 'heap' or 'bundle'; the five so-called aggregates which make up an individual. Since it deals with the makeup of the individual, it was of prime interest to Abhidharmists' analyses.

Sōka Gakkai – 'Society for the Creation of Value'; one of the largest 'new religions' of Japan. It draws much of its religious input from Nichiren Buddhism.

Sŏn – A Korean Buddhist Chan group that eventually broke into many individual branches.

Sŏnjong – Buddhist meditation school in Korea which was composed of the Chinese schools of *Vinaya*, Tiantai, and Chan.

Sōtō – Japanese school of Zen Buddhism, derived from the Chinese Caodong Chan tradition. It was introduced to Japan by Dōgen, and emphasizes *shikantaza* ('just sitting') and gradualism.

*śraddhā* – 'Faith' or 'trust'; emphasizing faith in the Buddha, his *Dharma*, and his *Sangha*. It is not to be taken in the sense of 'blind' faith, but rather that which is open to verification in the experiential realm.

*śrāvaka* – A 'hearer', or one who heard the Buddha's teaching directly. This title would thus apply to all of the Buddha's early disciples. The Mahāyānists use this term in the pejorative sense to represent those who cannot understand the teachings of *prajñāpāramitā*.

Sthavira – Literally 'Elder'; that title applied to the early schools of Buddhism which broke from the unified community and opposed the Mahāsāṃghikas.

*stūpa* – A memorial mound constructed over the relics of the Buddha or other important person. Around the turn of the Common Era, a cult grew up around the worship of *stūpas*. To this day, *stūpas* remain worthy of reverence in Buddhist countries.

Subhūti – One of the lesser-known of the Buddha's early disciples. In the *Prajñāpāramitā* literature, he emerges as the prime interlocutor, often exhibiting greater insight than the Buddha's foremost disciples.

Śuddhodana – Ruler of the Śākya tribe at the foothills of the Himalayas. He was the Buddha's father.

Sukāvatī – 'Land of Happiness' or the 'Pure Land'; that special sphere over which Amitābha presides, located in the Western region.

*Sukhāvatīvyūha Sūtras* – Two Pure Land texts, a larger and a smaller, in which formal devotion to the Buddha (*Buddha-bhakti*) appears. The larger text emphasizes the large stock of merit necessary for rebirth in the Pure Land, while the smaller text emphasizes the use of sound, particularly Amitābha's name, as a means for gaining rebirth in the Pure Land.

*śūnyatā* – The doctrine of 'emptiness' or voidness', stressed in many Mahāyāna *sūtras*. It goes beyond the early Buddhist position of *anātman* (not-self) in stating that even *dharmas* have no existence in their own right. One must be careful to understand that *śūnyatā* itself is not an ontological state, and that even emptiness is empty.

*sūtra* – Literally 'thread'; applied to the Buddha's sermons. Thus, the Buddha's sermons and discourses are called *sūtras*.

*Sūtra Piṭaka* (P. *Sutta Piṭaka*) – That portion of the Buddhist canon which gathers together all those sermons of the Buddha deemed canonical and authoritative. The *Sūtra Piṭaka* is broken down into five parts called *Āgamas* (*Nikāyas* in Pāli).

*svabhāva* – A traditionally Mahāyāna term meaning 'own-being' or 'own-nature'. It is the *svabhāva* which *dharmas* are said to be lacking and which contributes to their being empty (*śūnyatā*). If a thing had 'own-being', it would exist in itself, thus being outside dependent origination, and contradict Buddhist orthodoxy.

Tang Dynasty – Dynasty in China from 618–907 C.E. which marked the high point in Chinese Buddhist history.

Tan-luan – Chinese Buddhist (476–542 C.E.) who organized the Pure Land school of Buddhism in China. He is also reckoned as its first patriarch.

*Tantra* – Buddhist esoteric school originating in India around the sixth century C.E., and spreading to China, Japan, and Tibet, which emphasized techniques of spontaneity centered around the use of *mantras*, *maṇḍalas*, sexual imagery, and stirring psychological techniques.

Tāranātha – Tibetan Buddhist historian (1575–1634), a prolific writer, affording much in the way of the history of Buddhism.

*Tathāgata* – Literally the 'thus come one'; an epithet describing Siddhārtha Gautama after he achieved complete, perfect enlightenment. Also used to describe other Buddhas.

*tathāgatagarbha* – Doctrine found in Yogācāra which literally means the 'womb of the Tathāgata' and functions as a synonym for the *ālaya-vijñāna*.

*tathatā* – Literally 'suchness'; things as they really are. Perhaps a more modern rendering might be 'is-ness'. It functions as a synonym for enlightenment.

*Tenjur* – In the Tibetan Buddhist Canon, this division contains the commentaries. Following the hymns of praise, we find two general types of commentaries: commentaries on the *Tantras* and commentaries on the *Sūtras*.

Theravāda – 'Those Who Hold the Doctrine of the Elders'; one of the traditional eighteen sects of Nikāya Buddhism. This form of Buddhism emerged out of Mahinda's mission to Sri Lanka during Aśoka's reign. They represent the sole surviving sect of *Nikāya* Buddhism today.

Tiantai (Jap. Tendai) – School of Mahāyāna Buddhism in China which was organized by Zhiyi (538–597 C.E.). The basic text of this school is the *Lotus Sūtra*. This school represented a Chinese attempt to establish a great eclectic school recognizing all forms of Buddhism. The school gets its name from the mountain on which it was located.

Tilopa – The guru of Nāropa. He is described as being rather erratic, often only partially clothed and acting 'crazy'.

Toda, Jōsei – The second leader of the Sōka Gakkai school of Buddhism in Japan. He refined much of the teaching of the school.

Tokugawa Period – Period in Japanese history (1603–1867) when Japan was completely isolated from the outside world and Buddhism, as well as all areas of life, was strictly controlled by the military shoguns.

*trikāya* – The doctrine of the 'Three Bodies of the Buddha'. They include the apparitional body (*nirmāṇakāya*), enjoyment body (*sambhogakāya*), and the essence body (*dharmakāya*).

*Tripiṭaka* – The '*Three Baskets*' of the Buddhist scriptures, consisting of the *Vinaya Piṭaka, Sūtra Piṭaka,* and *Abhidharma Piṭaka.*

*triratna* – The 'Three Jewels' of Buddhism, including the Buddha, *Dharma,* and *Sangha.*

*tṛṣṇā* – Literally 'craving'; noted in the second Noble Truth to be the cause of suffering. Usually three kinds of craving are noted: sensual craving, craving for continued existence, and craving for extinction.

Tsongkhapa – Tibetan Buddhist (1358–1419) claiming to be in the lineage of Atīśa's Kadmapa (bKa-gdams-pa) sect and founding three monasteries in Lhasa. He is the founder of the Gelug (dGe-lugs) school of Tibetan Buddhism.

Udraka Rāmaputra – The second teacher under whom Siddhārtha Gautama studied in his quest for enlightenment. Udraka's system taught the attainment of the 'sphere of neither perception nor non-perception'.

Upāli – One of the Buddha's leading disciples and a specialist on the rules of the *Vinaya.* He was said to have recited the entire *Vinaya* at the first council, held at Rājagṛha.

*upāsaka* – A male lay disciple.

*upasaṃpadā* – Full ordination into the Buddhist monastic order.

*upāsikā* – A female lay disciple.

*upāya* – Literally 'skill in means' or 'skillful device'; those means by which the Buddha or *bodhisattvas* make the complex and difficult teachings of Buddhism understandable to persons of varying mental faculties. Sometimes cited as *upāya-kauśalya.*

Vairocana – Literally 'Shining Out'; a cosmic Buddha whose body is the emptiness of all things. In Chinese scholasticism he is sometimes regarded as the *Dharmakāya* of Śākyamuni.

Vaiśālī – Famous city in early Buddhism, perhaps best known for being the site of the second Buddhist council following the Buddha's death.

*Vajracchedikā Sūtra* – Literally the '*Diamond Sūtra*'; a summary of the larger *Prajñāpāramitā sūtras.* It is said to contain the essence of the teaching.

Vallée Poussin, Louis de la (1869–1938) – Great Buddhologist of the early twentieth century, offering translations of many critical Buddhist texts, and many books and articles on various Buddhist subjects. He is regarded as one of the 'superstars' of modern Buddhology.

Vasubandhu – Great Buddhist commentator who originally wrote as a Sarvāstivādin, producing such works as the *Abhidharmakośa,* but was later converted to Yogācāra by his brother Asaṅga. Among his major contributions to Yogācāra are the famous *Viṃśatikā* and *Triṃśikā*. With Buddhaghosa, he ranks among the most excellent of all Buddhist exegetes.

Vasumitra – Sarvāstivādin monk who served as 'President' of the Buddhist council held by King Kaniṣka. He is the reputed author of the *Samayabhedoparacanacakra* and the *Prakaraṇapāda*, the latter text being included in the *Abhidharma Piṭaka* of the Sarvāstivādins.

*vedanā* – Literally 'feeling'; the second of the five *skandhas*. It derives from the contact of our physical and mental organs with objects in the external world.

*vihāra* – Originally a hut inhabited by a single monk during the rainy-season retreat. As Buddhist monasticism developed, and the wandering ideal was abandoned, the word came to denote an entire monastery.

*vijñāna* – 'Consciousness'; the fifth of the five *skandhas*. It represents the resultant activity when our mental and physical organs come into contact with objects in the external world, and the input derived therefrom is integrated, identified, and acted upon. Traditionally, there are six *vijñānas*: eye, ear, nose, tongue, body, and mind (but the Yogācārins enlarge this list).

Vijñānavāda – Literally 'Holders of the Doctrine of Consciousness'; that title applied to the Yogācāra school of Buddhism which aims at being descriptive in terms of the doctrines held by the school.

Vimalakīrti – In Mahāyāna, a layman *bodhisattva* who, in spite of his worldly ways, has great insight and attainment. A famous Mahāyāna text, the *Vimalakīrtinirdeśa Sūtra*, was written about this figure, in which Vimalakīrti outshines all the Buddha's great disciples in his understanding.

*Vinaya Piṭaka* – The first 'basket' in the Buddhist canon, containing all the rules for monastic discipline, ethical considerations, and transacting monastic business.

*vipassanā* – Literally 'insight'; the second half of Buddhist meditational practice (the first being *samatha*) which leads to the experience of the four trances.

*vīrya* – 'Vigor' or 'striving'; the fourth of the perfections (*pāramitās*) practiced on the *bodhisattva* path.

*Visuddhimagga* – The '*Path of Purity*', a classic Buddhist text written by Buddhaghosa. It has become a standard guide to Theravāda meditation and, as a compendium of doctrine, includes precepts, legends, miracle stories, etc., all of which glorify arhantship. It ranks in brilliance with Vasubandhu's *Abhidharmakośa*.

*vyakāraṇa* – Literally 'prediction'; received by a *bodhisattva* (from a Buddha) who takes a vow to save all sentient beings. It notes when the *bodhisattva* will attain complete, perfect enlightenment.

*wu* – Chinese term literally signifying individual enlightenment.

Xuanzang – Chinese pilgrim who traveled to India and back between 629 and 645 C.E. to study the language and bring back Buddhist texts for translation into Chinese. He lived from 596 to 664 C.E. and played an instrumental role in organizing the

Jushe or *Abhidharma* school of Buddhism from Paramārtha's teachings and the Faxiang school of Buddhism, modeled on Yogācāra viewpoints.

Yaśodharā – Wife of Siddhārtha Gautama before he renounced worldly life.

*yathābhūtam* – Literally 'things as they really are'; it is this that is the goal for all Buddhists, but particularly emphasized by the Mahāyānists. One can say that to see things as they really are is to be enlightened.

Yogācāra – Literally 'Practice of Yoga'; Mahāyāna philosophical school founded by Asaṅga and innovating several new concepts in Buddhist thought, among them the eight consciousnesses, *trisvabhāva* doctrine, *vijñaptimātra*, and *tathāgatagarbha*. With Mādhyamika, it represents the driving force in Mahāyāna.

*zazen* – Literally 'sitting in meditation'; with the notion that the person is already a Buddha, this realization being clouded only by ignorance. *Zazen* provides an opportunity in which one's inherent Buddha nature may manifest itself.

Zen – Name of the Japanese school of Buddhism, based on meditation, that continues the Chan tradition of China. It first appeared in the twelfth century C.E., and has grown to become widely popular throughout the modern world.

Zhenyan – The 'efficient (or true) word'. It corresponds to the Buddhist *tantra*, and was introduced into China in the eighth century C.E. Zhenyan transliterates to '*mantra*' in Sanskrit.

Zhiyi – Chinese Buddhist (438–597 C.E.) who served as the major systematizer of Tiantai Buddhism in China.

# Index

Page numbers followed by an asterisk* refer to entries in the glossary. Those in *italic* refer to illustrations.